Y0-BSE-988

JIHAD, HINDUTVA AND THE TALIBAN

Jihad, Hindutva and the Taliban

South Asia at the Crossroads

Iftikhar H. Malik

OXFORD

UNIVERSITY PRESS

OXFORD

UNIVERSITY PRESS

Great Clarendon Street, Oxford OX2 6DP

Oxford University Press is a department of the University of Oxford.
It furthers the University's objective of excellence in research, scholarship,
and education by publishing worldwide in

Oxford New York

Auckland Cape Town Dar es Salaam Hong Kong Karachi
Kuala Lumpur Madrid Melbourne Mexico City Nairobi
New Delhi Shanghai Taipei Toronto

with offices in

Argentina Austria Brazil Chile Czech Republic France Greece
Guatemala Hungary Italy Japan South Korea Poland Portugal
Singapore Switzerland Thailand Turkey Ukraine Vietnam

Oxford is a registered trade mark of Oxford University Press
in the UK and in certain other countries

ISBN-13: 978-0-19-597790-5
ISBN-10: 0-19-597790-4

Typeset in Times
Printed in Pakistan by
Kagzi Printers, Karachi.
Published by
Ameena Saiyid, Oxford University Press
Plot No. 38, Sector 15, Korangi Industrial Area, PO Box 8214
Karachi-74900, Pakistan.

CONTENTS

CONTENTS

ACKNOWLEDGEMENTS

A volume of this nature, attempting to cover several regions and diverse but still not so dissimilar ideologies, has duly benefited from a wide variety of sources and authors. However, the inspiration for undertaking this project mainly came from all the jolting changes accompanying the dissolution of the global Cold War and subsequent developments including the escalation of ethno-sectarian wars, Islamophobia, the rise and fall of the Taliban, nuclearisation of the subcontinent and the two Gulf wars. The terrorist attacks of September 2001, the Anglo-American invasions of Afghanistan and Iraq, despite a massive public outcry to the contrary, and the second Intifadah, amidst a brutal repression through 'target killings' and a 12-meter high perimeter wall around 'Palestinian Bantustans', are the painful memories of the 'lost decade'. The reinvigorated Russian and Indian campaigns in turbulent Chechnya and Kashmir, the debacle of democracy in Pakistan amidst sectarian and Jihadist violence, and an overall greater emphasis on the so-called majoritarian nationalism in the entire South Asian region reflect the salience of violent means over civic and peaceful strategies. It is a new populism of fascist and violent portents that has blurred the erstwhile relationship between the state and society. Extremism, sometimes turned into sheer extermination of the vulnerable, has certainly been growing out of proportion. It may be spawned by mundane and modernist factors but equally receives its impetus from primordial and traditionalist trajectories.

Srebrinica, Sarajevo, Nablus, Ayodhya, Gujarat, Mazar-i-Sharif, Qali-i-Jangi, Tora Bora, Baghdad and so many other towns have been uniquely internalised in human consciousness, which continued to defy the war mongers by thronging the streets in London, Rome, Berlin, San Francisco, Calcutta, Tokyo and Cairo. Millions of pacifists espousing an alternative humanist globalism and showing a new 'consensus from below' defied the recourse to violence, deception and decimation. Whereas the 11 September attacks awakened the United States to its vulnerabilities, unleashing its vengeful campaigns, its Neo-Conservatives, more like the Serb Chetniks and Zionist expansionists, found themselves at home with the Hindutva exponents and Muslim exclusionists in South Asia. The promotion of violence both at the official and societal levels in recent years has only further marginalised the ethno-religious minorities globally, bringing pluralism under severe strain. In a sense, South Asia or the Middle East are not unique as they, like their counterparts elsewhere, reverberate the bitter lessons of modernity itself gone haywire. A selective blend of religion, demography, history and national identity is nefariously put together by a whole generation of ideologues, who are quite adept in applying modernist means and pretences to draw their pound of flesh from already marooned minority groups. The suggestions for a benevolent 'Western control' or 'lite imperialism' over and above the democratic prerogatives and judicious international law are too simplistic to resolve this predicament which is not merely confined to so-called 'conflict-prone' regions. In the same vein, the dictum of prioritising freedom over democracy, simply to suit some specific sections in the powerful North Atlantic regions is as fallacious as the premises of the clash of cultures, or the end of history. We are all in it together, and the solution has to come from various directions, especially through a global civic agenda, and not by pursuing annihilative military strategies.

This study, while putting South Asia in this agonising global context, also offers a comparative outlook from within the region. It is not an altogether lost case, only if the civil societies, resuscitated by humane heritage found in abundance in the region itself, can reinvent South Asia as a bastion of peace, pluralism, tolerance and democracy. That is why this book is not only a modest tribute to these silent and struggling masses, but has also been immensely inspired by their humanity and humility. I must thank my numerous friends and colleagues in South Asia, the Muslim world, Europe, and the United States for pointing me in the right direction. They are too numerous to be named. My colleagues and students in Bath, Oxford and elsewhere definitely deserve my sincerest thanks for their persistent prodding, whereas my family, as always, stood behind me during the taxing and stressful years of teaching and travelling. But the challenge has surely been worth it. At Oxford University Press, Ameena Saiyid is a resolute source of encouragement, whereas Ghousia Ali, Rehana Khandwalla and Soonita Wadia have duly kept me focused. My special gratitude to two anonymous readers for their constructive comments, though I personally undertake the responsibility of any errors of judgement.

Iftikhar Malik
Oxford, April 2005

ACRONYMS

AI	Amnesty International
AKRCP	Aga Khan Rural Support Programme
AL	Awami League
ANP	Awami National Party
ASEAN	Association of South East Asian Nations
ASI	Archaeological Survey of India
ASSP	Anjuman-i-Sipah-i-Sahabah, Pakistan
BJP	Bharatiya Janata Party
BNP	Bangladesh National Party (of Mrs Khalida Zia)
BNP	British National Party (a racist party led by Nick Griffin)
BRCS	Bangladesh Red Crescent Society
CLASS	Centre for Legal Aid, Assistance and Settlement, Lahore
CTBT	Comprehensive Test Ban Treaty
EU	European Union
HM	Hizbul Mujahideen (Kashmiri activists)
HRCI	Human Rights Commission of India
HRCP	Human Rights Commission of Pakistan
GATT	General Agreement on Trade and Tariff
ICRC	International Committee of the Red Cross
ISI	Inter-Services Intelligence (Pakistani intelligence agency)
JI	Jama'at-i-Islami
JM	Jaysh-i-Muhammad (a Pakistani Sunni militant group)
JUI (F)	Jamiat-i-Ulama-i-Islam (Fazlur Rahman Group)
JUI (S)	Jamiat-i-Ulama-i-Islam (Sami-ul Haq Group)
JUP	Jamiat-i-Ulama-i-Pakistan
LFO	Legal Framework Order (General Pervez Musharraf's unilateral amendments [2002] in the Constitution of 1973)
LJ	Lashkar-i-Jhangvi (a Sunni militant group)
LT	Lashkar-i-Tayyaba (a Sunni militant group)
ML	Muslim League (founded in 1906 in Dhaka, but now divided)
MMA	Muttahida Majlis-i-Amal
MNA	Member, National Assembly [Pakistan]

MPA	Member, Provincial Assembly [Pakistan]
MQM	Muhajir/Muttahida Qaumi Movement (mainly of Urdu speakers in Karachi)
MRD	Movement for the Restoration of Democracy (1983–4)
MRG	Minority Rights Group
NAP	National Awami Party (now ANP)
NCJP	National Commission for Justice and Peace
NGO	Non-Governmental Organisation
NPT	Nuclear Non-Proliferation Treaty
NWFP	North-West Frontier Province
OIC	Organisation of the Islamic Conference
PML	Pakistan Muslim League
PPP	Pakistan People's Party (established by Zulfikar Ali Bhutto in 1968, and now mainly led by his daughter, Benazir Bhutto)
RAW	Research and Analysis Wing (Indian intelligence agency)
RMMRU	Refugee and Migratory Movements Research Unit
RSS	Rashtriya Swayamsevak Sangh
SM	Sipah-i-Muhammad (a Shia militant group)
SS	Shiv Sena (lit: the followers of Lord Shiva. A fascist Hindutva party in Maharashtra)
SAARC	South Asian Association for Regional Cooperation
SPGRC	Stranded Pakistanis General Repatriation Committee
TNFJ	Tehrik-i-Nifaz-i-Fiqah-i-Ja'afria
UNHCR	United Nations High Commissioner for Refugees
VHP	Vishwa Hindu Parishad
WMDs	Weapons of Mass Destruction (presumably of Iraq)
WTO	World Trade Organisation

GLOSSARY

Akhand Bharat	United India
Alim	a Muslim religious scholar
Amir ul Momineen	Leader of the faithful
Anjuman	cultural or literary association
Ayatollah	pre-eminent Shia imam
Azan	Call for Muslim prayer
Bastis	Settlements
Bharat	ancient name for India
Chador	a loose wraparound for women
Chardiwari	Within four walls of the home
Chak	a rural settlement in an irrigated region
Diyat	blood money
Dhimmi/zimmi	a non-Muslim subject in an Islamic state
Fatwa	religious decree
Fiqh/Fiqah	jurisprudence
Fitna	feud, dissension
Ghazi	a Muslim holy warrior
Ghazwah	a battle led by the Prophet (PBUH)
Hajj	Annual Pilgrimage to Mecca, Arabia
Huqooqul Allah	Duties unto God
Huqooqul Iba'ad	Duties unto humanity
Ijtiha'ad	innovation
Imam	a religious leader
Imambargah	A place of religious significance for Shias.
Jalwah	lit: appearance
Jihad	To struggle in the name of God
Jihadi	holy warrior
Kalima	Statement reciting the unity of God and the prophethood of Muhammad (PBUH)
Khatam-i-nabuwwat	finality of the prophethood of Muhammad (PBUH)
Khutba	sermon
Madrassa	an Islamic seminary

Mahdi	Promised Revivalist (Messiah)
Majlis	a cultural association
Malai	Zikri religious leader
Mantra	panacea; treatment
Maulvi/Mullah	Muslim religious leader
Mujahid	One who undertakes *Jihad*
Mujahideen	pl. of *Mujahid*
Muhajir	Muslim migrant
Muhajireen	pl. of *Muhajir*
Mujta'ahid	Shia Muslim theologian
Murid	disciple of a Sufi or *pir*
Nabi	Prophet
Namazis	Sunni Muslims in Makran
Pir	Sufi saint
Qisas	lit: revenge, blood money
Ram Janambhoomi	Birthplace of Lord Ram
Rashtra	Homeland
Sajjada Nashin	Muslim dynastic sufi order
Sharia/Shariat	Islamic law; jurisprudence
Shia/shi'ite	Follower of Caliph Ali, a doctrinal Muslim sect
Silsilah	a sufi order
Sufi	a mystic
Sunni	lit. a follower of the Prophetic traditions, a majority doctrinal sect
Taliban	plural of *Taleb/Talib*: students
Tanzim	an organization/association
Taqli'd	uncritiqued imitation
Tariqa	Sufi way; order
Trishol	trident
Ulama	Muslim religious scholars (pl. of *alim*)
Ummah	Trans-national Muslimhood
Wadera	a big/feudal landlord in Sindh
Zakat	charity
Zikr	remembering God through repetitive phrases

Suicide bombing is the weapon of the weak. Killing from the air is the approach of the rich and powerful.
— Mary Kaldor, *New Statesman,* 26 May 2003

The suicide bombers who attacked Washington and New York on September 11th, 2001, did more than kill thousands of civilians and demolish the World Trade Center. They destroyed the West's ruling myth.
— John Gray, *Al-Qaeda and What it Means to be Modern,*
London, 2003, p. 1

Whatever the cause, in September 2001 it was better to be a Westerner in a Muslim country than a Muslim in a Western country.
— John Simpson, *News From No Man's Land,*
London, 2002, p. 82

Iraqis have paid a heavy price for the fall of Saddam Hussein's government.
— Kofi Annan, the UN, 10 April 2003

Blair tells Congress... 'History will forgive us'.
— *The Guardian*, 18 July 2003

Bush and Blair's crusade had been a righteous cause.
— Robin Moore, *Task Force Dagger: The Hunt for Bin Laden,*
London, 2003, p. 372

Far from becoming mahaan (great), India is going to the dogs, and unless a miracle saves us, the country will break up. It will not be Pakistan or any other foreign power that will destroy us: we will commit hara-kiri.
— Khushwant Singh, *The End of India,* New Delhi, 2003, pp. 314.

INTRODUCTION
The War on Terror and Beyond

In the last few years, a number of significant developments have completely transformed the South Asian political contours, reinvigorating populist forces seeking newer and pronounced roles in the polities. The most plural and populous region in the world experienced crucial societal movements, justifying themselves on primordial, ideological and demographic determinants. While spawning radical movements such as Talibanisation, Jihad, Hindutva, Sunni statism, mono-nationalism (such as the Khas Hindu movement in Nepal, Islamic Bangladesh, Buddhist Sinhalese nationalism or LTTE's Tamil Elam particularism both at the expense of each other and Sri Lankan Muslims, secessionism or even Maoist transformation), countries like Afghanistan, Pakistan, India, Bangladesh, Sri Lanka and Nepal have been witnessing greater volatility in the state-society relationship, of violent proportions. These new trajectories have equally generated intra-society chasms, especially for ethnic and religious minorities. These clusters have tried to offer alternative interpretations of national identity, occasionally advocating a forceful ethno-religious conformity. The religio-political creeds such as Sunni Islam and Hindu Rashtra as propounded by these groups, seek their legitimacy by claiming to be speaking for the so-called majorities. That is why they are occasionally identified as populist movements where fiery leaders offer a wide mix of old and new. Seeking sustenance from history, religious particularism, majoritarianism, and occasionally exhibiting anti-Western sentiment, they have definitely pursued modernist means and strategies to obtain their goals. To these redeemers, an idealised past still remains the reference point, which the post-independence Westernised elite have betrayed time and again. The resurrectionist claims are mostly anchored on highly romanticised and untested utopianism underwritten by an equal amount of intolerance and violence. The Promised Land has never been, but is to be. Still, it is as alluring to small town inhabitants as it is to tribal and rural communities.

POPULISM OR MAJORITARIAN FASCISM

While 'indigenous' elites lead these ultra right, populist movements, the foot soldiers are all trained in *madrassas* or temples harbouring an emotional hatred for an invisible enemy. The enemy could be from within or across the borders, but still immoral and pernicious! The enemy within, in particular, lacks authenticity and patriotism and is thus the root cause of all the ills. This enemy features as the fifth columnist in the so-called majoritarian discourse and is presumed to collaborate with the external adversary. That is where non-Muslims in Pakistan, Muslims in India, Hindus and Biharis in Bangladesh, Tamils for Sinhalese nationalists, and Tajiks and Hazaras for the predominantly Pushtun Taliban have been more often perceived as surrogates for external enemies. In most cases, the West evokes both an envy and multi-layered hostility besides providing a useful alibi. The West, in a cultural sense, is an immoral modernity whereas in its politico-economic embodiments, it is an American hegemony. The hyped-up anti-secularism, as defined by many of these movements, invariably converges with an undefined and varying mixture of anti-Americanism. Nativism as a major ingredient in these trajectories, however, remains rooted in a religious authenticity though the means may be simply modernist.[1] The forces share the rejection of 'alien' infrastructures and their replacement with more 'authentic' and native alternatives across the regional spectrum.[2] Other than being a majority-minority contestation, or its religious portents, the ideological conflict displays class-based characteristics. The post-colonial ruling elites are perceived as Western lackeys with their alien life-styles and ideological orientation, while the masses remain poor and disempowered. In-between, the emerging middle class stays thin, insecure, mostly state dependent yet very ethnicised and sectarianised. Either this middle class is too sparse and weak, or plainly lacks a strong unifying role, though it never lags behind in assuming patriotic and nationalist espousal. For instance, in India, the middle class remains divided between the secularists and proponents of Hindutva; in Pakistan, Sunni-Shia and ethno-regional fissures crisscross it. The Bangaldeshi middle class, despite its ideological divisions, overwhelmingly subscribes to a majoritarian nationalism anchored on Muslim Bengali credentials, leaving little space for Hindu Bangladeshis and no leeway for Biharis. In Sri Lanka, the Sinhalese-led majoritarian nationalism, in its contestation with its Tamil counterpart, has tried to overlook intra-

Sinhalese religious configurations, but at another level, both adversaries share a muted suspicion of Sri Lankan Muslims, who in most cases speak Tamil though they may trace their origins to the Arabs or even to early Ceylonese converts. In Nepal, the Khas Hindus—in the name of a Hindu Kingdom—continue to deny the plural prerogatives of ethno-religious minorities, who, in return, have begun to support the Maoists.

In the post-11 September 2001 simplistic jargon, one may be tempted to decry these ideological forces as mere terrorist outfits harbouring violent means to attain their narrowly defined objectives. However, a rigorous analysis demands an investigation of their historical and politico-economic roots. Religion is basically a ploy to overcome multiple grievances and a sense of hurt, and also operates as a major socializer. That is why it mobilises masses across the streets in Karachi, Lahore, Kabul, Kandahar, Ahmedabad, Baroda and Dhaka. It is this dominant religious idiom that attracts so many recruits—both from the emerging intermediate class and the have-nots. The Taliban, Lashkar-i-Tayyaba (LT), Jaysh-i-Muhammad (JM), Lashkar-i-Jhangvi (LJ), Rashtriya Swayamsewak Sangh (RSS), Hizbul Mujahideen (HM), Bharatiya Janata Party (BJP), Vishwa Hindu Parishad (VHP), Tamil Tigers and the Nepalese Maoist guerrillas, in their own distinct ways, reveal important facts including new class formations, state-society fissures, and majority-minority dissension. While they all invariably share an utmost disgust for the existing national and regional politics, they are eager to capture their respective polities to transform them into their own image. They may be the armies of Kalashnikov toting, bearded or saffron-clad fanatics, but in fact, many of them are the have-nots who were offered shelter, security, education, and even identity by their respective *native* lower middle class mentors. This is where madrassas and mountain hideouts become the rallying points and impart a unique seminary education, offering a mix of the lost glory and its reconstruction through a force justified by religion, history, racial traits or even nationalism. It could be, in other words, owing to the inefficiency of the public education system and economic adversity that hosts of underprivileged youths falling out of the safety net end up as mercenaries for Allah, Ram or Mao. Many of them have agendas confined to their own country, while others may have extra-regional ambitions, but they all have their global and diasporic backers and antagonists.[3] All of them complain of being misunderstood and insist on offering utopian, simplistic but authentic panaceas to rather complex problems. But the fact remains; they continue to hold camaraderie among the rural, tribal and small town supporters, who offer them financial and moral support.

The *enemy within* may also include human rights activists, especially those demanding empowerment of women and tribals. The fundamentalist movements among these outfits, excluding the Maoists and Tamils, profess a domestic role for women, almost denying them any public space. Their nationalist trajectory is unreservedly muscular. The religio-political groups in Afghanistan and Pakistan, since the 1980s, have been part of organised efforts to confine women to home and *chardiwari* besides offering them a restrictive education, and that too, in a non-coeducational set-up. Similarly, in India, women have been the victims of xenophobic attitudes since the nineteenth century when reformers demanded equal gender rights and greater women's participation in the public sphere.[4] After the military-led elections in Pakistan in 2002, the provincial regimes formed by the United Action Forum (known as Muttahida Majlis-i-Amal or MMA) in the Frontier and Balochistan began Islamicising the socio-legal structures. In addition to banning music and Western films, five-times prayers were made mandatory even for travellers, followed by several more strictures legislated through *Sharia* laws in the summer of 2003. In the same vein, in neighbouring Kabul, the Afghan chief justice in Hamid Karzai's regime outlawed satellite dishes beaming Western programmes, as they spread nudity and profanity. This is not to suggest that these powerful pressure groups do not enjoy support from specific women's cadres. In Pakistan, the Jama'at-i-Islami (JI), for instance, has the most organized and equally vocal women's group whereas the Tamil Tigers have their own women recruits and suicide bombers, some of whom have been conducting successful *kamikaze* attacks. The BJP also does not lack in women's support with some of them like Uma Bharati and Jayalalita holding important ministerial positions. However, Sri Lanka may be the only country in the entire region with the highest ratio of women's participation in the socio-economic sectors, while the other countries lag behind in equal opportunities. Simultaneously, it has to be noted that many women journalists, writers, lawyers and NGOs all across South Asia account for a major portion of the civil society who take a high-profile stance on human rights, environment and regional peace. Though South Asia has a unique tradition of having several women prime ministers, it is only the urban women from an emerging middle class who have been heralding civic causes and frequently confroning a backlash from some of these unilateralist outfits. Concurrently, women from amongst minorities, tribal and other underprivileged groups frequently fall victim to societal and official tyranny.

WHAT HAS GONE WRONG? MODERNITY, NEO-CONSERVATISM AND POLITICAL ISLAM

Within this periscope, one may be tempted to ask pertinent questions such as: Is South Asia, or for that matter the Muslim world, unique in experiencing this new wave of ultra right? Are we seeing a new societal populism against the traditional elites, or are we witnessing modernity gone haywire? Are we seeing new ideological fault lines emerging in South Asia and elsewhere, signalling major changes to come? Or, is it a reaction to a West-led globalisation that itself is the new name of modernity? Are the Anglo-American offensives part of a historical burden as propounded by their neo-conservatives or substantive efforts to plant democracies in the 'rogue' states by using military power in a post-cold war unipolar world? And, how far are Political Islam or the New Hindu Movement, despite espousing anti-hegemonic stances, themselves consciously attempting to establish newer hegemonies at the sheer expense of plural imperatives of their societies? Certainly, each of these questions deserves a separate theoretical formulation and an in-depth empirical research. At a conceptual level, these ideological crossroads may not be unique to South Asia as one witnesses a steady growth of a multi-polar intolerance towards ethnic pluralism, immigrants and asylum seekers in the North Atlantic region. The hawkish policies pursued by the Bush Administration, the unmitigated Israeli campaign against Palestinians, Russian atrocities in Chechnya and the Anglo-American invasion of Iraq in 2003 are some of the recent manifestations of this neo-conservative mode of politicking, which does not shy away from using blatant force in the name of pre-emptive strategy. Even electoral politics in several European Union states and a growing dependence of Blairite New Labour on the United States reveal greater 'pulls' towards exclusionary politicking.[5] In dealing with the Muslim Diaspora in North Atlantic regions, the focus has already shifted away from individual cases of 'suspect terrorists' to larger nationality groups such as Pakistanis, Algerians, Iraqis, Saudis and Iranians. The mass deportations, finger printing, vigilant surveillance, bans on several Muslim charities, visa restrictions on Muslim students and visitors, and the unilateral military trials of the Guantanamo Bay internees are some of the post-September manifestations of this cumulative campaign. In addition, there are numerous documented cases of individuals having experienced torture, verbal abuse, job discrimination and multiple forms of violence. Places of worship, Muslim women wearing *hijab* and bearded men have been occasionally targeted for verbal and physical abuse. Some commentators have designated it as the 'new anti-Semitism', which focuses on Muslims, though political leaders such as Bush and Blair have often differentiated between terrorists and Islam. Such a witch-hunt in the new Millennium poses serious ideological problems for the Left and Liberal groups as well, to whom class, more than anything else, mattered the most yet people have been victimised on the basis of creed and colour.[6] Thus, the issues of class, ideology, religion, immigration and pluralism have obtained a new significance in view of greater emphasis on national security, hyped-up patriotism, unilateral militarism and a gradualist squeeze on asylum seekers and immigrants, especially from the Muslim regions. As was seen on the media portrayal of asylum issues on 23 July 2003, thousands of callers to the BBC in Britain did not appear enthusiastic in offering hospitality.[7] Understandably, it is within this milieu of exaggerated fears that political parties like the British National Party (BNP) are able to gain several council seats in the local elections in England.

The slaughter of thousands of innocent Afghan and Iraqi civilians with the victims having no association with terror whatsoever, yet being subjected to aggressive campaigns, have raised serious issues of legitimacy of invasion, demolition of property and destruction of environment, especially in these two affected countries. The post-invasion debate on the illegality, immorality and intensity of military offensives has been accentuated both in the United Kingdom and the United States, the two main perpetrators and leaders of the anti-terror campaign.[8] The lack of proof on Iraq's hyped up linkages with Al Qaeda, or for that matter of the ordinary Afghans with Osama bin Laden's group, the non-discovery of the Weapons of Mass Destruction (WMDs) despite erstwhile diffusion of flimsy and often plagiarized evidence to the effect, and the continuation of extra-judicial killings of the Pushtuns and Iraqis have assumed serious legal and moral dimensions. The suicide of David Kelly on 18 July 2003, the British scientist working for the Ministry of Defence, in mysterious circumstances, followed by the US Congressional report on 24 July 2003 regarding the intelligence failure on the September attacks and the absence of linkages between Osama bin Laden and Saddam Hussein seemed to gradually attain the stature of an 'Iraqgate'.[9]

In a sense, the salience of fundamentalist and neo-conservative forces is not unique to the developing world where politico-economic factors may have put secular and moderate forces on the defensive.[10] Polities like the United States, and within the European Union, have embodied an enduring legacy of unitary nationalisms and specific attitudes towards pluralism, immigration and civil rights for a long time. In the recent past, discretionary policies towards ethno-religious communities have often bordered on sheer racism. The colonisation, slavery, missionary enterprise, scramble for markets and profits, intermittent wars and violence, the Holocaust, discrimination against minorities and the various forms of ethnic cleansing within Europe, the Western Hemisphere, Australasia and Africa (against the native millions) have been the major components of this historical tradition itself banking on an aggressive modernity. Thus, the resurgence of powerful pressure groups espousing exclusive and aggressive policies is nothing new or unprecedented, though the level of collective violence has certainly decreased within these democracies thanks to the evolution of alert civil societies and human rights groups. The politicians, media and racist outfits still use exclusive ideologies and primordial symbols to appease 'majorities', so as to increase their vote banks.[11] For example, in early 2003, prominent British politicians especially from among the Conservative Party and the racist BNP were juxtaposing asylum seekers with terrorists and illegal immigrants. Ian Duncan Smith, the Tory party leader, advocated the case for detention of all asylum seekers and refugees on their arrival in Britain. Such a dangerous ploy was being vociferously highlighted by dailies such as *The Daily Mail* and the *Sun*.

More than the Salman Rushdie affair in the early 1990s and the global recalcitration on Bosnia and Chechnya, the terrorist attacks in the United States followed by the American multi-pronged campaign have not only affected the Muslim–non-Muslim relationship, they have also reinvigorated the proponents of the 'clash of civilisations' theory. President Khatami's advocacy of dialogue among civilisations in the new millennium was overtaken by a new spectrum of events and rather ironic developments. The biases against the Muslim Diaspora and misimages of Islam came out into the open, and amidst profiling interrogation and strict immigration regimes, tolerance and celebration of pluralism appeared to be diminishing from within an enlarged Fortress West. The sustained bombing of Afghanistan, a continued silence on civilian killings in that unfortunate country, and the destruction of ecological zones through some of the heaviest bombings ever of an already devastated country generated an extreme anger in Europe and elsewhere. By 2003, Afghanistan was once again being left to the mercy of regional warlords and the promises of a new, peaceful and reconstructed Afghanistan appeared to have vanished. Emancipation became another long night of waiting and shattered hopes. The induction of NATO troops in the country in August 2003 still hinted towards the primacy of security concerns over reconstructive efforts. A plethora of books further demonising the Taliban, critiquing the entire ideology of Jihad and occasionally dramatising Political Islam have filled a growing demand and curiosity on this 'not-so-new-enemy'. The Bush administration, supported by Blair's government, resolved to attack Iraq for a regime change as countries like Iran, Syria, Yemen, Pakistan and others feared a larger hidden agenda targeted against their resources and weaponry. Many Muslim groups internalised a severe dose of anti-Americanism though saner voices cautioned for cool-headedness, yet the messianic American juggernaut appeared unstoppable.[12] Harold Pinter, Gore Vidal, Noam Chomsky, Arundhati Roy and several others felt that the double standards being pursued by Western powers, and especially by the Bush Administration, cannot be brushed aside.[13] President Bush's State of Union Address on 28 January 2003 and his press conference on 6 March unequivocally applied Christian and moral symbols to justify attacks on Iraq, reaffirming once again that the foreign policy was being largely geared by some religious zeal. According to Ed Vulliamy, 'President Bush's Christian faith—with its messiah shared by both Martin Luther King and the racist Right—is a complex political weave.... Friends say that evangelical faith underpins his every action.'[14]

Several Muslim observers felt that attacking Afghanistan and Iraq did not offer solutions to the terrorist threat, which came from altogether different causes and sources. Instead, the Western campaigns seemed to have assumed anti-Muslim undertones, despite the rhetoric to the contrary. On the eve of another invasion of Iraq by the Anglo-American alliance, it was felt by a wide variety of Muslims that the Western regimes were intent upon destroying emerging Muslim states one after the other:

Iraq may well capitulate even quicker than the ragtag Taliban army did. But what if there is another terrorist attack on US soil? Where and how will the US look for terrorists among 1.3 billion people? Will it start by interning the six million Muslims residing in the US? What happens to a country like Pakistan, with 140 million people, if some fanatics from here conduct terrorist attacks against the US? Will we all face collective punishment like Afghanistan? This is the fear that is sweeping through the Muslim world.[15]

It was baffling for many analysts that both the religious zealots of the type of Osama bin Laden and secularist dictators like Saddam Hussein were equally problematic for the US, which had, in fact, used them for its own interests in the past.[16] Bin Laden had been one of the favoured Mujahideen fighting 'the evil empire', whereas Hussein had pursued the eight-year-long war against Khomeini's Iran, generously supported by the West. During the 1990s, the erstwhile allies had become sworn adversaries.

Other than the well-known and equally disputatious clash of cultures view, the hypotheses about the ingredients, trajectories and motives of Political Islam, despite an ever-increasing historiography, still remain largely unexplored. The usual hypotheses are: it is a war between modernity and tradition; an ongoing clash between a rational West and an emotional East; a rage of the House of Islam due to a hurt pride; Islam hijacked by clerics; it is the new *old enemy;* bloodthirsty, age-old puritanism revived in the name of divine laws and Jihad; holy war against a presumed unholy West and the Rest; an ideology gone astray thanks to illiterate *mullahs*; Muslim governments using the West and Israel as scapegoats to let their critics ventilate their resentment; a sexist, violent, barbarian community thirsting for civilised, developed and urbane community; jealousy and reaction of the Muslim people against a powerful West; an unchanging ideology stuck in a time warp and refusing to change; Islam urgently in need of Renaissance and Reformation; authoritarianism ordained in the name of Allah against systems based on humanism and individual freedom; a new collective fascism against rational individualism of the West; an economic, sexist and militarist threat; a mish-mash of fatalism, otherworldliness; the house of Allah arraigned against the secular/mundane, this-worldly house of reason and so on! Most of these views stem from either ignorance or sheer arrogance. Some of them do posit partisan truth but are strictly anchored on dramatised and exaggerated views of threat perceptions and betray racist, hegemonic and Orientalist antecedents.

They are also justified in the name of Judeo-Christian morality and by a complete Othering of Islam. The most powerful exponents of such neo-orientalist views are scholars like Bernard Lewis and Daniel Pipes; evangelists like Pat Robertson and Frank Graham; media pundits such as Oriana Fallaci; politicians like Silvio Berlusconi; and strategists such as Richard Perle, Paul Wolfowitz and similar other groups led by ideologues like Ann Coulter.

To the neo-conservative elements within the Bush administration seeking to establish the age-old, Puritan-like American dream and control over the world, especially after the 'defeat' of communism, Political Islam turns out to be the main threat and destabilising force, especially for Israel, the closest ally. To them, this ideology is an antithesis to democracy other than being incorporative of all those ingredients listed above. Applying brutal military force against such a civilizational foe becomes both a moral and patriotic obligation. The invincibility of a hyper power is to be maintained only through a pre-emptive and massive use of military power, and in the process, democratisation and greater peace in the larger interest will come about. Thus to them, the salience of US power is synonymous with democracy, morality and rule of law—all the major components of the nineteenth century imperious ideology. In the same vein, their adversaries are not just the fundamentalist Muslims—the turbaned and bearded hordes—but also their 'liberal' sympathisers and Diaspora groups. Under such a McCarthyian presumption, the anti-globalisation, anti-war and anti-Zionist forces are defined as 'Muslim lovers' deserving no sympathy, and are the enemies within. Concurrently, Political Islam, in an exaggerated imagination, gets intertwined with global fundamentalism.

On the contrary, Muslim fundamentalists enthused by a simplistic view of the rest (West and pro-Western elite) believe that by using self-immolative strategies they can blast their way through all the hurdles. While some of them employ democratic symbols and promise egalitarian, corruption- and exploitation-free alternatives, they, in almost all the cases, are repressive and unilateral. While the Western neo-conservatives seek rewards in this world through a greater power and unchallenged primacy of market forces and related financial and military instruments, the Islamicists promise both a glorified hereafter and a global hegemony. In fact, both of them have more in common and are essentially hegemonic and militarist though the latter, unlike the former, do not have the extensive wherewithal except for conviction and rudimentary weapons. They seek to redress Muslim grievances all over the world and aim at establishing a New Canaan, just like their Judeo-Christian counterparts. While the former may be strong in terms of their resources, the latter solely depend upon a motivational ideology of sacrifice for higher ideals.

On the other hand, it will be incorrect to suggest that Muslims do not have similar views about the West, which also betray their misperceptions and biases. While the Western discourse reveals hegemony, power and arrogance, the Muslim images of the West, at the ordinary level, are also unrealistic. The West is all-powerful and glorious, or simply corrupt, manipulative and immoral. Other than these two opposite opinion groups, several emerging well-informed clusters on all sides emphasise interdependence, and seek out socio-economic tensions and geo-political factors underwriting reciprocal hostility. Instead of merely identifying themselves as rejectionists, antagonists or apologists, such opinion groups consist of synthesisers and cosmopolitans who posit Islam in the West, and West in Islam. To them, fundamentalism—Christian, Muslim, Jewish or Hindu—poses a grave threat to any society, especially to women, underprivileged communities, ethno-religious minorities and critical intelligentsia. Such a global civil society is definitely disparate yet part of an international humanism, purported to look at the socio-economic roots of the anomalous relationship. It also seeks the rise of fundamentalism, among other mundane factors, in reference to a massive disempowerment across vast sections of Muslim societies. To them, fundamentalism is a human phenomenon rooted in mundane causes yet shrouded in a religious cloak. It seeks its sustenance from literal interpretations of scriptures and justifies its case on the basis of a bygone yet attainable glorious past. Its articulation is through a mesmerising oratory or populist rhetoric, dished out by charismatic, apparently unpretentious, rhetoricians.

Within this context, a group of Muslim intellectuals—like their counterparts in other societies facing such ideological chasms—are starting to reconstruct a fresher Islamic discourse that imbibes humanism, equality, tolerance, critique and democratisation. Such activist scholars do not have a single platform and some of them may be simply theology-oriented, or living in exile in the West and thus at the forefront of a cross-cultural dialogue.[17] However, the spotlight on political issues merely as an *Islamic* problem or just a clash between a democratic West and a traditional Islam, though quite popular among the Western Neo-Conservatives, is not only simplistic but also overlooks the similarities in the two camps. For instance, Michael Ignatieff, an assertive North Atlantic ideologue, fails to see that the recent Western campaigns, despite early moral espousal, have not been aimed at a common good, democracy or even nation-building, at places like Kosovo, Afghanistan and Iraq. He does not appear sure-footed when he suggests: 'The essential paradox of nation-building is that temporary imperialism—empire lite—has become the necessary condition for democracy in countries torn apart by civil war.'[18] To a Russian-Canadian scholar at Harvard, the military control of conflict-ridden societies, which he calls 'empire lite' or 'temporary imperialism', is justified until they are able to establish harmonious and democratic systems. To him, for example, leaving a porous Pakistani-Afghan border without any such mechanism in place only led to chaos in the region and eventually the advent of terrorism under Al Qaeda. On the contrary, the fact remains that countries and regions such as Afghanistan, Pakistan, Palestine, Kashmir, Bosnia, Chechnya, Iraq or several Latin American polities became further fractious due to foreign interventions. In the same vein, most, if not all the contemporary conflicts, are rooted in colonial antecedents and arbitrary or hasty border demarcations by the receding colonial powers. Instead of ushering peace and democracy in these vast regions, colonialism only left them poorer, fractious and unstable. The emphasis on management and administration over governance and participatory democracy only retarded the evolution of empowered societies, though some historians may still like to romanticise this imperial past.[19]

Some balanced observers of Political Islam highlight various contemporary Muslim articulations on the relationship with the West and the rest. One group consists of intellectual activists such as Osama bin Laden, Ayman al-Zawahiri, Khalid Shaikh Mohammad, Omar Saeed Shaikh, Abu Doha, Abu Quttadah and Muhammad Atta, imbued with an idealised recreation of the Muslim past through scholarly, as well as armed struggle. These individuals have internalised a kind of history where Islam was a sublime and ideal civilisation, squandered by a corrupt and inept elite. The West, symbolising moral decadence, an enduring hostility towards Muslims since the early times, and intent upon exploiting Muslim regions and resources—in close conjunction with the surrogate Muslim elite—has to be encountered through Jihad. The inspiration for these people comes from the Muslim classical era, especially the Pious Caliphate. To them, the Afghan Jihad of the 1980s affirms their vision of defeating worldly powers like the former Soviet Union, today's United States, India and Israel or even some Muslim regimes through selective militarist strategy based on sublimation of self-sacrifice. To them, both the Western regimes and their Muslim surrogate rulers are the main enemies, and strategies like dialogue or democracy may not hold much water. To resist and die is a divine duty for a better life for fellow believers, over and above one's own family and material needs. They are Allah's soldiers in the tradition of early Muslim publicists and activists. These individuals are found all over the Muslim world, with varying degrees of training and intensity, and represent a new generation, successors to that of Syed Mawdudi and Sayyid Qutb. Their acts of self-sacrifice through suicide bombings or face-to-face encounters are not simply out of desperation or fanaticism, instead they represent dedication to a higher goal. Of course, Kashmir, Palestine, Chechnya, Iraq and Afghanistan are political issues where foreign powers—mostly non-Muslim—have invaded the lands and communities of believers, whose emancipation, according to pervasive Muslim consensus, becomes a communitarian duty. Since most of these invading powers are non-Muslim, a type of Muslim globalism becomes a natural bonding strand across the borders and divides. The fighters and guerrillas—both men and women—are, in the first instance, mostly native people, while a Muslim voluntary cadre would be willing to help them, though it may be an immensely uphill task, especially after 9/11, given all the restrictions and vigilance on trans-border movements. Bosnia offered a classic case since the UN-led embargo, common official Muslim apathy and lack of familiarity with the terrain and languages all posed serious handicaps for Muslim activists in reaching their Balkan co-religionists, yet the support for a common cause remained undiminished. The strategies to bomb them from the air or kill ordinary people *en masse*, deportation to camps such as Guantanamo Bay or even a complete occupation as of Palestine, Iraq or Chechnya are militarist strategies along with temptation and cooption that regimes have been pursuing selectively across these regions. As seen time and again, they have all failed in containing Muslim activism nor have they helped the local allies, since these bands are too numerous and scattered though they all share similar goals and perceptions of common enemies. Any news of more Muslims getting killed naturally further popularises their cause among the ordinary Muslims besides exacerbating the general anguish. That is why all the American claims of victories over militants appear further hollow as neither has the militancy been contained, nor have the frequency of massive attacks on hotels, Western targets and resorts been halted. However, it will be unwise to suggest that all these Muslim activists speak with one voice and have a common platform.

Another recent group of Islamicists comprises of individual militants who emerged in the 1980s and 1990s and have taken it upon themselves to displace political controls of the Muslim communities. Most of them are trained in the local *madrassas* or mosques and do not have the scholarly acumen and sophistication of the other two above-mentioned groups. Such groups are in large numbers, as unlike Catholicism, the Anglican Church, Reformed or Orthodox Judaism or even Shia hierarchies, they do not have a single church-like infrastructure. They may belong to different schools of thoughts, Sufi order, or of jurisprudence (*Fiqah*), and the prescriptions by writers such as Daniel Pipes, Bernard Lewis or Thomas Friedman advocating some kind of a renaissance of Islam does not hold any ground simply because Sunni Islam does not have a single church. Even Shia Islam, despite a tradition of *ijtiha'ad* and the institutions of *Mujta'ahid* and *Ayatollah*, would never accept any Euro-centric prescriptions. This cluster of Muslim organizations may include the Taliban, radical Algerian groups such as the Front Islamique du Salut (FIS), the Kashmiri Harkatul Mujahidin (HM) and the Lashkar-i-Tayyaba (LT). These clusters are neither totally middle class, nor do they represent illiterate laity, rather they consist of an emerging intermediate class, which is eagerly seeking its own role through a massive populism. Here the demographic changes such as urbanisation, greater mobility and awareness of global Muslim issues play an important role in establishing a Muslim camaraderie. These activists are seeking their own niche in the Muslim states by challenging their continued disempowerment and offer foot soldiers for all kinds of Islam-related movements. Despite some support from *sajjada nashins* and Sufi elements, they are predominantly literalists by choice, and are sectarian by intent, as seen in South, South-western and South-eastern Asia. The Lashkar-i-Tayyaba (LT), Anjuman-i-Sipah-i-Sahaba Pakistan (ASSP) and Lashkar-i-Jhangvi (LJ) are vocally anti-Shia because the former have been trained in a puritanical version of Islam, whereas Shias continue to challenge a Sunni consensus on the Pious Caliphate, the political successors of the Prophet (PBUH). The Deobandi forms of Islamic interpretations have certainly influenced some of these activists, whereas the others have been the beneficiaries of regimes such as those of Saudi royalty or General Zia. Some hasty analysts congregate them as *Wahabbis*, a hasty and simplistic identification given to all kinds of historical, political, economic and doctrinal variables. As witnessed in the recent past in Pakistan, they were the junior partners in the military regime's own regional trajectories and often fought as vanguard guerrillas in Kashmir. Their politicisation, instead of having been cast into some tangible electoral processes, was not only intentionally militarised by the regime and its external backers, but was also diverted to regional causes such as Kashmir and Afghanistan. This military–mullah axis remained a major retroactive political force denying space to other democratic forces, until the September attacks put new strains on it.[20] To all these groups, Islam is already a complete code of life, and by capturing political power either through the ballot or by the bullet, they have to promulgate it as the supreme law. They are definitely against *Ijtiha'ad* or reinterpreting Islam and only emphasise Jihad in its militarist incarnation, evading its scholarly or other humanitarian varieties. They stipulate a very limited role for women and a selective reading of Muslim history, combined with exaggerated and often conflictive views of the West, that underline their ideological convictions. Despite a devotional commitment to their causes, especially the liberation of occupied Muslim regions from non-Muslim regimes, they aim at imposing a unilateral system on their fellow believers. Such a majoritarianism, like that of Hindutva proponents in India, Neo-Conservatives in the United States, Zionists in Israel and such like groups elsewhere, is a spill-over from the contradictory imprints of modernity where the definition of a collective identity itself becomes a free-for-all contestation.

Perhaps the best theoretical framework to understand the rise of neo-conservatism such as Political Islam with its fundamentalist undertones and militarist strategy is through locating it within the discourse on democracy. Instead of seeing Political Islam as 'one-off' or sheer medievalist violence justified in the name of Jihad, we need to seek its modernist roots. Its slogans, strategies and symbolism, despite a traditionalist outlook, are inherently modern. It may desire an *ummah*, yet it is rooted in the very territorial grounds of a Westphalian nation state system. It equally reflects a power struggle and reaction to colonialism, Orientalism and industrialism, which continue to characterise a powerful West. It is a global class conflict without a clear replacement mechanism to enthuse adherents and is thus not an alien phenomenon. Like colonialism, it is masculine and self-righteous and like the Western neo-conservatives, uses morality to suit its jargons. Like fascism, communism, utopianism and globalisation, it is part and parcel of a larger human career and interaction at several levels since a movement of this scale would not evolve in a vacuum. Muslim polities dominated by Political Islam, like Saudi Arabia, Pakistan, Afghanistan, Iran and the Gulf States, invariably, have been closely linked in dependency relationships with the Western powers all the way from the colonial era to contemporary times. In the same manner, the main proponents of Political Islam such as Sayyid Qutb, Muhammad Qutb, Ismail Faruki, Abdallah Azzam, Syed Mawdudi, or even activists such as Osama bin Laden have been either students in the West or have had closer and often interesting interaction with Western institutions. These extra-ordinary figures, all seeking the resurgence of Islam, were influenced by modernity either by living directly in the West or interacting with its culture and power indirectly. Most of their formative ideas were, in fact, constructed through that formative interaction. For instance, Sayyid Qutb (1906–1966) the great thinker of Political Islam and the leader of the Muslim Brotherhood, formed his own opinion of Western 'immorality' during his stay in the United States. Syed Mawdudi (1903–1979) had a similar interaction with the Egyptian Sayyid Qutb, as well as with the West. To both of them, the West stood for nudity, free sex, individualism and materialism. Its secularist approach to politics was further distancing people from religious mores and the concept of the nation-state was basically a conspiracy to divide Muslims. The best way forward was to reject this Western heritage and rediscover the puritanical version of Islam away from all types of lateral synthesis. Muhammad Qutb, the younger brother of Sayyid Qutb taught at King Abdul Aziz University in Saudi Arabia and influenced individuals like Osama bin Laden, originally from a tribe in southern Hadharmaut. Osama came back to Islam after escapades in the Lebanon and elsewhere and joined the US-Saudi-Pakistani–funded Jihad in Afghanistan. Sayyid Qutb had been hanged by Gamal Nasser's regime in Egypt in 1966, but Saudi efforts to strengthen a puritanical brand of Islam coincided with US imperatives during the Cold War. The largest aid mission was undertaken by the CIA and other Western governments to help the Mujahideen against the Soviets at a time when Osama bin Laden landed in Peshawar.[21] His senior Islamist colleague, Abdallah Azzam, a Jordanian-Palestinian, was also based in Peshawar doing the groundwork for Al Qaeda until he was killed in 1989 and bin Laden succeeded him as the new supremo of this family-like network.[22] The other activists making news such as Ramzi Yusuf, Abdur Rahman—the blind Egyptian scholar—Jama'at-i-Islami's leadership such as Professor Ijaz Gilani, and several other individuals like Abu Hamza and Aimal Kansi were working in close collaboration with the Western regimes and agencies during the Afghan Jihad. The dissolution of the Soviet Union, the West walking away from Afghanistan and leaving its former allies out in the cold, and the state-led repressive policies pursued by Israel, India and Russia redirected the Jihadists and proponents of Political Islam to new ventures. Shambolic and equally violent developments in a bleeding Algeria shortly following the electoral victory by the Islamists, and denial of political power to them under the French dissuasion, all revived the images of a corrupt, immoral and pro-Zionist West. The emergence of the Taliban, in the meantime, offered both a well-needed sanctuary, as well as a hope for implementing the long-awaited project of Political Islam. The spineless Muslim regimes such as in Saudi Arabia were to be replaced by true Islamist governments, away from the exploitation and dependency of the Western 'crusaders and Zionists'. The United States, as viewed by Sayyid Qutb earlier, was the centre of this immoral, anti-Muslim and staunchly pro-Israel West, whose arrogance had to be shattered. The recruits, encouragement and money came from Saudi individuals already studying or staying in the United States—not the Taliban stragglers at all. The educated, motivated, affluent and well-organised Islamists were to take on the financial and military centres of the arch enemy, and on 11 September, they 'destroyed the West's ruling myth.'[23]

A more recent view within the diverse domain of Political Islam is a minority view of Muslim and Islamic secularists, to whom Islam is receptive to democracy, secularism and gender equality. Earlier, such a view was held by Muslim modernists such as Syed Ahmed Khan, Muhammad Abduh, Muhammad Iqbal and Fazlur Rahman, to be eclipsed by orthodox rejectionists. Though Muslim secularism was practiced at places such as Bosnia or Turkey, and was individually subscribed by scholars and political activists, it has, once again, resurfaced as a *possibility* and even a solution to Muslim predicament itself. Regimes like the Ba'athists in Iraq and Syria, Nasser's Egypt, Socialist Algeria and Kemalist Turkey have often pursued secularist policies selectively and also largely within a non-democratic context, and scholarly opinions on the desirability of Muslim secularism have remained sparse, even more so in the Diaspora. However, after a decade following the Revolution in Iran, the use of a narrowly defined Islam all over the Muslim world, both by the regimes and religious elements, has spawned a curious clerical-intellectual interest in secularism and democracy. This can be defined as Islamic secularism though it is still in its embryonic stage and is confined to some Shia theologians in Iraq and Iran, though in the latter case it remains a rather subterranean discourse due to official strictures. In an interview with a well-known American journalist in August 2003, Sayyid Iyad Jameleddine, a prominent Shia jurist in Baghdad, saw no conflict between Islam and secularism or Islam and democracy. He felt that Islam needed to be emancipated from the monopolistic holds of both the sacred and the state, as he observed:

> We want a secular constitution. That is the most important point. If we write a secular constitution and separate religion from state, that would be the end of despotism and it would liberate religion as well as the human being. The Islamic religion has been hijacked for fourteen centuries by the hands of the state.

A mentor of Sayyid Hussein Khomeini, the grandson of the late Imam Khomeini, Jameleddine, sounded a modernist view of reinterpreting the Holy Book, as he noted:

> The Koran is a book to be interpreted (by) each age. Each epoch should not be tied to interpretations from 1,000 years ago.[24]

Thus, to argue that Political Islam is a rejectionist monolith without any ideological or several other such diverse moorings is fallacious. Its numerous constellations and trajectories are as much a part and parcel of modernity, retaining an uneven relationship with the West and the rest, as the other way around. Concurrently, all are undergoing similar universal experiences with the Neo-Conservatives, Islamicists, Zionists and Hindu Kar Sevaks all attempting to establish, in their own distinct ways, larger-than-life utopias of *imagined* communities. The project(s) of Political Islam being still undefined, often seeks recourse in militarist ventures, the way the Neo-Conservatives are driven by an altruistic desire to pursue what several Western analysts define as non-benevolent Neo-Imperialism:

What we are seeing is in effect a re-visiting of the attitudes preceding nineteenth century colonial Britain. Now, as was the case then, there is a belief within the British and US governments that the people of the Muslim world are not capable of ruling themselves, that the so-called civilised nations of the West have every right to impose their will, because they've decided that is the way it is to be. This so-called War on Terror is barely disguised neo-imperialism, giving birth to oriental despotism as perfectly illustrated by the likes of Donald Rumsfeld.[25]

And 11 September came not merely as a wake-up call, but also as a sought-after opportunity to put such ideas into practice.

9/11 AND ...

The post-September American outrage, despite an early sympathy for the United States, soon began to feed into a predating anti-Americanism across the globe. The decimation of Afghanistan, deaths of its innocent civilians and a continued lack of interest in its reconstruction despite promises, only added to a severe criticism of the US hegemonic tendencies. The support for Sharon in his brutalisation of the Palestinians, the failure to censure Putin for Russia's manhandling of the Chechen republic, and an aggressive and trumped-up campaign against Iraq without any legal or moral justification, fuelled a strong critique of the Bush and Blair administrations. Washington's backtracking on the Koyto Agreement, revival of the Star Wars programme amidst the unprecedented highest defence hike in US history and a cold shoulder to the Europeon Union (EU) partners over trade, and other economic issues were translated as unchecked corporate capitalism and a 'go-alone' foreign policy setting the agenda for a new world order. The American unilateralism on global affairs, a growing disenchantment with the General Agreement on Trade and Tariff (GATT), World Trade Organisaiton (WTO), and highly publicised yet controversial globalisation were all perceived as unbound arrogance at the expense of larger human and ecological prerogatives. The ascendancy of neo-conservative hawks within the administration, many of them members of Bush Senior's cabinet, with their own unfulfilled agendas, was perceived as a continuation of unilateralist approach to intricate international issues. To many critics, the invasion of Iraq, despite a global and UN-led disavowal, and without tangible proof of the Weapons of Mass Destruction (WMDs) simply betrayed a desire to complete 'Daddy's War' or to meet the gluttonous American oil requirement. The 'conspiracy theory' advocates used such arguments forcefully, especially after the North Korean resumption of its nuclear enrichment programme, and a muffled response from Washington. The doubts about Bush's own presidential victory in 2000, though validated by the US Supreme Court, along with his linguistic travails simply multiplied apprehensions about various specific lobbies attempting to push their own interests.[26] Though Bush was defended as an objective leader by some of his detractors, still, the doubts about his capabilities and 'a war without causes but several excuses' continued to unnerve many opinion groups.[27] It should not be forgotten that where the United States does not lack in critics, it has its international share of defenders who feel that while dealing with Osama bin Laden and Saddam Hussein, Washington had been rather accommodative instead of jumping the gun.[28]

The post-September peace movement across the globe and especially in Euro-American regions has continued to grow, not essentially on the back of some anti-Americanism but for a more plural, peaceful and multilateral world. The issues of war, exploitation of ecology, and violence against asylums seekers have remained the major focal point, with the Anglo-American military campaigns against Afghanistan and Iraq catapulting the various ideological groups into a formidable coalition. The unique features of the peace movement have been its universality and multi-culturalism as it welded diverse ideological strands together for a better world. The anarchists, liberals, socialists, church leaders, students, Islamists, politicians, women, media and academics, all joined hands in a new internationalism from below against discriminatory regimes and restrictive and coercive policies. Such a phenomenon was never witnessed even during the height of the anti-Vietnam war movement. The year 2003 dawned with some of the largest demonstrations and peace marches ever seen in Washington, San Francisco, New York, London, Paris, Berlin, Madrid, Rome, Cairo, Lahore, Karachi, Calcutta, Jakarta, Sydney and Tokyo. Such powerful public opinion appeared to be the only deterrent against pre-emptive strikes, especially at a time when the United Nations (UN) seemed to have come under strong unilateralist pressures. Concurrently, when Germany and France dithered on a full-fledged Anglo-American attack on Iraq without a new UN resolution, Tony

Blair tried to hammer out a new alliance within the EU. The governments of Spain, Portugal, Denmark, Poland, the Czech Republic, Italy and the United Kingdom resolved to support the British-American invasion of Iraq. Such an initiative not only divided the EU on this crucial matter, but equally attempted to ignore the anti-war public opinion within these countries. *Le Figaro* called the alliance a 'Gang of Eight', whereas *Liberation* accused America for being 'keen to divide the Europeans in order better to rule them.'[29] The German newspaper, *Die Welt* characterised the move as 'the death knell' for a common EU foreign policy.[30] The Spanish papers, in most cases, censured Madrid for offering full-fledged support to the United States without allowing sufficient time to the UN arms inspectors. According to *El Mundo* opinion, polls in the country showed anti-war sentiments being the highest in Europe—almost 80 per cent—while the regime seemed to offer unqualified support to London and Washington. Barcelona-based *El Periodico* felt that the Spaniards will be 'disappointed' by political gestures aimed at 'distancing us...from France and Germany.'[31] The British liberal view held that Blair, despite his early enthusiasm for an integrated Europe and continent-wide adored social reformism, had turned away from Continental links in preference for trans-Atlantic bilateralism. Blair, despite being 'the first British leader in a generation to command true influence in Europe, has squandered it by playing lapdog to George Bush.'[32]

MUSLIMS: PERPETRATORS OR VICTIMS

Notwithstanding the destruction of yet another Muslim community after Afghanistan, Palestine, Chechnya, Kashmir, Bosnia and Gujarat, it is largely the disempowered and mostly an underdeveloped Muslim world that presents a massive spectrum of dismay, uncertainty and gloom in the new millennium. Gone are the hopes of a post-colonial bright future where dignity, sovereignty and prosperity were to be the order of the day. Half a century later, the majority still remain abysmally poor, uneducated and underprivileged, largely owing to a myriad of indigenous and external factors. Led by fiery clerics and their rhetorical outbursts, a neo-feudalism is taking its toll from amongst the minorities and women. To a wide array of Muslim opinion, the war on terror had already become a war on Islam, where no self-respecting Muslim country would be allowed to defy the hegemonic powers. General Musharraf's support for the United States after ditching the Taliban, and the official Muslim assistance to the Anglo-American alliance against Iraq deeply angered the Muslims, and by default, rehabilitated many fundamentalist groups. The 'return to Islam' in countries like Turkey, Pakistan, and Bangladesh through electoral processes or by dint of sheer street power, was embedded in a significant sense of hurt over continued Muslim disempowerment. While more than 90 per cent Muslims in Britain considered the war on Iraq to be basically a war against Muslims, the Muslim world at large, overwhelmingly refused to believe in the official propaganda emanating from London and Washington. The few efforts by Bush and Blair to portray the war as a campaign against a brutal regime and not against Islam, failed to convince the Muslim majority and other peace protesters. Washington's unquestioned support for Ariel Sharon angered Muslim masses and intelligentsia alike. The Anglo-American alliance, led by two practising Christian leaders, had lost the battle of the hearts, though after 9/11 there was a reservoir of universal sympathy for America in particular.

The internment of hundreds of Muslims across the EU and North America, the ill treatment of undefined prisoners in Guantanamo Bay, and lack of formidable evidence on the terrorists simply betrayed a misplaced official zeal contrasted with a widespread public uproar.[33] The perpetrators of the September attacks were highly sophisticated, well knit, immensely motivated individuals who exhibited a thorough proficiency in their planning and execution of terrorist activities, a world apart from the hapless figures interned amidst great guffaws. The news of their arrests was more often splashed with sensationalism and media indictment, soon to die out amidst lack of proof and substance, but not without doing damage to inter-community relations. The vibes against asylum seekers and immigrants—hastily characterised as terrorists and members of Al Qaeda—were hyped up routinely, as if the terrorists would seek such well-known, regulated channels to perpetrate their outrage.

The terrorist activities attributed to Al Qaeda have hurt Muslims the most besides the innocent victims and their families. This travesty cost the Afghans, Palestinians, Chechens, Indian Muslims, Iraqis and the Muslim Diaspora dearly. For a vast majority of Muslims the terrorist attacks on the World Trade Center were 'a violation of Islamic laws and ethics', and the claims of seven thousand British Muslims fighting for the Taliban proved untrue: 'I said that if they could find

seven, I would give them a medal. In fact, not a single British Muslim
fought against the British forces—the only ones who went there were
on humanitarian work,' observed Zaki Badawi, a leading British
Muslim intellectual.[34] Undoubtedly, the Muslim sense of loss and hurt
since the late twentieth century is comprehensible when one looks at
the rekindling of Neo-Orientalism with a strong tinge of racism in the
post-Salman Rushdie affair.[35] Like the colonial discourse anchored on
a strong racist typology, the Muslims were 'othered' as savage, uncouth
book burners. Islam was resurrected as an anti-liberal, anti-
civilisational and anti-democratic demagogy. Media and other opinion
groups only saw Khomeini as a Muslim persona. The Iran-Iraq war
was considered to be proof of some inherent Islamic penchant for
violence. The erstwhile fondness for valorous Mujahideen in
Afghanistan fighting 'the Evil Empire' quickly evaporated, to be
replaced by new damning caricatures. The Bosnians suffered the
longest siege in Europe's history but the international community
including the United Nations, and especially the Muslim regimes, failed
to undertake any tangible steps. Ethnic cleansing in the Balkans and in
Rwanda appeared far too distant and complex to be addressed through
resolute actions, but aggravated a sense of hurt and helplessness.

Reverberating the anti-war sentiments, Edward Said censured the
Arab leaders as well as the West in a widely publicised piece amidst a
growing war mania in Washington, with the Muslim world finding
itself rudderless:

> We are on the eve of a catastrophe that our political, moral and religious
> leaders can only just denounce a little bit while, behind whispers and
> winks and closed doors, they make plans somehow to ride out the storm.
> They think of survival, and perhaps of heaven. But who is in charge of the
> present, the world, the land, the water, the air and the lives dependent on
> each other for existence? No one seems to be in charge.[36]

Without subscribing to the clash of civilisations theory, one still cannot
ignore the partisan nature of the Western, and especially the American
policies towards the developing world, the Muslim world being a
major part of it. The dissolution of the Soviet Union has, by no means,
meant that the prerogatives of a properly interdependent world be put
aside for some specific interests. While many Americans may be at a
loss to understand why huge sections of world opinion felt
uncomfortable with their official policies, the critique by their
intellectuals such as Noam Chomsky or Gore Vidal certainly merited

wider public attention. Critics detected 'an increasingly perceptible gap between our need for social transformation and America's insistence on stability....'[37] Many observers believe that, to a significant extent, the Jihadi culture in several Muslim regions was revived by the United States during the cold war in the 1980s when Afghanistan became the battleground:

> I have seen planeloads of them arriving from Algeria, Sudan, Saudi Arabia, Egypt, Jordan, even from Palestine where at that time Israel was supporting Hamas against Al Fatah....These people were brought in, given an ideology, and told that armed struggle is virtuous—and the whole notion of jihad as an international, pan-Islamic terrorist movement was born. The US has spent billions in producing the bin Ladens of our time.[38]

Certainly, among its many other props, the grave politico-economic deprivation, as acknowledged by several Western politicians, has been spawning a vulnerability to extremist and terrorist tendencies.[39]

SOUTH ASIA: A NEW BALL GAME

South Asia is in a great flux and one needs to focus on some of the ideological formulations within the context of their historical antecedents and multiple strategies. The societal chasms within all the South Asian states converge with the regional incongruities and hostilities, which have more often been compounded by external interventions. Despite being on the 'periphery', the region has been a battleground for an erstwhile East-West Cold War, as witnessed in the competitive and conflictive polices pursued by the United States, the Soviet Union and China until the early 1990s.[40] With the dissolution of the Cold War, the South Asian states redefined their alignments in a unipolar world though the region, for a while, remarkably turned marginal in global politics. The salience of the BJP, despite its avowal for a uniformist and exclusivist nationalism—Hindutva—did not register any external resentment as India pursued electoral politics and an accelerated privatisation. Following a violent warlordism, a marginal Afghanistan came under the Taliban hegemony, whereas democracy in Pakistan suffered both from inertia and an army-led interventionism. Bangladesh experienced yet another phase of unmitigated inter-personality polarisation, still not as fiercely as was the case with Sri Lanka, yet party politics remained volatile. Its travails with India over border security and the widespread anti-Bengali feelings in Assam and the north-east continued to sour bilateral relations. The Indian papers frequently carried news of a rising tide of Islamic fundamentalism in Bangladesh, along with occasional tirades from the BJP politicians. The Sri Lankan government initially appeared to be moving towards a negotiated reconciliation with the Tamils, though President Chandrika Kumaritunga continued to express her reservations, and eventually the Tamil-Colombo peace parleys broke down. Soon, Nepal was to plunge into a harrowing civil war between the royal forces and a populist Maoist insurrection costing seven thousand casualties in seven years.[41] The internal political instability, especially after the assassination of the royal family, combined with a fully-fledged insurgency, cast its shadow over the Himalayan kingdom. Both India and Pakistan tested their nuclear capabilities in May 1998, though in February 1999, a short-lived thaw raised some hopes following Prime Minister A.B. Vajpayee's visit to Lahore. But the clash over the Kargil Heights in the summer of 1999, not only swept aside bilateral gains, the generals also lost patience with the electoral institutions. In October 1999, General Pervez Musharraf overthrew Nawaz Sharif's government and imposed yet another military rule over Pakistan, which already suffered from sectarian violence and global indifference due to its support for the predominantly Pushtun Taliban. After the October coup, Pakistan was completely isolated, like a pariah state, but the terrorist attacks in the United States in September 2001 changed the regional geo-political scenario, and Islamabad re-emerged as the closest ally against the Taliban and Osama bin Laden's Al Qaeda. Musharraf's newly found support from Washington and London, and similarly, eagerness by the latter to keep India on their side allowed both the regimes to pursue their own specific policies without resolving the Kashmir dispute or stabilised confidence-building measures to avert any miscalculation in their pursuit for nuclear weaponization programmes. Elections held in Indian Kashmir, Gujarat and Pakistan, in the closing months of 2002, failed to reverse the imbalances within the polities and their gaping fissures. India conducted elections in Kashmir in October 2002, and despite Mufti Saeed's postulations and Pakistani restrictions on cross-border infiltration into the Valley, peace and calm failed to return. Elections in the state of Gujarat brought back the BJP-led Narendra Modi's administration with an overwhelming majority, dismaying those forces in India and elsewhere, who felt that a regime so deeply tainted with anti-Muslim violence would be thwarted through an electoral verdict. The Hindutva proponents, including Deputy Prime Minister, L.K. Advani, who portrayed them as Pakistani agents and supporters of fundamentalism, were scapegoating the Indian Muslims. In the same breath, such elements equated Pakistan with terrorism, though Prime Minister Vajpayee appeared to distance himself from these elements in his party and desired a better relationship with the estranged neighbour. The fact remains that there has been a sea of change in the attitude of Indian Muslims over the last several decades. The emergence of the Taliban, insurrection in Kashmir and bickering with Pakistan have failed to change their loyalties towards their own homeland—India—-a fact admitted by many. B. Raman, formerly belonging to the Research and Analysis Wing (RAW)—the Indian counterpart of the Pakistani Inter-Services Intelligence (ISI)—is noted to have observed:

> In the 1980s, not a single Indian Muslim joined the mercenary force created by the CIA to fight against the Soviet troops in Afghanistan. When bin Laden created his International Islamic Front in 1998, many Islamic extremist organisations joined it. Not a single Indian organisation—not even from J&K—has done so. Hundreds of Muslims from all over the world rushed to Afghanistan to help the Taliban and Al Qaeda (after the October 2001 strikes). Not a single Indian—not even from J&K—has done so. [42]

General Musharraf's military regime conducted elections in the country by pre-empting them with his own controversial election to a five-year presidency through a dubious referendum and by inducting vital constitutional amendments under the Legal Framework Order (LFO) of August 2002. Both the measures turned the balance of power in Musharraf's favour as the Pakistani Army busied itself once again to tailor the country's politico-administrative structure through the intelligence agencies, aggravating its chronic problems of governance. The rising tide of anti-Americanism in Pakistan and exclusion of Benazir Bhutto and Nawaz Sharif, the two main political leaders in exile, had ensured greater electoral support for the religio-political parties. By early 2003, led by a Baloch tribal chieftain, Mir Zafrullah Jamali, Pakistan's political system, as crafted by the generals, embodied duality, where the real powers lay with the army chief and the ISI, while politicians stayed divided and unfocused. However, on the issue of the Anglo-American war on Iraq and Musharraf's contentious LFO, during the summer of 2003, they displayed an amazing amount of unity and consensus, though both the issues also reflected strong anti-American undertones. However, this crisis, largely created by the army to secure the General's own precarious position within the country's body politic, reaffirmed the long-held view that the polity suffered from severe internal imbalances. The imposition of a selective, and rather punitive form of Sharia law by the religio-political leaders in the NWFP equally dismayed the civic forces, who feared a gradual Talibanization of their country, owing to the vagaries of an ambitious military and the *mullahs*.

In 2003, South Asia still appeared stalemated into regional and domestic bickering. Though the troops from Indo-Pakistani borders had been withdrawn under US persuasion, the scheduled summit of the South Asian leaders was postponed amongst accusations and counter-allegations. The entire region seemed to be held hostage to an endemic Indo-Pakistani discord with fundamentalists and hardliners on both sides fanning the hatred, and their respective regimes swiping at each other. In the process, one-fifth of humanity, and in particular, the ethno-religious minorities found themselves in a precarious situation. The induction of Indo-Pakistani confidence-building measures following Prime Minister Vajpayee's offer for peace talks in April 2003, during his visit to Srinagar, beckoned a glimmer of hope, but the salience of formidably antagonistic forces on both sides contrasted with the weaker nature of regional civil societies, warranted a cautious optimism. The tumultuous changes in the backdrop of ideological contestations and trajectories such as Jihad and Hindutva require an academic investigation, so as to locate the contentious politics of identity among the major South Asian states, especially in reference to religion and nationalism. The internal and intra-state conflicts are being exacerbated by these dissensions with scarce resources being devoted to non-development sectors, while literacy, housing, healthcare, human rights and socio-economic development remain on hold. A societal divide, thanks to an increasing incidence of poverty aggravated by corrupt and inept administrative structures, exacerbated by an endemic regional discord, has allowed zealots to offer reductionist and xenophobic panaceas. The brainwashing of new generations through doctored texts and misinterpretation of histories to suit exclusive nationalist discourses—both validated in the name of majoritarianism and religion—have certainly put a plural South Asia at a testing cross roads.

Comparative studies on contemporary South Asia are few, and mostly historical in nature. These studies have usually concentrated either on the pre-1947 issues, or in their post-Partition perspective, have only researched individual states. The 'traditional' comparison between India and Pakistan has simply focused on secularism versus Islam, or on constitutional politics versus military takeovers. During the sixth decade of their existence, all the major subcontinental states are facing almost similar ideological challenges and appear vulnerable to a propped-up majoritarianism. What a military-dominated Pakistan did to its civic and plural institutions in the 1980s, Hindutva was bent upon doing under an elected regime. While the military regime in Islamabad in 2001–02 came under strong pressure to curb its support for militant and Jihadi elements—Taliban and others—the BJP-led regime in India continued spearheading the Hindutva campaign. Its self-congratulatory attitude over the Gujarat massacres and Modi's victory was perceived as a dress rehearsal of a similar sinister strategy to be implemented in the other states in the Indian Union. Afghanistan under Karzai showed some semblance of stability but lack of a countrywide political consensus, his own dependence on the American security forces, and the lack of global interest in the reconstruction of Afghanistan has regenerated serious concerns about its future. While the warlords pursued their own autonomous agenda amidst growing poppy cultivation, Karzai's writ remained confined to Kabul. Though on his foreign visits, he received a warm welcome, his appeals for a greater global financial and political engagement in his country remained unheard. Not only did the Afghans share a sense of betrayal, especially after massive American bombardment, the Pushtun majority equally felt that they were being denied their due representation in the new set-up. Political Islam and ethnicity seemed to be gradually re-emerging, amidst a pervasive sense of loss.[43] Bangladesh seems equally to be on the verge of a similar polarisation despite its successful transition to electoral politics. Sri Lanka has been progressing haphazardly towards a cherished peace through the peace parleys, but the dream of a 'New Hong Kong' stays dashed at the moment. Nepal, the quiet Himalayan Kingdom, is in the throes of civil war and political instability, whereas politics in Afghanistan and Pakistan remain uncertain and unaccountable. Such developments necessitate a comparative study, linking the societies and states in reference to their identity politics, civil societies and policies towards ethno-religious minorities. Benefiting from the realms of intellectual history and contemporary ideological debates on human rights in South Asia, the present study aims at exploring regional commonalties, as well as divergences.

Unlike the hasty and rather alarmist works focusing on Jihad, this research looks at this powerful Islamic tradition in its classical, early modern and more contemporary perspectives. It investigates some Jihadi elements including the Taliban and their gradual cooption of the *madrassa* culture in addition to highlighting the need for a steady reinterpretation of this significant trajectory, which is often assumed to be the sixth pillar of Islam. While the alarmist writers of the various shades simplify Jihad into a mere bloodletting ideology of vendetta and self-immolation, the apologists see in it a recourse to re-establish a lost glory. While regimes and several ideological clusters have appropriated the ideology of Jihad to suit their own prerogatives, a continued lack of consensus on its portents and situational imperatives has been seriously impacting the postulations of Political Islam. Undoubtedly, Jihad remains a major component of Political Islam, but the inherent ambiguities and uncritiqued anomalies not only seriously hinder a fresher discourse on collective Muslim identity, they also engender an unnecessary and misdirected violence. Consequently, Islam, instead of being recognised as a civilisational heritage, turns into a repressive dogma, monopolised by a few fundamentalists. A creed otherwise in its pristine form celebrating humanity and equality by thwarting hegemony, racism and exploitation itself becomes an oppressive and dismissive conformity. The second chapter explores the origins of Hindutva and its underlying historical and intellectual ingredients, purporting a more holistic and rather uniformist transformation of India. It seeks the background and the fall-out of an ever-present Ayodhya Mosque-Temple issue, both as a symptom and the cause of a larger ideological malaise, and its continuing imprints upon political, communal and regional domains. The next chapter delineates the course of civil society in Muslim South Asia both in its historical and contemporary phases, and flags the greater relevance of intellectual history of Islam in South Asia. It posits the problems of governance in Pakistan in reference to a continued and equally harmful relationship between an embryonic civil society and the vetoing statist institutions such as the army. The US-led Western alliance against terror zeroed in on Afghanistan with serious human, ideological and regional repercussions including increased Indo-Pakistani tensions over Kashmir. These thematic issues and their human cost have been analysed in the fourth chapter. The subsequent two chapters revisit the issues of nationalism, pluralism and identity politics in Pakistan and Bangladesh. The disenfranchisement of religious minorities in Pakistan since the 1980s is a human rights issue and a major challenge for its civil society. Based on extensive fieldwork, this section highlights the legal, constitutional and electoral dimensions of the predicament. The chapter on Biharis in Bangladesh—the *stranded Pakistanis*—in fact, highlights the problematic of national identity in both the predominantly Muslim countries, where a fellow ethno-religious community has been left asunder across 'the no-man's land'. It is premised that nationalism in South Asia remains a contested paradigm and the forces of globalization may make it even more contentious, where religio-ethnic minorities may face further marginalization. The Epilogue offers a brief resume of the quest for identity in South Asia within the changing regional and global contours.

NOTES

1. The Iranian Revolution of 1979, salience of the BJP in India in the late 1990s, the anti-Soviet resistance, and the ascension of the Taliban in Afghanistan during the 1980s and 1990s, all owed to modernist means and weaponry. Even the very acceptance of the given territorial statehood has been in apparent contradiction of trans-regional aims of such movements. All the three movements maintained the same state structures and many of the policies of their forerunners. In 2003, despite all the electoral promises for Sharia-based governance, the religio-political parties ruling the Frontier Province (NWFP) and Balochistan operated within existing rules and structures. However, their demands in March–April 2003 for the repeal of Musharraf's unilateral constitutional amendments under his preemptive Legal Framework Order (LFO) of August 2002, and a strong anti-American sentiment due to Anglo-American campaign against Iraq, engendered an atmosphere of grave suspicions. Such moves were soon followed by the imposition of Sharia law.

2. This emphasis on nativism, mingled with all its diverse components, is not merely a Third World phenomenon. The anti-immigration regimes, profiling of certain ethnic groups and strict border controls, amidst a growing accent on an exclusionary nationalism, have been evident across the board. All the way from Australia to Europe and North America, one sees these barriers being erected in the name of national security. For instance, the 'three-tiered frontiers' are meant to keep the United States 'safe' from eastern, southern and northern directions. Europe, while needing more human labour to operate its industrial and service sectors, ends up raising a fortress around it which poses serious dilemmas: 'How do you stay open to business, and stay closed to people,' asks an observer, who answers it herself: 'Easy. First you expand the perimeters. Then you lock down.' Naomi Klein, 'The Rise of Fortress Continent', *The Nation,* 16 January 2003.

3. Many charity organisations or individuals in Diaspora offer assistance to such
   organisations. The groups in Kashmir and Pakistan have been helped by external
   financial and moral support, whereas, the more recent exposé of the Vishwa Hindu
   Parishad (VHP), and its leading role in financing the Hindutva campaign have
   confirmed the external sources of support. A Britain-based Hindu charity, SEWA,
   despite a commendation from Prince Charles, was found to have sent funds and
   volunteers to Gujarat. Channel Four TV, on 12 December 2002, presented an
   investigative documentary on the links between charity and terror. Jonathan Miller,
   'Funding Gujarat extremists', Channel.com/news/home/z/stories/20021212/guj.html.
   Also, 'India's hard men' (leader), *The Financial Times*, 24 February 2003. The BJP
   and VHP have both been supporting the Khas Hindu project of keeping Nepal as a
   unitary Hindu Kingdom by negating the due rights of plural communities and the
   concept of *janajati*—the plural nationalities. For more on this, see, Bal Gopal
   Shrestha, 'Ethnic Nationalism in Nepal', *IIAS Newsletter* (Amsterdam), 30 March
   2003, p. 22. In Bangladesh, the anti-Hindu and anti-Christian campaign gathered
   momentum following the alliance between the ruling Bangladesh National Party
   and Jama'at-i-Islami. Prime Minister Khalida Zia denied any *Talibanisation* of
   Bangladesh, yet the Amnesty International and country's own civic groups remained
   concerned over the rising tide of fundamentalism. For details, see, John Vidal,
   'Britain ignores Bangladeshi persecution', and 'Rape and torture empties the
   villages', *The Guardian*, 21 July 2003.
4. For a historical background, see, Charu Gupta, *Sexuality, Obscenity, Community:
   Women, Muslims and the Hindu Public in Colonial India*, New Delhi, 2002, and
   Seema Kazi, *Muslim Women in India*, London, 1999.
5. Following the 11 September terrorist incidents, more than 200 Muslims were
   detained in Britain amidst a hyped-up media reportage but even after several months
   not a single one of them had been convicted. The 150-strong police raid at 2 a.m.
   on a London mosque run by a fiery *mullah* (Abu Hamza) on 20 February—first
   time on a place of worship—also failed to bring out any results. Such raids took
   place at a time when anti-asylum sentiments were quite high in the region. A
   journalist wrote: 'For all the hysterical headlines warning of a Bin Laden in our
   backyard, the reality is a picture of political repression of Muslims that is starting
   to resemble the experience of Northern Ireland's Catholics throughout the Troubles'.
   Faisal Bodi, 'Fear and loathing', *The Guardian*, 21 January 2003. On Tony Blair's
   risky alignment with the Neo-Conservatives in the United States, see, Will Hutton,
   'The tragedy of this unequal partnership', *The Observer*, 30 March 2003. This is
   not to ignore the fact that like their counterparts elsewhere, the neo-conservatives
   have their own powerful proponents. See, Ann Coulter, *Slander: Liberal Lies about
   the American Right*, London, 2002. The American Muslims have been equally
   sceptical of the US policies towards the Muslim world and criticised the military
   invasions of Afghanistan and Iraq. However, many senior officials in the Bush
   Administration continued to have their own specific views about American Muslims,
   which did not reflect ease with the Muslim critique of US policies. For an insider's
   view, see, David Frum, *The Right Man*, London, 2003.
6. This dilemma has led to an interesting discussion and soul searching among such
   groups, resulting into a vast array of debate in papers such as *The Guardian, The
   New Left Review, New Internationalist* and *New Statesman*. An analyst observed:
   'In many ways, we are in an analogous position to that of the liberal left in the 80s:

then the battles for about the ordering of the economy; for the next decade and beyond, they will be about civil liberties and international law'. Madeleine Bunting, 'The fight for tolerance', *The Guardian,* 20 January 2003. Some intellectuals felt that both the Left and Islamic activists needed to re-evaluate their respective stances, and a pervasive Muslim anger amidst a growing disempowerment may lead to a shift to more liberal and leftist strategies. See, Chris Harman, *Prophet and the Proletariat: Islamic Fundamentalism, Class and Revolution,* London, 2002. Also, *New Internationalist* (Islam, Resistance and Reforms), Special Issue, 345, May 2002.

7. While the Panorama highlighted the discrepancies in the system through an undercover agent, the two discussion sessions and phone calls from thousands of viewers mostly reflected strong reservations towards offering asylum to the cases involved. The next day, Home Secretary David Blunkett, in an article, tried to project a policy balancing the just asylum cases with the needed immigrants and warned against witchhunt. David Blunkett, 'A return to Powellism', *The Guardian,* 24 July 2003.

8. Though Bush and Blair led the campaign on terror, Australia and several other 'Western' countries were not to be left behind. For instance, John Pilger, 'George Bush's other poodle', *New Statesman,* 20 January 2003.

9. The 900-page Congressional report on the failure of US intelligence agencies was followed by another on the lack of contacts between Saddam Hussein and Al Qaeda. The report was highly critical of the Saudi role and the Democrats demanded an explanation from the Republication administration. *The Guardian,* and BBC 24, 25 and 26 July 2003.

10. To some analysts, similar ideologies are in conflict with each other with Osama bin Laden representing one strand, whereas the hawks in the Bush Administration as the other. For interesting and comparative perspectives, see, Tariq Ali, *The Clash of Fundamentalisms,* London, 2002; Joseph Nye Jr., *The Paradox of American Power,* Oxford, 2002; Fareed Zakaria, *The Future of Freedom,* New York, 2003, and, Benjamin R. Barber, *Jihad Vs. McWorld,* London, 2003.

11. Angus Roxburgh, *Preaching of Hate: The Rise of the Far Right,* London, 2002, and, Norman Mailer, *Why Are We At War?* New York, 2003.

12. An eminent academic felt that the United States was acting to reshape the world in its own dream and interest, unencumbered by any formidable opposition from any quarter, especially after the dissolution of the cold war. It was seen merely as a mundane project without being overtly against Muslims. See, Pervez Hoodbhoy, 'Is it War on Islam', South Asian Citizens Wire (www.sacw.com), 16 January 2003.

13. Several observers felt that the unprecedented hike in the American defence budget and eagerness to attack Iraq stemmed from some hidden agenda, where oil played a crucial role, while others felt that it was the age-old Orientalist discourse that had been rekindled by certain groups. See, John Lloyd, 'Radical Islam as the new evil empire', *The Financial Times,* 10 January 2003. Harold Pinter's poem on the US war mongering and his other writings censored the war mania. Noam Chomsky, Arundhati Roy and Bianca Jagger in their lectures and articles, criticised the militarist approach towards the developing world.

14. Ed Vulliamy, 'The President rides out', *The Observer,* 26 January 2003. Even the former president, Jimmy Carter, himself a practising Christian, alluded to the

Southern Baptist Convention in the American South for their eagerness to redesign the Middle East, and a 'commitment to Israel' before the second coming of Jesus Christ. Carter remained critical of Bush's policy on Iraq. See, Jimmy Carter, 'This will not be a just war', *The Guardian*, 12 March 2003.

15. Imran Khan, 'Who's the real villain?' *The Guardian*, 24 January 2003.

16. Peter Bergen, 'This link between Islamist zealot and secular fascist doesn't add up', ibid., 30 January 2003. Bergen is the author of *Holy War Inc.: Inside the Secret World of Osama bin Laden* (New York, 2002). Bergen had interviewed bin Laden in Kabul in 1998. Even some serious critical studies failed to differentiate between state-led totalitarianism and group-led terrorism. See, Paul Berman, *Terror and Liberalism*, London, 2002; and its critique in Mary Kaldor, 'Armageddon myths', *New Statesman*, 26 May 2003.

17. Some of these individuals have been discussed in some recent studies. See, John L. Esposito and John D. Voll, *Makers of Contemporary Islam*, New York, 2001.

18. Michael Ignatieff, *Empire Lite: Nation-building in Bosnia, Kosovo and Afghanistan*, London, 2003, p. vii. In the same vein, other early works such as by Rubin, of seeing countries like Afghanistan falling apart without an overarching Western support, belittle the internal and human dynamics of those societies.

19. Unlike earlier works by eminent historians like Eric Hobsbawm or Victor Kiernan, the new generation historians utilising camera, may find empire to be a rather positive project. See, Niall Ferguson, *Empire*, London, 2002.

20. For a useful categorisation of Muslim activists, see, Jason Burke, *Al-Qaeda: Casting a Shadow of Terror*, London, 2003. Such a symbiotic relationship between religious and political authorities is not merely confined to the Muslim polities, as India under the secular regimes of Indira Gandhi and Rajiv Gandhi, also used ethno-religious groups for numerous ventures in the former East Pakistan, Sri Lanka and East Punjab. Even in the Middle East, Israel has often used specific groups in the Occupied Territories and Lebanon to suit its own security interests or to divide Arab resistance. In Southwestern Asia, the United States, and earlier, the Soviet Union, never shied away from establishing unique interfaces with several religio-political elements to further specific policy interests in the region. The American support for Sunni Islam against Khomeinite Iran and the communists in Kabul is already well-known and same has been the case with the People's Republic of China in assisting Mujahideen in Afghanistan all through the 1980s.

21. For a revealing study, see, George Crile, *My Enemy's Enemy: The Story of the Largest Covert Operation in History. The Arming of the Mujahideen by the CIA*, London, 2003.

22. For interesting and revealing studies, see, Malise Ruthven, *A Fury for God: The Islamist Attack on America*, London, 2002; and, Rohan Gunaratna, *Inside Al Qaeda: Global Network of Terror*, London, 2002.

23. John Gray, *Al-Qaeda and What it Means to be Modern*, London, 2003, p. 1. John Gray has made a very persuasive argument in this small volume, though some early country specific studies such as on Iran had hinted towards such linkages.

24. Thomas L. Friedman, 'Dinner with the Saiyyids', *International Herald Tribune*, 11 August 2003. Mr Friedman is certainly an influential columnist for *New York Times* and has been on the forefront in supporting war on Afghanistan and Iraq. Despite distancing himself from the Neo-Conservatives, he still believes in the American re-ordering of the world and has been ardently supportive of George W.

Bush's policies in the Muslim world. For instance, in the above-quoted column, he opined: 'If the West is going to avoid a war of armies with Islam, there has to be a war of ideas within Islam'. For his influential columns, see, Thomas L. Friedman, *Longitudes and Attitudes: Exploring the World Before and After September,* New York, 2003. For an interesting review of his book, see, *The Guardian,* 5 August 2003.

25. Samia Rahman, 'Meeting William Dalrymple', *Emel* (magazine), London, September-October 2003, p. 18.

26. A number of books, some by American authors as well, not only dwelt on the unilateralist policies of the US-controlled multinationals but also critiqued Bush Administration's turn-about on global covenants. See, Naomi Klein, *Fences and Windows,* London, 2002; Ziauddin Sardar and Meryl Wyn Davies, *Why Do People Hate America?* London, 2002; Michael Moore, *Stupid White Men,* London, 2002, and, Jeremy Fox, *Chomsky and Globalisation,* London, 2002. Also, Fidel Castro, 'Voice of the dark corners', *The Guardian,* 6 March 2003; and John Pilger, *The New Rulers of the World,* London, 2003. The world opinion, after a universal support in the aftermath of 9/11 has been turning against the U.S. policies. The invasions of Afghanistan and Iraq have seriously eroded this goodwill, and the trends are not just confined to the Muslim world, as is duly recognised by the American think tanks such as the Pew. For details, see 'What the World Thinks in 2002?'; 'America's image further Erodes' (18 May 2003), and, 'Views of Changing World' (June 2003), www.people-press.org.

27. Bob Woodward's *Bush at War* (New York, 2002) is a very strong defence of Bush's personality and presidency during the war on terror; also, William Safire, 'Let us get on with the war', *The Guardian,* 7 March 2003. Hillary Clinton did not find anything wrong in supporting the Bush administration and has been quite vocal in her support of Israel. See Hillary R. Clinton, *Living History,* New York, 2003. In the same vein, Blair resolutely supported Bush's stance on Iraq, and despite massive public disapproval decided on a military attack. For first hand information, see, Peter Stothard, *30 Days: A Month at the Heart of Blair's War,* London, 2003. To the former editor of the *Times,* Blair's controversial decision stemmed from political and related considerations and not for any reasons on the ground. See, p. 87 in particular. However, Bush, as well as Blair have been taken to task by a number of critics, especially after the non-discovery of the WMDs. See, Scott Ritter, *Frontier Justice, Weapons of Mass Destruction and the Bushwhacking of America,* New York, 2003. Religion has played very important role in bringing Bush and Blair together besides influencing their policies, as was recorded repeatedly by various observers: 'George Bush likes his Bible—as more quietly, does Tony Blair—and is reported to have scriptural advisers to have highlight daily passages relevant to his presidency'. Mark Lawson, 'Seeing is believing: Why does Bush feel he now has to resort to head-on-a-stick politics?' *The Guardian,* 26 July 2003.

28. *The Times,* January 2003.

29. *Le Figaro,* 31 January 2003; *Liberation,* 31 January 2003. These views were reiterated on 18 July during Blair's visit to the United States amidst the ongoing controversy over the non-discovery of WMDs and the allegations of exaggerating Iraqi threat both by Washington and London.

30. *Die Welt,* 31 January 2003. The Austrian newspaper, *Die Presse,* opined as if the Iraq crisis 'has split Europe apart'. *Die Pressse,* 31 January 2003.
31. *El Mundo* and *El Periodico,* 31 January 2003. However, *La Razon* supported the Madrid's policy.
32. John Kampfner, 'Politics', *New Statesman,* 3 February 2003.
33. Among the 1200 detainees within the United States by January 2003, a vast majority came from Muslim countries. The US Immigration and Naturalization Service (INS), in a bid to show its performance especially after coming under public scrutiny, started profiling male visitors from 24 countries, 23 of them being Muslim. Curiously, the INS had issued student visas in the early 2002 for two terrorists who had long been killed after slamming the hijacked aircraft into the World Trade Center. Under attack for such dysfunctionality, the INS turned over-vigilant. In January 2003, they arrested Ejaz Haider, a well-known Pakistani journalist, and a fellow at the prestigious Brookings Institute in Washington. He was brought back to his office and then put in a lock-up. A personal friend of Mr Mahmud Khurshid Qasuri, the foreign minister of Pakistan, who was in Washington to talk about the issues of detainees and deportation with Attorney-General Ashcroft, Mr Haider was interrogated by the INS. It was with the intervention from Strobe Talbott and Professor Stephen Cohen, the senior executives at the Institute that Mr Haider was finally released. Professor Cohen was reported to have said: 'Fortunately, we were able to contact people...and get him released without bail....For me, the personal irony of all this is that I have four times over the last 25 years made calls to the Pakistani government to release a Pakistani journalist from one of their prisons. I never thought I would be making a plea to our own government to release a Pakistani journalist from one of our jails.' *The Washington Post,* 30 January 2003. For more on the sad plight of the internees at the Delta Camp, see, *The Observer,* 6 July 2003. By July 2003, 82,000 Muslim 'aliens' in the United States had been registered and 12,000 of them were deported to their home countries: 'America just loves immigration—it's immigrants who aren't popular, as Muslims are finding out now', Hugo Younge, 'Wish you weren't here', *The Guardian,* 14 July 2003. Even Tony Blair agreed to accept the military trial of British internees in the Delta Camp despite a growing public criticism at home reflecting a deeper apprehension of American military tribunal passing on death penalty. The death penalty was banned in Britain in 1965, and some Britons have been executed in America in the recent past over and above public protests. In April 2003, David Blunkett, the British Home Secretary, signed an extradition treaty with John Ashcroft making it easier for the United States to shift British suspects to America. The official justification for this new treaty superseding the bilateral agreement of 1976 was mainly to bring the UK policy in line with that of the other EU nations. But the human rights watchdogs felt as if the Americans were dictating the British policies in a vital area. For further details, see, http://news.bbc.co.uk/1/hi/uk_politics/2920563.stm. In fact, the common view was that the British Government did not want the trials of the British internees within the United Kingdom. David Blunkett was aware of the fact that the allegations against these suspects would not hold any ground in the British courts and they would be released. Thus, the parleys between the British Attorney-General, Lord Goldsmith, and John Ashcroft only focussed on modalities of the trials outside Britain. In one of its reports, the Amnesty International took Washington to task for establishing a dangerous precedent by holding military

trials of Guantanamo suspects, over and above their civic rights. It was worried that many other governments may be tempted to 'infringe human rights' of similar cases in the future. The report was summarised in the BBC 24 report on 19 August 2003, monitored in Oxford.

34. Quoted in Jack O'Sullivan, 'Defender of his faith' (an interview with Dr Zaki Badawi, head of the Muslim College, London), *The Guardian,* 15 January 2003. Many of these internees including the British were simply picked up by the Americans, facilitated through intelligence agencies.

35. The American scholars such as Bernard Lewis and Daniel Pipes and the Religious Right spokespersons like Pat Robertson reinvigorated their efforts to portray Islam in their own specific ways. Amidst a growing debate, it was felt that the negative portrayal of Islam as the driving force behind terrorism was a fallacy and ahistorical. See, Mark Mazower, 'Religion's role in world affairs', *The Financial Times,* 23 December 2002. Some of the leading critics of war mania included the Pope, the Archbishop of Canterbury and Nelson Mandela, though Italian Prime Minister, Silvio Berlusconi considered Islamic civilisation inferior to its Christian Western counterpart. For a defence of the Neo-Conservatives, see Patrick J. Buchannan, *Death of the West,* New York, 2001; and, Oriana Fallaci, *The Rage and the Pride,* New York, 2003.

36. Edward Said, 'When will we resist?', *The Guardian* and *Al-Ahram,* 25 January; *Dawn,* 26 January 2003. Some Israeli groups also criticised US-Israeli policies. Characterising the Bush administration as 'a missionary regime which wants to be top dog in the world', Amos Elon, an Israeli writer, felt pessimistic for the region. He believed that expansionists had hijacked Zionism. For his views, see, Jonathan Steele, 'A cold eye on Zion', *The Guardian,* 1 February 2003. Concurrently, some Indian magazines reported of growing mutualities between Diaspora Hindu organisations and Zionist groups, both within and outside the Congress. Such meetings ironically carried a clear intent and content of anti-Muslim discourse. The 'threat' from 120 million Muslims 'besieging Israel' was likened to that of 120 million Muslims to India. For details, see, Zahir Janmohamed, 'Gowalkar, Savarkar...And Jews', 17 July 2003, *Outlook,* in www.outlookindia.com.

37. Eqbal Ahmad in dialogue with Samuel P. Huntington as quoted in Eqbal Ahmad, *Confronting Empire,* London, 2000, p. XXIII.

38. Ibid., p. 91. At that stage, America and other anti-Soviet powers were not interested in demonising fundamentalists, rather Political Islam was considered to be an asset: 'The issue is who is more likely to ensure the safety of the oil resources that the United States or its corporations could control?' Ibid., p. 51.

39. '...we will never deal with terrorism and other threats to world peace if we don't deal with the hunger and misery and frustration across the developing world.' Patricia Hewitt, the Labour Secretary of State for Trade and Industry, as quoted in John Kampfner, 'Terrorism: the price we pay for poverty', *New Statesman,* 3 February 2003.

Another journalist lamented: 'Africans should open their doors to our goods while we continue to restrict their exports to us. Instead of extending the ideas of social justice that we take for granted, we have, all too often, allowed our companies to deny Africans those very standards. How fair is it that a cocoa farmer in Ghana should get less than one penny from the proceeds of a bar of chocolate that sells for 90p in Britain? Why did it take a court battle in South Africa in 2001 to persuade the great pharmaceutical businesses that some people couldn't afford their AIDS drugs!' George Alagiah, *A Passage to Africa,* London, 2002, p. 4. As the UNDP's annual Human Development Reports on the Middle East, South Asia and Latin America amply reveal, the issues of economic stratification and poverty have never been so severe as they are now. The Arab and Muslim anger, in that sense, typifies a great sense of deprivation where their natural resources have been exploited mostly over and above their heads. Countries like Afghanistan, Iraq, Turkey, Pakistan and Algeria feel seriously disadvantaged and discriminated. Even without a pervasive Pan-Islamism, it takes a few rhetoricians to build it into a war between an exploitative West and a marooned Muslim world.

40. For a useful background, see, Robert J. MacMahon, *The Cold War on the Periphery: The United States, India and Pakistan,* New York, 1994.

41. *The BBC World Service,* news bulletin monitored in Oxford on 1 February 2003. For a detailed and on-the-spot, report, see, Sandra Jordan, 'Children go to war as villagers', *The Observer,* 2 February 2003 (Full report on: www.observer.co.uk/worldview). The Maoist leader, Prachanda, wanted to establish a People's Republic on the basis of equality while abolishing monarchy, caste system and other feudal institutions. Nepal: Raising the Red Flag, a film by Christopher Kendall, Channel 4, 21 February 2003.

42. Quoted in Praful Bidwai, 'How terror feeds terror?' *The News International,* 27 December 2002. Following the bomb blasts in Bombay on 25 August 2003 resulting into several fatalities, it was feared that the anti-Muslim and anti-Pakistan feelings will spiral out of control in the Hindutva heartland. The bombs exploded on the day when a group of archaeologists submitted a report affirming the existence of a temple on the Babri Mosque site. L.K. Advani and several other BJP officials promptly blamed Pakistani militant outfits such as LT for the blasts, though Islamabad condemned the terrorist attacks. It appeared as if the communal and inter-state conflicts had become intertwined in South Asia. *The Guardian, BBC Online, Dawn,* 26 August 2003.

43. President Hamid Karzai, in his visit to the United Kingdom on 5–7 June 2003, was knighted by the Queen though his appeals for global aid to the tune of 15–20 billion dollars did not elicit any response. During his visit abroad, the violence back-home intensified with 47 deaths in Spin Boldak on 6 June attributed to a shoot-out with the Taliban, whereas a suicide bomb in Kabul the next day, killed six German peace keepers besides injuring several others. In his well-attended lecture at Oxford, Karzai expressed deeper security and financial concerns and a fear of increased drug and gun-running if the country was once again left on its own. However, he avoided critiquing the US role, especially the bombing, continued incidents of mine explosions and the American prioritisation of militarist pursuits over reconstruction. Hamid Karzai, 'Reconstruction of Afghanistan', a public lecture at St Antony's College, Oxford, 6 June 2003. For an interesting perspective on post-invasion Afghanistan and Iraq, see, John Pilger, 'Bush's Vietnam', *New Statesman,* 23 June 2003. In early July the situation between Kabul and Islamabad was again tense over border skirmishes and following General Musharraf's alleged reference to Kabul regime lacking a multi-ethnic consensus.

Fighting is prescribed for you, though it is distasteful to you.
— *Al-Quran*, 2:216

Fight in the name of Allah those who fight you but do not provoke hostility, verily Allah loveth not those who provoke hostility.
— *Al-Quran*, 2:190

Whenever the Prophet (PBUH) appointed a commander over an army or detachment, he enjoined upon him to fear God regarding himself and regarding the treatment of the Muslims who accompanied him. Then he used to say:
'Fight with the name of God and in the path of God. Combat those who disbelieve in God. Fight yet do not cheat, do not break trust, do not mutilate, do not kill minors.

If thou encounterst an enemy from among the Associators (infidels), then offer them three alternatives. Whichever of these they may accept, agree to it and withhold thyself from them.

So ask them to embrace Islam. If they accept, then agree to it and withhold thyself from them. Then ask them to immigrate from their territory into the territory of the migrants (i.e., Muslim State), and inform them that if they do that they will have same rights as the migrants and same obligations as they. If they refuse to migrate, then inform them that they will be considered as Bedouins (wandering) Muslims, the same divine laws being obligatory on them as on other Believers, except that they will not benefit by booty and other State income unless they join forces and fight along with the Muslims.

If, however, they refuse, then call them to pay the jizyah (protection tax). If they accept, then agree to it and withhold thyself from them. If they refuse then seek help from God and combat them.'
— Original from Muslim, *Sahih* in Muhammad Hamidullah,
Muslim Conduct of State (Lahore, 1961, reprint), pp. 305–6

By even conservative accounts, the Green Berets sent more than 40,000 Islamic fundamentalists to their afterlife. Whether or not Allah and his multitudes of virgins ever welcomed them upon arrival is a moot point.
— Robin Moore, *Task Force Dagger: The Hunt for Bin Laden*,
London, 2003, p. xvii

1

Jihad, Political Islam, and the Taliban: Islamic Discourse on War and Resistance

The prevalent images of Islam as a violent religio-political ideology, with gun toting hordes of bearded men, chest beating and bleeding mourning crowds or groups of terrorists and suicide bombers engaged in bomb blasts and killing sprees have become pervasive in the Western popular consciousness and elitist discourse. The rise and fall of the Taliban, the controversy about Jihadi outfits in Muslim countries such as Pakistan, spotlight on Osama bin Laden and Mullah Omar symbolizing the turbaned Muslim activists all the way from Algeria, Lebanon to Afghanistan, Palestine, Kashmir, Iraq, Chechnya, and the Philippines, despite their diverse and indigenous agendas, are not only seen inherently as anti-Western, but have been allocated the unenviable status of Muslim terrorists, posing a threat to global peace.[1] Following the dissolution of the Soviet block, Islamic fundamentalism, to several observers and analysts, has become the major civilizational threat sponsoring a wave of terror against minorities, women and human rights activists. Certainly, fundamentalism in its sectarian, official or ethnic forms, poses a serious threat to fragile Muslim civil societies, yet it will be simplistic and injudicious to link it with some specific Islamic lust for bloodshed and violence. Where it is equally injudicious to brand every movement in the Muslim world as a terrorist one, in the same vein, denigrating Jihad merely as a killing spree is incorrect. Political Islam, though still largely undefined, has many manifestations, varying from fundamentalism to moderate reformism, though it is the fundamentalist postulation that stays newsworthy.[2] The economic stratification, gnawing underdevelopment, elitist monopoly of state and resources in the name of socialism, democracy or Islam, feudalist hold on society, and a pervasive authoritarianism varying from political to religious circles make Islam, despite various attendant intellectual ambiguities, a rallying force and a corrective alternative for protestors.[3]

Islam, in the recent years, provided vanguard resistance to foreign occupation, and since the 1980s has become a battle cry to fight corruption and criminalization of the state structures. In several cases, disempowered groups—ethnic, class-based or religious minorities— have sought legitimacy in Islamic rhetoric, and in the process, have become violent. The Ayatollah Khomeini-led revolution in Iran in 1979 was both anti-capitalism and anti-communism, and turned the Muslim attention towards the hegemonizing nature of foreign powers like the United States. Such a sentiment received wider acclaim as it soothed a pervasive Muslim sense of hurt and loss due to a continued humiliation at the hands of non-Muslim states including Israel and her supporters.

However, during the Afghan crisis, the resistance to the Soviet occupation crucially depended upon American support and ostensibly did not exhibit any anti-Americanism. But when the Americans and the rest left the Afghan Mujahideen in the doldrums after the Soviet retreat in 1989, the anger against the United States began to gather momentum. The unquestioned Western support for Israel, inaction in Bosnia, Kashmir and Chechnya contrasted with a quick offensive against Iraq, along with the continued Western exploitation of inter-state differences in the Muslim world to suit the former's geo-political interests only multiplied anger towards Western opportunism. The support and protection for Salman Rushdie across the North Atlantic region was also perceived as a sustained Western animus against Islam. The militants who had been earlier drawn and recruited by international agencies to fight against the 'evil empire' erstwhile occupying Afghanistan, now directed their ire against Washington. The incompetence of the Arab elite in resolving their domestic problems and a sheer inability in diminishing Iran-Iraq and Iraq-Kuwait hostilities only aggravated this resentment against the ruling elite, generally seen as spineless surrogates. The disillusionment with the nationalists across the Muslim world including the post-Soviet Central Asia, offered a fertile ground for radical forces to gain recruits and sympathetic ears. Osama bin Laden may have been brought into Afghanistan by the Americans to fight the Soviet Union but his anti-Americanism sprang from the continued US military presence in Saudi Arabia—the holy land—and Washington's exploitative and divisive policies across the Muslim world, as perceived by the former. He became a symbol of the underdogs, who are found in large numbers in the Muslim world. The Jihadis of the new millennium have been immensely politicized groups who mostly come from seminaries—*madrassas*—after inculcating idealism based on a glorious Muslim past. They embody an idealism of ridding the Muslim world of foreign occupation, Western hegemony and restoring past glory through an armed struggle. Their political and militarist project has been based on an Islamic internationalism, and is deeply rooted in the massive disempowerment of the Muslim masses. These ordinary 'brothers' are the *Che Guevaras* of an Ultra Right, which seeks empowerment and justification by confronting the United States and its military might. Despite their limited human and other resources, they have fatalistically banked on their will power and divine assistance, given their unquestioned belief in the self-righteousness of their cause. The failure of the state-led educational system, largely due to misplaced priorities, and owing to a total negligence by rather self-centred elite has spawned Jihadi Islam from these seminaries. Though these *madrassas* symbolize an age-old tradition in learning, their transformation into hotbeds of activism is rooted in politico-economic factors. It would not be superfluous to suggest that the seminaries are the abodes of the Islamic proletariat eager to dismantle the corrupt and monopolist elitism. In the post-Cold War unipolar world, the United States emerges as the main foci of anti-Americanism, curiously shared by both the socialists and Islamicists, who, for their own reasons, consider America solely responsible for all the misfortunes of the contemporary world. Its allies, especially the British government and Israel, receive the same level of antagonism, largely because of being hands-in-glove with Washington on all global issues. On the other hand, Japan, several European Union nations, Scandinavia, China, and such other countries are not perceived as enemies, due to their 'apolitical' and uncomplicated relationship with the Muslim world. In that sense, it is a political contestation, refurbished by both groups with similar trajectories—hegemony versus hegemony—and is definitely not a clash of civilizations.[4]

The world of Islam is astir and in agony, as violence accrues due to inter-state conflicts, inter-ethnic dissension and inter-sectarian cleavages. In a sense, the contemporary spectre of violence is linked with a dismissive modernity and is not merely a religion-based crusade.[5] Studies and interviews across the Muslim world amply reveal that the Muslim activists/Islamicists are eager modernists[6] in their objectives and strategies, though they are deeply weary of an abrasive Westernization.[7] The repressive politico-economic structures only add to Muslim frustrations, whereas feudalist and clerical forces, while perpetuating their own interests, seek status quo. Violence within the Muslim world, as mentioned above, is because of these dichotomies, and like any other obscurantist and repressive nomenclature, women, dissenters and minorities frequently fall prey to it. Thus fundamentalism, more than anybody else, is a debilitating threat to Muslim civil societies themselves and must be tackled through holistic measures and judicious policies, since mere retaliatory policies based on brutalization and ill-defined military pursuits will prove abysmally counter-productive.

Within the context of an uneven and often ambiguous relationship between the Muslims and the West, especially following the advent of colonization and North-South divergences, the Muslim predicament is aggravated by indigenous factors engendering intolerance and violence. The newness of the Muslim diaspora and a growing idiom against immigration in the aura of nationalist redefinition across Western Europe and North America, especially after the Salman Rushdie affair, and the terrorist attacks on the United States in 2001, have only widened and deepened the chasm.[8] Islamophobia, in a reductionist manner, provides a convenient scapegoat.[9] Several sections in Western societies either dislike Muslim minorities or totally remain indifferent towards their predicament reflected in an institutionalized discrimination rooted in colour, class and culture-related factors. For instance, a reputable study in early 1997 based on a countrywide survey conducted by the Runnymede Trust confirmed that a vast majority of Britons simply disliked Muslims.[10] Such a dismissal may be owing to a lack of proper information, slanted views on the *Islam versus Christianity* scenario, and the routine media portrayal of Muslims. Such mis-images are also closely linked with turbulent Middle Eastern politics, where it is only the Muslims who are *seen* as the enemies.[11] Islam in the Middle Eastern and Asian context has come to be associated only with militant organizations. At the Western popular level, Islam, fundamentalism and terrorism are all synonymous, whereas at the academic level, however, there is a growing interest to see the complexities and tribulations of diverse Muslim communities. Though not very pervasive, such an academic view goes beyond the archetypal 'Islam versus West' equation by deconstructing the myth of a terrorist, monolith Islam poised against the rest:

Islam is not a united force, as demonstrated, for example, by the war between Khomeini's Iran and Hussain's Iraq and the Afghan civil war. Although Muslim states have military arsenals and contribute to the supply of oil, and while Islamic fundamentalism is not likely to disappear, the Islamic world is not omnipresent and does not provide a serious economic, social or political threat to the West.[12]

Due to its centrality within Islamic teachings and history, and its radical yet misunderstood role, any discussion on Muslim views on violence has to incorporate a theoretical and semantic overview of Jihad, Muslim statecraft and pursuance of war and peace in reference to spoils, prisoners of war, and the status of non-Muslim minorities within the Muslim state. However, during the past fourteen centuries of Muslim history, Jihad has meant differently to different generations of Muslim religious and political elite. Jihad has been both a contemporary response to various external threats, and a clarion call to meet any internal *fitna* (disorder). Jihad was the medium for fighting in the name of Allah at the expense of one's own life, family and worldly possessions to seek divine pleasure and a better status in the world hereafter by welcoming *shahadat* (martyrdom). Fighting for God was to follow the Prophet's way—*ghazwah*—to become a *ghazi* or a *shaheed*. It was not an Islamized form of *razzia*, prevalent amongst pre-Islamic Arabs to gather booty.[13] All the way from the Battle of Badr (626) fought between Prophet Muhammad (PBUH) (570–632), and the Makkans to the Afghans fighting the Soviets, the Chechens trying to gain freedom from the non-Muslim Russian hold, and Hamas and Hizbollah taking on Israel have been sanctioned in the name of Jihad. Thus, Jihad is both an act and a high state of religious ideology to achieve sublimity. However, one must notice the fact that the Muslims, especially in recent years, have contended among themselves over the conditionalities, necessity and extrapolation of Jihad itself. Without totally rejecting it as a purifying act, several Muslim thinkers have tried to demilitarize it. Such rethinking has come about due to a constant Western critique of Islam legitimating violence with Jihad as the main instigator of a fundamentalist, collectivist assault on extra-Islamic institutions. The Muslim revisionists may see a mere defensive strategy in Jihad, whereas to the non-Muslims, it is a vicious battle cry and a sheer act of self-immolation.

Within the entire spectrum of Islamic traditions and practices, Jihad remains the most misunderstood and equally controversial concept. On the one hand, it is perceived as the ultimate step in the programmic evangelical mission incorporative of active force legitimating violence to spread the word. Concurrently, it is interpreted as a non-violent yet self-reformative process to synchronize both the individual and collectivist lives within an Islamic ideal. Jihad, because of its wider and diverse connotation, an assertive symbolism and communitarian outreach, is both an ideology and an activism. In a more recent period, its protagonists—the classicists of the early Islamic era, nineteenth century semi-classicists and the contemporary apologists—as well as its critics, including the orientalists, imperialists, modernists, socialists or non-Muslim missionaries, have more often tended to agree on its profundity and complexity. Jihad, in a very powerful sense, has remained a motivational ideology and a major mobilizing strategy periodically applied by Islamic scripturalists, spiritualists and secular nationalists. Whereas the early enthusiasm for Islamic propagation developed Jihad into an assertive, self-righteous ideology, the anti-colonial *silsilahs* and Sufi orders in North Africa, the Caucasus, Central and Southern Asia found in it a transformative ideology for decolonization.[14] However, the Muslim modernists of the twentieth century found it more prudent to distance themselves from a militarist postulation and have instead tried to emphasize the educational, purific and tolerant aspects of Jihad by playing down its militant and activist components. The cases like Algeria, Palestine, Afghanistan, Bosnia, Kashmir, Abkhazia and Chechnya have, however, rekindled the anti-colonial aspect of Jihad in more recent years, whereas the Iranian revolution tried to incorporate its transformative, liberationist and defensive postulations all through the 1980s. Emancipation from the Shah's Westernized regime by replacing it with a radical Islamic ethos, a defiant anti-Westernism and adulation of the *watan*—the motherland—following the Iraqi invasion provided the three major ingredients of the Khomeinite revolution. To the Iranian revolutionaries, Khomeinism was a Jihad to restore the long-promised *hukumat-i-Ilahiya*—the Divine rule. But a militant defiance is not the only form of Jihad since *Jihad bil qalam* (struggle against ignorance through knowledge) or *Jihad bil nafas* (struggle against one's own destructive tendencies) are also vehemently and routinely pronounced, both from the official and religious pulpits across the Muslim world. However, it is the military-style struggle legitimated in the name of Islam, Muslim honour or homeland, which has remained the centrepiece of any discourse on Jihad. But considering the entire tradition of Jihad merely as Islamic terrorism, as suggested by some recent authors is problematic, since it refuses to recognize the historical, diverse and evolutionary processes operative within the heuristics of Jihad.[15]

Our chapter looks at the meanings of the term, its diverse interpretations in reference to classical, colonial and contemporary times within the context of *darul Islam* (house of peace) and *darul harb* (house of war). We will also try to explain how any such discussion on Jihad may not be deemed merely introspective due to Western criticism as it may itself operate as a reconstructive discourse for communitarian consensus. An intra-Muslim debate on redefining a non-military Jihad to create a consensus among the *ummah* (community) may inherently be a reinvigorative strategy to eradicate intellectual inertia. Such a conscious discourse could be aimed at restoring Islam as an ideology of peace and co-existence by dispelling suspicions for inciting violence.

The initial section of our discussion deals with the articulation and implementation of the classical and prophetic view of Jihad and statecraft, followed by a reappraisal during the caliphate. The Zangis during the Crusades rekindled the Islamic views of limited warfare for defence and the propagation of Islam. Jihad enthused various Turkic Muslim conquerers but lost its role as a political ideology of the state in the early modern period. However, some ulema and Sufis while confronted with Western colonialism, tried to build up a new communitarian consensus around the Islamic concept of Jihad. These neo-classicists were soon confronted by the modernists/apologists, to whom the military aspect of Jihad had to yield to a more reconstructive and instructive dimension, where the West needed to be perceived as a source of inspiration rather than antagonism. However, the debate and dissensions remain unresolved, with Jihad still operating as a major source of massive political mobilization in North Africa, the Middle East, South Asia and the Caucasus.

JIHAD WITHIN PURIST ISLAMIC POLITICAL THEORY

Jihad, usually translated as the holy war or Muslim crusade in English, in its inceptive formulation and implementation did not mean warfare or any other such militarist enterprise. It, however, emerged as the cornerstone of Muslim political ethics in the early years of Islam, especially after Prophet Muhammad's (PBUH) migration to Medina

(622) and the evolution of a Muslim city-state. Apart from mere fighting, Jihad stood for a departure from traditional warfare, diplomacy and relationship with non-Muslim communities within and outside the Islamic polity.[16] Though largely symbolizing the act of fighting, Jihad literally means: strife, struggle or strenuous effort—both individual and collective—as is revealed in a verse: 'He who exerts himself (*jahada*), exerts only for his own soul' (29:5). Despite its multifarious meanings and methods, Jihad, in its classical definition, comes to symbolize military preparedness both for offensive and defensive purposes. However, every war in subsequent Muslim history cannot be defined as Jihad, unless in the larger benefit of community, though various *amirs* or Muslim rulers have tried to project their wars as Jihad, so as to gain mass-based support. Sometimes, the ulema equally tried to project such 'mundane' ventures as Jihad, but in its strictest sense, Jihad would definitely denote a godly effort beyond individual motives and gains. Jihad, in early Islamic history, emerged as an ideology to spread the word amongst non-believers and polytheists, though a differentiation was made between the People of the Book (*Ahl-i-Kitab*) and the rest.[17] Similarly, there was a clear understanding of difference between defensive war and offensive campaigns. Jihad assumed such a major profile that, in an informal sense, it became the sixth major pillar (*rukn*) of Islam. Even now, for the Muslim sect of the Kharijites, Jihad, like prayer and fasting, is an essential feature of Islam.[18] Jihad proved a powerful strategy to de-tribalize the Muslims of the early period to cement them into a single united bond.[19] Thus, Jihad became the cornerstone of Islamic universalism over and above tribal and localist affiliations, and a perpetual state of war kept the feuding tribes engaged in communitarian activities. Both for the defence of Islam, as well as to propagate the word, sheer manslaughter or unbridled violence were strictly forbidden. The enemies were always to be first invited to Islam through proper preaching and peaceful negotiations, and warfare was only allowed as a last resort, following which their women and children would be spared. After the conquest, the non-Muslim community would co-exist as *dhimmies* (protected citizens) without any obligation to fight for the Muslim state. Such an elaborate arrangement, in fact, led to the development of an Islamic concept of statehood, warfare, peace and diplomacy, which received its sanction from the Quranic verses and the traditions of the Prophet. 'The classical doctrine of *jihad* is to be understood in its historical context: it has a "situational" character and

is the product of an "atomistic" approach.'[20] For latter Muslims, the career of the Pious Caliphs and several Muslim dynasts and jurists provided the main corpus of this classical ideology which did coopt several of the preceding Greek, Roman or Sassanid traditions.[21]

A derivative of *jihad/jahd/jahada*, literally meaning effort, 'Jihad' occurs several times in the Quran and does not always mean warfare, for which there are separate Arabic terms like *harab* and *qital*. However, as mentioned earlier, the Muslims in the early period did use Jihad to signify warfare against non-believers in the name of Allah though such a usage, to some recent interpretations, is post-Quranic and post-classical.[22] Various derivatives of *Jihad* such as *jahada, jahadoo, johd, jahidoo, mojahidoona* appear fourteen times in thirty-six verses of the Quran.[23] Jihad, in its 'juridical-theological meaning is exertion of one's power in Allah's path, that is, the spread of the belief in Allah and in making His word supreme over this world. The individual's recompense would be the achievement of salvation, since jihad is Allah's direct way to paradise.'[24] Khadduri considered Jihad more than mere warfare or fighting since any effort in the path of Allah could be achieved both by peaceful and violent means. In a way, he partially agreed with Cheragh Ali and the subsequent Ahmadiyya interpretation of a non-militarist Jihad that to many Muslim writers appears apologetic. However, he does not ignore the militarist tradition and desire for universal proselytization which meant that either people belonged to the Muslim *ummah,* or if not, then were subordinate to an Islamic superstructure. Such an evangelization allowed the assumption of various means including war and peace.[25] To him and several neo-classicists, Quranic verses unequivocally defined Jihad as an ideology to convert *darul kufr* into *darul Islam* as was revealed in the following sura:

O ye believe! Shall I guide you to a gainful trade, which will save you from painful punishment? Believe in Allah and His Apostle and carry on warfare (Jihad) in the path of Allah with your possession and your persons. That is better for you. If ye gave knowledge, He will forgive your sins, and will place you in the Gardens beneath which the streams flow, and in fine houses in the Gardens of Eden: that is the great gain. (Quran, LXI, 10–13)

PERMANENT OR RESTRICTED WAR

Several Muslim scholars and activists, who believed that Jihad meant fighting in the name of Allah, quoted extensively from some of the post-Hijrat Quranic verses to rationalize a constant state of war:

> Fight against those who fight against you in the way of Allah, but do not transgress, for Allah does not love transgressors. Kill them whenever you confront them and drive them where they drove you out. (For though killing is sinful) wrongful persecution is even worse than killing. Do not fight against them near the Holy Mosque unless they fight against you; but if they fight you kill them, for that is the reward of such unbelievers. Then if they desist, know well that Allah is Ever-Forgiving, Most Compassionate. Keep on fighting against them until mischief ends and the way prescribed by Allah prevails. But if they desist, then know that hostility is only against the wrongdoers. (2:190–3)

These verses from the second chapter of the Quran clearly delineate the way for Muslim strategy on defensive warfare simultaneous with some major preconditions. While differentiating between unaccounted killing and necessary offensive, the verses restrict warfare to warring men by sparing their dependants, animals and property. To Muslim jurists, Jihad and *qital* (manslaughter/killing) are both to be undertaken in the name of Allah but every Jihad would not imply killing since it would be undertaken only for (a) defensive purposes or, (b) once after the invitation to Islam has been properly made to and rejected by the unbelievers.[26] *Qital*, like Jihad, is totally forbidden against fellow Muslims unless there is a definite worry of *fitna*. The above-quoted verses appeared in Medina proving that the Muslims were no more a persecuted community and 'were commanded for the first time to unsheathe their swords against those who had resorted to armed hostility against their movement of reform'.[27] It was shortly after this revelation that the Battle of Badr—the first armed encounter between the Muslims and their Makkan enemies—took place, followed by many more until the Prophet was able to return to Mecca victoriously. Following the Hijrat, Muhammad's (PBUH) community had come of age and was ready to begin a new chapter in its history. Rather than assuming a very low-key profile and exhibiting endurance against torture and persecution, the Muslims in Medina could stand up for their rights. Both Hijrat and Jihad evolved as complementary processes with an integrationist and forward-looking role for the community.

They became the cornerstone of this new ideology of resistance and regeneration. However, such a major transformation, subsequently led to the Orientalist depiction of Islam as a violent movement depending upon the sword for self-propagation.

The above-quoted verses also signify a major strategic rethink beside their centrality in establishing important restrictive conditionalities on the pursuance of Jihad. The Muslims are directed not to fight for material interests, and should only resort to arms against those who actively oppose their faith. The rest are to be spared. In a very powerful way, the Quran forbade Muslims from assuming unscrupulous means of violence like indiscriminate killing or pillage of property, which were routine activities in the pre-Islamic era. Such a prohibition outlawed the killing of women and children and devastation of fields, wells or destruction of livestock, which were defined as brutal acts. The Prophet's traditions, as will be seen subsequently, further elaborated these prohibitions. The Quran, in another verse, exhorts for a limited warfare to end *fitna*, which may be translated as disorder, mischief, chaos or persecution. It also devises the way to distribute the booty:

> And fight against them until the mischief ends and the way prescribed by Allah—the whole of it—prevails. Then, if they give up mischief, surely Allah sees what they do. But if they turn away, then know well that Allah is your protector—an excellent Protector and an excellent Helper. Know that one-fifth of the spoils that you obtain belongs to Allah, to the Messenger, to the near of kin, to orphans, and the needy, and the wayfarer. This you must observe if you truly believe in Allah and in what we sent down on Our servant on the day when the true was distinguished from the false, the day on which the two armies met in battle. Allah has power over all things. (8:39–41)

The concept of limited war emphatically lays down divine guidance for the distribution of spoils, so that the community may not fall back upon its traditional pursuits of plunder and clannish rivalries. Following the Battle of Badr, it prioritized the societal prerogatives over individual needs by reminding the faithful to distribute the spoils among the needy and deserving in the community. Thus, the Islamic concept of Jihad, while ordaining it as a holy duty, encompasses a restrictive communitarian activity to restore peace and order, and is to be pursued in the general welfare of the needy over and above personal motives.[28]

The Muslims are rather sternly told to provide assistance to the persecuted Muslims, left behind in Mecca, making Jihad a rescuing offensive:

> How is it that you do not fight in the way of Allah and in support of the helpless—men, women and children—who pray: 'Our Lord, bring us out of this land whose people are oppressors and appoint for us from Yourself, a protector, and appoint for us from Yourself a helper. Those who have faith fight in the way of Allah, while those who disbelieve fight in the way of *taghut* (Satan). Fight then, against the followers of Satan. Surely Satan's strategy is weak. (4:75–6)

In another Quranic verse, the believers are exhorted to participate in Jihad as it is the best for them though they may not be fully aware of its positive implications: 'March forth whether light or heavy and strive in the way of Allah with your belongings and your lives. That is best for you if you only knew it.' (9:42)

However, it is the military and war-related component of Jihad that seems to reverberate in various commentaries. Thus, the Muslims propounding militant solutions or simply offering apologia, failed to highlight the cohesive and evolutionary nature of the entire concept of war and peace, anchoring a full-fledged political philosophy. The single-factor explanation has only damaged the *raison d'être* of Jihad, which was actually a means to establish a *darul Islam*, and not to convert the world around into *darul harb*. The division between *darul Islam* and *darul Kufr* did not mean that Muslims must be on the militant offensive all the time.

PEACE OVERRIDES VIOLENCE

The restrictions put on the conduct of war by providing protection to women, children, animals and sources of income made Jihad a strictly restrained affair. It was posited as a strategy for a larger ideal and not an ideal unto itself. The Prophet (PBHU), who himself implemented the Islamic political philosophy and practised Jihad as one of its major ingredients, pursued warfare as a last resort. It was adopted either for defensive purposes or for deterrence. His letters to various rulers and tribal chieftains for conversion to Islam were not instigatory in nature; instead they fitted his role as a messenger and evangelist. His numerous traditions underline the message of Islam as an ideology of peace with warfare being the last resort. He is quoted to have said: 'I am the prophet of mercy, I am the prophet of battle.' On another occasion, he observed: 'Both I smile and I fight.' He would quote the Quranic *sura* to his followers to restrain any vengeful tendencies amongst some of them who, in particular, had suffered due to conversion and eventual migration: 'The forbidden things are reciprocal. So one who attacketh you, attack him in like manner as he attacked you and fear God. And know that God is with those who fear (Him)' (2:194). The Prophet cautioned against any adventurous spirit and advised for calm as he is quoted to have said: 'Do not be eager to meet the enemy, perhaps you may be put to test by them, but rather say: O God Suffice for us, and keep their might away from us.' The Prophet would prefer peace to war, negotiation over confrontation, and limited action to outright plunder. In the same vein, while defining the classical and pristine concept of Jihad, he emphatically differentiated the just war from an unwanted and unnecessary war. The just war was to defend the *darul Islam*; aimed at assisting fellow Muslims; was punitive action against hypocrisy and apostasy, and was in the name of Allah—*fi sabeel Allah*—rather than for limited personal and material goals or even for the sake of mere lusty bloodshed. The evil was to be challenged by precedent, force, good intentions and by oral denunciation, force being one of many options. For Muslims, according to the Prophetic view, wars were neither to be 'deserved or to be sought after'.[29] Peace was to be prioritized even amidst a war in case the enemy asked for it: 'So do not falter, and invite to peace when ye are the uppermost. And God is with you, and He will not grudge (the reward) of your actions' (47:35). At another place, it was reiterated: 'And if they incline to peace, incline thou also to it, and trust in God' (8:61). The Prophet, quite minutely, outlawed several acts during a war, which were otherwise quite common in contemporary societies. For instance, women, children, slaves, prisoners, the blind, hermits, elderly or insane individuals were never to be tortured. Physical mutilation of any of these or of prisoners of war was strictly forbidden. The devastation of harvests, trees and plants was not sanctioned; animals belonging to the enemy were not to be slaughtered at random except when needful. No excess of any type on the person or property of the enemy was allowed, and Muslims were strictly prohibited from committing adultery. Severing of the head of the fallen enemy or usage of poisonous weapons was completely banned. In addition, even during a war or in hot pursuit, Muslims were required to restrain from transgressing the terms and conditions of various treaties earlier signed with the opponents. Surrender was to be respected without any physical harm accruing to the enemy, and the sick and wounded were to be provided with medical care and shelter. All such meticulous guidelines made Jihad a holy and just activity rather than wanton violence. The Prophet (PBHU) also appointed spies, and devised uniforms and flags, so as to create a regular discipline amongst his followers who were already radicalized with an inspiring ideology. Women were trained to play a crucial role in helping Muslim soldiers, a major departure from contemporary Arabian, Persian or Byzantine practices. The Prophet entered into a peace treaty with the people of Medina on a reciprocal basis, followed by similar other treaties with several other tribes. His treaty with the Qurashites at Hudaybiyya (628), despite early reservations from some of his own companions, aimed at affirming Islam as a religion of peace.

The Prophet outlawed bloodshed amongst Muslims by creating an Islamic fraternity over and above race, colour and nationality. It was easy for anybody to become a part of the *ummah* by simply entering the house of Islam. Similarly, his peace parleys with the Meccans after the fall of the city (630), show his magnanimity, when he could have razed the town to the ground, especially after two decades of suffering and tribulations. Even the declaration of Jihad, though contingent upon a leader or *imam*, was not so simple since his credibility and integrity had to reflect the rational and religious preconditions of waging a war. Muslims were disallowed to undertake any such venture without proper assessment and evaluation, since warfare remained an undesired occupation. However, once the community came under attack or circumstances dictated a mass mobilization, Jihad would become compulsory for all Muslims. Jihad, despite being an individual responsibility, was a collective effort, and as long as there were groups of people waging a Jihad, not every member of the community was required for active military service. Unbound and frequent sanctioning of many posthumous feuds and movements among the Muslims of a dubious nature in the name of Jihad only stigmatized Islam as a religion of violence: 'It will be interesting to note that Islam has contributed to mitigate the horror of war and made it more humane.'[30]

The division of the world between the two communities aimed at strengthening intra-communal bonds and not to carry out a war of attrition and tension. The non-Muslims could live as *dhimmis* amongst the Muslims whose protection was the paramount responsibility of the Muslim state. It has been opined very often that the non-Muslims—both the People of the Book or non-believers—were categorized as second-class citizens in a Muslim state because of their relegation to a *dhimmi* status. In hindsight it may appear so but within the contemporary time-span, guaranteeing safety and security without incurring any defence responsibility was no less than revolutionary. For the payment of a tax—*jizyah*—the non-Muslims could pursue their own businesses and life-styles without being compelled to fight war for the state itself. To several Muslim observers, non-Muslims within the Muslim state were 'better off' than many Muslim fellow citizens. Other than *jizyah*, no other taxation or conscription was expected of them.[31]

After the demise of the Prophet (PBUH) in 632, his successors, known as the Pious Caliphs or *Rashidun* (632–661), followed their mentor to the letter in their pursuit of quelling *fitna* and apostasy. Enthused with a dynamic transformative message and its obligatory diffusion, the caliphs sent expeditions to introduce Islam to the neighbouring regions in the Middle East and North Africa. Like the Prophet, Jihad, to the Rashidun, was the means to propagate the divine word without unleashing persecution or terror and it is instructive to note that even before the arrival of the Muslim armies, communities converted largely due to the guidance and evangelical efforts of the companions. The military expeditions aimed at universalizing the Islamic religion from its erstwhile Arabian frontiers and were internalized as the prophetic mission. Abu Bakr (632–34), the first caliph after Prophet Muhammad (PBUH), would personally address the troops to observe the *sunnah* of the Prophet and avoid extremities and bloodshed by observing:

People! stop. I enjoin upon you Ten Commandments. Remember them: Do not embezzle, do not cheat, do not break trust, do not mutilate, do not kill a minor child or an old man of advanced age or a woman, do not hew down a date-palm not burn it, do not cut down a fruit-tree, do not slaughter goat or cow or camel except for food. Maybe, you will pass near people who have secluded themselves in convents; leave them and their seclusion. And it may be that you pass near people who will bring you dishes of different foods. If you eat one after the other, then utter the name of God over them.[32]

Umar (634–44), the second caliph, was very particular about the behaviour of Muslim commanders and soldiers. He would not allow them any laxity in behaviour, or coercion upon the conquered peoples. He himself undertook a long and austere journey to Jerusalem as desired by the local priests. His successors, Usman (644–56) and Ali (656–61), followed the precedents established by their predecessors. However, with the transformation of the caliphate into a dynastic hierarchy, the emphasis turned more to grandeur and worldly pursuits. Still, dissenting voices from amongst the family members of the Prophet and ulema did confront the Ummayyid caliphate (661–1031) on its waywardness. Hussain's martyrdom at Karbala (AD 680) while fighting Caliph Yezid's autocratic and dissipatory rule (680–3) was a reminder to the Muslims that the Islamic mission must remain prioritized over territorial expansions. Imam Hussain, the Prophet's grandson, along with his companions, was killed in Karbala in Iraq fighting fellow Muslims to arrest corruptive tendencies.

It was a few years later, with the ascension of Umar bin Abdal Aziz as the Ummayyid caliph, that a thorough revision of the caliphal structures and institutions took place. Umar the Second (717–720) revived Jihad as a means of Islamic propagation, by rejecting it simply as a mundane venture for amassing wealth and territory. His austere lifestyle and rigorous Islamic discipline reoriented the Ummayyid polity but only for a short while. However, mass-based participation in Jihad, accepting it as the ultimate source of sublimity did not diminish the supply of Muslim volunteers to fight in distant lands. The conquests in Europe, Africa, Central and Southern Asia all owed to a greater sense of commitment and sacrifice engendered by Jihad. The Muslim armies consisting of warriors, artisans, publicists and academicians propagated Islam and played a vanguard role in presenting it as more than a mere political or military movement. Tolerance, equality and simplicity won them followers without applying force too often.

CLASSICAL INTERPRETATIONS OF JIHAD

The Abbasids (749–1517) and various Turkish rulers (945–1925) maintained the momentum built up during the Ummayyid period, though there was a greater emphasis on learning and sharing. The early Abbasids sought the help of the disgruntled Shias to avenge the murder of Hussain and his descendants, but like their predecessors, avoided converting the state into a theocracy. However, the salience of monarchical order and Jihad becoming a dormant affair led to a strenuous effort by various jurists to codify and interpret Islamic *Sharia*. These *ulema* felt an urgency to elaborate Islamic principles and thus interpretive Sunni and Shia schools of jurisprudence emerged without diverging on the basics of Islam. Earlier, the Kharijites had, however, found their own separatism by insisting on Jihad as a fundamental of Islam that could never be abandoned. To them, Prophet Muhammad (PBUH) had spent all his life in Jihad and the Islamic society was basically a garrison community which must continue waging Jihad even without a leader—*imam*. The Kharijites pursued war with full violence, not sparing even children and women and thus, their obsession denied them a mainstream following. On the other hand, one does not find any major doctrinal differences between Shia and Sunni views on Jihad. The Sunnis would interpret Jihad as a guaranteed way to heaven, whereas for the Shias, Jihad could not be undertaken without an *imam*. Due to the absence (*ghaiba*) or occultation of the *imam*, to them, Jihad had become less significant. Only the *imam* being the infallible leader/ruler could judge the rationale and strategy of Jihad for the entire community. He was equally empowered to enter into peace with the enemy whilst the rest of the community was to follow.[33] However, some recent interpretations find a 'marked' difference between the Sunni and Shia positions on Jihad.

> For Imami or Twelve Shi'is, who comprise the majority of the Shi'ite community, *jihad* is not indefinitely deferred, nor is it held in abeyance till the return of the hidden Imam. *Jihad* is constantly extolled, and it can be waged not only by the hidden Imam but by one who has been chosen by the Imam, an individual whose scholarship and piety ensure that he has been commissioned by the Imam, that is, a Shi'i cleric.[34]

Despite emotional rhetoric, one does not find any serious Shia postulation on Jihad inclusive of fellow Muslims. The classical view on Jihad makes warfare against fellow Muslims totally forbidden, so any view considering Shia denouncement of the Sunnis or vice versa, or the violent sectarian clashes between the two cannot be defined as a Jihad.

In early Islam, scholars like Abu Hanifa (died 768) and al-Shaybani (died 804) made no explicit declarations that jihad was a war to be waged against non-Muslims solely on the grounds of disbelief. On the contrary, they stressed that tolerance should be shown to unbelievers, especially the scripturalists (though not idolaters and polytheists), and advised the Imam to wage war only when the inhabitant of the daral-Harb came into conflict with Islam.[35]

A leading Sunni jurist, Al-Mawardi of the Abbasid era, distinguished between Jihad against non-believers and fellow believers. To him, three types of Jihad were permissible against believers: Jihad against apostasy (*al-ridda*); second, Jihad against dissension (*al-baghi*); and third, against secession (*al-muharibun*). Some other jurists added categories such as defence of the frontiers (*al-ribat*) and fight against the People of the Book.[36] Caliph Harun al-Rashid (died 809) used violence against the Banu Taghlib, a Christian tribe settled near his borders 'on the grounds of their alleged sympathy with the Byzantines. Shaybani, who was consulted on the matter, said in no uncertain terms that the Banu Taghlib did not violate the treaty and that an attack on them was unjustified, although he did not necessarily imply that if the Caliph issued an order, his order should not be obeyed.'[37]

The Crusades proved a turning point, as a centralized Muslim political power had weakened resulting in several regional contestations. The loss of Islam's third holiest place in Palestine was both a moral and military reversal, which despite a shared anger as articulated by famous Muslim scholar and mystic, Abu Hamid al-Ghazzali (1058–1111) and others, failed to motivate a unified front until the Zangis undertook the initiative. Still, the essence of Jihad as the fulfillment of a duty in Allah's path remained the consensus.[38]

Averroes (born 1126), the well-known judge at Cordova and a philosopher of international repute, interpreted Jihad as a part of *Sharia* though, to him, its major purpose was not conversion, rather the expansion and defence of the Islamic state. A Malakite by his creed, he finished his treatise on Jihad in 1167, affirming his belief in the centrality of the state within the Islamic ethos. However, to him, Jihad was 'a collective and not a personal obligation'.[39] Only the healthy adults, after seeking prior permission from their parents, were to participate in Jihad as 'there is no blame upon the blind, the lame or upon the sick'.[40] The prerequisite for warfare is that the enemy must have heard the summons for Islam prior to any attack, but to Ibn Rushd, the Prophet (PBUH) did make night attacks without prior warning since open hostilities had already ensued.[41]

Though the Almovarids (1056–1147), a ruling dynasty in Muslim Spain, and the Fatimids in Egypt (910–1171) invoked Jihad for territorial expansion and military consolidation, it was Salah-ud-Din (died 1193) who protected Egypt from the *guerre sainte* of the Crusaders. Imam al-Din Zangi (died 1146) and his son, Nur al-Din Mahmud Zangi (died 1174) had filled the leadership vacuum with the task being completed by Salah-ud-Din Ayyubi. Imbued with the spirit of Jihad, he decided to capture Egypt first, which to him, had a predominantly Christian army of Nubians and Armenians. He 'envisioned a vast Islamic front stretching from the Indian Ocean to Muslim Spain facing Western Christianity in the East and Europe; first uprooting the Crusades completely from the East with its combined forces (this is the defensive *jihad*), then following this with the *jihad* against the enemy in Constantinople and Europe (offensive *jihad*).' Like other Muslim jurists, he felt that the early Muslim defeats were a form of divine punishment, and redemption was possible only through Jihad.[42]

The recourse to Jihad in dynastic or territorial wars by Muslim sultans and kings has been a frequent occurrence since the Crusades. The Sultan of Ghazna, in his seventeen attacks on India, built a crusading momentum in the tenth century, though he never thought of establishing an Indian empire which was left to another Turk conqueror, Shahab-ud-Din Ghori, beginning his campaigns in India in 1191. It was Qutub-ud-Din Aibak, the slave king, who became the founder of the Delhi Sultanate in 1206 until it was overthrown by the Mughals in the early sixteenth century. Tamerlane's armies destroyed the Muslim capital of Delhi in 1398–9, and killed its citizens wantonly for three days. However, the 'Ghazi', instead of taking the responsibility for the carnage, passed it on to unreprimanded soldiers.

Jihad—The Early Revisionism

Ibn Taymiya (died 1328), a great revivalist during a turbulent period, while reiterating responsibility of the Muslim state in protecting Christians, reinterpreted Jihad not as a permanent state of war, but rather as an ideology for self-defence. At a time when the Crusaders and Mongols threatened the Muslim polities and communities everywhere, he strictly advised against attacking the unbelievers without any provocation or even for propagation of Islam by force. This was a vital departure from the early era when Jihad was frequently invoked by various caliphs to justify military offensives for religious propagation and territorial acquisition. However, such a departure, to Ibn Khaldun (died 1406), was itself a great social transformation since Islam had come of age and Jihad as a permanent war was no more essential. Muslims, to him, had already matured into an urban civilization from a warlike society. Thus, it was not a sign of weakness or exhaustion, rather a natural process dictated by social realities and changed circumstances. Ibn Khaldun divided wars into four categories: tribal warfare, feuds and raids in the primitive style, wars prescribed by the *Sharia*, and wars against rebels and dissenters. The first two were unjustified, whereas the latter two were just. Unlike his predecessors, he considered wars to be a natural phenomenon, which needed to be fought with proper planning and strategy. As a realist, he objected erstwhile Muslim abhorrence for war since to him wars were a part of human life and would remain so despite their undesirability.

Tamerlane's great-grandson, Babur, the founder of the Mughal dynasty in India, before the decisive Battle of Khanwah with Rana Sanga in March 1527, renounced alcohol and enthused his followers in the name of Jihad. His grandson, Akbar (1556–1607), for his own political and personal reasons, tried to pilot an innovative hodge-podge of religion—*Din-i-Ilahi*—much to the annoyance of several ulema and Sufis like Shaikh Ahmed Sirhindi (died 1624). However, it was left to the last great Mughal emperor, Aurengzeb (died 1707), to implement a puritanical form of government in a country where 90 per cent of the inhabitants were non-Muslims. His battles against Sikhs, Marathas, and even fellow Muslim Pushtuns and Shias weakened the empire, though the resolute emperor fought resiliently until his death. It was his death and the advent of the European powers that left the Muslim elite in a dilemma. India had become *darul harb*, and *darul Islam* was in tatters.

REVIVALISTS

The political setbacks across the Muslim world, especially while confronted with a reinvigorated Europe and internal factionalism, led to two divergent views on Jihad—revivalism and apologia. Both these responses emerged in Muslim India. The loss of Muslim political power and a pervasive disillusionment motivated reformers like the well-known theologian Shah Waliullah (died 1763) to undertake multiple initiatives including translation of the Quran, intellectual reformism beside extending an invitation to the neighbouring Afghan ruler, Ahmed Shah Abdali, for an onslaught on the rising tide of Maratha power threatening the Muslim heartland in India.[43] Shah Waliullah's influence proved far-reaching in replenishing an activist debate on Muslim identity especially during the European colonization.[44] His descendants and followers like Sayyid Ahmad and Shah Ismail (died 1831), known as *shaheeds*, began a full-fledged Jihad movement to restore Islamic glory.

Jihad, along with its corollary of *Hijrat*, reemerged as an anti-colonial ideology by providing impetus to a number of Muslim movements in India, Central Asia and North Africa. Rudolph Peters enumerates seven such movements in these regions, which despite their sustained efforts, failed to defeat Western imperialism. British India, largely due to the influence of Shah Waliullah, and also because of the minoritarian nature of the Muslim community, emerged as the earliest focal point in resistance. Following the Battle of Plassey in 1757, the British East India Company was gradually able to expand and consolidate its control of India, especially after defeating the rulers of Bengal, Oudh and the Deccan (1764). The defeat and death of Tipu Sultan of Mysore (died 1799) removed the last vestige of resistance to the Raj. But, by that time, the Sikhs led by Ranjit Singh were able to establish their control of the Punjab and the trans-Indus region neighbouring Afghanistan, which itself suffered from segmentary politics. The loss of political power, divisiveness of Muslim communities, consolidation of alien control, and the demand for greater revenues led to a serious intellectual debate in Delhi, leading to the famous *fatwa* (decree) declaring India as *darul harb* by Shah Abdul Aziz, the son of Shah Waliullah. Amongst the various protest movements, the *Tariqa-i-Muhammadi* led by Sayyid Ahmad Barelwi (1786–1831) and Shah Ismail (1779–1831) focused on the ideology of Jihad and migration. In addition to its intent to wage an armed struggle against alien rule, it aimed at purifying Islam of various innovations (*bida'a*). Due to its rather zealous nature, Sayyid Ahmad's movement, also known as *Tehreek-i-Jihad*, was maligned as a Wahabi movement, though it had no link with its counterpart in Arabia. Shah Ismail recorded Ahmad's teachings in his *Sirat-i-Mustaqim*, and extolled the virtue of classical Jihad as an armed struggle to restore the Islamic state and to achieve ultimate divine glory: 'One should know that jihad is an advantageous and beneficial institution. Mankind derives benefit from its advantages in various ways, just like rain, the advantages of which are imparted upon both plants, animals and men.'[45] After his return from pilgrimage in 1824, Ahmad started his campaign to organize Jihad to rid India of the British occupation.[46] However, he and his companions decided to embark on *Hijrat* towards the north-western frontier with a view to pioneer an armed defiance to the Sikh rule by concentrating on the Muslim majority region neighbouring Afghanistan. The *Hijrat* took place in 1826 and after a long and winding journey avoiding the Sikh heartland, Ahmad, Ismail and their followers, known as *Mujahideen*, reached Pushtun territory. After a few initial victories including the significant conquest of Peshawar, Sayyid Ahmad, Shah Ismail and most of their followers were killed in an encounter with the Sikh army in 1831 at Balakot. After his death, several people began harbouring Ahmad's return as the *Mahdi*. The longer and arduous supply lines, betrayals by some local notables and efficient British propaganda of an alleged Wahabiism, resulted in the isolation of the Jihad movement. However, the movement kept itself alive by moving into Sittana, inside Pushtun tribal territory (with a simultaneous centre in Patna), and staged a number of incursions into British India. During the revolt of 1857, the *Mujahideen* once again tried to make it into a popular uprising but without any conspicuous result. The Jihad movement on the Frontier, however, kept on irritating the British government, which undertook a major military expedition against 'the Wahabis' in 1883.

While Sayyid Ahmad's movement concentrated on north-western India, another leader of *Tehreek-i-Muhammadi*, Titu Mir was active in a similar Jihad movement in Bengal. His was a peasant-cum-religious revolt against the Hindu landlords and the British administrators. Following a military campaign, Titu Mir was finally killed in 1831. Another contemporary revivalist movement in Bengal, called the Faraidhi Movement, founded in 1804 by Haji Shariatullah (1781–1840) was reformist by nature, to cleanse Islam of *bida'a* and avoided an armed confrontation with the British.[47] His son, Dudu Mian (1819–1861), transformed it into a social protest movement against the Hindu moneylenders, landlords and the British indigo planters. He declared India to be a *darul harb* and did not permit Friday congregational prayers.

During the Balkan wars, the Indian Muslims were astir with Pan-Islamic sentiment, which multiplied with the Turkish entry into the First World War. After the War, when the Allies were in the process of deciding the future of Turkey, and the Greek forces threatened the very survival of the last vestige of the Muslim caliphate, a mass-based Khilafat Movement began in India. Led by the Ali Brothers, Hakim Ajmal Khan, Maulana Abdul Bari Farangi Mahal, Mukhtar Ansari and several other regional leaders like Abdul Ghaffar Khan, the Khilafat Movement deeply politicized Muslim India. As a consequence, several thousand Indian Muslims undertook *Hijrat* from *darul harb* for Afghanistan. Known as the Tehreek-i-Mawalat, this migration was not merely the rejection of alien control but also an effort to establish a common cause with the Kabul regime, which had been engaged in a war with British India. Earlier, several Indian revolutionaries, in league with Turkish and German sympathizers, had established the Provisional Government of Independent (*azad*) India. These revolutionaries were helped by several Hindu and Sikh rebels who had been actively involved in the Ghadr movement and similar other acts of armed resistance. In India, during the Balkan wars, Muslim religious schools across India pursued an effective chain of coordinating their rebellious activities by sending symbolic silk handkerchiefs from one place to the other. The leaders of this campaign were mainly two Muslim ulema, Maulana Mahmood Hasan and Maulana Ubaidullah Sindhi, who, while abroad, had developed underground contacts with the Turks, Afghans and Germans.[48] The post-Khilafat party politics in Muslim South Asia inherited the mantle of radicalism without openly declaring an armed resistance against the British. Such an ideal, though internalized by the Jamiat-i-Ulema-i-Hind, Red Shirts, Tehreek-i-Khaksar, Majlis-i-Ahrar and Jama'at-i-Islami, was never made public. However, these movements, in their own ways, remained anti-colonial, and their leaders occasionally referred back to the glorious past of Islamic conquests and military expansion.

There were several Jihad movements with clear anti-colonial postulations in North Africa, varying from Algeria to Sudan to Morocco. The resistance in all the three countries owed to a Jihadist ideology with minor variations. Inspiration came largely from the Sufis and the ordinary masses, making anti-colonial struggle both a religious, and class-based defiance. The French captured Algeria in 1830, after defeating the Turkish troops. Here the resistance was put up by the Arab and Berber tribes who were enthused by the ideology of resistance rooted in Jihad, and leaders like Ahmed Bey and Abdal Qadir campaigned against French control. By the 1880s, the French had been able to quash the popular Jihad-based resistance like the British whose contemporary confrontation with the Mahdi Sudani's movement had resulted in their victory. The Russian expansion in the Caucasus and Central Asia, despite armed resistance by the Tatars, Chechens, Uzbeks, Tajiks and other Turkic communities, remained transcendent all through the nineteenth century. These isolated Muslim communities could not defeat the Czars like their counterparts in Sinkiang, who fell easy prey in the 1860s to a rather weak and corrupt Manchu government. In these Eurasian regions, Sufism substantiated the resistance and frequent invocation of Jihad kept the rebellions alive. However, lack of proper preparedness, absence of external support, limited resources and the divisive nature of communities could not demolish the foreign occupation. Islam as a major identity marker and Jihad as a *subversive* defiance against Moscow kept the flames alive until the crucial 1990s, when the Soviet Union itself fell apart. These sentiments were revived, when Boris Yeltsin in the mid-1990s, mounted a campaign to crush the Chechen rebels. Despite a brief interlude of independence, the Chechens yet again fell victim to a massive military campaign under Vladimir Putin. The US-led campaign against terror offered a golden opportunity to the Russian government to malign the Chechens and some of the worst human rights violations took place in the region, where a political movement was depicted as a terrorist campaign. Earlier, the decolonization of North Africa led to the establishment of independent Muslim states, though not without a cost. The Algerian war of liberation in the late 1950s and 1960s, itself cost several thousand deaths of freedom fighters to whom fighting meant more than independence.

APOLOGISTS

Overawed and largely subdued by the apparently invincible power of European colonialism, several Muslim intellectuals adopted apologetic views on Jihad. Instead of armed resistance, they spoke of cooperation with the new rulers, immersion into Western scholarship and sciences and chose to de-emphasize the evangelical aspect of Islam. Like the pioneer revivalists coming from South Asia, the early apologists were also Indian Muslims with Sir Syed Ahmad Khan (1818–1898) being the most prominent. To him, the British, instead of trying to convert the Muslims, were protecting the latter, and waging a Jihad against them would be unlawful. His views were supported and opposed by several contemporary ulema.[49] His leading protagonist was Cheragh

Ali, who undertook to prove that Islam had spread through non-violent means. Operating in the backdrop of the failed revolt of 1857, and the resultant British coercion against Muslims in particular, several Muslim elite found it prudent to support the Raj. The contemporary Orientalist writings attacking Islam as a violent ideology put Muslim intellectuals like Ali on the defensive. In his major study, published in 1885 and dedicated to Sir Syed, he observed:

> In publishing this work, my chief object is to remove the general and erroneous impression from the minds of European and Christian writers regarding Islam that Mohammad waged wars of conquest, extirpation, as well as of proselytizing against the Koreish, other Arab tribes, the Jews, and Christians; that he held the Koran in one hand and the scimitar in the other, and compelled people to believe in his mission. I have endeavoured in this book, I believe on sufficient grounds, to show that neither the wars of Mohammad were offensive, nor did he in any way use force or compulsion in the matter of belief.[50]

To a large extent, Ali was reacting to what was being written about Islam as a violent ideology as he quoted from William Muir: 'He [Muhammad] now occupied a position where he might become the agent for executing the divine sentence, and at the same time triumphantly impose the true religion on those who had rejected it.'[51] Maulvi Karamat Ali, another noted Muslim scholar in the latter half of the nineteenth century, while speaking on behalf of the Muhammadan Literary Society of Calcutta, declared British India to be *darul Islam* and exhorted Muslims to cooperate with the Raj: 'Now, if anyone were to wage war against the Ruling Powers of this Country, British India, such war would be rightly pronounced rebellion; and rebellion is strictly forbidden by the Muhammadan Law. Therefore such war will likewise be unlawful...'[52]

By the late-nineteenth century, the landowning and middle class Muslims had started supporting the British, and on occasions, several decrees by ulema advocated complete loyalty to British imperial power. With the outbreak of the War, and the revolt by Sharif Hussein of Makka against Ottoman Turkey, an interesting and equally contentious scenario emerged. While Sharif proclaimed his revolt to be a Jihad, the Turks declared their participation in the War as a holy act and leaders like Anwar Pasha were proclaimed *Ghazis*.[53]

However, an extreme view immersed in apologia on Jihad emerged with the Ahmadi movement in India in the early twentieth century. A

Muslim publicist, Mirza Ghulam Ahmad (1835–1908) at Qadian in Punjab, who had earned his fame by holding public debates with Christian missionaries, founded it. Eventually, to the chagrin of other Muslims, he claimed to be a *Mahdi* [Messiah], besides refuting the finality of Muhammad's prophethood. His followers came to be known as Ahmadis.[54] They have been sceptical of the classical meanings of Jihad and only believe in Jihad *bil nafs* (against one's own body) or *bil ilm* (for/with knowledge).[55] In 1930–1, when several Punjabi Muslims entered the princely state of Kashmir to wage a Jihad against the Maharaja's oppression, Mirza Bashir-ud-Din Ahmad, the contemporary leader of the Ahmadi community, headed the convening Kashmir committee.[56] However, a number of Muslims like Muhammad Iqbal refused to serve on a committee led by an Ahmadi.

One of the recent *imams* of the Ahmadi movement, Mirza Tahir Ahmad, has published a critique of the neo-classical view of Jihad as articulated by Sayyid Abul Ala Mawdudi (1903–1979). To Ahmad, the wars fought by the Prophet (PBUH) were defensive and the terms like *ghazwa* or *sariya* do not stipulate war or conflict at all, rather simply imply expedition and campaign. Tahir Ahmad censures Mawdudi for spearheading a rather extreme view of Jihad due to the latter's favouritism for Abdul Rashid, an Indian Muslim, who had killed Swami Shradhanand, a Hindu revivalist. Ahmad also criticizes Sir Muhammad Iqbal for writing a letter to Pandit Jawaharlal Nehru in 1936, in which he had allegedly advocated the declaration of Ahmadis as a minority. Ahmad is not happy with Khomeini's usage of Jihadist symbols and is equally annoyed with Qaddafi and Hizbollah who, to him, malign Islam by perpetrating violence against non-Muslims.[57]

MODERNISTS

Like British India, Egypt, during the period between the two Wars, also witnessed an interesting contestation between the apologists and neo-classicists. For instance, Mahmud Shaltut (born 1893), Dean of Sharia Faculty at Al-Azhar University in Cairo, in his treatise published in 1933, suggested that Allah wanted people to be converted through education and reflection, and not by force. To him, Jihad had not been abrogated, rather needed reinterpretation according to each arising situation. According to Shaltut, only three occasions necessitated fighting: repelling aggression; protecting the Islamic mission; and defending religious freedom.[58] Another such modernist view was presented by another Egyptian scholar, Abu Zahrah, who like many other Muslim interpreters, believed in contextualizing Quranic verses through an *ijtiha'ad* (innovative inference).[59]

NEO-CLASSICISTS

This category includes those Muslim intellectuals and revivalists who subscribe to a holistic view of Jihad and consider it to be the only possible way to retrieve the pristine ambience of the Rashidun. Sir Muhammad Iqbal (1875–1938), the famous poet-philosopher, challenged a submissive view of Islam in several of his poems and other writings and sought glory in a more activist, liberationist and radical Islamic ideology. In more recent years, Muhammad Hamidullah's exhaustive and well-argued work has established him as a prominent Islamic intellectual. His volume is certainly a cohesive restatement of Islamic postulation on Jihad and related state affairs.[60] Amongst the Muslim religio-political groups, the Ikhwan [Muslim Brotherhood] in the Middle East and Jama'at-i-Islami in Pakistan have been activist propounders of this neo-classical view.[61] According to Mawdudi, the founder of the Jama'at-i-Islami (1941), Jihad aimed at getting rid of oppressive regimes and was not purported for conversion. In other words, it engineered an end to human enslavement by fellow human beings so as to establish *hukumat-i-Ilahiya* (divine rule). He observed:

> So, just as it incorrect to say that Islam uses sword to convert people, it is equally wrong to say that the sword has played no part in propagating Islam. The truth lies in between the two, namely, that the call to Islam (*tabligh)* and the sword have both contributed to the propagation of Islam, just as is the case with any civilization.[62]

However, the question arises that if the conquest, as Mawdudi suggests, is not meant for religious conversion, then why undertake it?[63] However, Mawdudi tried to articulate 'a rational exposition' of Jihad to refute the allegation that it was 'the most visible vestige of Islam's violent nature'.[64]

More recent implementation of Jihad within its neo-classical interpretation has been witnessed in five case studies: Iran,

Afghanistan, Kashmir, Palestine and Chechnya. Ayatollah Khomeini and Ali Shariati in recent times have recast the Shia conceptualization of Jihad by espousing the dissolution of an unjust order and foreign invasion. Shariati, a progressive scholar, rekindled the memory of Hussain's martyrdom as a model for resisting evil and for establishing 'justice, equity, human brotherhood, public ownership of wealth and, most important of all, a classless society.'[65] On the other hand, Ayatollah Mutahhari invoked a more puritanical view of Jihad, which, to some, may be the articulation of the distinct Shia view of Jihad, different from that of the Sunnis.[66] The Afghan resistance[67] against the Soviets, combined Sunni and Shia interpretations, though Bosnia, quarantined by the Western powers, failed to receive massive material support from several willing Muslim volunteers from across the globe. However, the Bosnians avoided applying Jihadist symbols to their resistance so as not to annoy the Western powers, despite the fact that the Serbs and the Croats openly proclaimed fighting for Christiandom. On the contrary, Greek officials and several pressure groups considered it their utmost duty to help and fight for the Serbs, the fellow Orthodox community. The Serbs under Slobodan Milosevic were considered to be fighting for Christianity against American hegemony and Islamic fundamentalism. At the time of Milosevic's extradition to the Hague to face trial for crimes against humanity, eighty members of the Greek parliament passed a resolution calling upon Belgrade to stop his expulsion.[68] On the contrary, the Bosnian modesty was not based on any opportunism or lack of courage, rather it stemmed from a bitter realism.[69] The resistance in the Kashmir Valley against the Indian control has always been defined by most of the Kashmiris as a Jihad and that is why support from numerous Muslim communities becomes so readily available. After 2001, the perspective totally changed as many of these groups, with their Pakistani backers, were categorized as terrorist outfits. *Intifadah* by the Palestinians against the Israeli occupation and repression is largely viewed as a Jihad, where struggle is projected as a sublime duty, over and above personal or territorial gains. The Israeli repression and curbs on Yasser Arafat not only backfired, they equally turned *Intifadah* into an armed struggle through all means including suicide bombing by teenage girls. It was in 2002 that for the first time, the world watched girls volunteering to carry out such suicidal operations. The resistance by the Chechens, anchored on a long-time pursuit led by the Sufis against Moscow, hardened amidst periodic pogroms by the Russian troops, and despite the lack of any major external material support, was valiantly carried to a victory in 1996. However, the massive military operations by Boris Yeltsin, and again by Vladimir Putin in the recent past, characterized by indiscriminate killings, decimation of urban and rural infrastructure, including the poisoning of the water resources, compelled many Chechens to assume a Jihad form of resistance, also identified by their supporters as a just war. Islam and nationalism have both more often joined hands together to wage liberationist, defensive Jihad in Algeria, Afghanistan, Kashmir, Palestine, Iraq and Central Asia. Interestingly, the credentials of such a just war are not questioned across the Muslim world, though one may differ on their modalities and strategies.

Islamic discourse on Jihad and warfare over the centuries has reflected the changing patterns of power in Muslim societies. From a defensive and just war aimed at establishing a divine rule, it became a major preoccupation for Muslims until the weakening of the caliphate. The congregative, reformative and other-worldliness of the ideology of Jihad played a levelling role in enthusing Muslims with a common mission. Following the colonization and an uneven relationship with the Western powers, a new articulation assumed apologetic dimensions. The efforts to overthrow authoritarian regimes in the national period are increasingly receiving impetus from a Jihadist ideology as was seen in Iran. Islam as an alternative ideology for the poor and underprivileged, and a vehicle for mass mobilization. continues to substantiate that numerous movements in Muslim society are but a mere vengeful violence, which without a substitution in place, may degenerate into full-fledged anarchy. Muslims need to establish just orders but must guard against wanton violence and sheer intolerance towards pluralist forces. Equally, the application of Jihad to enhance education by fighting ignorance can be immensely constructive.

TALIBAN, *MADRASSAS* AND THE JIHADI CULTURE

The rise and fall of the Taliban has been a dramatic development both in the South Asian and global perspectives, but was not so unexpected. Warlordism, with all its worst portents, had reemerged in a country that had suffered so grievously following the Soviet invasion in 1979, and when the time came to reconstruct it, the world looked the other way. The predominantly Pushtun tribals, the war veterans, and the orphans from the refugee camps across north-western Pakistan joined forces to establish the Islamic Emirate of Afghanistan by promising to rid the country of rapine warlords and pervasive dismay. The Western agencies such as the CIA, and oil companies like Unocal and Bridas saw the Taliban—the graduates of religious seminaries on the Frontier—as the new stabilizing force in a country that was crucial to strategic and energy pipeline links between Central Asia and the rest. The Pakistani military intelligence—the ISI—once again played a vanguard role in organizing and training these predominantly Pushtun tribals to undertake the gigantic task of unifying this retribalized country. The Taliban (lit. students) promised peace, security, unity, and above all, *Sharia*—the Islamic law. They offered themselves as a moral alternative to anarchy, and in 1994, began their campaign from Kandahar. Soon Herat, Kabul, Jalalabad, and eventually Mazar-i-Sharif fell before the Taliban, known for their flowing beards, big turbans and Japanese mini trucks. The Taliban owed their dramatic rise to a pervasive revulsion against internal schism due to internecine warfare among the Tajik, Hazara and Uzbek groups, and were led by a mysterious but charismatic leader, Mullah Mohammad Omar, a hardened anti-Soviet warrior. They represented vital demographic changes within Afghan society, where the clerics rose to the centre stage, ousting the erstwhile *khans*—the tribal chieftains. The Soviet invasion and the resistance led by the *khans* and clerics had brought the latter into mainstream politics, and after the Soviet withdrawal, the anarchic conditions under the Mujahideen commanders—mostly from the north—helped these clerics to offer themselves as a better alternative. Ahmed Shah Masood, the famous anti-Soviet *Mujahid*, had been unable to offer unity and peace to Afghanistan due to rivalries from other warlords such as Abdur Rashid Dostum, the Uzbek general, and Gulbaddin Hekmatyar, the Pushtun commander. Mullah Omar's emirate drew the former resistance commanders and the youthful students from *Sharia* schools, and the Taliban began their rule by invoking the prophetic traditions of the early Islamic state. Its eventual transformation into a repressive and intolerant set-up dismayed most of its external supporters, though they could not find a better alternative, until the terrorist attacks brought in Western bombs and troops.

No other Islamic movement has received so much coverage in recent years as did the Taliban, and that is largely due to the US-led campaign against them following the terrorist acts in New York and Washington on 11 September 2001. In addition, the Taliban proved their own worst enemies by pursuing intolerant policies towards women, non-Muslim vestiges and through brutalizing their own Muslim opponents. One may suggest that other than the global demonization in the wake of the Anglo-American aerial strikes, the Taliban's own obduracy and oppression led to their decapitation. Their medieval solutions to more contemporary problems, assaults on women's schools, severe punishments of their victims, justified by them in the name of *Sharia*, and a stubborn attitude towards changing realities, brought them down from an immensely advantageous position. They had risen like a storm and soon captured 90 per cent of their country; with a single decree of Mullah Omar, they eradicated the total poppy production and equally wiped out the local regional warlords who had earlier preyed on the poor Afghans through unfair means. However, the Taliban's own repressive policies, lack of tolerance for differences and debate and further more, their single-minded pursuit of fighting on so many fronts—local and regional—weakened their hold. Their leaders, despite their incorruptibility, displayed an extreme ignorance of the changed realities of their own country and of external pressures. Their outmoded means of governance and uncoordinated efforts to put up some diplomatic or moral front to the American campaign, like their rise, brought a quick end to their oligarchy. By hosting Osama bin Laden and his Al Qaeda group, they earned American wrath and even after the 1998 bombing of their country, did not fully comprehend the extent of American military and political power, which would eventually prove to be their death knell. In the name of Islam, they committed several blunders, including the summary executions in Herat and Mazar-i-Sharif, and annoyed all their Muslim neighbours especially Iran, Turkey and the Central Asian republics. For Pakistan, they initially proved to be a semblance of 'strategic depth', but eventually became a liability. Many Pakistani religious extremists took refuge in Afghanistan and under the pretext of Jihad, engaged in killing sprees of Shias and others. The Taliban themselves, coming from *madrassas*, felt a closer affinity with the Pakistani and other Jihadi elements who, like religious outlaws, found shelter in Afghanistan. Anyway, Afghanistan's outmoded structures and porous borders could not quarantine the country from foreign elements. The comparatively isolated location of Afghanistan, the hospitality of its tribal people, and the global indifference towards the human imperatives of this unfortunate land, encouraged many of these religio-political exiles as the new harbingers of a global Jihad to restore Muslim glory by militarily taking on exploitative, non-Muslim states such as the United States, Russia, India, Israel and others. Such an idealism, justified in the name of holy war, was couched in a simplistic reading of Islamic scriptures and a reductionist view of the Western powers. Simple religiosity, fraternal bonds and outdated kalashnikovs in an extremely poor country were no match for the world's advanced economies, and highly sophisticated and immensely destructive weapons. Led by a rather naïve president, who was himself eager to make his mark on the global scene, Afghanistan once again, like in 1998, proved an easy scapegoat for Washington to cover up the serious failure of its intelligence agencies. The domestic disenchantment, regional isolation and a global assault, as expected, quickly broke down Taliban power with the reemergence of tribal warlordism. The Western powers installed a confidante, Hamid Karzai, the former go-between for the Unocal and the Taliban to facilitate the anti-Osama campaign.

The emergence of the Taliban owes to both short-term and long-term causes, and once again, reveals the lack of a constructive discourse on Jihad among Islamicists and shows the minimalist international sensitivity to human and doctrinal problems faced by Muslim societies, thus proving that the West can easily conjure up alliances with Muslim regimes to mount selective campaigns and 'mopping up operations' against defiant or totally independent Muslim polities and communities. The forces of Muslim dogmatism are accompanied by annihilative forces from the West with Palestine, Afghanistan, Iraq or Chechnya as sad reminders of Muslim marginalization, as well as ideological confusion. In the specific sense, the Taliban were one more group in a line of Islamicist groups that have been struggling for the last three centuries to revive lost Muslim glory by taking up weapons to challenge several times more powerful foes. Islam, as during the colonial period, is used as the rallying force, where Jihad is offered as the legitimizing ideology to gain recruits and the process of self-immolation takes place with a total predictability.

The Taliban, in a powerful way, showed the emergence of clerical power amongst the Pushtun Afghans, over and above the discredited tribal chieftains—the hated warlords. Further expanded, it could be seen as Pushtun nationalism rooted in religious clericalism and widely subscribed by otherwise disempowered peasantry geared up to establish its hegemony in the urban centres. With their archaic reductionism, anti-urban attitudes and a crass dismay with the native warlords and external forces, the Taliban initially offered healthy, pristine and frugal alternatives, soon to become a repressive oligarchy. There is no doubt that the sustained American military campaign in Afghanistan not only cost more than 40,000 Afghan deaths, but also unleashed further instability and anger across the vast swathes of the Pushtun heartland straddling the Durand Line. The politics of temptation and selective cooption unilaterally offered to the Northern Alliance against a predominantly Pushtun Taliban only increased anti-American and anti-Musharraf sentiments. While Karzai is ethnically Pushtun, his sole dependence upon the Americans and a helpless kowtowing to the Northern Alliance, has only aggravated hostility towards him. With an unpopular Anglo-American presence in Iraq and the subsequent complications for the occupying forces, the Taliban elements have bided for time and gradually increased their guerrilla activities against the US-controlled Kabul regime.[70] It will be a while before one would be able to evolve a more balanced interpretation of the Taliban experience, away from a total demonization or uncritical adulation, unleashed in the wake of the American offensive. Questions such as the continuous failure of the various models of Political Islam to offer a positive alternative to widespread disempowerment, class-based exploitation, social fragmentation, all compounded by injudicious Western policies in the Muslim world, remain unanswered. Did the Taliban ascendancy symbolize the rise and fall of a Sunni activism where lack of any hierarchical order, unlike its Shia counterpart, failed to consolidate itself? Was it the ideological inefficiency—a weakness of Islamic ethos—because of not going through some internal critique that Political Islam in Afghanistan failed to deliver? Or, is it the case of Political Islam, once again, operating as the ideology of displacement, but failing to offer a systemic replacement? Was it really 'Mullahism' or a genuine Islamic movement, which suffered due to the usual structural problems within the Muslim world while being faced with the Western hegemony? Was the Taliban hegemony a majoritarian backlash against the Tajik, Hazara and Uzbek minorities? Does the focus of a newer research need to be only on the religious components or politico-economic props of such movements? These are some of the vital questions whose answers may help one understand the rise and growth of a militant version of Political Islam, legitimated in the name of Jihad. In many cases, several Muslim states or their functionaries seem to have contributed towards the rise of such informal groups, either to wage unofficial, proxy wars against their neighbours, or merely to eliminate domestic critical opponents. But, still it will be too simplistic to suggest that the Jihadi elements have been totally surrogate or holistically autonomous movements, nor can a single-factor explanation help us in properly comprehending the dynamics and popularity of such movements.

A major media and official focus, especially in the West in recent times had been on the *madrassa* culture. For the average non-Muslim, *madrassas* are nothing more than terrorist dens, whereas to critical Muslim opinion, they are, in fact, schools whose scholastics and structural problems have begun to veto their benefits. To the *madrassa* proponents, these religious seminaries are the successors to the age-old Islamic tradition of intensive learning and religious knowledge. There is no doubt that the *madrassas*, mostly attached with mosques, like the early Western colleges, provided housing and tutoring to young boys committed to a life-time clerical career. But other than providing leaders for prayers and Friday sermons, the *madrassas* in classical Islam offered discussion of secular, scientific and extra-curricular pursuits. The old seminaries in Medina, Damascus, Cordova, Granada, Baghdad, Delhi, Lahore, Patna, Constantinople, Nishapur, Herat, Kufa, Shiraz, Samarkand, Cairo and Timbuktu offered multifarious courses to scholars-in-residence and the contemporary regimes offered them land grants through *waqf*—estate attached to the seminary—to bear the expenses. These seminaries were not totally apolitical and played a crucial role in forwarding, as well as occasionally resisting the political agenda of contemporary regimes. However, major politicization of several *madrassas* began during the Western colonialism. Many seminaries and even Sufi circles began rearticulating Islamic history and learning to imbibe a cumulative sense of resistance. North Africa, Central Asia, Southern and South-eastern Asia witnessed the emergence of Islamicist movements in the last two centuries, such as the Wahabis in Arabia, Salafis in North Africa, Imam Shamil's followers in the Caucasus, Deobandis and Brelvis in India. The return to purist Islam and an emphasis on collective organization were offered as the only way out to resist Westernism, which, with its political and cultural onslaught was seen as a 'Christianizing' project. The former Deobandis opened branches across South and South-western Asia, including the well-known seminary at Akora Khattak in the North-West Frontier Province. After Independence, the continued dominance of 'alien' influences and surrogate forces further politicized the *ulema*, whose chance to obtain military training came with the popularization of the Jihadist ideology in Afghanistan in the 1980s. Most of the Western countries, largely motivated by their own cold war imperatives, and several Muslim regimes for their own reasons, sponsored Jihadi elements to fight in Afghanistan. Mullah Omar and several of the Taliban leaders were not only former *Mujahideen*, they were also the graduates of Darul Uloom Haqqania at Akora Khattak and the Binori Uloom-i-Islamiyya in Karachi. Such seminaries received Pakistani, American and Saudi support during the Afghan Jihad and after a grievous sense of betrayal, some of the Taliban supporters from Arab countries turned immensely anti-American. While there is a greater need to bring these seminaries into the mainstream educational set-up through proper standardization and quality control, they also need to be recognized as shelters for the have-nots. In addition, it is imperative to look at the rise of religious militancy in reference to serious imbalances within the state-society relationship, otherwise simply curbing the institutions without a positive alternative may simply produce angrier youths.[71]

WAR AND VIOLENCE AMONG THE MUSLIMS

So far, we have only discussed Muslim views on war and violence in reference to their relationship with non-Muslims, by concentrating on variable definitions of Jihadist ideology all through the Muslim experience. Violence within the Muslim world, like many other regions in the developing world, has been an agonizing fact accruing out of political, economic, religious and socio-linguistic reasons. Inter-state bickering,[72] state-led oppression against civil society,[73] brutalization of state structure,[74] outbursts against religious minorities,[75] sectarian violence,[76] inter-class dissensions,[77] conflicts between the state and ethnic groups or among the ethnic communities,[78] and violence against women,[79] press,[80] human rights groups,[81] peasants or impoverished dwellers[82] are various recurrent manifestations of violence across the Muslim world. Despite the fact that Jihad is not the guiding ideology for Muslim states *per se*, peaceful evangelical efforts in some areas do persist in accordance with the Prophetic tradition. Most of the conflicts mentioned above are largely confined within the Muslim world, except for those where they are still fighting for liberation, or in such cases where Muslims live as beleaguered minorities vulnerable to majoritarian chauvinism.[83] However, redemption has to come about through multiple, reformative and consensual measures.

The problematic of Jihad as a major component of Political Islam is both an academic and populist dilemma. For the non-Muslims— excepting a few solitary academic voices—it simply symbolizes violence and bloodshed, sanctified in the name of Islam. To the Muslims, especially the minority communities, it is equally baffling and impractical. Despite a rhetorical demagogy emanating from contemporary clerical groups, in its military form, Jihad's reinterpretive discourse is missing, owing to statist and societal restraints. Our discussion also shows that over the last several centuries, Jihad, despite its signification of a defensive or offensive militarist enterprise, has undergone some transformative interpretations. The expansion of the Muslim world yet its inherent ethnic, sectarian and politico-economic diversity, coupled with the evolution of the Muslim Diaspora amidst the non-Muslim milieu, do not warrant the pursuance of a *traditional* Jihad, unless it stipulates resistance or decolonization. In the latter case, it is again a combination of religion and nationalism *per se*, not simply aimed at a forced propagation of Islam.

Though the Muslim world, in several cases, remains a hotbed of activism in various forms, it does not engage in any cumulative offensive campaign aimed at non-Muslims. The survival of non-Muslim communities in the Muslim heartland, and the minoritarian nature of Muslim communities in cases like India, despite historic Muslim domination for longer periods speaks volumes for mainstream Muslim tolerance towards non-Muslims. Such cases, while compared with the sixteenth century revivalist Spain or Bosnia of the 1990s, affirm the Islamic preference for co-existence. The violence within the Muslim world is a diverse and painful experience and sporadically engulfs minorities. It accrues out of multiple causes like the weak nature of civil society, low rates of literacy, feudalist and monopolist nature of societal and statist structures and such other mundane and psychological factors. The stark realities of massive poverty, elitist arrogance, political marginalization and authoritarianism simply underwrite such violence. The ideological vacuum in several non-democratic polities, and a constant dismissal of Islam only exacerbate cases of self-immolation. In the absence of mediatory institutions, violence only breeds violence. There is no doubt that, in several cases, violence is perpetrated in the name of Islam, which is of course, equally responded to with a communitarian disgust and sheer despair. Any attempt aimed at depoliticizing Islam or de-Islamicizing politics will prove foolhardy. The best way forward would be to undertake rehabilitative and reconstructive efforts based on cooption, conciliation and constitutionalism. The reinterpretation of Islam as a humane, egalitarian, tolerant, non-hegemonic and cooptive ideology implemented through multiple, positive politico-economic and cultural initiatives can decrease the level of violence. It is by strengthening civil society and a better understanding of the forces of tradition and modernity that a new Islamic discourse with pragmatic alternatives can be generated.

Political empowerment in the form of substantive democratization, universal literacy, eradication of poverty, realization of basic needs, safeguards for civil society, legal protection for minorities, and curbs on sectarianism can deliver the Muslims from a horrid and recurrent spectre of violence. It is crucial to retrieve the intellectual heritage of a peaceful, tolerant and dynamic Islam to enthuse a community still lost in rituals and simultaneously victimized by unrepresentative regimes, coercive feudalist structures and obscurantist clergy, often supported from the outside. These are naturally human problems and only human efforts can seek their solutions. Collective efforts are needed to coincide with the corrective measures. The non-Muslim world cannot afford to be simply dismissive, indifferent or hostile towards Muslim concerns as a shared understanding within a just global order can help achieve a more interdependent and tolerant world for all.

NOTES

1. In addition to frequent media reports, several serious analysts, in a rather alarming manner, believe in a *given* polarity between Islam and the rest. See Samuel Huntington, *The Clash of Civilizations,* London, 1997. Earlier, Francis Fukuyama predicted the triumphal universalisation of Western political and liberal traditions which, to Huntington, is doubtful due to new and old cultural 'fault lines'. Francis Fukuyama, *The End of History and the Last Man,* London, 1992. For a different perspective, see, Iftikhar H. Malik, *Islam and the West,* Oxford, 1994.
2. There is a growing literature on intra-Muslim relationship and quest for identity among the Muslim minorities *vis-a-vis* the non-Muslim Western majorities within the Islamic context. See, Jacob Landau, *The Politics of Pan-Islam,* London, 1994; and, Gilles Kepel, *Allah in the West,* Oxford, 1997; and, *Jihad: The Trail of Political Islam,* London, 2003.
3. Ibrahim M. Abu Rabi, *Intellectual Origins of Islamic Resurgence in the Modern Arab World*, Albany, 1996.
4. In his latest book, a socialist critic calls it a clash of fundamentalisms. See, Tariq Ali, *The Clash of Fundamentalisms,* London, 2002.

5. A. Jerichow and J. Simonsen, *Islam in a Changing World*, London, 1997.

6. Even the Iranian revolution has been viewed quite modernist in its contents and methods. See, E. Abrahmian, *Khomeinism*, London, 1993.

7. For several such groups, differentiation between modernisation and westernisation remains obfuscate.

8. Several authors including Edward Said have written on this subject. To some, it is an irretrievable situation since misimages can never be dislodged from the Western consciousness. See, G.H. Jansen, *Militant Islam*, New York, 1979.

9. When, in a speech, the Prince of Wales, urged the West 'to be taught by Islamic teachers how to learn once again with our hearts, as well as our heads', Muslims across the world were jubilant. But, the letters appearing in the leading British newspaper (four out of five) simply caricatured Islam as anti-women, anti-intellect and anti-West ideology. See, *The Times,* 14 December 1996, and 21 December 1996. The profiling of Muslims in the West, surveillance of diasporic Muslim groups, and unmitigated bombing of Afghanistan for months causing major displacements and deaths, were viewed as neo-Semitism. The state-led terrorism focusing on Chechens, Kashmiris and Palestinians made many Muslims fearful of a wider anti-Muslim campaign. See, Seamus Milne, 'The innocent dead in a coward's war', *The Guardian,* 20 December 2001; Jonathan Steele, 'Fighting the wrong war', ibid., 11 December 2001; and, Martin Woollacott, 'It is still America against the world, war and no war', ibid., 30 November 2001.

10. 'British found to be a nation of Muslims haters', *The Independent*, 21 February 1997. In a heated debate on the BBC Newsnight, Tony Blair was confronted by his lack of proper understanding of the Muslim predicament in the United Kingdom and elsewhere, following a hyped-up anti-Iraq campaign. A woman questioner quoted the increase in the incidence of violence and racial discrimination against Muslims after 9/11. He tried to suggest that the military action in Kosovo and then in Afghanistan were in support of Muslim communities living there. The BBC TV 2, 6 February 2003.

11. A study by the Institute of Jewish Affairs observed: 'The most serious threat to Jewish security currently lies in Islamic anti-Semitism...[It] is so widespread and potentially violent that it could eclipse all other forms of anti-Semitism over the next decade'. Martin Kramer, *The Salience of Islamic Fundamentalism,* No. 2, London, 1995, p. 1.

12. Fred Halliday, 'Does Islamic Fundamentalism Pose a Threat to the West?' (a report by the Institute for Jewish Policy Research), No. 2 (1996), p. 1.

13. W. Montgomery Watt, *Islamic Political Thought,* Edinburgh, 1968, pp. 14–19; also, *The Majesty That Was Islam,* London, 1974, pp. 32–34.

14. To Maxime Rodinson, the anti-colonial character and commitment for an unexploited society remain the salient features of the Jihadist ideology. Maxime Rodinson, *Islam and Capitalism*, trans. by Brian Pearce, London, 1974.

15. Such a view largely stems from a rather hasty judgement on some recent militant movements in the Middle East. For a case study, see, Fouad Ajami, 'In the Pharaoh's Shadow: Religion and Authority in Egypt', in James Piscatori, (ed.) *Islam and the Political Process,* New York, 1983, p. 34.

16. For an exhaustive discussion see, Rudolph Peters, *Islam and Colonialism. The Doctrine of Jihad in Modern History,* The Hague, 1979.

17. A Quranic verse exhorted the Prophet to 'slay the polytheists wherever you may find them'. (9:5) The Prophet is reported to have said: 'I am ordered to fight polytheists until they say: "there is no god but Allah".' One must not forget that certain revelations and traditions addressed specific situations rather than implying a universal application.

18. *The Encyclopedia of Islam*, Vol. I, Leiden, 1913, p. 1042.

19. 'The importance of the jihad lay in shifting the focus of attention of the tribes from their inter-tribal warfare to the outside world; Islam outlawed all forms of war except the jihad, that is the war in Allah's path. It would, indeed, have been very difficult for the Islamic state to survive had it not been for the doctrine of the jihad, replacing tribal raids, and directing that enormous energy of the tribes from an inevitable internal conflict to unite and fight against the outside world in the name of the new faith.' Majid Khadduri, *War and Peace in the Law of Islam*, Baltimore, 1955, p. 62.

20. Mustansir Mir, '*Jihad* In Islam', in Hadia Dajani-Shakeel and Ronald A. Meissier, (eds.) *The Jihad and Its Times*, Ann Arbor, 1991, p. 115.

21. For more on this, see, Fred M. Donner, 'The Sources of Islamic Conception of War', in John Kelsey and James Turner Johnson, (eds.) *Just War and Jihad: Historical and Theoretical Perspectives on War and Peace in Western and Islamic Traditions*, New York, 1991, pp. 31–69.

22. This argument was forwarded by Maulvi Cheragh Ali, a follower of Sir Syed Ahmed Khan in India during the nineteenth century. His views on Jihad, though aimed at refuting the European accusations of Islam being a religion of violence, have been interpreted as apologia by several Muslims. See his, *A Critical Exposition of the Popular 'Jihad'*, Calcutta, 1885.

23. Ibid., p. 166.

24. Majid Khadduri, *War and Peace in the Law of Islam*, Baltimore, 1955, p. 55.

25. Ibid., pp. 51–53.

26. For instance, the following Quranic verse, considers Jihad to be more than mere warfare: 'Believers: Fear Allah and seek the means to come near to Him, and strive hard in His way; maybe you will attain true success.' (5:35) Sayyid Maududi, in his explanation, refers 'to solicit all means which might bring them close to God and enable them to please Him'. He also disputes the English nuance of Jihad as something oppositional as he notes: 'The true sense of the Qur'anic injunction "strive hard" in the way of Allah is that the Muslims ought to use all their strength and engage in vigorous struggle against those forces which either forcefully prevent them from living in obedience to God or force them to live in obedience to others than God. It is this struggle which is likely to lead man to his true success and bring him to a close relationship with God.' Sayyid Abul Ala Maududi, *Tafheem Al-Quran: Towards Understanding Islam*, trans. by Zafar I. Ansari, Vol. II, Leicester, 1989, p. 158.

27. Ibid., Vol. I, Leicester, 1988, p. 151.

28. 'The purpose is two-fold. Negatively speaking, the purpose is to eradicate "mischief". The positive purpose consists of establishing a state of affairs wherein obedience is rendered to God alone. This alone is the purpose for which the believer may, rather should, fight. Fighting for any other purpose is not lawful. Not does it behove men of faith to take part in wars for worldly purposes.' Ibid., Vol. III, Leicester, 1990, p. 153.

29. Hamidullah, op. cit., p. 160.
30. Ibid., p. 157.
31. Ibid., p. 107.
32. *History of Al-Tabari*, as quoted in ibid., p. 307.
33. The disappearance of the *imam* led to different views on the capacity of the *mujtahid* (authentic interpreter) to declare Jihad. However, Imam Khomeini and Allama Shariati in the 1960s and 1970s radicalised Jihad amongst their followers to rekindle Hussain's tradition of Karbala.
34. The same author finds the conceptualisation of Jihad by Rudolph Peters 'flawed', as it downplays the Shia differences with the Sunnis. To him, Shias identify several groups as their enemies and quotes Etan Kohlberg, to whom, Shia definition of enemy includes 'the entire hateful Sunni world, a world held responsible for all the harassment and persecution to which the Shi'is were subjected throughout the ages'. See, Bruce Lawrence, 'Holy War *(Jihad)* in Islamic religion and Nation-State Ideologies', in John Kelsey and James Turner Johnson, op. cit., pp. 146–7.
35. 'It was Shafi'i (d. 204/820), the founder of the school of law bearing his name, who laid down a framework for Islam's relationship with non-Muslims and formulated the doctrine that the jihad for its intent the (sic.) waging of war on unbelievers for their disbelief and not only when they entered into conflict with the Islamic state'. Some jurists like al-Tahawi (d. 933 AD) followed Abu Hanifa, that Jihad was obligatory only in a war against unbelievers. On the other hand al-Sarakhsi (d. 1101) believed that fighting against the unbelievers was 'enjoined until the end of time'. Majid Khadduri, *The Islamic Conception of Justice*, Baltimore, 1984, pp. 165–6.
36. Khadduri, op. cit., (1955), p. 74.
37. Ibid., *(*1984), p. 166.
38. Ibn Rushd (Averroes), *Kitab al-Muqqaddimat al-Mumahhidat* as referred in Khadduri, (1955), p. 102.
39. Averroes, *Bidayat al-Mujtahid* (Legal Handbook), in Rudolph Peters, (ed.) *Jihad in Medieval and Modern Islam*, Leiden, 1977, p. 1.
40. Ibid., p. 2.
41. Ibid., pp. 19–20.
42. Hadia Dajani-Shakeel, 'Perceptions of the Counter-Crusades', in Hadia Dajani-Shakeel and Ronald A. Messier, op. cit., p. 62. She is correct in refuting Bernard Lewis, to whom, contemporary Muslims were disinterested in Europe. For his view, see, B. Lewis and P.M. Holt, (eds.) *Historians of the Middle East*, Oxford, 1962, p. 181.
43. For his views see, *Hujjat Allah al-Baligha*, trans. by Marcia K. Hermansen, Leiden, 1996.
44. While reinterpreting Jihad, he felt that the Muslims had to depend on spoils *(ghanima)*, since they could not simultaneously peruse Jihad and tend to their trade or agriculture. Ibid., p. 359.
45. Quoted in Rudolph Peters, *Islam and Colonialism. The Doctrine of Jihad in Modern History*, The Hague, 1979, p. 47.
46. For more on this see, ibid., pp. 45–48; M. Mujeeb, *The Indian Muslims*, London, 1969; I.H. Qureshi, *The Muslim Community of the Indo-Pakistan Sub-continent, 610–1947*, The Hague, 1962; and K.A. Nizami, 'Muslim Political Thought and

Activity in India during the first half of the 19th Century', *Studies in Islam*, 4, (1967).

47. Abdul Bari, 'The Fara'idi Movement' in, *Proceedings of the Pakistan History Conference*, 5th session, Karachi, 1955, pp. 197–208.

48. For more on the Ghadr movement, Kabul Provisional Government and the Silk Handkerchief campaign, see, Iftikhar H. Malik, *U.S.-South Asia Relations, 1784–1940: A Historical Perspective*, Islamabad, 1988, pp. 123–258. It is interesting to note that several posthumous Sikh radical movements in British Punjab like Babbar Akalis and Shaheedi Jhathas adopted Islamic symbols of martyrdom.

49. For further details, see, Rudolph Peters, op. cit., (1979), pp. 50–52.

50. Maulvi Cheragh Ali, op. cit., p. a. He further observed: 'All the defensive war (of Muhammad), and the verses of the Koran relating to the same were strictly temporary and transitory in their nature.' Ibid., p. 115.

51. William Muir, *The Life of Mahomet*, London, 1877, p. 211.

52. Quoted in Rudolph Peters, op. cit., p. 51.

53. Later on the same title was extended to Mustafa Kemal, the founder of modern Turkey who abolished the institution of Khilafat itself.

54. Sometimes they are addressed as Qadianis, a term they do not favour. In 1974, Pakistan's parliament declared them a non-Muslim community, and several of them migrated to Britain where their present head of the mission resides. They are quite active in propagation in Africa and denounce other Muslims as unoriginal imitators.

55. On the Ahmadiyya views on Jihad, see, Hazrat Mirza Bashir-ud-Din Mahmud, *Invitation to Ahmadiyyat*, London, 1982, p. 52; and, Yvonne Y. Haddad and Jane I. Smith, *Mission to America: Five Islamic Sectarian Communities in North America*, Gainesville, 1993, p. 58.

56. For further discussion on resistance to the Maharaja, see, Alastair Lamb, *Kashmir: A Disputed Legacy, 1846–1990*, Hertingfordbury, 1991, pp. 89–90.

57. For his views, see, Hazrat Mirza Tahir Ahmad, *Mazhab Kay Naam Per Khoon* (Murder in the Name of Religion), trans. by Syed Barakat Ahmad, Cambridge, 1990.

58. Mahmud Shaltut, *The Treatise 'Koran and Fighting'*, trans. by Rudolph Peters, Leiden, 1977.

59. For more on him, see Mustansir Mir, op. cit.

60. Hamidullah, a Paris-based scholar of South Asian origins, researched for his study before the decolonisation began and the volume has since been printed several times. See, Hamidullah, op. cit.

61. See, Hasan al-Banna's article on Jihad in H. Banna, Sayyid Qutb and Abul Ala Mawdudi, *Al-Jihad fi Sabil Allah*, Cairo, 1977.

62. Sayyid Abul Ala Mawdudi, *Al-Jihad fil Islam*, Lahore, 1947, p. 158. The 600-page Urdu book was written when the author was 26 and was first published in 1927, and until late 1980s had undergone several editions. It has not been translated into English though a small section has been rendered into Arabic and published together with essays by Hasan al-Banna and Sayyid Qutb.

63. For a critique see, Mustansir Mir, op. cit., p. 119.

64. Sayyed Vali Reza Nasr, *Mawdudi and The Making of Islamic Revolution*, Oxford, 1996, p. 22.

65. E. Abrahamian, *Iran Between Two Revolutions*, Princeton, 1982, p. 466.

66. For more on this see, Bruce Lawrence, op. cit.

67. See, Olivier Roy, *Islam and Resistance in Afghanistan,* Cambridge, 1984.

68. The Serb leader, Radovan Karadzic in his visits to Greece during the 1990s, used to pronounce that after God it was only Greece that stood with the Serbs. The Greek volunteers helped the Serbs in their ethnic cleansing of the Muslim population, especially in the notorious Srebrnica massacre of 1995, when around 10,000 unarmed Muslims were killed by their forces. For the inside details from a Greek writer, see Takis Michas, *Unholy Alliance: Greece and Milosevic's Serbia,* Houston, 2002.

69. The Bosnian holocaust, largely unreprimanded for so long by the Western powers, posed a serious moral and intellectual challenge to Muslims across the globe. The terms like 'New Jews' and 'Andalusia Syndrome' reverberated across the West among the diaspora Muslims, and especially over the unmitigated cruelty to the Bosnian citizens, so soon after the Gulf war where an immense amount of enthusiasm had been exhibited for the 'turkey shoot'.

70. These figures are given in a recent study that claims to have benefited from first-hand information on military ventures in Afghanistan. The book claims to offer an inside view of unreported guerrilla activities by the Anglo-American Special Forces and the resultant massive Afghan casualties, unlike some familiar media coverage of the aerial bombardment and the fall of Kabul. See, Robin Moore, *Task Force Dagger: The Hunt for Bin Laden,* London, 2003, p. xviii.

The American aerial campaign in 1998 followed by a more sustained and equally massive one in 2001–2, led to a 'rediscovery' of Afghanistan, and a host of writings have appeared on the country, Taliban and the terrorism, though many of such works are hasty and meant to whet a massive demand for such works. However, there are several serious works by analysts which merit deeper attention. The recent studies include: Ahmed Rashid, *Taliban: Islam, Oil and the New Great Game in Central Asia,* Oxford, 2000; Kamal Matinuddin, *The Taliban Phenomenon,* Karachi, 1999; William Maley, (ed.) *Fundamentalism Reborn: Afghanistan and the Taliban,* London, 1998; Peter Marsden, *The Taliban: War, Religion and the New Order in Afghanistan,* London, 1998; Michael Griffin, *Reaping the Whirlwind,* London, 2001; Peter Bergen, *Holy War Inc.,* London, 2001; Simon Reeve, *The New Jackals,* London, 2000; Tom Carew, *Jihad,* Edinburgh, 2001; Adam Robinson, *Behind the Mask of Terrorism,* Edinburgh, 2001; Fred Halliday, *Two Hours that Shook the World,* London, 2001; and, Ahmed Rashid, *Jihad: The Rise of Militant Islam in Central Asia,* New Haven, 2002; and, Jason Burke, *Al-Qaeda: Casting a Shadow of Terror,* London, 2003. Excepting a few works, most of these books are scholarly studies of militant Islam, the Taliban, rise of Jihadi elements and their regional impact.

71. One cannot deny the fact that the perpetrators of terrorist acts in the United States were not the graduates of these traditional seminaries but were sophisticated graduates with competent knowledge of aviation and geography. The Taliban and their supporters across South Asia were no match for the sophistication of the terrorists. However, the suicide bombers in Palestine reveal serious imbalances in the Muslim-West equation where Israel—a nuclear power and also defiant of numerous UN resolutions—is continuously protected by the West, very much at the expense of genuine Palestinian rights. Anguish and utter dismay, and not any special fondness for killing has spawned these acts of utter frustration.

72. The Iran-Iraq war, polarity between Saudi Arabia and Nasser's Egypt over Yemen, antagonism between Morocco and Mauritania, Iraq-Kuwait war and other such inter-state conflicts in post-independence years have to be resolved through bilateral or multilateral arrangements.

73. Reformative views held by women's groups, journalists, judges, academics and human rights activists are simply not tolerated in many Muslim countries.

74. Unlimited powers enjoyed by the police, intelligence agencies and military establishments in various Muslim countries have made life unbearable for the masses.

75. Violence against Sunnis in Iran or against Shias in Pakistan, or a unilateral hold on power by the Alawites in Syria reflect monopolistic patterns and extreme intolerance.

76. Non-acceptance of pluralism both by the state and societal forces cause such violent outbursts. Over the last decade, hundreds of Shias have been killed by Sunni outfits such as LJ in Pakistan. The Shias have retaliated as well through selective killings but their tally has been lower. On 4 July 2003, three Sunni militants killed fifty-three Shias and injured more than two hundred in an attack on a mosque in Quetta. Subsequently, their video, containing a confession and emotional rhetoric was given to the local BBC correspondent. A few days earlier, twelve Shia Pakistani police cadets had been killed in a similar attack in Quetta. See www.bbc.co.uk/southasia, and for detailed facts and figures on Sunni-Muslim killings, see, Massoud Ansari, 'Valley of Death' (cover story), and Shahzada Zulfiqar, 'Seeds of Discord', *Newsline,* August 2003.

77. In several authoritarian or even in pseudo-democratic countries, elite—military, dynastic or feudal—control the power while the societies overwhelmingly remain disempowered resulting in all sorts of retaliatory violence. Jihad, here, is applied to get rid of oppressive regimes and to implement Islamisation.

78. Ethnic violence is a major issue in the Muslim world especially where ethno-regional forces are very strong like in Pakistan, Turkey, Indonesia, Sudan, Lebanon, Iraq, Syria and Afghanistan.

79. Typologies of violence cover domestic, societal and statist sectors, where women are routinely abused. Marginalisation of women in all walks of life, and violence exacerbated though feudalist structures against poor women, cases of mass rapes in revenge or in state penitentiaries, exploitation of foreign maids or simple harassment of women activists, are some of the bitter realities across several Muslim countries. A weak development sector, traditional sexism and intolerance towards dissent refurbish such chauvinist attitudes.

80. It is only in a few solitary cases like Pakistan, Bangladesh, Malaysia or Turkey that the press is comparatively free, otherwise its role in almost every other country is conformist.

81. It is a new development but odds are heavily against it. State functionaries and clerics gang up against such groups by simply decrying them as foreign agents.

82. The landless peasants, their families, slum dwellers or, in cases such as the oil-rich states, unskilled workers are routinely exploited and manhandled by the landlords, state functionaries and individual sponsors.

83. Muslim minorities in India, Bosnia, Philippines or in the former Soviet Union fall victims to periodic violence mostly masterminded by fascist groups posing as majoritarian communities.

The Bharatiya Janata Party's campaign, which caught fire after the broadcast of the Ramayana, laid the foundation for what might be permanent oppression of the Muslim minority.

— Ved Mehta

The Ayodhya movement has given a shot in the arm in bringing the concepts of nationalism, secularism, socialism, communalism, minorityism and fundamentalism in the correct perspective.

— Girilal Jain

Germany has shown how well–nigh impossible it is for races and cultures, having differences going to the root, to be assimilated into one united whole, a good lesson for us in Hindustan to learn and profit by.

— M.G. Golwalkar,
the Rashtriya Swayamsevak Sangh (RSS) ideologue, in 1925

Yesterday's report by the archaeological survey of India (ASI) appears to support them—and claims that a Hindu temple did indeed exist on the disputed religious site long before the mosque. The report deals a blow to India's Muslim community—and appears to be a blessing to Hindu vandals who plunged India into a communal crisis.

— Luke Harding, 'Amid the ruins, new verdict on holy site',
The Guardian, 26 August 2003

2

Beyond Ayodhya: Hindutva and Implications for South Asia

The Bharatiya Janata Party (BJP) and its allies from amongst the other extreme parties, could not have found a more opportune time than 6 December 1992, to demolish the contentious Babri Mosque in Ayodhya in the state of Uttar Pradesh (UP).[1] With an unabated 'ethnic cleansing' in contemporary Bosnia, reinvigorated expulsions of the Palestinians from Israel, and the United States engaged in another showdown with Saddam Hussein during the final phase of its presidential campaign, it certainly appeared that such an action in a region already notorious for communal upheavals would pass largely uncensured. Within India, the assassination of Rajiv Gandhi in 1991 had left the Indian National Congress (INC) without a charismatic leader carrying the dynamic legacy of the Nehru family as the Italian-born Sonia Gandhi still resolutely dismissed any effort to woo her for the party leadership. The Hindu fundamentalists led by the BJP and other outfits such as Vishwa Hindu Parishad (VHP), Shiv Sena, Bajrang Dal, and Sang Pariwar had aimed at capturing political power for a long time to transform the Indian polity and this was the ideal opportunity to bait Islam. The age-old dream of transforming a plural India to a *Hindu Desh* (*Bharat Versha/Hindu Rashtra*) never appeared so easy as the forces of Hindutva, Akhand Bharat and Hindu nationalism converged to rewrite the history and politics of the subcontinent. The time was considered ripe to aggressively launch the 'New Hindu' movement in India, where culture, politics, religion, foreign policies, and the entire gambit of identity politics would reflect the Hinduist unilateralism or Hindutva. Other than the domestic incentives, the South Asian regional scenario appeared equally ideal to undertake such a long-desired project. A politically unstable Pakistan, after having suffered the longest and the most oppressive military rule, did not pose any major challenge, since her main political leaders, Benazir Bhutto and Nawaz Sharif, instead of resolving its problems of governance were single-mindedly engaged in annihilating each other. The country's economy was in the doldrums; Karachi was restive with ethnic tensions and incessant strikes called by Altaf Hussain, and both Kabul and Kashmir did not signal any major political hope for Islamabad despite the Soviet departure from Afghanistan four years earlier. Sri Lanka had been unable to resolve its ethnic conflict, and democratic institutions in the post-General Ershad Bangladesh still were in their infancy. Delhi was managing the insurgency in Kashmir, despite its hot and cold phases, without causing any international concern, and in any case, such a rebellious Muslim valley could prove another asset to drum up support amongst the ultra-right Hindu zealots. That is how the Ayodhya mosque became a casualty in the full glare of cameras and enthusiastically egged on by the BJP leaders such as Lal Krishna Advani, Murli Manohar Joshi and K.R. Malkani.

For some outsiders, communal volatility in South Asia may be an enduring fact. However, communal riots during the Partition in 1947 were to a large extent spontaneous, but their counterparts in the 1980s and 1990s have represented newer and ever-widening ideological polarization within the Indian society, aiming at the establishment of a Hindu *rashtra* (homeland).[2] Ironically, soon after the demolition of the mosque—also called *Ramjanam Bhoomi* (the birthplace of the Lord Ram)—the riots spread to Bombay and Surat, where Muslim protesters initially faced retaliation by the police as the Shiv Sena, a chauvinist ultra-right organization, took the metropolitan administration into its own hands.[3] Bombay, the most cosmopolitan city and the cultural and commercial hub of India, could not guarantee safety to its Muslim inhabitants whose only obvious option was to flee from the tarnished slums.[4] Such a major development raised a number of serious ideological issues within the Indian political spectrum and their regional and extra-regional ramifications, as ten years later, while the Rama Sevaks, the activists from the VHP, planned the construction of the contentious temple contrary to the judicial stay order, and India was once again thrown into the throes of severe communal riots. In 2002, Muslims in Gujarat faced the Hindu wrath as a planned ethnic cleansing was set into motion in Ahmedabad, Surat and other towns across the western state. The anti-Muslim campaign took place largely to engineer the BJP's electoral victory in December 2002, once again, by using the 'Ayodhya card' and stirring communal hatred.

On 27 February 2002, a special train full of Ram Sevaks returning from one more *yatra* at Ayodhya, caught fire at Godhra station. Fifty-eight passengers in one compartment were burnt alive in the mayhem, which was publicized as a pre-planned Muslim ambush on the Sabarmati Express. Within a few hours of the incident, the entire state was engulfed in some of the most organized and brutal attacks on Muslims, their shops, properties and places of worship. It was maliciously given out that the local Muslims had ambushed the train and thus revenge was in order. It is important to note that it was only on 2 July, as reported by the Indian media and the BBC, that the real circumstances leading to the death of fifty-eight Hindu pilgrims were made public. Accordingly, it was suggested that the Muslims were not responsible for the fire, as it had broken out due to some inflammable material in one of the carriages. According to another view, the returning travelling Kar Sevaks had molested a Muslim girl and then humiliated Muslim vendors on the platform before the train moved on until it slowly reached a predominantly Muslim neighbourhood where it caught fire. The Muslim culpability in the incident is not tenable, given the fact that such an operation could not be mounted so quickly following the incident at the train station. But the irreplaceable damage had already been done triggering a year-long annihilative anti-Muslim campaign across the state. The Kar Sevaks, VHP and Bajrang Dal, with the full connivance of the state administration, kept on blaming Muslims for the deaths at Godhra and even the publication of several challenging reports did little to defuse the hatred. The orchestrated campaign focused on Muslim localities in inner towns and villages, and through pamphleteering Hindus were persuaded to boycott Muslim businesses. The BJP-led Narendra Modi administration in Gujarat totally failed to protect its Muslim citizens, who were instead selectively hunted down by the Hindu mobs receiving official patronage. For instance, on the eve of Prime Minister Atal Bihari Vajpayee's official visit to Ahmedabad on 3 April 2002, five Muslims of the same family were burned alive and still the central government refused to hold an inquiry into the serious lapses on the part of state government. Curiously, Modi instead blamed the Muslims for the entire saga and intentionally wasted precious time in calling in troops to protect the Muslim minority across his state. Consigned to inner town ghettoes as well as in far-flung villages, Indian Muslims, like the Dalits, proved vulnerable to a well-orchestrated campaign of terror. Following the Godhra incident, at least two thousand Muslims were slaughtered with another 150,000 forced into refugee camps at a time when most of the Indian troops had been posted on the borders with Pakistan. On 27 June 2003, twenty-two attackers of the Best Bakery in Vadodara in western Gujarat, where twelve Muslims had been burnt alive, were released due to 'lack of evidence'. The arson attack had occurred on 1 March 2002, and it was only after the persistent demand of the Human Rights Commission of India that the courts agreed to a retrial. During the first trial, sixty witnesses had been threatened by the police and Kar Sevaks of retaliation, in case the former divulged the real information to the courts. The fierce anti-Muslim campaign even expanded to the states of Rajasthan, Haryana, Kerala and Karnataka, where communalized police forces moved aside to let the Hindu fundamentalists vent their venom. Ayodhya, once again, had pushed India into grievous turmoil underpinning the growing tensions within the polity. In February 2003, after meeting some senior Hindutva leaders, Prime Minister Vajpayee agreed to approach the Supreme Court to allow Hindu worship at the disputed place. In its initial report on 11 June 2003, the team of archaeologists from the Archaeological Survey of India (ASI), digging at the disputed site, found no traces of any temple which could have substantiated the BJP's stance. However, in a subsequent report on 25 August 2003, they confirmed the existence of a temple predating the Babri mosque. The same day, Mumbai experienced two major bomb blasts resulting in several deaths and numerous casualties, not only causing serious concern of a new anti-Muslim campaign in the city run by Shiv Sena but also a downward spiral in Indo-Pakistan relations. Observers feared that the Hindutva would seek a major pound of flesh from the Indian Muslims and with the elections taking place in the next few months, such anti-Muslim tirade would prove a timely vote-catcher for the BJP.

Far from being an aberration, the mosque-temple controversy has awakened many concerned Indians to the growing menace of Hindutva with its severe domestic, ideological, regional and extra-regional portents. The contentious issue highlights the serious imbalances within the Indian polity, where the erstwhile Nehruvian model of secularism seems to have been thwarted by vast sections to redesign India as a Hindu nation. This major development has signalled a serious threat to Indian plural realities where minorities, especially the Muslims have

been put on the receiving end. Exploiting anti-Muslim sentiment across
the globe in the wake of the Anglo-American war on terror, the dream
of turning India into a unilateralist polity and society is being converted
into a reality. While to some Indian analysts, Indian democracy and
civil society would eventually lead the country out of this greatest
threat to its fabric, the more skeptic voices refuse to take it as a mere
aberration or a temporary outburst. In the wake of growing inter-state
tensions, absence of people-to-people contacts and fundamentalist and
militarist forces on a constant rise, with the constitutionalists and
moderates such as the Congress and the communists either being
marginalized or staying on the defensive, the future may certainly
look bleak. While India discusses and redefines its collective identity,
the Muslim clusters across India reflect a disparate reality of divisions,
morass and alienation. While several Indian Muslim politicians,
intellectuals, journalists and activists—mostly of secular and liberal
persuasion—stay upbeat, the vast majority of this largest Muslim
minority in the world undoubtedly feel extremely vulnerable. The usual
mantra of blaming Muslim politicians and the British Raj for
partitioning Indian Muslims in 1947 and for all the other ills, does not
hold ground six decades later. While India has fallen into a serious
ideological chasm, its Muslims have also failed to offer a consensual
leadership—away from the extremes of apologia and alienation. Within
this milieu, only a greater cooperation among all the Indian minorities
in alliance with the tolerant forces from amongst the majority could
offer a way out, which may be further augmented through a long
overdue Indo-Pakistani regionalization.

AYODHYA: THE DOMESTIC RAMIFICATIONS

The demolition of the disputed Babri mosque at Ayodhya in 1992, an
act anticipated, yet not prevented, left one uneasy about the political
future of pluralism within India and its regional implications. While
the riots, largely rooted in religious passions, were engineered by
manipulative forces banking on communal sentiments, they equally
reaffirmed the rising tide of the Ultra Right in Indian politics.[5]
Jawaharlal Nehru and other founding fathers had both genuinely and
expediently espoused and followed a supra-communal national
dispensation, yet the Indian masses persistently remained religio-
centric. The old polarity between the secularists and the saffronists

had been rekindled in the post-1947 decades, due to a growing weakening of the old liberal elite and a continued accent on exclusionary nationalism. The half-century conflictive relationship with Pakistan characterized by denigration and open warfare had allowed the ultra Right to assume centre stage. While polities like Iran and Pakistan were being pushed towards Islamicization by their clerical and military leadership, Hindutva forces felt justified in transforming India into a more Hinduist mould. The evolution of a middle class, bearing the characteristics of religious conservatism and espousing exclusionary nationalism, sought to play up intolerant forces to rewrite the history of India and Hinduism. They rekindled an emotional debate on Partition by apportioning blame to Muslims and Jinnah who had caused the vivisection of Mother India and now desired to further balkanize it. They exaggerated the Muslim population ratio in India, cast aspersions on their patriotism and accused the Indian National Congress leadership all the way from M.K. Gandhi and Jawaharlal Nehru to Rajiv Gandhi, for appeasing the Muslims. While basing their case on a majoritarian nationalism, they demanded new textbooks heralding Hindu heroism and the vilification of Muslims as outsiders and invaders who had robbed India of its heritage. The saffronization of India, in a sense, is not merely the destruction of a few hundred mosques, but has been a multi-dimensional and enduring project of intermixing Hinduism with an extreme form of nationalism. It aims at replacing India's identity of a plural and secular democracy with that of a Hinduist nationalism, where Hindus as a majority would hold the veto position. Without openly demanding the conversion of Muslims or some other minorities, it, in fact, espouses a cultural conversion of these sections, since to them, the reality of India as a plural, democratic and tolerant country has been the appeasement of the Muslims who needed to be put in their proper place. Though initially, Hindutva stood for Hindu cultural identity, reassertion and self-actualization, it quickly transformed into a multi-dimensional project. It professes a complete end of the Indo-Islamic culture, advocates full-fledged nuclearization, and espouses a greater and rather hegemonic role in regional affairs. It has sought a preeminent international profile for India, duly proportionate to her population and military power. In other words, Hindutva can be viewed as a sheer irredentism of ambitious proportions that has openly aimed and unequivocally worked for a complete transformation of the polity and society in India.

Whereas earlier on, Indian nationalism with its supra-religious con-
notations had found listening ears among India's Westernized,
cosmopolitan intelligentsia, it has gradually come to rest upon religious
extremists intent upon bringing it closer to, in their view, the native
and demographic realities. Such an ideological transformation—already
under way in India since the early 1990s—represents a major shift
within the Indian political spectrum.[6] State and society have been
witnessing an intense struggle between the bi-polar forces of Indian
secularism and Hindu nationalism, where the former has been put
largely on the defensive. At another level, ethnic nationalism,
especially in the 'peripheral' areas like Kashmir, Punjab or north-east
India, has been adding tangible strains on the polity itself, allowing
Hindutva extra mileage to play upon the insecurities of the Indian
populace.

Soon after independence, state-led nationalism had visualized an
overarching and supra-religious Indian identity, which, during the
nationalist era, was in its embryonic form. Conveniently, the struggle
for national self-determination led by the Indian National Congress
and other parties was equated with a binding composite nationalism. It
was simplistically assumed that secularism, as espoused by the leaders
(despite its frequent violations), and pursued by the state with its
powerful role as a modernizing agent, would eventually lead to a
broad national consensus. Secularism, in its Indian incarnation, still
symbolized modernization and development which Jawaharlal Nehru
and his colleagues believed would resolve India's age-old problems of
poverty and underdevelopment. It was assumed that they would level
the socio-ideological divergences and cleavages as the country would
move towards a more cohesive nationhood. However, modernization
left its own imprints and rather, by default, intensified the quest for
identity amongst several groups. In addition, the state took upon itself
a greater role as the sole modernizer with societal forces having been
left behind or disarrayed. Like the former Soviet Union and other
developing countries, India's heavily bureaucratized and largely
centralized state apparatus pursued monopolistic policies within a
political system which suffered from steady erosion in authority due
to inertia and growing corruption. Its colonial roots and preferences
were not substituted with more egalitarian and participatory
institutions. The body politic itself became synonymous with the Nehru
dynasty. Growing disenchantment among the ideological groups,
tribals, underprivileged castes and ethnic communities, especially in

the outlying areas, met with official coercion instead of political adjustment. Branding serious and often justified dissent as a mere
administrative problem to be met through *ad hoc*, centralist and
coercive measures—as in neighbouring Pakistan—only aggravated the
situation, leading to an intense majority-minority relationship. It was
not simply the Indian nationalism of Nehru and Gandhi *per se* which
was being confronted by separatism in Punjab, Kashmir, Assam or
elsewhere; rather these communities perceived it as a manifestation of
heightened, enforced, majority rule over ethnic and religious minorities.
To them, Delhi was not only 'distant' but was equally insensitive to
minority needs. For several of these minority groups, the so-called
majoritarian forces were already ruling India, as all the politico-cultural
symbols manifested steady Hinduization and Hindiization. The official
machinery itself did not undertake any fresh initiatives to dispel this
growing perception which, indirectly, ended up offering legitimacy to
a gnawing Hindutva.

Centralization and a growing use of force to resolve problems in
the 'peripheral' regions facilitated the entry to the forces, promising
prompt solutions to the 'internal threats'. The policies of Indira Gandhi
exacerbated sectional schisms in the country and instead of offering a
new 'social contract', she simply pursued a more viceregal tradition.
Her own assassination in 1984 was interpreted as a failure of the
Nehruvian model, secularist politics and pluralism, as India was feared
to be threatened from within. The brutal killings of the Sikhs in revenge
in Delhi, and the official inefficiency in bringing the perpetrators to
book were seen as cracks in the higher echelons, offering concurrent
threats to India's integrity and opportunities for alternative leadership.
Indira Gandhi's emergency, her eventual ouster and the establishment
of the Janata government had already exposed the vulnerability of the
INCs grip on the country's politics. Rajiv Gandhi's regime elicited a
sympathy vote, but his political naïveté, mishandling of Tamil
secessionism in Sri Lanka, and allowing the Muslims to follow their
Shariah-based Family Law deeply infuriated the Hindutva forces.[7]

India, with the world's largest middle class of 270 million, is
occasionally posited as a promising market, especially with its
liberalization policies, and due to the fact that it produces more
scientists and engineers than France and Germany put together. But it
has its own Ulsters, which bespeak of the failures of official policies.
Today, South Asia has the world's largest concentration of the poor,
with standing figures of 420 million, while India, the core country,

remains the world's fourth largest military power.[8] The stark regional contrasts in the quality of human life are reminders of the pursuit of larger-than-life roles at the very expense of basic needs for its teeming millions. With a raging consumerism and partisan administration, nativists and religious chauvinists in the garb of BJP or Shiv Sena fall upon the slum-dwellers not simply for Ram but for Mammon as well. The politics of hate and derision with its fascist contours can be helpful in acquiring vote banks, both from amongst the middle classes and the ordinary masses. The BJP's juggernaut has seen a steady increase in its power base with the electoral graph going up all the time. In 1984, it had only two seats in the Lok Sabha, the lower house of the Indian parliament. Five years later in 1989, the BJP had eighty-nine seats whereas in 1993—soon after Ayodhya—the total jumped to 180. In 1996, the BJP was the ruling party with Vajpayee as the Prime Minister. In 2002, on the eve of the crucial elections in states like the UP, Punjab and Jharkhand, the BJP had already created war hysteria in India, with its armed forces in attack preparedness on the borders with Pakistan. In addition, a Ram Rath Yatra was sponsored to travel to Delhi across the UP to drum up support for the BJP by demanding construction of Ram Mandir (temple) on the controversial site. Certainly, this intense atmosphere led to another spate of Hindu-Muslim riots in Western India in February and March 2002, deeply damaging the morale of her moderate citizens in addition to discouraging further foreign investments. Though Pakistan and Bangladesh, to a large extent, escaped a major communal backlash against their Hindu populations, yet the pressures on these already marooned minorities multiplied. For instance, in Karachi, Pakistani Hindus demonstrated against the BJP policies and even threatened to convert to Islam *en masse*, whereas more cases of rape of Hindu girls and evictions were reported in the press.

IDEOLOGICAL DIMENSIONS: ISLAM, PARTITION AND THE HINDUTVA DISCOURSE

Since 1947, Indian Muslims have suffered from an identity crisis exacerbated by growing suspicion from their fellow citizens. The departure of the Muslim middle class and other articulate groups to Pakistan in 1947 left the rest of the community rudderless and depressed. Party politics came to depend on religious elements that lacked the proper institutional and intellectual wherewithal to transform the community according to changing times. The Indo-Pakistani discord, communal killings in the wake of Partition, and the greatest migration in human history were serious dislocating developments and Hindu organizations like the RSS and Mahasabha blamed the Muslims for everything. Overnight, Indian Muslims became the 'other' for such ultra nationalist elements. Mahatma Gandhi attempted to assuage Hindu anger while simultaneously trying to protect the remaining Muslims. His efforts to put the Indo-Pakistani relationship on a balanced keel further infuriated Hindu zealots and eventually the Mahatma was killed by Nathuram Godse, a Chitbavan Brahmin, for being 'soft' on Muslims and Pakistan. The Mahatma had been demanding the transfer of assets due to Pakistan and had begun a fast to address the rising tide of anti-Muslim sentiment across India. In the RSS-Mahsabha parlance, Partition was a non-condonable crime; the Indian Muslims were Pakistani agents, separatists and fifth communists who had to be reined in. The Muslims responded to this by accepting a low-key profile status just like the newly freed slaves in the American South without the benefit of having a leadership of the stature and vision of Frederick Douglass and Booker T. Washington. Scattered all over India, Muslims in general supported the Indian National Congress in elections, though in Kerala, a regionalized version of the Muslim League operated as a frontline party. Some Muslims even supported leftist parties simply because they were opposed to communalism, though on religio-cultual matters, Imam Bokhari of the Shahi Mosque in Old Delhi emerged as a significant voice.

The 'secularization' of the Indian Muslims in the changed circumstances displayed their pragmatism, dismissing the allegations of their being inherently communal or parochial. However, the lack of any tangible India-wide platform and ever-escalating Indo-Pakistani tensions did not leave much space for Indian Muslims to manoeuvre. Their continued dispersal, economic underdevelopment, both due to despair and discrimination, characterized Muslim politics all the way until the 1980s. The new generation of Muslims, well ensconced in their Indian identity, increased mobility due to jobs and exposure in the Gulf region, and the emergence of local parties offered some incentives to selected sections. The growing Hindiization and Hinduization of Indian society and politics were, of course, not helpful indicators, especially at a time when the penetration of Saffron groups had already been on the ascendance. The Muslim predicament in India

sadly remained a solo fight except for some occasional moral support
from the liberal and leftist sections, yet it is a fact that the minorities
could not offer any combined strategy and platform to fight any class
or caste-based discrimination. Muslims suffered like the Jews in
Europe, though the Dalits led by B.R. Ambedkar, tribal groups and
Sikh elements tried to pursue several strategies of resistance and
communitarian regeneration. The Sikhs, in general, were coopted; Dalit
conversion to Buddhism was tolerated, though not any more, but the
Muslims became the 'new untouchables'. The Dalit conversion to
Buddhism was acceptable to Hindu extremists until recently, but their
conversion to Islam or Christianity was not, as both these religions
were perceived foreign. The Muslim strategy for survival vacillated
between sheer surrender to introversion and occasional resistance.[9]
The communal riots took their toll through an intense ghettoization of
Muslims. Indian Muslims have felt all along as if they were expected
to show extra-nationalist commitment with an inherent renunciation of
their Muslimness. While the national parties like the Congress treated
them as convenient vote banks, communalist organizations used them
as levers and bait to gain populist support.

Such a multifaceted crisis confronted by the Indian Muslims has
only hindered their wider participation in the country's political and
economic life.[10] Intermittent riots further marginalized the Muslims,
who gradually resigned themselves to the role of a divided, depressed
and introverted underclass.[11] Younger Muslims eager to assert their
profile on the basis of equal citizenship, have more often met with
stronger majoritarian forces, which are given to viewing equal
opportunities as the official appeasement of a minority at the expense
of a majority. Allegations of Muslim extra-territorial loyalties in the
uneasy relations with Muslim Pakistan, and subsequently with
Bangladesh, found an ear among several Hindus. Events in
Afghanistan, Iran and Central Asia, growing defiance in Kashmir and
strained relations with Pakistan and Bangladesh were put forward to
substantiate the exaggerated fear of a Muslim 'fundamentalism'
harbouring extra-regional support and pretensions.[12] Indian Muslims
were portrayed as 'the enemy within', in cahoots with Pan-Islamic
forces elsewhere. Though Pakistan's intelligence agency, the Inter-
Services Intelligence (ISI) was projected as the Trojan Horse behind
these anti-India campaigns, catch-phrases like 'Jihadis' and 'Jihadi
culture' and 'trans-border terrorists' had not yet ventured into the
official verbiage. To broaden their constituency at a time when India

suffered an ideological and leadership crisis, they engaged in a populist campaign, offering exaggerated statistics on Muslim population growth and representation in jobs.[13]

In fact, Muslims in India do not retain a higher rate of population growth, nor do they retain better jobs commensurate even with their proportion to the country's population. The Indian Muslims, making up 12 per cent of the population, do not have even 4 per cent of the higher positions in the central and state governments. In terms of symbols, the names of all the states are in Hindi, the national anthem is in Hindi, places and offices of national significance are named in Hindi, and the country is constitutionally named *Bharat*, overwhelmingly symbolizing the pre-Islamic past. Every notable Indian Muslim, occasionally, ends up identifying some kinship with some Hindu to assuage suspicions about his loyalty towards India.[14] To some observers, the rise of Hindu nationalism in recent years signifies the consolidation of 'Hindu Zionism' as an organic nationalism which perceives Muslims simply as alien. By stressing a 'back-to-roots' legacy, the ideological conflict is actually between India and *Bharat*, with obscurantism and enmity against Islam reinforcing the forces of 'New Hinduism'.[15] While for many Muslims, the growing ascendancy of such forces in India has unleashed further insecurity, to a few optimists it may also symbolize the emergence of a new and regionalist leadership within the Indian community itself.[16]

While discussing the rising forces of Hindutva, it is imperative to look at the entire legacy of communalism and its disputatious contours within the academic and ideological realms in recent South Asian history. The secularists-nationalists have generally attributed the rise of communalism to the colonial politics of divide and rule, and have seen the creation of Pakistan within that context. The Muslims amongst them keep focusing on the uninevitability of Pakistan, without accepting the plural reasons for the evolution of a polity or the usual processes of decolonization hinging on Partition as seen in Ireland, the Middle East, Eastern Europe and Africa time and again. Meanwhile, the contrary Hindutva view anchors itself on two conflictive premises; firstly, it sees Islam as foreign and the 'other' of what is indigenous to India. The second premise subsumes Muslim identity within a larger Hindu cultural identity. In other words, a superarching Hindu culture becomes synonymous with the Indian culture(s). Beyond these two mainstream prevalent views, scholarly interpretations have looked at the subcontinent as a multi-national region lacking a single and cohesive nationhood. This is a retort to the secular viewpoint, which posits any religion-based divide either totally irrelevant or simply anachronistic. Interestingly, all these interpretations end up substantiating respective nationalisms—Indian and Pakistani in particular—and are characterized by a dangerous reductionism. In their zealotry, they tend to be either totally irredentist or simply divisive. The construction of Indian and Pakistani nationalism merely on the basis of Hinduism and Islam is simplistic and inherently communal, and has been dangerously fanning intolerance. While religious identities cannot be ignored as being the significant part of the cultural nationalist discourse, they should not be allowed to overshadow other complex configurations and factors. The aversion to religion by secularists has backfired in all the three South Asian states. Rather than encouraging a more openhearted discourse, it has inadvertently allowed Hindutva to steal a march on the former. In the same manner, the Islamicists in Pakistan and Bangladesh, helped by the dictatorial regimes, hushed an open debate and have merely fed into religious separatism. In the case of Pakistan, the formation of the fifth largest state in the world was reductionistically essentialized to a sacrosanct religious divide.[17]

Irrespective of the discussion on communalism, the issues of Partition remain quite crucial in understanding the post-1947 Indo-Pakistani (and Bangladeshi) mindsets. They see in Partition a reiteration of their respective nationhood though within the nationalist projects, Partition is viewed both as a cut-off, as well as an inaugural point. While the Indian nationalists saw Partition vivisect a historically ordained/monolithic India, the Hindutva forces have posited it as a great betrayal to Mother India. Pakistanis have also built upon the literary narratives of Partition and migration where the elements of loss and grief for the sake of a greater cause—Pakistan—have been highlighted. This is not to suggest that Partition as a subject has been totally ignored in Pakistani historiography, though it seems to centre on the high politics of a Indian-Pakistani schism rather than focusing on the human and socio-psychological dimensions. In addition, the discussion on factors such as violence, gender and family remains absent from such studies.[18] Studies from outside the subcontinent in the last few years have tried to offer some comparative analysis, both by the Punjab specialists or scholars from the Punjabi diaspora.[19] However, studies of a comparative nature on Bengal remain even fewer than on the Punjab.[20] The element of sacrifice is seen within the tested tradition of martyrdom, and any talk of confederation or a revisit to pre-Partition common heritage is deemed heretic. Such an aversion is more apparent in central Punjab and amongst the Urdu speakers. Whereas in India, several studies on Partition have documented the issues of grief, gender abuse and dislocation, Pakistani discourse is still largely shying away from confronting Partition.[21] This is mainly due to the overall underdeveloped nature of historiography in the country, and a single-factor explanation of the country's history as ordained by the successive military regimes.

The amassing of Hindutva literature, over the last decade, has tried to develop its own history, textbooks and altogether a new historiography, almost displacing the secularist-nationalist mainstream. The Hindi literature on India has focused on themes including the Indus Valley Civilization, Aryans, Hinduism, the advent of Islam in South Asia, Muslims in the modern subcontinent, and their possible reconversion to Hinduism in the post–1857 era. Where the encounter with modernity led to a redefinition of identity in reference to primordial and instrumental determinants, it increasingly assumed more communal characteristics. The encounter with the High-Noon Raj itself engaged in redefining India as the Oriental core of a congeries of primordial identities, and came to focus on essentialized religious, regional and lingual denominators. The brief inter-communal bonhomie in Northern India during the Revolt of 1857 was soon overshadowed by the Hindi-Urdu controversy, cow slaughter, the socio-economic competition over jobs and eventually over political representation. For instance, the Hindi-Urdu controversy in the UP edged Muslim leaders such as Sir Syed Ahmed Khan (1817–1898) towards cultural separatism. Similarly, in the Punjab, the most plural of all the British Indian provinces, the Urdu-Devnagri-Gurmukhi controversy started to draw demarcations among the Muslims, Hindus and Sikhs. The antecedents of cultural nationalism in the latter half of nineteenth century India were even evident in Bombay and Bengal, though the non-Hindi belt was still not as affected by it. The Bengali Muslims— mostly in the eastern portions—were largely landless peasants working for *bhadralok*, for whom the *pothi* literature assumed a definitional role as a distinct community.[22] The groundwork among the Bengali Muslim peasants had already been done by Dodu Mian and other Muslim activists such as S.M. Latif. In the UP, the Deobandis and Brelvis were spearheading religious revivalism, whereas Aligarh and Nadwa concentrated on a more intense intellectual renaissance. In the

Bombay region, while Muslim commercial interests did not find the same intensity of communalization, the local elite tried to establish linkages with both the Indian National Congress and trans-regional Muslim bodies. Like the Punjabi Muslims, they engaged themselves in convening *anjumans* and other cultural and educational institutions, though most of them remained confined to Bombay.[23] A sense of morass as well as new opportunities and facilities provided by the Raj led to a whole plethora of debate on cultural redefinition of all the Indian communities.

The Bengali Hindu renaissance coincided with the Muslim intellectual renaissance in Lahore and Amritsar in the closing years of the nineteenth century. Bankim Chatterji's novel, *Anandanath* (The Abbey of Bliss, 1882) and the ideology of foreignness of Muslims played a very important role in *othering* the Indian Muslims. Chatterji challenged the myth of Muslims being 'martial' and through his populist song, *Vande Matram* ('Hail to thee, Mother') tried to inject an aggressive Hinduist national ethos. This was certainly the triumphal march of the 'print capitalism' which was being articulated both in political and *communal* terms. By the turn of the century, the cultural issues merged with political demands, especially within the Indian National Congress as leaders like B.G. Tilak, Lala Lajpat Rai, Madan Mohan Malaviya, Lala Hardayal, Sri Aurobindo, Dayananda Saraswathi, Shardhanand and Swami Vivekananda pushed the debate towards a vocal Hindu consciousness. The partition of Bengal in 1905 and the success of the Swadeshi Movement led by the Hindus in its annulment in 1911, proved a landmark in this march for a Hindu Right. The Muslims had been offered Separate Electorates and mandated seats through the legislative reforms of 1909, and Indian pluralism started to show growing strains. The colonial state, instead of ensuring a greater dialogue and harmony, found it more convenient to exploit these growing schisms. The Lucknow Pact of 1916 between the All-India Muslim League (AIML) led by Jinnah and the Indian National Congress, followed by the Khilafat Movement under the leadership of Gandhi and the Ali Brothers, were the last significant developments to forestall this growing communalization of Indian politics, though they failed to offer an enduring politico-constitutional arrangement. In the meantime, movements like Sangathan and Shuddhi focused on converting Muslim peasants to Hinduism whereas the Muslims responded with the Tablighi Jama'at.

The ideology of *Ram Raj* or *Ramrajya* (the rule by Lord Rama) was in its full swing when, in 1925, Keshnav Baliram Hedgewar established the RSS, the precursor of the BJP. The event followed a few months after some serious communal riots in Nagpur and Western India. Madhav Golwalkar, who succeeded Hedgewar, likened Indian Muslims to the Jews in Nazi Germany. To him, if Hitler could eliminate the Jews, Hindus could do the same to Muslims to establish Ramrajya, or a pure Hindu rule.[24] By now, this ideology of Ultra Right had become a mish mash of selective historical facts, exclusionary racism and ideological irredentism. It reflected unashamed imprints from contemporary fascist ideologies, so popular in Europe and Japan. Though the Muslims were the main targets of this xenophobia, Dalits and Christians also came under a negative spotlight. Even Gandhi's contemporary thoughts seem to support the 'foreignness' and 'bullish' nature of the Indian Muslims due to their centuries-long rule in India.[25] The respective movements for Muslim Raj and Hindu Raj were pulling India apart until Partition became a *fait accompli*. While both the Indian National Congress and the All-India Muslim League were largely led by modernist elements from amongst the Hindus and Muslims, despite their varying definitions of nationalism in India, the religious parties from amongst these two major South Asian communities tended to subscribe to almost exclusionary versions. After independence, the erstwhile INC-AIML contention was replaced by intra-Indian and intra-Pakistani polarities, with the religio-sectarian elements in both the countries pulling polities towards 'majoritarian' nationalism. The 'domestic' forces were now challenging the composite model of nationhood as projected by the anti-colonial discourse. The Nehruvian model was contended by the Mahasabhai/ RSS version, whereas in Pakistan, Islamicists tried to capture the polity either through sheer street power or by working as junior supporters of Zia's military regime.

The last quarter of the century, as noted above, proved a threshold for Hindutva. To Ved Mehta, the campaign for Ramrajya, as sponsored by the VHP, RSS and BJP, began earnestly in 1987, with its clear anti-minority and anti-Muslim contours. Despite the controversy over the Babri Mosque/Ram Janambhoomi since the 1850s, the real concessions were made in post-independence years. After the ban on Mahasabha and the RSS following Gandhi's assassination, Shyama Prasad Mukherji established Bharatiya Jana Sangh in 1951, which was the precursor of the present-day BJP. Initially, they espoused regeneration and moral renewal but gradually began to assume more extreme and communal political views.[26] While the Indian National Congress leadership allowed a back-door entry to saffron elements, the visual media, largely controlled by government, revitalized Hindutva forces in the 1980s by serializing *Ramayana* and *Mahabharata*. The Doordarshan version of these epics provided official recognition of Hindu mythology, shrank the place for secular forces and bolstered a romantic yet intolerant view of a glorified past. Such populism was deeply exploited by the Hindutva leadership who now planned to demolish Babri mosque to take a bigger stride towards Ram Rule. The consecration of the bricks for the temple to be built following the demolition, had begun in September 1989. Each Hindu community, including those in Diaspora, were asked to send in special bricks for this holy project, until egged on by *Sadhus* and politicians, the mosque was razed to the ground within thirty-six hours. The city of Leicester in East Midlands (UK), also called 'Little India' in general parlance, had sent a golden brick along with a huge donation for the Ram Temple: 'The vandals and their leaders were such a well-trained band and did their work with such dispatch that it was hard to escape the conclusion that the entire operation had been planned.'[27]

The demolition of the mosque took place despite advance warnings to the effect, and judicial rebuke, though the Indian National Congress government of P.V. Narasimha Rao, a Brahmin himself, failed to stop Hindutva from carrying out this act. The destruction of the historic mosque dismayed Muslims amidst the growing communal frenzy in which several thousand lives were lost. Like the Bosnian Muslims, the Indian Muslims feared a new wave of militarist onslaught on their cultural and historical vestiges. However, in a significant way, the act also intensified the ideological debate within India. While the middle class Indians were largely polarized on the nature of their polity, the Muslims felt betrayed by the secular and Hindutva groups. Indian nationalism was earlier being perceived without them and now it was being articulated at their expense. Several secular Indians felt that the Hindutva forces had only harmed themselves by demolishing the mosque but had reached the tether end of their campaign by killing the cause itself. Some observers, both from the Hindutva groups and elsewhere, opined that India had gone back to its 'real roots', and Jinnah stood vindicated. However, the optimists in the early 1990s still believed that by committing such an irresponsible act, the Hindutva had depopularized itself amongst the masses and thus had committed self-immolation.[28] However, as subsequent events showed, this proved to be a short-lived optimism. The ensuing debate among the leading Indian analysts also reflected their own ideological moorings and biases. Some lamented the turning of the tide, while a few others came out of the closet and justified Hindutva as a historic, ultimate and democratic vision of India. Some critics, however, felt that the change signaled more than sheer symbolism and traced its roots to colonial times. While faced with a powerful Christianity and a still largely intact Islam, many Hindus, as well as the Orientalists had tried to 'semiticize' Hinduism and in the 1990s, the process appeared to have reached its maturity.[29] Unlike the early Hindi literature, the populist literary works of the 1980s are more subtle and massive, in addition to their successful utilization of multi-dimensional channels for diffusion. Contemporary Hindutva exponents have enormous expatriate funds and resources at their disposal, and since 1996, a supportive regime, which was ensuring a steady rewriting of history texts to inculcate specific teachings and precepts of Hindutva. In other words, the new phase was enduring, highly intellectualized, well-planned, resourceful and multi-pronged. In a crucial way, it had the support from an expanding middle class, both at home and in the Diaspora, which had converted it into a dominant Indian discourse by peripheralizing secularism, liberalism and other class- or caste-based issues. It is not to say that the liberal and secular elements in India had resigned to this fate but the resistance put up through alternative discourse by the leftist and subalterns was unable to forestall the gigantic Hindutva assault. The political strategies by the local parties, ethno-ideological groups and the Indian National Congress were unable to roll back the Hindutva juggernaut which has been attempting to keep the Ayodhya issue alive, and by fanning anti-Muslim, anti-Pakistan and anti-Bangladesh sentiments to stay supreme in the national consciousness. Nuclearization, militarist policies towards smaller neighbours, demonization of Pakistan and changing the text books have been used as shots in the arm by the BJP strategists and it may require concerted efforts to roll back its remit.

The 'new' Hindutva discourse in post-mosque years shows increased self-confidence, invincibility and an amazing amount of clarity on the issues of pluralism. In other words, there is more sophistication than ever before, and amidst a growing economy, and by denigrating any political movement as a foreign-sponsored terrorism, Hindutva seems to be successfully playing up xenophobic forces. Some of its ideologues see the new millennium as a long-awaited breakthrough. For instance, the late Girilal Jain, a noted journalist, while reflecting the views of a whole generation of fundamentalist Hindus, considered December 1992 'as a process of self-renewal and self affirmation'.[30] To him, the struggle for Ram Raj was nearing its maturity as Nehru's socialism and secularism were already dead, and *Janambhoomi* symbolized long-awaited Hinduization of India. He found Hinduism different from Islam and Christianity by being inclusive with a political struggle spread over two centuries. To his mind, power, had already shifted from the Muslims to the Hindus, and India was emerging as a civilizational state once again after losing to the former in the second millennium. The two factors—the British Raj and the Muslim intransigence—according to Jain, had played a crucial role in the reemergence of Hindu civilization. To him, the Indus Valley Civilization was basically a Vedic civilization and not Dravidian, a view that had been held earlier on by historians and archaeologists.[31] Jain considered both Buddhism and Jainism to be components of a larger and overarching Hindu civilization. While talking about Partition and more recent events, Jain offered an interesting, though no less ironical view of Jinnah and Pakistan. For instance, to him, Jinnah 'was the greatest benefactor of Hindus in modern times, if he was not a Hindu in disguise.' Partition was the best thing to have happened as it allowed Hinduism to reemerge both as a consolidated state and revitalized civilisation.[32] Revealing his anti-Muslim animus, he opined that Muslims all over the world were on a rapid decline since their various socio-political 'movements have promoted ghetto psychology', and consequently, were opting out from a more proactive life.[33] They had lost their dynamism and aggression, and the *ummah* remained closeted in a time warp with urban-rural and Sunni-Shia schisms dissipating its energies. While this has been happening to the Muslims, India, on 6 December 1992, 'has taken another big step towards self-affirmation'.[34] While one may go on quoting extensively from such other 'serious' leaders of the BJP, Shiv Sena and the RSS, still even after their occasional electoral lapses, they tend to reappear in newer and more dangerous forms.[35]

The post-Ayodhya populist literature only reveals anti-Muslim rhetoric in its extreme and reflects efforts under way to project Islam as a global threat. For instance, an author observed in the mid–1990s: 'The Muslim problem anywhere by its very nature remains a never-ending problem. As long as there are Muslims in any country, that country will have to live with Muslim problems. This is so because Islam does not tolerate parallel existence of any other ethos or way of life.'[36] The *rath yatras*, aggressive postures on Kashmir, and a continued hostility towards pluralism have kept adding adherents to the BJP from amongst the youth and women. The hope of a moderate element within the Hindutva, as opposed to sheer fascists may yet be wishful thinking, as the total transformation of India both from above or below may further deny space to more tolerant and plural elements. The battle for a plural and democratic India is not totally lost as electoral politics, and a greater sense of security and responsibility, may tame its 'McCarthyism' of conjuring up images of a dreamland that had its glory in by-gone centuries until the Muslim barbarians struck.[37] Even after their defeat in the elections of May 2004, the Hindu extremists are hopeful of a new opportunity emerging in the new millennium for Hindutva to put India back on its path to a lost glory.

AYODHYA: THE REGIONAL IMPLICATIONS

Apart from a more radical ideological shift, and an accompanying electoral victory through an adroit use of religio-political upmanship,[38] the new configuration between the state and populist forces has serious implications for South Asia. Areas like the rudimentary channels for regional cooperation, ethno-national movements, relationships with extra-regional powers and nuclear proliferation have borne the strains of intra-Indian developments. The Ayodhya controversy is neither a culmination point in the majority-minority relationship, nor an endgame in itself, as it engenders various crosscurrents in South Asian politics, some of which may turn sharper in the future. By 2002, India was already a nuclear power with growing stockpiles of nuclear weapons and delivery systems including inter-ballistic missiles, named after Hindu gods and heroes. The relationship with Pakistan had nose-dived, especially with New Delhi mounting its one-million strong army on Pakistani borders, all geared up for a showdown with the arch rival. The Indian extremists wanted to seek a pound of flesh from Pakistan, at a time when the latter was catapulted into being a frontline state in the Anglo-American war in Afghanistan. Though Pakistani president, General Musharraf had accepted many of India's demands to curb militant movements, the Vajpayee regime, largely egged on by

Advani, Malkani and others, refused to relent. Instead of pursuing a meaningful debate on Kashmir, India started eyeing Azad Kashmir. Regionally, India had developed tensions with Sri Lanka and Bangladesh—especially after the latter's elections in October 2001— and the South Asian Association for Regional Cooperation (SAARC) summit could not take place for several years simply because the BJP regime would not accept Musharraf at his word. Globally, India has drawn closer to the United States, and in the process, has developed proximity with Israel. The Nehruvian non-alignment, support for the Palestinian right of self-determination, and a pronounced accent on anti-hegemonic policies, all evaporated in the new milieu. Domestically, the BJP was able to pursue two-pronged policies: firstly, it successfully roller-coastered new text books and ensured further Hindiization and Hinduization of several cultural institutions. Secondly, it ensured penetration of all the important institutions with Hindutva supporters further marginalizing the liberal, plural and secular elite. With the economy showing a persistent 5 per cent growth, and India's global prestige on the rise, Hindutva forces had never had it so good, though electoral worries kept its leadership on tenterhooks. Victory in Gujarat, however, offered a great boost, and 2003 began with a renewed call for Ayodhya to be made accessible for Hindu worship.

Policies to use a military-led Pakistan as bait, especially after the US bombing of Afghanistan and a global negative spotlight on Muslims, reflected BJP's increased self-confidence in India's military might. On occasions, it even went to ironic extents just to manoeuvre Pakistan into some strategic miscalculation, including a botched hijack attempt to start hostilities, or at least alienate Washington from Islamabad. Though there were signs of some thawing during the summer of 2003, South Asia still remained one of the most militarized and restless regions in the world. In terms of its regional politics, South Asia, even after the end of the global Cold War, remained a hotbed of bilateral rivalries, triggering an arms race and almost uncontrollable population transfers. While India retains 76 per cent of the entire regional territory with a corresponding proportion of population and resources, its relationship with the six other regional neighbours has usually been less than cordial. The image of a grand and united India has been propounded, both by the Congress and its rival Hindu parties such as the outlawed Mahasabha, RSS, Jan Sangh, Shiv Sena or the ruling BJP, for their own respective reasons. However, this ironical convergence, shared both by the secularists and ultra nationalists, assumed a pronounced hegemonic dimension under Hindutva, spawning centrist policies within the country, parallel with an attitude towards neighbours characterized by indifference, ambiguity or occasional hostility. It is not just the size of the country itself, but also the advocacy of Akhand Bharat and such other unilateral formulae, varying from regional preeminence to a kind of Monroe Doctrine, that has inculcated fear among its neighbours. Though some Indian nationalists frequently counseled accommodation with the Muslim League, the bitterness over Partition has never allowed any meaningful dialogue.[39] After Independence, the mass migrations, disputes over princely states, natural resources and assets bedeviled Indo-Pakistan relations which fluctuated from fear to active warfare. Like Jinnah,[40] some Indian leaders occasionally advised compromise with Pakistan over such issues, but misperception of Pakistan as the very reminder of Muslim separatism never gave way to good-neighbourliness.[41] Nehru, Kripalani and others kept on expecting Pakistan's eventual amalgamation into India, though, in private, many extreme elements were gleeful over offloading Muslim majority territories and the resultant helplessness of Muslim minorities left in India.[42] When Pakistan, contrary to such presuppositions, managed to survive despite numerous hardships,[43] Indian leadership, incensed over the disputatious nature of Kashmir, resorted to denunciation of Pakistani alliances with Western powers. Such a dismissive attitude not only added to mass-based Pakistani resentment, but equally pushed the young state to find favour among its co-religionists in Western Asia. In such an aura of oversimplification and rigid mistrust, the Indo-Pakistan relationship has never been able to reach common ground. Keeping Pakistan at bay has had severe repercussions on India's own inter-communal relationships, which are apparent to any student of modern Indian history. Of course, Pakistan had to pay a huge price as well. Here, not only did the military become the most dominant political force at the expense of democracy and socio-economic development, but an anti-India fervour dangerously strengthened xenophobic attitudes towards Hindus. For many Pakistanis, India's intervention in former East Pakistan in 1970–1971 was not rooted in some sublime fraternal idealism for Bengalis, but accrued from sheer anti-Pakistan sentiment.

A common slogan applied by the BJP and Shiv Sena—'Pakistan Ya Qabristan!' (Pakistan or graveyard!)—aims at pressurizing Indian Muslims to accept Hindu civilization as the mother civilization while maintaining their cultural distinctness as Muslims.[44] In other words,

Muslims must be Hindus first to symbolize their 'Indianness', followed by their Muslimness, and that too in a strictly cultural sense. Being Hindu and Indian is synonymous to them.[45] Thus Pakistan, without being, or willing to be a party to intra-Indian politics, remains a major factor. While the secular nationalists *needed* Pakistan to prove that India was not a theocracy, the present-day Hindu nationalists need it to drum up their anti-Muslim propaganda. Similarly, when the Ayodhya mosque was demolished, the strongest reaction came from Bangladesh, where a fifty-thousand strong protest demonstration tried to cross into India forcibly, causing a shoot-out by border troops.[46] Since the riots in India portrayed xenophobic nativism and narrowly-based nationalism, fears among other religious and ethnic minorities within the country multiplied. The cross-currents of nativism, religious extremism and chauvinistic nationalism mingled together in India at a time when one expected a new, post-Cold War South Asia led by the forces of cooperation, peace and demilitarisation.[47] The BJP, RSS, VHP and Shiv Sena—often collectively called *Sang Parivar*—and such other nativist groups have often taken up cudgels against economic refugees from Bangladesh, who, apart from smaller numbers, are mostly Muslims, but provide an opportune issue in the Indian political arena. In the same vein, the Hindu refugees from the turbulent state of Kashmir are conveniently portrayed as victims of Muslim fundamentalism approaching from the North and further West. The changed Indian ideological scene and its growing proportions as recorded in many Indian opinion surveys, show an increasingly weakened and retreating secularist ideology faced with overpowering regimentation.[48] The ascendance of expansionist and intolerant forces believing in racial and cultural superiority only signal the security of South Asia to be at risk, unleashing forces of instability which could subsequently engulf the neighbouring areas of the Gulf and Central Asia. The very Indo-centric nature of the subcontinent and its status as a non-priority region in global geo-strategy, even if, after nuclearization it allows India to play a pronounced regional role, shuns its hegemonic intentions. A weak Congress-led or coalition government could play a policy of appeasement to totalitarian forces as was seen earlier on, when Rajiv Gandhi tried to buy Hindu votes in the temple-mosque controversy by opening the disputed site to Hindu pilgrims. In 2002, Sonia Gandhi stopped short of challenging the Hindutva's rising offensive in turbulent Gujarat. The feeble stance of the Congress on serious communal violence only afforded more space to Narendra

Modi's camp followers. Except for the varying degree of sophistication, the Taliban-style Islamic fundamentalism, Jihadi groups and Hindutva are similar to one another in their inception, ideological mindset, scapegoating minorities and a high level of obduracy, though some may appear more *modern* than the rest.

One may pause here to observe the less-than-effective role of SAARC, which was mistakenly viewed as a 'gang-up' against India by some hawkish elements. Even after two decades in existence, it has not 'taken off' since it excludes political, economic and military matters while concentrating on less significant subjects. Even the annual SAARC summits fall frequent victims to contemporary bilateral dissensions, as was seen between 1999 and 2004. Unlike the ASEAN and EU, the SAARC reflects an uneasy stalemate in South Asian inter-state relationships, though support for its invigoration through appropriate initiatives remains undiminished throughout the region. Civil societies in all the seven nations are eager to move forward, yet the states are invariably failing their aspirations for cooperation and fraternity.

ETHNICITY AND IRREDENTISM IN SOUTH ASIA

Even after witnessing the world's largest migration in 1947, South Asia continues to experience an unprecedented number of population movements in recent years owing largely to geo-political, economic or religious factors. Such movements have been taking place both within the respective countries and between them. Never in the history of the subcontinent have so many huddled masses been on the move. The developments in Afghanistan in 1978–79 pushed more than three million Afghan refugees into Pakistan with serious human and politico-economic repercussions, whereas revolution in Iran caused the exodus of a number of Iranian nationals to Pakistan. Many of them continue to stay on. During the 1970s, while Pakistan agreed to accept a number of Biharis—generally known as stranded Pakistanis—from Bangladesh, the repatriation of many more remained a major emotive issue in both the countries. While about 250,000 Biharis have continued to live in designated camps in their former homeland, in Sindh, local, parallel ethnic movements have made their repatriation a contentious issue.[49] As the Urdu-speaking community in Sindh led by the Muhajir Qaumi Movement (MQM) demanded their immediate repatriation, the native

Sindhis agitated against 'becoming American Indians on their own soil'.[50] While General Zia and Benazir Bhutto largely avoided repatriation for its political implications in Sindh, the Nawaz Sharif regime did begin the process of their rehabilitation in Punjab rather than Sindh.[51] However, the number of repatriated Biharis was still quite meagre. After the Soviet withdrawal from Afghanistan, a number of Pakistani Baloch exiles came back to their own province while the Afghans began trickling home, though with the unabated civil war among the warlords, many Afghan refugees still stayed on in Pakistan. Following the anti-Taliban military strikes in 2001 and 2002, many more Afghan refugees tried to come into Pakistan, though most of them remained displaced on their own soil. During the 1980s, many Sri Lankans, especially the Tamils, had sought asylum in India, receiving Indian moral and material support. The events in contemporary Punjab led to an exodus of Punjabi Hindus and others from the troubled province, followed by two-way migrations from the Kashmir Valley, both to India and Pakistan since the beginning of an armed defiance in 1989. Due to inter-ethnic tensions in Nepal and Bhutan, one noticed growing population movement and the resultant inter-state tensions. Nepal seemed to have lost its erstwhile political stability in 2001, when the crown prince, in a furious bout, killed the king and other members of the royal family. The instability only increased the violent unrest in the rural areas, largely sponsored by the communists since 1996. It was being feared that if the insurgency went out of hand, it might trigger Indian intervention, which could escalate Sino-Indian rivalry in the Himalayan regions.

In Punjab, Maharashtra, Bihar, Assam and Jharkhand, the nativist movements became more vocal in demanding the expulsion of the non-natives who had come there seeking jobs and seasonal employment. In a cosmopolitan and otherwise forward-looking Bombay, Shiv Sena triumphantly articulated its anti-alien campaign, demanding Maharashtra for the Maharashtrans and organized itself into a formidable parallel administration. By adding a very communal ingredient to its ethnocentricity, Shiv Sena became a vanguard in the anti-Muslim campaign and has since broadened its following. Bal Thackeray has virtually controlled the politics of the state and has established his countrywide leadership on sheer communal animosity. His audacity would not allow even a cricket match between India and Pakistan. It appeared as if the South Asian urban centres, instead of developing an overarching composite ethos, had fallen prey to criminalized ethnicization and dangerous atomization.

Ethno-regional heterogeneity, like religious diversity, may prove a bane for any plural, representative system, and if not handled judiciously, can be an immensely implosive factor for any multiple society like India or Pakistan. Due to the Indian polity gradually becoming dependent on a centralist and elitist state structure, ethnic, communal and regional identities have become extremely politicized. Primordial factors such as language, religion and region have been operative in identity-formation activated through an ambiguous or hostile interaction with the state itself. All the way from Kashmir and Punjab to the North-east, ethno-regional movements embody defiance against the official authority by falling back upon primordial loyalties to varying degrees. In all such cases of ethnic and cultural nationalism in India, one notices an indigenous revulsion against a perceived majority-led irredentism. Where such a scenario reflects basic impediments to the evolution of a pluralist Indian nationalism, one detects a permeating uneasy relationship between the majorities and minorities and between the centre and the constituent units. If the Hindu majority, on the basis of its numerical strength, was ever able to consolidate a vetoing power within a centralist structure through electoral or other means, the separatist aspirations of various cultural and ethnic nationalists, especially on the peripheries, could gain further momentum, ushering South Asia into a conundrum of convulsions. Both ethno-nationalism and majoritarian irredentism are capable of changing the contours of South Asian politics either through massive population transfers with accompanying 'ethnic cleansing', or by simply triggering inter-state hostilities.[52]

Already one has witnessed escalating tensions between India and Pakistan over Kashmir in 1984, 1987, 1990 and 2001–2003. The Indo-Sri Lankan dissension increased after India's anti-Tamil military operations in that country, which eventually cost Rajiv Gandhi his life. So far, South Asian states seem to be managing the regional low-intensity conflicts rather successfully without any major cost, but any larger change within the Indian body politic could radically change the status quo. In 1999, following the Pakistani and Kashmiri incursions into the Kargil region of Kashmir, there was a possibility of a fully-fledged Indian attack on Pakistan, while in more recent years, Indian troops were positioned to move into Pakistani-controlled Kashmir to cow down Pakistan. The Hinduist forces blame Indira

Gandhi for not imposing humbling conditions on a defeated Pakistan in 1972, and are determined to rectify the legacy.

The forces of Hindutva envision a trans-regional India as reflected in ancient scriptures, negating pluralism within Indian society and even the existence of separate sovereign states in the region. It allows only a caste-based diversity but that too within a strictly defined Hindu hierarchy. Such a conviction stipulates a twin-pronged policy. While it aims at remoulding the ethno-regional diversities into a monolithic mainstream culture (not without caste distinctions), it equally challenges the existence of neighbouring states. Such views, however unrealistic they might appear, are essentially irredentist in nature and strategy.[53] The porous borders, easy availability of weapons in open markets, problems of underdevelopment with an insurmountable number of unemployed in otherwise exceedingly youthful South Asian societies, and a consistent 'cold war', could veto any effort for peaceful co-existence. Following the nuclearization of both the rival neighbours and an increase in the frequency of crisis including the strict visa restrictions, and the stoppage of all contacts and expulsion of diplomats, it is widely worried that any miscalculation on either side could trigger a nuclear exchange with horrid consequences for the entire region.

NUCLEAR PROLIFERATION ON THE SUBCONTINENT

While India and Pakistan carry on an unrestrained race to acquire missiles to carry their nuclear payloads, the US and its allies like Japan have tried to ascertain a regional *quid pro quo*, either through confidence building measures or through better warning systems. Since the late 1990s, the US relationship with both countries allows it to play a more effective role in restraining them from an all-out war. Both the countries have used similar arguments of deterrence underwriting their nuclearization and missile development technologies but nuclearization has neither stabilized the regional security nor has it decreased the dependence and expense on the conventional weapons. The erstwhile American policy of pressuring both the countries into signing the Non-Proliferation Treaty (NPT) failed to contain weaponization nor has Washington been successful in making them sign Comprehensive Test Ban Treaty (CTBT). Musharraf's reiteration of a nuclear-free South Asia and offer of a No-War Treaty, both have evinced no positive response from India. However, including Vajpayee, there are elements within the BJP and the INC who may like to redefine the relationship with Pakistan by agreeing on some formula to resolve the Kashmir dispute. Both the military rulers in Pakistan and the Indian leadership will have to labour hard to evince support from their jingoistic followers for such a breakthrough.

India's supporters in America have been advocating the acceptance of India's full-fledged entry into the 'haves' club and her regional preeminence as a 'natural' reality rather than demanding a rollback. To them, this 'privilege' must signify 'more than a reward for [her] civic achievement', even if 'there is a whiff of a cave-in'.[54] The US singled out Pakistan in 1990 'by choking off aid' over its nuclear programme, followed by a demand of a Pakistani retreat on the Kashmir issue.[55] Pakistan, without any guarantee for its territorial integrity, saw in its nuclear programme, a credible deterrent, and despite the aid blockade, largely resisted American pressures. Instead, Pakistan proposed the idea of holding a conference on the issue of nuclear proliferation in the region involving the five permanent members of the Security Council besides India and Pakistan. Pakistan received support from all these countries, but India showed no enthusiasm. Japan, too, has been critical of Pakistan's nuclear programme, and despite assurances to the contrary by Nawaz Sharif, refused to release a grant of $450 million. Periodic reports in the Western media carrying exaggerated accounts of 'clandestine' Pakistani nuclear and missile development programmes with Chinese or North Korean assistance were seen as bringing further pressure to bear.[56] Pakistanis perceived such reports as being part of a well-orchestrated campaign of 'Muslim bashing', while India, Israel, and until recently, South Africa, pursued their weapon-oriented nuclearization with impunity. In addition to its parallel strategic aspects, the nuclearization symbolized an officially sponsored nationalism intrinsically linked with sovereignty. To date, Pakistan has resiliently resisted severe pressure to sign the CTBT. After China's adherence, India's reluctance, grounded in the question of sovereignty or contradictions within the NPT and CTBT, gave Pakistan a strong additional argument to support its case. The American and the Japanese demand for CTBT was also momentarily rebuffed by both the South Asian nations and especially after the new Afghan imbroglio, and the second Anglo-American invasion of Iraq, the former diverted their attention to other areas of interest. However, the links between North

Korea and Pakistan on the mutual exchange of nuclear and missile capabilities reverberated in the media as Islamabad was confronted with new American sanctions on its nuclear research facility at Kahuta in April 2003.

THE KASHMIR SAGA

Kashmir, closely linked with other regional divergences, has been witnessing a new phase in massive defiance since 1989. India's official retaliation has already caused more than sixty thousand deaths, numerous cases of gang rapes and arson.[57] In addition to the involvement of some half-million Indian troops, the dispute has already caused three major wars in the past between India and Pakistan, with the possible spectre of another confrontation of nuclear dimensions in 1990–1991 and then again during 2001–2002. The saga of Kashmir began in 1846 with the British sale of the entire territory (equal in size to the United Kingdom), to a local chieftain for a paltry sum. Kashmir, a Muslim majority region, remained under the dynastic rule of the Dogra Maharajas for the next century, whose last claimant in 1947 initially dithered on the future of his princely state.[58] Faced with indigenous revolts, he was 'arm-twisted into acceding to India', conditional upon a reference to the people.[59] India, while accusing Pakistan of interference, took the issue before the UN in 1948, which enforced a cease-fire to be followed by a plebiscite. Pakistanis and the Kashmiris base their case on the UN resolutions, demanding a plebiscite while India has vacillated between different positions. Until the 1970s, it considered Kashmir as a regional irritant while, more recently, it portrays it as a 'domestic' issue.[60] India has traditionally accused Pakistan of aiding and abetting the Kashmiri activists, while the latter reaffirms its moral and political support to the Kashmiris by virtue of being a historical party to the dispute, as confirmed by the UN resolutions and bilateral agreements signed in 1966 and 1972. Since 1989, Kashmiri ethno-nationalism has turned into a full-fledged rebellion, with India intent upon crushing the mass-based defiance in the predominantly Muslim Valley using brutal force besides some cooption.[61] The BJP, while believing in a unitary India, has occasionally desired to settle the Kashmir Valley with millions of Hindus to outnumber its Muslim majority. It also advocated an open war with Pakistan on Kashmir, and has often demanded the abolition of Article 370 from the Indian constitution, which allots a special status to Kashmir. In 1991, the BJP-led *ekta yatra* (unity march) had led to further spates of violence in Punjab and Kashmir. Murli Manohar Joshi, the leader of the BJP, was specially flown into Srinagar with seven companions in a military helicopter, while the city remained under strict curfew so that he could terminate his 'long march'. Similar marches on the Pakistani side of the Line of Control (LOC) had only been stopped by force. On the eve of the British Prime Minister's visit to India in January 1993, the Indian security forces, in pursuit of a scorched earth policy, ran amok in the town of Sopore, killing more than fifty civilians through indiscriminate shooting besides torching hundreds of shops and dwellings.[62] Kashmir is not only a major regional flash point, it is also an ongoing human agony which needs to be rectified before further accentuating the existing polarization in South Asia. In more recent years, the unrest in Kashmir has been assuming more communal dimensions with severe ramifications to the entire region.

By the late 1990s, with the ascendance of the Taliban in Afghanistan, Kashmir once again became a hotbed of militarism and official repression. In 1999, India and Pakistan dangerously got embroiled in the Kargil conflict followed by the hijack of an Indian aircraft in 1999, which led to the release of a few militants. For the next few years, the Kashmiri militancy remained on the rise with several militant organizations supported by Pakistani intelligence agencies, and the Kashmiri Diaspora operated against the Indian troops. With the American offensive against the Taliban, and greater pressure on Pakistan for controlling the Jihadi groups such as Lashkar-i-Tayyaba (LT) and Jaysh-i-Muhammad (JM), India expected a gradual end to Kashmiri militancy though, in the process, the dispute got further internationalized. The Kashmiri groups like the Hurriyat and the Jammu Kashmir Liberation Front (JKLF), have persistently sought Kashmiri inclusion in any Indo-Pakistani talks on Kashmir, whereas the Vajpayee administration had been resisting efforts for arbitration. The BJP government continuously insisted on the stoppage to 'cross-border terror', whereas Musharraf desired a frank talk on Kashmir as the core issue. His meeting with Vajpayee in Agra in July 2001 ended on a sheer reiteration of their receptive stances. Both the rivals were back to hostilities within a few weeks of the Agra Summit. In the early 2002, their armies were in an 'eyeball-to-eyeball' situation on the LOC and across the international borders, leading to a flurry of international diplomatic activities due to a possible nuclear flare-up. The elections in the Indian Kashmir in October 2002 were seen as a remedial step by Delhi to pacify Kashmiri Muslims, though Pakistan remained insistent on a fully-fledged dialogue. However, the cross-border infiltrations, as well as the incidents of violence within the Valley and Jammu region, decreased considerably by early 2003, though Indo-Pakistani bilateralism remained volatile. Several Pakistanis felt that after Musharraf's significant about turn on Pakistani support for insurgency, India should have reciprocated with substantive measures to ease regional tensions instead of insisting on a 'pound of Pakistani flesh', especially during the latter's dire security environment. In April 2003, Vajpayee announced his desire to mend fences with Pakistan and a number of confidence-building measures were put into effect by both the rivals. Amidst a growing hope for *détente*, underwritten by a cautious realism, civil societies on both sides displayed a keen desire for regional peace.

HINDUTVA AND GLOBAL GEO-POLITICS

Historically speaking, the regional geo-political incongruities, as reflected in embittered inter-state relations, saw to it that South Asia found itself seeking allies among extra-regional powers. Pakistan sought help both from the Western and Muslim countries to compensate for its severe security concerns, while India tried to assume a non-aligned stature in the Afro-Asian world. The American interest in Pakistan, and the Soviet interest in India, grew out of their global strategic thinking, though after the Sino-Indian war of 1962 both the rivals discovered a mutual convergence in arming India against China.[63] The Chinese threat deflated Nehru's stance on neutrality besides revising his erstwhile policy on a nuclearization programme. The separation of East Pakistan, made possible through an Indian military intervention under a Soviet umbrella, demoralized Pakistani leaders, who despite a Westernized orientation sought a closer relationship with the Muslim Near East. Pakistanis were dismayed that despite their alliance-based relations with the USA, the latter did not help them in Kashmir and in wars with India, and instead left them stranded. Both in 1965 and 1971, Pakistan, despite an executive agreement of 1959 with the USA, was equated with India by the global power in its imposition of an arms embargo. Zulfikar Ali Bhutto's efforts to build

Pakistani defence capabilities both in conventional and nuclear areas met stiff resistance from Washington. Again, during the 1980s, with Pakistan enjoying closer security collaboration, the Americans did not let it off the hook by keeping its nuclear programme under constant scrutiny. Subsequently, upon the dissolution of the Soviet Union, the Clinton Administration was eager to develop closer relations with India while pressurizing Pakistan to withdraw on Kashmir and roll back its nuclear programme.[64] Pakistan faced severe American sanctions after its nuclear tests in 1998, and the military coup in 1999 led by Musharraf further isolated the country. It was suspended from the Commonwealth and Musharraf was shunned from the Western capitals. But following the terrorist attacks in the US, Pakistan reemerged as an active partner from a pariah state. Amidst increased Indo-Pakistani hostilities, their Western friends shied away from offering any substantial arbitration to help them resolve their conflictive relationship. The focus was instead on easing tensions and dissuading India from attacking Pakistan in hot pursuit, that could have led to a nuclear clash. Tony Blair's visit in 2002, in fact, meant to sell weapons worth one billion pounds to India, whereas Colin Powell urged for restraint. In other words, their external allies, either find the Indo-Pakistani discord intractable or simply seem less eager for a resolute initiative.

While South Asian states remain wary of a growing tide of extreme Hindu nationalism and its repercussions on Indian minorities, and resultant geo-political and economic ramifications both for India and her neighbours, Russia and the Western countries have been reappraising their bilateral relations with India. While enthused by India's liberal market-oriented policies, these extra-regional powers are still sensitive to implosive forces within the country, and the region around it. South Asia, more open to foreign investment and eager to develop democratic traditions, is occasionally idealized as a potential area of commercial significance with accompanying geopolitical interests,[65] but significant foreign investors have usually shied away from the region. The inter-state and intra-state conflicts and the instability of states such as Afghanistan, Nepal and Burma do not offer any major incentives for greater economic activity. Not only is South Asia notorious for bureaucratic inertia, its reputation as the hotbed of fundamentalist organizations feeding into terrorist ventures, equally dissuades foreign capital. Despite the high level of technical know-how, especially in India, the low-intensity conflicts, greater communalization of politics, and a persistently feeble nature of the social sector has continued to exclude the region from mainstream economic zones. The Indian economy has made significant progress in areas such as IT and communications—without forgetting the extra-regional role for Indian films—but its rate of growth is not that immense. The 28 per cent hike in the defence budget in 2001, and the missile tests during 2002–03 reflected a prioritized non-development sector and a disincentive for foreign investments. South Asia's inter-state trade remains very low; expenditure on defence stays high and spiralling; and the outward flow of trained professionals is also high, though within the region there is due apprehension of illegal trans-border population movements. In this context, substantial regional cooperation away from inter-state schisms could offer a long-awaited breakthrough. For that, the forces of Hindutva and Islamic militancy, often supported by official hierarchies, will have to give way to moderate and mundane priorities. The energy sector, more than other economic areas, needs a long overdue regional harmony so that oil pipelines, power transmission infrastructures and regional communications, besides a judicious use of water resources, could play a vanguard role towards full-fledged economic development. Peaceful South Asia can prove a useful linkage with Central Asia and the Middle East in developing complementary economies where, after all, the pronounced forces of Hindutva and Islamic fundamentalism are perceived inimical to regional security.

Given the volatile communalism in India and its vivid repercussions for regional stability and security, and even for the country's own territorial integrity, it is imperative to persuade India to play a more responsible regional role by resolving various bilateral irritants. While Kashmir, distribution of water resources and mutual trade can be sorted out with bold initiatives, the nuclear issue can be tackled only through an Indo-Pakistani 'standstill agreement'. One should not forget that it was the Congress government which introduced the nuclear factor into South Asian politics while visualizing an enhanced military role 'at the expense of improving conditions of its people'. The BJP wanted to outdo its rival in currying favour with its supporters by suggesting a masculanized nationalism: 'We don't want to be blackmailed and rated as oriental blackies. Nuclear weapons will give us prestige, power, standing. An Indian will talk straight and walk straight when we have the bomb.'[66] After the acquisition of nuclear bombs, the emphasis has turned to missile technology and both India and Pakistan are engaged in developing long-range missiles, which ironically carry the names of their respective Hindu and Muslim leaders from their past.

The evolution of Hindutva is not a unique phenomenon in the global politics, but its consolidation through a longer rule, helped by a weakened opposition and divided civil society may herald serious challenges for India's plural society. The substantial changes in the curricula and a greater accent on the so-called majoritarianism may have long-term ramifications irrespective of who rules the country. The Muslims and Hindus are already bearing the brunt of the campaign for Hinduization which may simply be expanded to other communities.[67] In more recent years, Indian Christians have also incurred organized violence and even official strictures against conversion have been put in place in Tamil Nadu. Many Indian secularists continue to perceive Hindutva as an aberration and assume that it may go away once things settled down.[68] But wishful thinking of this kind is not borne out by realties on the ground. While the Indian constitution still stipulates a secular polity, the substantial changes across the country have already unleashed irreversible processes. The weakening of the secular forces and their lack of fresher alternatives on the national and regional policies only allow more space to Hindutva: 'The killings of innocent Muslims in the laboratory of Hindutva, Gujarat, followed by the forcing of the Ayodhya issue by the Hindu extremists, is ominous for the future of the world's largest democracy.'[69] While the world may counsel the BJP-led India to 'stay calm', as it may trigger a nuclear holocaust,[70] it is for the Indians themselves to decide what kind of ideology may suit their plural nation, and what guiding principles should lead the largest democracy in the world. The challenge of being taken seriously as a big power is attainable only through humane and generous deeds, and not merely through destructive weaponry and hateful rhetoric. However, it is certain that any deconstruction of inter-state hostility may go a long way in ridding the entire region of militant forces flourishing on denigration and spite.[71] Being the largest and well-established country in the region, India needs to provide a generous leadership to South Asia, rather than hiding behind puny excuses and merely looking for scapegoats in smaller and equally turbulent neighbours. The strictures against its own inhabitants, repression in Kashmir and undiminished diatribes against neighbours have to give way to a fresh start, as peace within and without, is in India's own premier interests.[72]

NOTES

1. The Babri/Baburi Mosque was originally constructed during the reign of Zaheer-ud-Din Babur, the Turkic founder of the Mughal empire in India. Mir Baqi, one of his generals, built it in 1528. During the British period, a number of Hindu leaders believed that the Mosque actually stood on the site of Ram's *Janambhoomi* (birthplace) and thus symbolised Muslim aggression. It was in an article in 1936, that the claims of a temple being demolished to build the mosque upon the site were made by a Hindu scholar, S.K. Bannerji. However, the claims lacked any documentary evidence on any preexisting Ram Temple. Mir Baqi's jubilant description of the mosque as *Mohibi-i-Qudsiyya* (the place of descent for celestial beings) was misinterpreted out of context to make an outlandish claim. (For details, see, S.K. Bannerji, 'Babur and the Hindus', *Journal of the United Provinces Historical Society*, 9, 1936, 76–83. For further details, see, Richard H. Eaton, *Essays on Islamic and Indian History*, New Delhi, 2001, pp. 110–112.) During the night of 22–23 December 1949, the idol of Ram was sneaked into the premises, and the Mosque was closed down by the government though it allowed worship by Hindu holy men. On 1 February 1986, it was made open to Hindu worshippers. In 1989, Rajiv Gandhi allowed laying of the foundation stone for the Ram temple. In 1990, the BJP tried to cash in on the Mosque/Temple controversy as its leader, L.K. Advani, led a *rath yatra* (chariot march) causing massive bloodshed. In 1991, the BJP won 119 seats in the lower house of the parliament and established its government in the UP, where the site is located. The BJP was also able to establish its governments in three other states of Rajasthan, Himachal Pradesh and Madhya Pradesh. In April 1992, all the buildings, trees and even graveyards around the Mosque were demolished and a temporary Hindu shrine was built, until on 6 December, the Mosque itself was completely destroyed. On 15 March 2002, the Kar Sevaks gathered at the contentious site to install the prefabricated structures for the temple, but the higher court once again banned the activity, averting a major crisis at least for the time being. In its party convention in July 2003, the ruling BJP reiterated its resolve to build the Temple on the disputed site, though some leaders advised for negotiations with the Muslims, much to the chagrin of extremists.

2. Some of the well familiar Hindu organisations are as follows:
   • Rashtriya Swayamsevak Sangh (RSS), established in 1925 as a non-political, socio-cultural organisation, aimed at the reorganisation of the Hindu society.
   • Bharatiya Janata Party (BJP), itself evolved from Bharatiya Jan Sangh (1977–79), which had been founded in 1951, strictly as a political party espousing Hindu ideology.
   • Vishwa Hindu Parishad (VHP) was formally established in 1964 as a religious organisation and since 1984 has been mobilizing Hindu public opinion for the construction of the Ram temple at Ayodhya. It has world-wide branches and receives ample funding from its UK and US affiliates.
   • Bajrang Dal was established as a youth organization on the fascist pattern with a massive membership. Named after the monkey god, Hanumann, its trained members wear saffron bandannas and carry tridents in their hands.
   • Shiv Sena was established in Bombay (Mumbai) in 1966, to espouse the nativist cause of 'Maharashtra for Maharashtra', and propagated expulsion of 'others' from

the state. Its founder, Bal Thackeray, a former cartoonist, is vehemently anti-Muslim and has joined the BJP-led bandwagon subscribing to Hindu nationalism.

3. 'Might vs. Right', *Time International*, 18 January 1993. Not only the police, but even their telecommunication network was used to single out Muslims and their properties in the city. While the police shot at Muslim protesters, their radio transmissions quite unabashedly led the Hindu extremists on Muslim localities and commercial properties. *International Herald Tribune*, 6 February 1993.

4. 'More killed as Muslims flee Bombay riots', *The Times*, 13 January 1993. The Shiv Sena activists came with marked electoral lists to carry out their anti-Muslim programs in the slums while many businessmen and civil rights activists felt that only martial law could save the city from the carnage. See, *The Observer*, 13 December 1992; and, *The Independent* and *The Guardian*, 13 January 1993.

5. In an interview, Bal Thackeray, the leader of Shiv Sena, explained his policy towards Indian Muslims: 'I want to teach Muslims a lesson.... If they are going, let them go. If they are not going, kick them out. If Pakistan feels Muslims in India are being harassed, let it, please, take this lot back.... This is a Hindu *rashtra* [nation].... In politics it's Shivaji. The third eye is now opening. Burn them!' *Time International*, 25 January 1993.

6. Shashi Tharoor, 'India in the Plural: Save This Ethos From the Dividers', *International Herald Tribune*, 12–13 December 1992.

7. In fact, the issue of Muslim alimony caused a major stir. A Muslim woman of senior age, Shah Bano, was divorced by her barrister husband after 42 years of marriage. The court asked the barrister to pay her alimony of 25 rupees per month. He challenged it in a superior court on the plea of Sharia where alimony is allowed only for three months after the consummation of divorce. The controversy raised quite a storm as the Muslim fundamentalists sought the prioritisation of Sharia while modernists and feminists supported Shah Bano. Eventually, Rajiv Gandhi's administration, through legislation, allowed Muslims to pursue the Sharia Personal Law, which deeply incensed many Hindu groups. Interestingly, to appease them, Rajiv Gandhi allowed them access to the Babri Mosque. Both the steps showed the official retreat on secular policies and pandering to fundamentalist demands.

8. South Asia has more people below the poverty line than their counterparts elsewhere put together. For statistics, see, United Nations, *Human Development Report 2001*, Oxford, 2001; also, Human Development Centre, *South Asia in 2001*, Islamabad, 2001.

9. Academics have differed in their explanation of Muslim experience in India. Imtiaz Ahmed would see localism and closer networking offering safeguards. To Robinson, it has been the religio-spiritual articulation and corresponding seminaries to keep the community from going totally under. In the recent past, the Hindutva proponents built its case by portraying Muslims as a major threat to Hinduism and 'Hindu girls are not safe with Muslims around'. Quoted in Alkananda Patel, 'Gujarat Violence: A Personal Diary', *Economic and Political Weekly*, 14 December 2002. Such extreme views are similar to those of the racists in the American South during the nineteenth century.

10. Akbar S. Ahmed, 'The History-Thieves: Stealing the Muslim past?' *History Today*, 43, January 1993, p. 12; also see, Kai Friese, 'Hijacking India's history', *The New York Times*, 30 December 2002.

11. Such riots until recently were interpreted as the machinations of *goonda* elements intent upon pursuing their own nefarious aims by using the communal card. For a historical perspective, see, Mushirul Hasan, *Legacy of a Divided Nation: India's Muslims since Independence*, London, 1997.

12. Internationally, with the dissolution of the Soviet Union, Islamic fundamentalism was see,n as a threat to the new world order. Islam began to be see,n as an authoritarian ideology like communism, eventually to give way to the marching forces of democracy and liberalism. One can refer to a host of writings espousing such a new ideological bi-polarity. For instance, see, Francis Fukuyama, 'The end of history is still nigh', *The Independent,* 3 March 1992; and, *The End of History And The Last Man,* London, 1992, pp. 45–6; and, Judith Weinraub, 'The End of History? Well, Not Quite', *International Herald Tribune,* 19 March 1992.

13. While to any non-partisan observer, such a threat may appear unfounded, it went well with frenzied crowds who quoted from instances such as the Shah Bano case, to prove that the Muslims were being promoted at the expense of the Hindu majority. It is interesting to note that the Hidutva forces have been focusing on young generations by inculcating a greater sense of pride in being a Hindu and transforming India into a specific mould. These khaki-clad youths are indoctrinated at specific schools and parade grounds, which are sponsored by the VHP largely through expatriate funding. Curiously, when in a special television programme, Mark Tully asked a young trishol-carrying Hindu trainee for his reason to acquire martial training, the boy said: 'I want to fight Pathans'. 'Hindu Nation with Mark Tully', BBC 4, 11 August 2003.

14. A leading Indian thinker finds such symbols very significant as they add to existing ambiguities in the Hindu-Muslim relationship in India. To him, the Hindus also feel aggrieved over the stereotypes about their being a 'flawed race' which was first governed by the Muslims and then by the British, and the efforts for 'Neo-Hinduism' receive wider acclaim. They quote the *Muslim* character of Pakistan and Bangladesh while, to them, in their own state, despite an overwhelming majority, they are not allowed to do so. Professor Bhiku Parekh expressed these views in his paper in a workshop, *India after Ayodhya,* held in Oxford on 6 February 1993. In the absence of a 'Neo-Islam', according to Professor Parekh, the slogans for 'Neo-Hinduism' do not make any sense.

15. In addition to a weakened party system, the strife revolves around the basic question: 'Who is an Indian?' Neville Maxwell, 'Back on Track', unpublished paper presented at the workshop, Oxford, 6 February 1993.

16. Such optimists believe in the inner strength of an Indian composite nationalism, where Ayodhya might lead to a much-needed catharsis eventually tempering down fascist tendencies. Talmiz Ahmed (Minister for Information in Indian High Commission, London), 'Do Muslims have a future in India?' in above.

17. For more details on Islam in South Asian historiography, see, Iftikhar H. Malik, *Islam, Nationalism and the West: Issues of Identity in Pakistan,* Oxford, 1999, pp. 38–71.

18. For instance, Chowdhury Muhammad Ali, *The Emergence of Pakistan*, New York, 1967. The books by Pakistani writers including I.H. Qureshi, Sharifal Mujahid, Latif Sherwani, K.K. Aziz, Abdul Hamid, Aziz Ahmed, S.M. Ikram and Khaliquzzaman look at the larger issues, whereas the studies by Ayesha Jalal, Ian Talbot, David Gilmartin, David Page, Imran Ali, Taj Hashmi, Anita Inder Singh,

Yunas Samad, Tazeen Murshid, Farzana Shaikh, Sarah Ansari, Andrew Roberts, Alastair Lamb, and Patrick French are based on research completed outside South Asia mostly as doctoral dissertations, or are personal efforts. The recent studies by Wiqar Shah, Aslam Malik and Dushka Sayid are new additions focusing on region and gender.

19. For a pertinent study, see, Ian Talbot, *Freedom's Cry: The Popular Dimension in the Pakistan Movement and Partition Experience in North-West India,* Karachi, 1996.

20. For a useful comparative compendium, see, Ian Talbot and Gurharpal Singh (eds.), *Region and Partition: Bengal, Punjab and the Partition of the Subcontinent,* Karachi, 1999; also another holistic effort focusing on Punjab only, see, Shinder Thandi and Prtiam Singh (eds.), *Punjabi Identity in a Global Context,* Karachi, 1999.

21. It must be noted that many of these studies are quite recent: Urvashi Butalia, *The Other Side of Silence: Voices from the Partition of India,* New Delhi, 1998; Ritu Menon and Kamla Bhasin, *Borders and Boundaries: Women in India's Partition,* New Delhi, 1998; and Gyanendra Pandey, *Remembering Partition: Violence, Nationalism and History in India,* Cambridge, 2001.

22. This has been amply discussed by Raifiuddin Ahmed in his *The Bengal Muslims, 1871–1906, A Quest for Identity,* Delhi, 1981.

23. Some of the urban Indian Muslims such as Allama Abdullah Yusuf Ali and Syed Ameer Ali built linkages with Jinnah, Sir Muhammad Iqbal and Aga Khan. The Nawabs of Dhaka promoted such efforts, and eventually hosted the meeting in December 1906 that led to the formation of the All-India Muslim League. Earlier, Aga Khan, in October 1906, had led a delegation of Indian Muslims to Simla to apprise the Viceroy of the aspirations and demands of the Indian Muslims.

24. Madhav S. Golwalkar, *We or Our Nationhood Defined,* Nagpur, 1938, p. 27. For a recent study by a known Indian Muslim, see, A.G. Noorani, *Savarkar and Hindutva: The Godse Connection,* Bombay, 2002, and its review by Christophe Jaffrelot in *Outlook,* 30 December 2002.

25. *Young India,* 29 May 1924, and 30 December 1926. For pertinent discussion on the evolution of cultural movements in modern India, see, Kenneth Jones, *Socio-Religious Reform Movements in British India,* Cambridge, 1989; and, Antony Copley (ed.), *Gurus and Their Followers: New Religious Reform Movements in Colonial India,* Delhi, 2000.

26. For a semi-official history of the BJP, see, Gurdas M. Ahuja, *BJP and the Indian Politiccs. Politics and Programmes of the Bharatiya Janata Party,* New Delhi, 1995; Deendayal Research Institute, *How Others Look at the RSS.,* New Delhi, 1989; K. Jayaprashad, *RSS and Hindu Nationalism: Inroads in a Leftist Stronghold,* New Delhi, 1991. Based on a doctoral thesis, it concentrates on how the Hindutva have been challenging the leftist politics in Kerala. Also, Jay Dubashi, *The Road to Ayodhya,* New Delhi, 1992. This is a collection of articles on almost every subject within the Hindutva which had been published by the author in *The Organiser,* the official mouthpiece. Harsh Narain, *The Ayodhya Temple-Mosque Dispute: Focus on Muslim Sources,* Delhi, 1993. This work goes back to Persian sources to prove that the mosque was built on a temple.

For two balanced studies on the emergence of ultra Right in the Indian politics, see, Craig Baxter, *Jana Sangh: A Biography of an Indian Political Party,* Delhi,

1971; Walter K. Anderson and Shridhar D. Damle, *The Brotherhood in Saffron: The Rashtriya Swayamsevak Sangh and Hindu Revivalism,* Boulder, 1987.

27. In fact, after the Shah Bano case, Hindus were allowed to put statues in the Mosque though the court had debarred these groups from demolishing the original mosque structure. The frenzied crowd, in the full presence of the police, raised it to the ground. The visual media had already created a utopian vision of a lost glory, which the Kar Sevaks were now determined to restore. For media's impact on the Hindu militancy, see,, Arvind Rajagopal, *Politics After Television: Hindu Nationalism and the Reshaping of the Public in India,* Cambridge, 2001.

28. Contemporary Indian press, especially in English, is full of such diverse commentaries. Also see,, Madhu Limaye, *Religious Bigotry: A Threat to Ordered State,* Delhi, 1994.

29. Analysts saw this as a new phase in the conflictive relationship between tradition and modernity, while others felt that it was more than a political game plan. For an interesting mix of ideas, see, Upendra Baxi and Bhiku Parekh (eds.), *Crisis and Change in Contemporary India,* New Delhi, 1995. For this particular term, I am obliged to Sudipto Kaviraj, who has used it in his article: 'Religion, Politics and Modernity', in ibid., p. 312.

30. Girilal Jain, *The Hindu Phenomenon,* New Delhi, 1944, p. v.

31. Ibid., pp. 11 and 21–2.

32. Ibid., p. 56.

33. Ibid., p. 60.

34. Ibid., p. 114.

35. Interestingly, soon after the demolition of the Mosque and riots, many BJP leaders, in their statements in the Lok Sabha, tried to distance themselves from these 'irresponsible' acts. But that has not stopped them from offering full-fledged support to build the Temple. For the speeches by MPs and Swamis, see, A.B. Vajpayee, L.K. Advani, Swami Chimayanand and Professor Rajendra Singh, *Hindus Betrayed,* New Delhi, 1995.

36. B.W. Jog, *Threat of Islam: Indian Dimension,* Mumbai, 1994, p. vi. Also, Baljit Rai, *Is India Going Islamic?* Chandigarh, 1994. He blames Urdu Mafia, Muslims including secularists like Rafique Zakaria, the ISI and Bangladesh, for all the troubles in India. For Zakaria's views, see, *The Widening Divide: An Insight into Hindu-Muslim Relations,* New Delhi, 1995. Some other notable Indian writers on the subject include Asghar Ali Engineer, Mushirul Hasan, A.G. Noorani, Imtiaz Ahmed, Ejaz Ahmed, Shakir Moin, Muhamamd Talib and Muzaffar Alam. The Nadwa tradition of Indian Islam was largely led and embodied by Maulana Abul Hasan Nadwai until his death in 2000. Imam Bokhari of the Shahi Mosque in Delhi has traditionally held a very important position among the North Indian Muslims. On the other hand, southern Muslim groups like the Muslim League in Kerala have usually pursued mainstream politics.

37. Gyanendra Pandey (ed.), *Hindus and Others: The Question of Identity in India,* New Delhi, 1993, pp. 2 and 12. See, its chapter on women *Kar Sevakas* by Tanka Sarkar, pp. 24–45. The Hindutva remit seems to be expanding including the conversion of several thousand mosques to temples, or simple destruction of other historic monuments, including the Taj Mahal and Qutub Minar. In the late December 2002, following Modi's re-election in Gujarat, VHP and the Bjarang Dal planned a *puja* at Qutub Minar in Delhi. For details, see, Rajeev Dhavan, 'Puja at the Qutub

Minar', *The Hindu,* 27 December 2002. The VHP finances the training of its men and women cadres to subdue Muslims and other minorities. Even young Hindu girls are emotionally incited to undergo military training to fight the 'impure' Muslims. For a recent account, see, Prajnan Bhattacharya, 'Training camps worrying India's minorities', *Los Angeles Daily News,* 12 July 2003. The internet and Hindu diaspora both have helped each other in globalising Hindutva over and above Hinduism. Thousands of web sites such as Global Hindu Electronic Network (GHEN) are maintained by VHP volunteers from among the Hindu scientists and students to spread selective propaganda on cybernet. The revisionist, un-referenced, mostly incorrect and exaggerated information is offered on India as the Aryan birthplace, Muslim rule as the bloodiest past and the Taj Mahal as being a Hindu monument, nefariously attributed to Mughals by Muslim-loving Hindus. On the Hindutva web sites, it is called Tajmahlay. Some boistrous claims such as Argentina being the land of Arjuna, Vive Canada for Vivekananda, Denmark as 'Dheng Marg' (the land of cows), are some of the familiar travesties given out in the name of Hindu globalism and invincibility. For further details, see, Vinay Lal, *The History of History: Politics and Scholarship in Modern India,* Delhi, 2003. When *Indian Express,* on 6 August 2003, excerpted the final chapter of this book, the US-based author was deeply criticised by VHP, and other proponents of Hindutva. Lal, a Hindu academic, was called 'a Hindu basher, a communist, a lover of Aurangzeb....One commentator says that I am the kind of Hindu who would sell his mother and wife (presumably to a Muslim)'. Email message received on 11 August 2003.

38. For an historical background and then focus on Central India, see, Christopher Jaffrelot, *The Hindu Nationalist Movement and India Politics, 1925 to 1990s: Strategies of Identity-building, Implementation and Mobilisation,* London, 1996.

39. See, B.R. Ambedkar, *Pakistan or the Partition of India,* Bombay, 1946.

40. Jinnah, in his speeches of 14 October 1944, and 15 November 1946, had suggested a joint defence between India and Pakistan. See, Jamil-ud-Din Ahmad, (ed.) *Some Recent Speeches and Writings of Mr. Jinnah,* Vol. II, Lahore, 1947, pp. 225 and 474.

41. For instance, see, Jayaprakash Narayan, 'Our great Opportunity in Kashmir', *The Hindustan Times,* 20 April and 14 May 1964.

42. Sardar Patel, as recorded by Maulana Azad, the Congress president, felt that 'acceptance of Pakistan would teach the Muslim League a bitter lesson. Pakistan would eventually collapse in a short time.' A.K. Azad, *India Wins Freedom,* Calcutta, 1960, p. 242. Pandit Nehru and Krishna Menon justified the acceptance of partition mainly to get rid of the British. See, Jawaharlal Nehru, *Jawaharlal's Discovery of America,* Delhi, 1950, p. 144; and, *The Statesman,* (Calcutta), 14 October 1947.

43. 'Few states emerged from colonial rule with as many disadvantages as Pakistan. There were over seven million refugees to absorb. There were two wings divided by over 1000 miles of hostile territory to defend. There was no integrated economy; partition thoroughly disrupted the transport systems, communications and trade of colonial India—separating raw materials from manufacturers, suppliers from customers, and hinterlands from ports.' Francis Robinson's review of Ayesha Jalal's *State of Martial Rule. The Origins of Pakistan's Political Economy of Defence,* in *Modern Asian Studies,* 26, 3, (1991), p. 626.

44. 'India lurches towards Hindu state', *The Observer*, 13 December 1992.
45. In his interview, Bal Thackeray, the leader of the militant party, Shiv Sena, who virtually controls Bombay, observed: 'I want to teach Muslims a lesson. Our fortitude has gone too far.' *Time International*, 25 January 1993.
46. When hooligans demolished some Hindu temples in Pakistan as a protest against the demolition of the Babri mosque, the RIP took up the issue with the Pakistani High Commission in New Delhi and 'warned Pakistan of a backlash'. *The Daily Telegraph*, 15 December 1992.
47. Shiv Sena, originating as a nativist movement espousing strong resentment against Tamils and others, has taken upon itself the mantle of an anti-Muslim organization. Even Bombay's 'Bollywood' see,ks security from Shiv Sena. See, 'Indian actors join real world', *The Independent*, 2 February 1993. Ten years later, Sajjan Kumar, the accused facing charges of anti-Sikhs riots in Delhi in 1984, was acquitted on the basis of lack of evidence. Not a single person was convicted for committing heinous crimes against Sikhs following the murder of Mrs Indira Gandhi. As a commentator write: 'In fact the judiciary's record of punishing those who have allegedly played a provocative role during the communal riots has been dreadful. Every time a riot takes place, inquiry commissions are set up, they publish voluminous reports that should become the basis of trial and exemplary punishment, but no-one is ever convicted. The Srikrishna Commission published a detailed report of the Mumbai riots of 1992–93, but the state government has so far taken no action on it'. 'Crimes of Evidence' (editorial), *The Indian Express*, 25 December 2002. For a more recent detailed analysis on the anti-Sikh riots in Delhi after Mrs Indira Gandhi's assassination, see, Katherine Frank, *Indira*, London, 2001, pp. 497–500.
48. For statistical information on such attitudinal changes across India, see, *India Today*, 15 January 1993. This issue assumed a serious dimension in early 2003. The deputy prime minister, L.K. Advani accused Bangladesh of sending millions of economic refugees into India, while Dhaka responded by defining them as Indian Bengalis and not Bangladeshi citizens. However, hundreds of gypsies and traditional entertainers were stuck across the Indo-Bangladeshi borders with both countries refusing to accept them as their citizens. Soon, both the countries engaged in parleys but in an atmosphere of mutual accusations. See, BBC World Service (South Asia) bulletins in February 2003 on www.bbc.co.uk/southasia.
49. For further details, see, Ben Whitaker, et al., *The Biharis in Bangladesh*, MRG Report No. 111, London, 1982.
50. Feroz Ahmed, 'Pakistan's Problem of National Integration', in Asghar Khan, (ed.) *Islam, Politics and the State. The Pakistan Experience*, London, 1985, pp. 229–230.
51. 'Biharis reach Pakistan after years in Bangladeshi camps', *The Guardian*, 11 January 1993.
52. It is only in recent years that ethnicity has been recognised as a crucial factor in global politics, and multiple societies in 'imbalanced' regions like South Asia have been subjected to further intensive research. Myron Weiner, 'Peoples and states in new order?' *Third World Quarterly*, 13, 2, (1992), p. 317.
53. L.K. Advani, Murli Manohar Joshi and other leaders of the BJP and its forerunners have articulated such views unequivocally in their writings and party manifestos. The *Rath Yatra* or long march, led by Advani in 1991 was originally meant to unite

Hindus on this point. Despite being responsible for more than 1500 deaths, the march was followed by another one—*Ekta Yatra*—under the leadership of Joshi which ended in Kashmir, basically to reaffirm the credentials of united Hindu rule. In his interview with the Western press, Bal Thackeray, the leader of Shiv Sena, denied the existence of a hidden agenda since their programme was already clear. He observed: 'We don't need stepping stones. This is a Hindu *rasthra* [nation].' *Time International*, 25 January 1993.

54. Stephen S. Rosenfeld, 'Do We Bow to a Bomb in India?', *International Herald Tribune*, 18 January 1993.

55. Stories like the secret transfer of sophisticated technology and delivery systems from China are frequently 'leaked' in the press to malign Pakistan. For instance, see, 'China Said to Deliver Missiles to Pakistan', *International Herald Tribune*, 6 December 1992. Even after the nuclear tests in May 1998, reports of secret technology transfers from various external sources to both India and Pakistan have frequently appeared in media. In early 2002, a CIA report identified the sources of such procurements, as well as the intensive development of missile technology programmes by the two rivals. Reported in *Dawn* (Karachi), 2 February 2002.

56. See, Amnesty International, *India, Torture, Rape and Deaths in Custody*, London, 1992, pp. 18–20; Human Rights Watch, *Human Rights in India: Kashmir Under Siege*, (An *Asia Watch Report)*, New York, May 1991; and 'End Kashmir's Misery', (ed.), *The New York Times*, 22 March 1992. The subsequent yearly Amnesty and Human Rights Watch reports have offered further details on extensive violations.

57. For an excellent study, see, Alastair Lamb, *Kashmir: A Disputed Legacy, 1846–1990*, Hertingfordbury, 1991.

58. 'Kashmir. A Lifetime ago', *The Economist*, 31 October 1992.

59. For various positions on Kashmir, see, Raju G.C. Thomas, (ed.) *Perspectives on Kashmir*, Boulder, 1992; also, Victoria Schofield, *Kashmir in the Crossfire*, London, 1996.

60. Frequent reports of Indian violations of human rights including indiscriminate killings of civilians, rapes and arson have been reported in the world media. See,, Christopher Thomas, 'Indian army uses torture in Kashmir', *The Times*, 12 November 1991; 'Kashmir and the Bomb', (editorial), *The Washington Post*, 5 May 1992; and 'The Pain of Kashmir', *Newsweek*, 7 December 1992; also, Shyam Bhatia, 'India's Shame', *The Observer Magazine*, 17 January 1993. Following the American action in Afghanistan in 2001–02 and the heightened Indo-Pakistan bickering over Kashmir, the global coverage both in print and visual media became quite extensive.

61. 'India Admits Police Ran Amok in Kashmir', *International Herald Tribune*, 8 January 1993; 'Outcry in Delhi over Kashmir massacre', *The Independent*, 8 January 1993; and 'Major's Visit to India: Separatist Reminder', *International Herald Tribune*, 27 January 1993.

62. Pakistan has been denying its role in abetting the terrorists and has taken a number of steps to prove that the nuclear issue is deemed intrinsically linked with national sovereignty and regional security.

63. One is led to believe that political stability guaranteed by the BJP might result in a major policy shift towards it in the Western capitals. Historically, South Asia has remained a peripheral region in the global geo-politics. For a useful background, see, Robert J. MacMahon, *Cold War on the Periphery: The United States, India,*

and Pakistan, New York, 1994. However, many recent studies, while basing on India's economic growth, regional pre-eminence, 'revitalizing' cultural movements, and military might have predicted her status as an Asian/global power. See, Stephen P. Cohen, *India: Emerging Power,* Washington D.C., 2001.

64. 'Nuclear South Asia', (ed.) *The New York Times,* 1 February 1993.

65. 'Nuclear arms will do little to ease India's more pressing domestic needs, nor will its display of nuclear pride do much for its prosperity and unity', Ibid.

66. Ibid. For a detailed study on India's nuclearisation and its regional and global impact, see, George Perkovich, *India's Nuclear Bomb: The Impact on Global Proliferation,* Berkeley, 1999.

67. Like the assassination of Mahatma Gandhi, the demolition of the Mosque, anti-Muslim rioters and even the killers of the Christian priests are all lionised as heroes. There is a *Dara Sena* (Dara's army) to idealise Dara Singh, who had murdered Bishop Graham Staines and his two children. *The Hindu,* 22 January 2002.

68. Based on extensive interviews in India, Western Europe and North America. However, the anti-Muslims tirade in Gujarat and the BJP's electoral victory have dampened down such optimistic views. See,, 'Letter from Gail Omvedt', 25 December 2002, in www.aiindex.mnet.fr; Kancha Ilaiah, 'The Rise of Modi', *The Hindu,* 26 December 2002; N. Muthu Mohan, 'Hindutva Fascism', a paper presented at Progressive Writers' Union at Calicut on 22 December 2002, on www.sacw.com; and, Satadru Sen, 'Danger of Hindutva', 1 Janaury 2003 on h-Asia.h-net.msu.edu.

69. Ian McDonald, 'A nation on the brink?', *THES,* 22 March 2002. This British academic had the rare opportunity to observe the military training workshop, convened by the RSS, in Nagpur in 1998. Kuldip Nayar, a leading Indian journalist and politician, felt horrified at the extent of anti-Muslim campaign in Gujarat in March-April 2002. He criticised the BJP administration for its dangerous liaison with the Kar Sevaks in their anti-Muslim campaign. His eye-witness accounts of the destruction and killings offer a chilling record of events. See, *The Indian Express,* 3 April 2002. Khushwant Singh, another leading columnist, in his column, lashed at the 'medieval mentality and practices', being promoted at the expense of pluralism and secularism. *The Hindustan Times,* 30 March 2002. The pogroms in Gujarat accompanied the well-orchestrated campaign of annihilating the Muslim heritage from the state. For instance, the tomb of Wali Daccani, the pioneer poet of Urdu, was desecrated in March 2002, by Kar Sevaks to be followed by a complete demolition under official orders. Within a few days, a road was built upon the site. In addition, rare historic monuments including mosques, hand-written copies of the Quran and walls exhibiting calligraphy were decimated with an official connivance. For further details, see, Luke Harding, 'Gujarat's Muslim heritage smashed in riots', *The Guardian,* 29 June 2002. The articles by Arundhati Roy, Praful Bidwai, Mushirul Hasan, Romila Thapar and several other prominent Indians published in the papers and circulated widely on internet, lamented the loss of plural values and the opportunistic and dangerous tactics being played by the BJP and its associates. For a comprehensive collection of such contributions, both by the Indians and Pakistanis, see, www.sacw.com. When, on 27 June 2003, the twenty-two Kar Sevaks accused of an arson attack on Best Bakery in western Gujarat killing, twelve Muslims were released on the lack of evidence, the analysts were shocked and expressed their apprehensions about the future of pluralism and secularism in India.

This was one of the most publicised five massacres in the state during 2002, and the Indian Human Rights Commission had sought its inquiry by the Central Bureau for Investigation (CBI), since the state police was considered to be corrupt and partisan. *The Independent*, 28 June and 1 July 2003. Basing his study on available data, one Indian observer found 90 per cent culprits involved in communal killing being acquitted. See, Asghar Ali Engineer, 'Justice Aborted in Gujarat', *Secular Perspective*, 16–31 July 2003.

70. 'India must stay clam', *The Daily Telegraph*, 13 January 2002; also, 'India's hard men' (leader), *The Financial Times*, 24 February 2003. The Indian Diaspora is the strongest in the United States and the United Kingdom in terms of human and monetary resourcefulenss. Several of its Hindu elements have been supportive of VHP, and have funnelled funds to establish temples and training camps in India. Their support for Narendra Modi's policies became quite obvious when the controversial chief minister was invited to London on a visit in August 2003. He was feted by his prosperous Gujarati and other pro-Hindutva elements, while Gujarati Muslims and other South Asian solidarity groups would demonstrate outside such venues demanding his trial. For details, see, *The Guardian*, 18 August 2003. All through 2003, there were reports of growing mutualities between Hindu Diaspora and Zionist groups, which were further invigorated by multiplying Indo-Israeli military and economic exchanges. In the United States, the anti-Muslim animus of such meetings was not lost on some Indian observers. For instance, see, Zahir Janmohamed, 'Golwalkar, Savarkar...And Jews', www.outlookindia.com.

71. 'In cricket, Hindu self-assertion has taken the form of subjecting Indian Muslims to a Tebbit-style cricket test, and refusing to play against Pakistan. It has been routine for some years for any lull in okay at an international match in India to be punctuated by mass chants of "Pakistan—Hai! Hai!" (down with Pakistan).' Mike Marqusee,, 'India is put to the test', *The Guardian*, 21 December 2001.

72. Isabel Hilton, 'Repressive measures: India and China have seized on the rhetoric of anti-terrorism to steamroller opposition', ibid., 15 December 2001; also, Bronwen Maddox, 'India should budget for action on Kashmir', *The Times*, 27 February 2002.

In India, if bare leave be deigned
His prayer-prostration,
Our dull priest thinks Islam has gained
Emancipation.
— 'Hindi Islam' [Islam in India], by Muhammad Iqbal, in *Poems from Iqbal,* trans. by Victor Kiernan, 1999, p. 172

And while he [Musharraf] still believes that the Pakistan army is the solution to the country's problems, he shows no sign of accepting that, in fact, it is part of the problem.
— Owen B. Jones, *Pakistan: Eye of the Storm,* 2002, p. 290

3

Civil Society and South Asian Muslims: Issues of Governance in Pakistan

The problems of governance, uneven development, fundamentalism, ethno-sectarian and inter-state conflicts, and sheer authoritarianism in the post-colonial, and specifically post-Cold War, world have led historians and human rights groups to focus on the issue of civil society. It is widely agreed among the various intellectual groups that several of these problems can be resolved through a full-fledged empowerment of civic forces, and by redefining the symbiotic relationship between them and the organs of state. A growing consensus across the board suggests that state-led unilateralism, without it being moderated and humanized through civic forces, has been spawning intra, as well as inter-state schisms. The weaker civil societies and unrestrained official hierarchies—more often vulnerable to pernicious influences from outside—underpin the identity crises faced by these countries. The misplaced official emphasis on security, simply as an external paradigm and obsession to stockpile weapons amidst euphoric rhetoric on 'othering', equally feed into social unrest. Before one can address the urgency for a newer and positive equilibrium between these crucial trajectories, one needs to respond to various ongoing academic, and even not so academic queries. They may include questions such as: Is civil society a Western construct alien to non-Western polities such as in South Asia? Is it possible to expect an essentially *Muslim* [or *Hindu, Buddhist,*] civil society, without raising serious questions about long-held social traditions? And, how far is the concept of Hindutva and Hindu Rashtra inimical to the prerogatives of a vibrant civil society, the way a narrowly defined Sunni Pakistan, Buddhist/Sinhalese Sri Lanka, Hindu Tamil

Elam, Muslim Bengali Bangladesh, Khas Hinduist Nepal, Buddhist Bhutan—could threaten their respective civil societies and minorities? As one can see, all the existing models in the developing world varying from secular state(s) to theocratic polities, or from one-party governments to military regimes, the issues of national identity in reference to ideological dispensations remain problematic, and the serious imbalances invariably bedevil all the polities.[1]

This chapter, following a brief historical introduction, problematizes civil society in reference to various religio-national traditions in South Asia, though the focus remains mainly on Muslims. It also explores the changing relationship between Islam and the state in South Asia over the years within the context of the politics of pressure groups. Taking Pakistan as a case study, it dwells on a cross section of public opinion over vital issues, where the state has been lacking both resolve and initiative. Despite their diverse ideological trajectories, all the states in South Asia are confronted with similar problems of internal dissensions, augmented by external tensions. To a great extent, South Asian states can resolve their identity crisis, minimize the economic disparities, and counter a fundamentalist threat—Hindutva or Talibanization—by taking aboard this societal consensus. But these initiatives have to accompany the deconstruction of inter-state discords and hegemonies, which have been nefariously feeding into a dire communalization of the region.

CONCEPTUALIZING CIVIL SOCIETY

'Civil society' involves various mediating institutions seeking a redefinition of state-society interdependence, as well as intra-societal equilibrium. It comprises of those institutions which are rooted among the populace, and operate as a bulwark against any infringement. Human rights groups, untainted NGOs, women's and minority constellations, independent think tanks, objective groups with reformative agenda such as ecology, constitutionalism, regional peace and sociopolitical egalitarianism, judiciary, academia, and certainly, the media, all collectively form an ideal and vocal civil society. In addition, the political parties and independent groups such as those of lawyers, intellectuals, artists and other clusters resisting authoritarianism or unilateralism are important pillars of an alert civil society. Thus, an ideal country would have a vibrant, independent and flourishing civil society, effectively restraining official unilateralism and equally offering healthier alternatives. Civil society is the lifeline of democracy and democracy in return is nourished by free debate, human rights, peace, tolerant policies and accountable administration. In any authoritarian set-up, civil society will remain bruised and suspect, and in the process, the populace at large is likely to become hostage to the whims of a sectional or ideological particularism. The communities with weaker or non-existent civil societies frequenty fall victim to authoritarianism. Thus, an empowered civil society and a responsive state will follow mutually supportive, rather than conflictive policies. Authoritarianism does not necessarily come from statist institutions; it may even stem from dominant or majoritarian ethno-sectarian groups as the slave-owners in America, the Nazis in Germany, and the Zionists *vis-à-vis* the Palestinians.[2] Apart from demographic factors, other determinants such as economy, religion, regional politics and ethno-nationalism also have a deep impact upon the composition and direction of civic forces. While continued economic stratification or dependence over foreign sources can damage the social fabric, the superimposition of religious or any ethnic uniformity can take place only by disavowing diversity and plurality. In the same vein, regional peace and cooperation offers multiple benefits, and through a substantial 'de-othering' of the neighbours, domestic inter-communal coexistence and harmony can also be achieved. While ethnic nationalism may assume immensely destabilizing and intolerant postulations for any society, it can equally help attain decentralization.[3]

The concept of civil society is neither new nor region-specific, though most of the current literature will trace its origins back to post-French Revolution Western Europe. An alternative explanation may be resentful of this eurocentricity and would see non-European societies trying to 'reinvent' themselves at different stages in their past. The sufis, *bhagats* or such other tolerant elements, even in the otherwise patriarchal societies empowering and protecting the underprivileged sectors were the arms of *traditional* civil societies. But, since all these societies were localistic, even during the imperial era, the civil societies functioned in a localist milieu, seeking resuscitation from a defined morality. Religion was a major component of such nascent civil societies, whereas with the evolution of modern democracies within the context of territorial statehood, sustained efforts highlight the societal and often secular prerogatives. The relocation of power in the West from state—absolutist monarchies or otherwise—to the echelons of society took centuries to happen and such processes may not be totally applicable to other human communities given their own sets of specific circumstances, yet cannot be denigrated as the negative portents of modernity.

The study of the Indus Valley Civilization reveals a greater human bonding and generally peaceful coexistence of the various communities, until the invasions from outside changed the cultural and demographic contours of the subcontinent. The subsequent emphasis on the caste system and degradation of the 'untouchables' spawned Buddhism, Sufi Islam, and the Bhagati movement, celebrating universal equality. The Gandhian movement and the Dalit consciousness largely eroded the invincibility of the caste-based divisions, yet even non-Hindu societies have continued to show similar, if not that intense, caste-based divisions.

Within this context, Islam, in its pristine and classical sense, may be seen as a major trajectory of civil society through its prioritizing of human rights—*Huqooqul Iba'ad*—over everything else including *Huqooqul Allah*—the duties owed to God. Prophet Muhammad's own life as a poor orphan, associating closely with the downtrodden in the society, his employment *under* a woman, followed by his marriage to her through *her* initiative—though she was senior to him by fifteen years—and his teachings celebrating humanity, specially the weaker elements, offered a revolutionary charter on human rights. The Prophet Muhammad (PBUH) greatly personified one of the earliest and holistic civil societies based on justice, help and kindness, all reflected in his own life, as well as through the state of Medina that he created. Muhammad's role as a prophet and statesman created a unique parallel in human history where a religion had created its own state rather than waiting for some existing polity to adopt it. Consequently, this led to an intricate inter-dependence between religion and politics. Islam was accepted across the world, largely because it empowered the underprivileged and oppressed by offering them equality and optimism.[4] The Muslim Sufis, and even many *ulema*, led this tradition of defiance against ruling hierarchies, opposing the prevalent tradition and trepidation of conformity where several of their colleagues may have been coopted by the regimes.[5]

Islam accorded new respect to the rights of women, slaves and other oppressed minorities, yet its appropriation in the subsequent centuries by feudalist and clerical oligarchies, and a deeper sense of

loss due to colonialism have turned it into a conservative and statist
ideology. The traditions of *ijtiha'ad* (interpretation and innovation)
gave way to *taqli'd* (imitation), and in the process, weaker Muslim
groups have suffered marginalization. Islam's encounters with
modernity unleashed several complex responses, including severe
introversion, as well as efforts to reinterpret the Islamic heritage. In
the meantime, the issues of poverty, health and illiteracy aggravated
the situation, making it an uphill task for any reformer. The colonial/
nationalist era was characterized by an ideological polarity between
the reformers and conformists, which in the post-colonial period,
reemerged with greater intensity due to growing disillusionment with
the ruling elite. No wonder, every Muslim polity is characterized by
this ideological polarization. The continued politico-economic
disempowerment of massive sections of Muslim societies and the
serious sense of grief, loss and helplessness over an inability to resolve
conflicts such as Palestine, Bosnia, Iraq, Afghanistan, Chechnya, and
others, have all engendered various manifestations of Political Islam.
Rhetoric, bullet and ballots are all used variably to create an untried
Islamic utopia which, to many non-Muslim elite, may be nothing more
than Islamic terrorism. While it will be incorrect to deny the existence
of fundamentalist groups among Muslims, and their own repression of
civic and plural groups including minorities and women, it is equally
dangerous to perceive it as a uniquely *Muslim* problem. The
cohabitation between a fundamentalist form of religion and an
exclusionary nationalism is not merely confined to Muslim states,
instead it is a global phenomenon with variable intensity. However,
Political Islam in its current manifestations such as in Taliban-run
Afghanistan, or Iran, Algeria and Saudi Arabia, or through specific
outfits such as Al Qaeda is neither incidental nor universal, it has
numerous embodiments in all Muslim societies. Theoretically speaking,
Political Islam is a forceful mechanism and a powerful ideology of
defiance and displacement, seriously lacking a viable, durable and
consensual replacement mechanism. Thus, even accomplishing a rather
heroic job of decolonization and dehegemonization, it has, so far,
failed to usher ideal societies and polities away from repression and
poverty. On the contrary, in most cases including South Asia, the
Middle East and North Africa, it is more often seen as self-immolative,
bent upon destroying civil society by trampling upon human rights. In
other words, while promising and fighting one set of alien hegemony,
Political Islam—just like Hindutva and ultra Zionism—itself tends to

turn into a new hegemony. While religion will remain closely associated with the politics of identity—irrespective of individual choices—it is all the more imperative to understand it as a historical force, which needs a better understanding, and of course, a constant reinterpretation. For instance, in the case of Islam, the discourse may focus on the *humanity* of the Prophet (PBUH), the constant reinterpretive reconstruction of *Sharia*, empowerment of the masses through full-fledged democratization and an increased emphasis on Islam's peaceful, tolerant and this-worldly portents. After all, the prophetic wars were altogether confined to just a few days/weeks in his twenty-three year long career of proselytizing. Similarly, the doctrinal interpretations of Islamic jurisprudence—such as Hanafi, Malaki, Jaafri, Hanbli and Shaafai Fiqh of the Abbassid era—evolved many centuries after the Prophet and deserve persistent revisiting if Islam is to meet contemporary and increasingly complex challenges. Such efforts, to some extent, took place in the early modern period, especially in India and Egypt, when a modern vision of Islam was attempted in the last two centuries by reformers such as Al-Afghani, Syed Ahmed Khan, Muhammad Abduh, Muhamamd Iqbal, Muhammad Taha, Fazlur Rahman and Allama Shariati. Like any other homogenizing ideology, Islam requires periodic reconstruction in mundane areas dealing with human issues, though one may take its *Huqooq Allah*—duties unto God—sacrosanct. However, it has been seen time and again, that while promising a divine polity for the ultimate betterment of humanity, the proponents and activists of Political Islam end up denying and damaging human rights. This is where not only is a new equilibrium urgently needed, but also a fresher perspective of interpreting Islam as a *human* heritage—more than a mere divine obligation or a dogma.

ISLAM AND CIVIL SOCIETY IN SOUTH ASIA

While discussing the quest for identity among diverse regions and sections of South Asian Muslims in more recent centuries, the contemporary historiographical debate has mostly tended to centre on 'High Islam,'[6] allocating it a kind of monolithic and overarching essentialism. The missionary, colonial, Orientalist, nationalist and even proto or post-nationalist schools either remain confined to these parametres, or simply dwell on the inevitability of respective nation-states (Pakistan, India and Bangladesh). Partition, as discussed in the last chapter, has left a rather indelible imprint on this discourse as the reductionist typologies of secularism/modernism and traditionalism/ communalism simplistically retain their ascendancy in a dialectical manner. The role of religion and politics, and of diverse communitarian manifestations in reference to class, gender or identity formation, has not yet been fully investigated. Islam in South Asia has been perceived through narrowly focused prisms, in most cases, succumbing to nationalist prerogatives. The India-Pakistan hostilities have also not helped a comparative discourse. Anyone talking of Islam in post-1947 India has been usually derided as a communalist or a Pakistani agent, something which many secular Muslim writers in India rather voluntarily imposed upon themselves. Thus, the studies on Islam in South Asia began to zero in mainly on Pakistan, which the Pakistani historians readily accepted. This squeeze of Islam into one territorial confinement did not let critical scholarship flourish, whereas in India, a Muslim scholar writing on Islam would either be apologetic, or simply end up supporting Indian secularism. The disowning of Islam by several Indian Muslims at the expense of their own identity, so as not to appear *communal* is quite obvious.

Both Islam and Pakistan have sadly become problematic for the Indian secularists, though in reality it does not have to be so. On the one hand, the Indian state and majoritarian nationalism pressurise for such disavowal, while concurrently, the class-based interests of some Muslim elite underwrite these negative attitudes. Moreover, coupling Islam with a mere medieval theocracy—despite the sheer negative reductionism of such a premise—ends up neutralising Muslim credentials of such elements.[7] The rise of the BJP and other outfits espousing Hindutva[8] should have inadvertently made it easier for many scholars erstwhile suffering from self-denial to revisit Islam. The essentialisation of secularism with India and of Islam with a communal interpretation of Pakistan now appear simplistic, and one can hope for a fresher perspective, though the damage to Indo-Muslim culture has already been done to a great extent. An Indo-Pakistan normalisation may also help relinking Islam in a greater historical and cross-regional periscope. The imperial, nationalist, secular and leftist schools of historiography have found 'Islam' problematic, and have more often avoided researching it. Even an historian like Ayesha Jalal while earlier writing on Muslim politics, chose to concentrate on three or four main personalities, totally ignoring cultural, ideological or class-based realities within Muslim India.[9] The tradition of intellectual history, as pioneered by Aziz Ahmad, still remains rather weak despite the valuable additions by Rafiuddin Ahmed,[10] Farzana Shaikh and Taj Hashmi, though Mushirul Hasan's otherwise passionate study also ends up falling within the usual trap of India-Pakistan nationalist subjectivity.[11] Without suggesting any fallibility or the alternative of the movement for a Muslim homeland, we need to locate the debate on Muslim identity in the nascent civil society during the colonial era. Pakistan may not have been the ideal solution for the Indian Muslim predicament, but to see its evolution as a mere incident of history is also an understatement. All post-colonial countries including India can be simplistically characterised as mere artifacts, but merely seeing in Pakistan the root cause of the Indian Muslim tragedy after more than fifty years of separate statehood, does not offer a sound argument, and at its most, is escapism and not just an euphemism. The debate on Islam in South Asia has to move away from the simplistic pillar posts of separatism and syncretism, as they both subscribe to a bland subjectivity.[12]

During the late-Mughal times, civil society took on a regional and proto national character. Sultan Hyder Ali, Tipu Sultan,[13] the Jihad movement, the Faraidhis, the peasant and tribal constellations or individuals such as Ahmed Khan Kharal pursued resistance vis-à-vis the British East India Company's expansionism and racist overtones.[14] The protagonists and the antagonists vacillated in their respective strategies, though South Asian Islam, both in the Sufi and scriptural traditions, remained uncomfortable with this major dislocation, as the loss of political power coupled with Western missionary enterprise, bleakly exposed Muslim vulnerabilities in India. The construction of Occidentalism—as a counterpoise to Orientalism—owed itself to the Muslim elite such as Mir Abu Talib Khan, Muhammad Husain, Itisam al-Din and others who had a closer experience of working with Sir William Jones and other administrator-scholars.[15]

It is following the Revolt of 1857, a great debilitating development for Muslims in particular, that the *ashra'af*—combining Islamic and Western learning—initiated regenerative efforts which despite their various strands, converged on the need for Muslim revitalisation. Here regionalism, as well as emerging trans-regionalism became the two major characteristics of such efforts. The efforts by Syed Ahmed Khan (1817–1898) for the socio-educational uplift of the Indian Muslims by emphasising the relevance of modernism, and those of the Deobandis,

Brelvis, Nadwis, and of the Tablighis are well known and can be
defined as trans-regional, whereas efforts by the regional *tanzims* and
anjumans still remain quite underresearched. These *tanzims* operated
within the praxis of an Islamic discourse cooptive of Western
educational and scientific precepts. They could also be considered as
the early modern forms of an embryonic Muslim civil society in South
Asia. This educational and cultural dimension eventually led to a
political discourse, seeking to define the place of Muslim community
in a plural and changing India. The schemes such as those of a separate
state, of a composite nationalism, or regional pluralism were being put
forth amongst the trans-regional groups long before the Partition.[16]

GOVERNANCE AND CIVIL SOCIETY IN PAKISTAN

The post-independence fragmentation of an India-wide Muslim
community simultaneous with the consolidation of a major section
within a nation-state [Pakistan] were certainly radical developments of
intense ramifications. In 1947, the emerging trans-regionality among
South Asian Muslims stood tarnished, and a sizable Muslim minority
had been left rather rudderless in India as the bourgeoisie and elite
had gone across the borders. Within Pakistan, after Jinnah's death in
1948, the concept of security and nation-building became co-terminus
with the extraneous factors increasing the militarist forces at the
expense of an emergent civil society. The relative openness and
tolerance in Pakistan, as seen in the 1950s, despite weaker democratic
traditions, eroded before the statist unilateralism and societal emphasis
on a rather exclusivist Islam.[17] Pakistan's partition in 1971 owed to
mismanagment, partisan policies and brutalisation of civil society under
a military dictatorship, further made possible by the Indian
intervention. The post–1972 Pakistani state, initially trying to stay on
a balanced and more worldly course, soon began to seek refuge in a
religious symbolism which subsequently turned into sheer
obscurantism, especially under General Zia. Over the past twenty-five
years or so, official authoritarianism seems to be increasingly
cohabiting with societal nihilism, at the expense of civil society.
Consequently, the human rights groups, journalists, women activists,
some NGOs, and such other elements have been put in a precarious
situation. The regional geo-politics and global misperceptions of Islam
only add to the furies of *mullahs* and their sympathisers in the military.

Even under the weak democratic regimes of the 1990s—the second major phase in the evolution of civil society—the state remained wary of the latter. The intelligence agencies increased their preponderance of the national structures at the expense of civil liberties. The press, women, human rights activists and even political opponents were often harassed and penalised, whereas the agencies ran their own parallel policies and agendas to the extent of forming and deforming governments and political alliances. The elected regimes either succumbed to totalitarian tendencies of deinstitutionalisation or simply allowed the ongoing criminalisation of the state structures.[18]

It is important to explore three related areas with their direct bearing on civil society in contemporary Pakistan, and they are: political economy, the military, and Islam. Following General Musharraf's coup in October 1999, one sees the unbridled salience of intelligence agencies to impose a self-serving political system by simply bypassing the organs and imperatives of civil society. On 20 June 2001, Musharraf, just a few weeks before his visit to India, directly assumed the presidency by virtually dismissing Rafiq Tarar, the erstwhile elected president. He now combined all the highest military and civil offices in his person. During all this time, the press has been quite bold but the judiciary seems to have lost its vigour and direction.[19] The religious elements—known as the 'Jihadi groups'—who, in many cases, were created or reinvigorated by the agencies as junior partners during the 1980s, were now seeking a full Talibanization of Pakistan.[20] With a weaker civil society and a self-serving military leadership intent upon perpetuating its own rule even if it was in total conflict with democratic norms and national prerogatives, the *mullahs* saw a life-time opportunity to impose their hegemony.[21] Politically and economically disempowered Pakistan, brimming with anti-Americanism, became a fertile ground for fundamentalism, and a bleak graveyard for its civil society.[22] Musharraf's turn-about on Jihadis and withdrawal of support for the Taliban in 2001, came about only after the US pressure to that effect. It was his predecessor, General Ziaul Haq (d. 1988), who had, in fact, brought these elements into mainstream national life and coopted them for prolonging his own rule. Now, another general promised reverting to the liberal, Jinnahist model of Pakistan, but only after Western pressures mounted up, otherwise civil society in the country had been demanding the same for so long to no avail. The pressure on Pakistan multiplied, following the bomb blasts in India and Indian-held Kashmir in 2002, with Indian troops dangerously poised for a swift military operation. The Pakistani generals responded with missile-testing, but the global worries for a nuclear flare-up led to a flurry of diplomatic efforts. In Pakistan, all the vital decisions were being made by a small coterie of generals, showing an extremely thin base causing demand for Musharraf, either to resign, or at least establish an interim government involving politicians. Eventually, he opted for a well-tested dualism. Through some basic unilateral amendments under the Legal Framework Order (LFO) in the Constitution, he amassed powers in his office of presidency, which he had secured by a contentious referendum held in April 2002. The establishment of a coalition regime of elected politicians led by Mir Zafrullah Jamali in 2002, following horse trading, rekindled memories of the 1980s, when the military had assumed a *de facto* role within the polity. It equally confirmed the premise that Pakistan's governability problems were far from over and the country still needed some bold, transparent and accountable policies and civic structures. The Musharraf-Jamali Duo was not only confronted by a parliamentary furore over the LFO, the legislation of *Sharia* in the NWFP assembly under the Deobandi aegis proved equally unnerving.

The problems of governance in Pakistan can be addressed through the prism of various factors, including history, politics and economy. Despite all the conducive forces for national harmony, progress and peaceful coexistence, the country often appears rudderless. One does not see any interface between the official institutions and societal prerogatives, rather they seem to be working in conflict with each other. The state has come to symbolise coercion, corruption and inefficiency. This is largely because the successive regimes have rigorously maintained a colonial structure based on the prioritisation of administration over governance, and by seeing security only in the regional/external context, instead of focusing on domestic politics and economy. The colonial politics of patronage through a high-handed executive have been maintained to its letters by the successive regimes and substantive restructuring, devolution and democratisation have not taken place at all. From the administrative decision of a huge country, to the very local level, the state has remained resistant to change and reforms.

Military rulers like Ayub Khan, Yahya Khan, Ziaul Haq and Pervez Musharraf, who have controlled the destiny of this nation for more than half of its existence, have been simply status-quoists like their civilian counterparts. However, some politicians in the early 1950s, and then Zulfikar Ali Bhutto in the 1970s, tried to induct a few minor changes including modest land reforms and some administrative preening. The feudal nature of Pakistan's economy still remains faithful to this proto-colonial state where khaki and civil bureaucrats operate as latter-day colonial *mai bap* (lit: mother and father, paternal). The worst form of internal colonisation was in the former Eastern wing (now Bangladesh), which eventually broke away, leaving West Pakistani elite to persist with the legacy. Musharraf's scheme of Devolution 2000, akin to that of Ayub Khan's 'basic democracies', offered a smaller and 'manageable' electoral college rather than a mass-based democratisation which was anathemic to the generals. His amendments to the constitution on the eve of national elections in 2002, converted Pakistan's political system into a presidential unilateralism. General Musharraf's main preoccupation has been to prolong his own rule, even at the expense of national prerogatives and participatory institutions. Like other generals in the past, he not only kept the country's constitution in abeyance, but also inducted unilateral amendments into it without involving the elected representatives. Such a cyclic mutation of nation-building institutions through a 'bogus referendum' only signalled the advent of the 'most factious period of instability' in the country.[23] Moreover, the nascent middle class has remained dependent upon state largesse with the intermediate class falling back upon primordial denominators like language and religion, and in the process, has become gullible to ethnic and sectarian chasms.[24] This class is conservative and more regional, rather than national, in its approach and character, and shirks from its civic responsibility including payment of taxes and loans. It equally shies away from a progressive outlook. In several cases, the middle class, based in urban areas, is more vulnerable to foreign temptations and thus a major proportion of NGOs lacks credibility. Concurrently, the intermediate outfits such as the Muhajir Qaumi Movement (MQM), Anjuman-i-Sipah-i-Sahaba (ASSP), and the Tehreek-i-Nifaz-i-Fiqh-i-Ja'afria (TNFJ) that emerged in the 1980s, have tried to push the polity towards specific agends, based on denying space to other ethno-sectarian communities. By the late 1990s, like a rising tide of communalism in BJP-led India, sectarianism in Pakistan and severe pulls towards a Taliban-style Islamic polity [in Bangladesh as well] became quite apparent. Private militant outfits such as Lashkar-i-Jhangvi (LJ), Lashkar-i-Tayyaba (LT), Sipah-i-Muhammad (SM) and

Jaysh-i-Muhammad (JM) grew in strength in Pakistan, espousing militant strategies on sectarian and regional issues. In league with the ISI, they became the instruments of Pakistani foreign policy on Afghanistan and Kashmir. The support from intelligence agencies, generally known as the 'hidden hand' in Pakistani parlance, took place at the expense of civic imperatives, as they equally witch-hunted vulnerable minorities and dissenter groups.

It would be sterile to suggest that Pakistan, or for that matter, South Asia has remained static; on the contrary, migrations and other demographic changes have generated several processes. Both integrative and conflictive postulations characterize this recent phase in inter-community relationship. The lack of respect for constitutionalism, frequent military coups, and a shrinking development sector, all feed into the privatization of Pakistani politics and economy through small networks working independent of the state, and in some cases, operating as mafias. The corruption and criminalization of a redundant state system have made the drug-and-gun culture rather more apparent since the 1980s, thanks to the Afghanistan crisis and self-serving regimes in Islamabad. Since no elected government has been allowed to complete its term, the political system has come to depend on the strong arm of the state. The intelligence agencies run various conflictive agendas and have been openly interfering in the making and unmaking of regimes. Pakistanis welcome every new ruler, hoping for a breakthrough, but they usually turn out to be a bigger disappointment than the last. The politics of personalities has always vetoed institutional imperatives, and the so-called strong men feel no qualms in denting civic institutions.

The judiciary's role has been quite mixed, though judges continue to defend their judgments with a crucial bearing on Pakistan's political culture.[25] The judgment by Pakistan's Supreme Court in May 2000, not only validated the military coup, but also curiously allowed General Musharraf to amend the constitution. The highest court of the land, instead of protecting and simply interpreting a constitution, has justified its suspension, and more significantly, has allowed a coup leader to amend it. The judgment has been based on the age-old law of necessity applied several times before in Pakistan, whereas the second prerogative, to many experts, opened a Pandora's box.[26] The generals have amended the constitution through the LFO to suit their whims and interests, and the court verdict may be used as a precedent in similar future political scenarios. There are serious implications in this verdict, and only time will tell how future political developments will be affected by it. At another level, the courts are overworked, with several judges vulnerable to corruption and underhand temptations.[27]

Pakistan's long-standing financial crisis seems to have gone from bad to worse in recent years. Not only the heavy defence expenditure, but also the massive external and internal loans and increasing deficit amidst stories of corruption, aggravate a pervasive dismay. Only half a million taxpayers in a population of 145 million, the massive loan defaulting, and the generals and judges being exempted from accountability while politicians bear the brunt, reveal a rather piecemeal and selective campaign. The generals, while dismissing the entire political set-up in October 1999, had promised accountability across the board, but by exiling a convicted Nawaz Sharif, they have merely displayed their own expediency.[28] Thus, the imbalances in economy and politics, aggravated by a largely corrupt system, make the forces of civil society easy prey to brutal attacks from all sides. However, any persuasive analysis of Pakistan's political economy has to go beyond state-centric paradigms incorporating changes and newly formed alliances within the society, and their interaction with official institutions.

The Pakistani armed forces have attracted a vast historiography, usually centring on their extra-professional role, the ambitions of the generals, and similarities or differences with their Indian counterpart.[29] The critics, including dismissed politicians, see in the Pakistan army, a state within a state, which would never allow the proper and autonomous functioning of a political regime. To them, the most it can tolerate is a pliant and dependent oligarchy of weaker politicians. According to this view, the army has been at the helm of affairs for so long, and now deems dictating domestic and foreign policies as its birthright. The civic groups feel that the army was initially dragged in by political leaders, who have found it hard to extricate it from its multiple and equally controversial role. The democrats want an immediate end to the military's domination of Pakistan, whereas some moderate voices counsel gradual strategies and cool headedness. Many observers feel that as long as India remains the enemy, the army will keep on ruling the roost. To some, the Indian hawks need generals ruling Pakistan, so as to malign the *other*. When General Musharraf and his colleagues brought about the coup in October 1999, some civic groups took it as a temporary respite, since Nawaz Sharif had foreclosed all possibilities of an in-house change. But such elements were again deeply disappointed, as the army failed to bring about any systemic changes, and the problems of governance, economy and regional security remain unmitigated.[30]

The generals are seen to be following their other khaki predecessors, by attempting to depoliticize and manipulate the country's vital institutions, so as to stay at the helm for a longer time.[31] In an intricate relationship between the politicians and generals, the former seem to have been marginalized. In fact, Benazir Bhutto, Nawaz Sharif and Altaf Hussain, the leaders of the main three parties—the Pakistan People's Party (PPP), Muslim League (ML) and the MQM—are already in exile, while their followers in most cases have been striking deals with the generals. While to its radical critics, the army is praetorian and neo-colonial as proven through several coups and by brutalization in the former eastern wing; to its detractors, it remains the *only and the last* institution to save Pakistan from a total collapse. The predictions about Pakistan as a failing state are more apparent now due to an uncertain political culture, weak economy, sectarian conflicts and a vindictive India seeking a bigger pound of flesh on Kashmir.[32] On the contrary, the generals project the armed forces as an asset, and refuse to accept responsibility for the muzzling of civil society, the brutalization of fellow Pakistanis in 1971, and the continued defamation of Pakistani politicians.[33] The publication of the Hamoodur Rahman Commission Report in August 2000 across South Asia, earlier suppressed by Islamabad, temporarily reinvigorated the debate on the military's entrenched role in national politics, but it was soon submerged due to an escalation in Indo-Pakistani tensions in 2002.[34] There have been constant demands from within Pakistan and Bangladesh to take the perpetrators to court, but the military government has been evading the debate and civil society seems to be totally helpless. The Report highlighted the brutalities, graft, and professional incompetence of several officials, and demanded a proper legal recourse besides suggesting the implementation of structural reforms within the armed forces. Neither the trial, nor the reforms have taken place.

It needs to be remembered that other than retired military officials drawing major benefits in the form of new jobs, plots and huge pensions, the military has quite a few supporters from amongst ethnic Punjabis. The Punjabis, especially from the central and north-western [Potowar] regions, are themselves heavily represented in the armed forces, followed by Pushtuns, making it a very ethno-regional specific force which causes serious resentment in the provinces of Sindh and Balochistan. Both the Punjabis and Pushtuns are from up country, and boast of strong *martial* traditions since the Raj. The lifestyles of the senior military officials reflecting a separate class of privileged and well looked after sections with vast land-holding in rural and urban areas allotted to them, engender all sorts of social tensions in a country where millions of university graduates remain unemployed with scores committing suicide.[35] The role of the army in the wars of 1965, 1971, 1980s (Siachen) and 1999 (Kargil) has become controversial, and demands for an inquiry are routinely hushed up. It is a fact that every time the generals have ruled the country, the ideological tensions and weakening of political culture have accompanied Pakistan's loss of yet more territory to India. During the 1980s, while military officials were flogging their critics and small-time criminals, India captured a vast portion of the Siachen Glacier in the disputed region of Kashmir. In 1999, the misadventure of the Kargil Heights in Kashmir cost Pakistan major humiliation, and the generals still refused to hold inquiries. Instead, they put the blame either on the ousted regime of Nawaz Sharif, or simply evaded the issue, and nobody was held accountable for several hundred deaths of Pakistani troops and Kashmiri youths.[36] The more recent Indian build-up across Kashmir's LOC and the main Indo-Pakistani borders also bleakly exposed the myth of nuclearization as an ultimate deterrent. It is a known fact that Musharraf's turn-about on Kashmir and American pressure dissuaded the Indians from mounting a military campaign in 2002, allowing Pakistani generals more time and space to continue controlling the country's destiny.

Military intelligence agencies such as the ISI have been behind various acts of defamation and harassment of politicians, and even of financing political alliances. For instance, General Aslam Baig, the former Chief of Army Staff, distributed 140 million rupees through the ISI, to the MQM and other such outfits to defeat the PPP but the irony remains that despite all the evidence, including a video of General Baig's press conference, the Supreme Court did not issue an assertive verdict, simply contenting itself with a toothless ruling. This eventually encouraged many of Nawaz Sharif's followers and cabinet members in late 1997 to physically storm the court premises in the full glare of cameras. In 1999, during the Kargil conflict, the generals had reportedly planned to prepare missiles for a possible launch without the knowledge of the Prime Minister, Nawaz Sharif. It was only during his visit to Washington that Nawaz Sharif came to know of the plan through President Clinton. Earlier, Benazir Bhutto, as prime minister, did not have any exact information on the Pakistani nuclear programme, showing the distrust and low opinion that the generals hold for politicians. The ISI—and likewise other military-led intelligence agencies—covertly operate Pakistan's foreign policy on Kashmir and Afghanistan, and would go to any extent to retain their unilateral hold on national policies, including the rise and fall of civilian regimes.[37] It is clear that the main opposition to Pakistani civil society other than from the fundamentalists is from the defence establishment itself. Pakistanis, for generations, have tried to disengage the military from its extra-professional and extra-constitutional role, but a series of martial laws, summary military courts, unaudited funds, huge tax exemption for defence-controlled ventures, sheer repression and intermittent take-overs have taken a heavy toll, and that is why the worries about Pakistan's vulnerability sometimes appear real. The huge loans—mostly for the non-development sector including defence—cannot be met by more indirect taxes, with the poor shouldering the major burden, in a country where poverty has already increased from 25 to 42 per cent of the total population.

PAKISTAN: A BETRAYED IDEAL

The movement for Pakistan aimed at ameliorating Muslim underdevelopment in Muslim majority provinces offering neutral supra-regional dispensation.[38] Thus, Islam became a rallying point incorporating economic, religious and political ideals, and *Pakistan* was visualized as a progressive utopia for a massive, trans-regional underclass. A country comprising of more than ninety per cent Muslims should apparently have no worry or confusion over its Islamic identity, yet with Pakistan being a plural country without a sustained participatory system, the political dissent and economic disenchantment are more often aired mainly through religious idiom or ethnic militancy. The domination of Punjab over civil and military cadres, and the failure of the Westernized elite in offering a tangible solution to the problems of basic needs have pushed huge sections of the populace towards a rhetorical Islamic ethos. Many disgruntled youths feel that a reductionist form of Islam is the remedy for all their problems, and distressed by Muslim agonies in Bosnia, Kashmir,

Palestine, Iraq, Afghanistan, and elsewhere, they feel that the world is arrayed against them. The Afghan Jihad in the 1980s offered free training to a whole generation exposed to traditional *madrassas*, and with the rise of the Taliban in Afghanistan, they saw a model for the entire Muslim world. The failure of state sector education and growing poverty have pushed many youths towards these *madrassas*, which, through their own well-organized networks and occasional support from the ISI, have been engaged in various regional ventures.

In a way, populist Political Islam is a rebuke to elitism and a retort to superficial Westernism as represented by the ruling elite. It is also a strategy by several religio-political parties to mount street power since they had been constantly weak in building up electoral power. Pakistani analysts would proffer an argument that since such parties did not have more than 5 per cent electoral support in the country, Pakistan did not risk being Talibanized. Certainly, it has been wishful thinking. The religio-political parties have the street power to cause a major economic and political setback to any government. In 2002, on the back of anti-Americanism, and a pervasive disillusionment across Pakistan, these parties under the banner of Muttahida Majlis-i-Amal (MMA), were able to bag a considerable percentage of the votes and easily established provincial governments in the NWFP and Balochistan. Soon, they began implementing their narrowly-defined Islamization of cultural life in these two vital regions, and civil society became a major casualty before their onslaught. These elements had in the past collaborated with the authoritarian sections, and an occasional nod from the defence establishment would send them into action, destabilizing any programme for full-fledged democratization. However, having once obtained massive electoral and street power, they have been less amenable to the military's dictates, unless it suits their own interests. However, with a newly realized self-confidence they have become critical of unilateral changes in the constitution inducted under the LFO, as it deprives them of their political power. By joining in the like-minded generals such as Generals Zia, Hamid Gul and Yaqub Nasir, these fundamentalists played havoc with civic forces in the past, and subsequently, upon their massive electoral performance, have the wherewithal to mount their own specific programmes.

Contrasted with this, Jinnah's vision of a tolerant, progressive and egalitarian society where everyone would have the same rights and privileges is still a consensus point. He, of course, desired a Muslim state, but never espoused for a theocracy. Jinnah considered Islam as a moral code, but was also clear that minorities will have equal rights. But the harrowing question of legitimacy confronted by various non-representative regimes like that of Zia, brought clerical groups across the Rubicon and into the mainstream arena. The imposition of Separate Electorates for minorities under Zia further eroded their civil liberties and equally emboldened the fundamentalist elements. The ambiguous demands for *Sharia* persistently put forth by several *ulema* received impetus from Zia, whereas after him, both Nawaz Sharif and Benazir Bhutto constantly kowtowed to them. Movements like Jamiat-Ulama-i-Islam (JUI) with both its factions (led by Fazlur Rahman and Sami ul Haq, respectively), Ahl-i-Hadith, Tehreek-i-Shariat of Maulana Sufi in Malakand, and Malik Akram Awan's Al-Ikhwan in the Salt Range share mutual rivalries yet have demanded the imposition of an unexplained *Sharia*.[39] Their support for the Taliban cost Pakistani civil society quite heavily, though Musharraf under American pressure promised to rein them in. However, the formation of governments in two vital provinces, a major share in the national parliament, and a strong anti-American rhetoric seem to have circumscribed Musharraf's manoeuvres to liberate the polity from ultra pressures. His own single-minded endeavour to concentrate all power in his person concurrently, both as the president and army chief, simply negates democratic norms and allows the proponents of Political Islam a greater space in the political arena. In other words, Pakistan's polity and civil society remain besieged by military-led authoritarianism and fundamentalist totalitarianism, and both the latter have never shied away from joining hands together to deny greater space to the former.

Similarly, a forward policy on Kashmir through the religious volunteers, once again, almost isolated an otherwise aligned Pakistan. Pakistan, prodded by successful Indian diplomacy and global aversion to any separatism was, however, compelled to rein in the militants. Like the dramatic changeover on Afghanistan, this major shift on Kashmir also proved to be a waste of scarce resources on irresponsible ventures. But to many observers, that was a temporary arrangement, given all the contradictions in Pakistan's power structures, and worst of all, due to the stratified educational system. It was felt that the *madrassas* and the intelligence outfits had already created a steady stream of volunteers to fight in Kashmir, and these trained militants may continue to remain active informally, despite official restrictions. It is believed that the best way to tackle this onslaught is through proper educational reforms, reorganization of syllabi, banning of private militia outfits and a low-key profile on regional issues. The redefinition of security in reference to internal cohesion and peace has to come about, over and above the externalized perspective. All this is possible by the salience of democracy, human rights and an open debate on Islam and the politics of identity.

As seen above, the challenges for Pakistan are largely the same as those which confront its civil society. The style of policies and politicking so far pursued by successive regimes has either been at the expense of civil society or has simply bypassed it. If Pakistan is to prosper and develop as a harmonious, peaceful and forward-looking nation, it must seek consensus, strength and guidance from its own people by trusting their opinions. The various surveys across the country—both formal, as well as informal—reveal an amazing range of consensus on all kinds of internal, regional and global challenges. The challenge is to take them on board, and ensure their implementation. But before one gets into the semantics of these two vital challenges, there is a need to look at such a consensus across the nation.

NATIONAL CONSENSUS ON CIVIL SOCIETY

Like any other developing society, the challenges for Pakistani civil society are far too many. It has to work at the local, national, regional and global levels to create a conducive interface with the organs of the Pakistani state, besides societal clusters and external forces which directly impinge upon the former. There is no doubt that the realities of political economy and establishments varying from the police, intelligence agencies to the army are unresponsive to civic dictates, and the regional and global apathy or sheer indifference towards this large Muslim nation are not helpful at all. Civil society survived in the 1980s, perhaps the worst and most repressive time in its history, when the generals, through brutalization were superimposing barbarian punishments and a retrogressive form of Islamization. Democracy has always been put on hold in the country thanks to the above factors, but there is one major redeeming factor in the form of a clear public opinion on several issues. Civil forces, reformers and human rightists have to align themselves with these popular sentiments, and succeed where others have failed. As was seen in 1997, in a countrywide comprehensive survey of public views on fifty crucial issues confronted by Pakistanis, the trans-regional consensus of opinions was quite amazing.[40] Such opinion surveys have persistently revealed a high level of politicization, critical analysis on crucial themes including the status of women, minority rights, democratization, corruption, Islam, relations with India, Kashmir, Taliban, and such other important areas. Certainly, the people of Pakistan have a clearer view of the policies that could ultimately move their country towards a Jinnahist dream, rather than making it an abode of retrogression and dismay. They see a future in democratization and prioritization of the social sector over everything else. They are largely a tolerant society, whose major sections support equal rights for women and minorities, and aspire for a better and friendly relationship with India. These seemingly disparate issues are interrelated and require bold initiatives, deeper democratization and radical reforms.

PROGNOSIS FOR CIVIL SOCIETY IN PAKISTAN AND SOUTH ASIA

One way of looking at the realities in Pakistan might be that the civil society has no future due to overpowering forces of state and ethno-sectarianism. On the contrary, one may premise that the civic forces have seen far rougher times than the present, and can survive yet another authoritarian onslaught. After all, media shows greater self-confidence; there is a wider acceptance for the NGOs, especially after the laudable work done by the Edhi Foundation, Orangi Pilot Project, Citizens Schools Foundation, the Aga Khan Foundation, the Human Rights Commission of Pakistan, and Imran Khan's The Shaukat Khanum Memorial Cancer Hospital & Research Centre. In addition, Aurat, Shirkatgah, Asma Jahangir's shelter project for battered women, conservationists from the National College of Arts and Indus Valley School of Art and Architecture, the Hamdard Foundation, and various investigative reporters across the land are beacons of hope. No doubt, there are also frequent stories of corruption of several NGOs, where former bureaucrats have been reportedly pocketing donated sums, otherwise meant for development.[41] The NGOs face strong resistance from the fundamentalist religious groups for obvious reasons, not least because the former consider them working for foreign interests, giving away national secrets to the latter. This is not merely confined to

Pakistan, as some NGOs in India and Bangladesh have similar problems of transparency and acceptance.

There are numerous ways to fight the malaise: First, the NGOs must develop an in-built accountability mechanism which should preclude any possibility of corruption, misuse of funds or valuable information at any level. Second, the money and help from abroad should be made totally transparent through a rigorous audit. Third, the NGOs should attempt for an autonomous space, away from the regimes, and less dependence upon the Western donors. Their reliance upon Western donors simply compromises their integrity and objectivity. Fourth, they must indigenize themselves in their orientation. It is interesting to note that only the West-supported NGOs come under severe attack. Their lifestyles, language, class background, and closer associations with the power elite, largely alienate them from the locals. Fifth, the NGOs should form their own networks holding seminars, coordinating complementary efforts, and educating the public on their shared goals and strategies. In addition, there should be a clear and fair system for their registration and audit.

The civil society sector can easily work through an independent and supportive media on defining societal objectives, benefits of democratization, and a greater respect for pluralism. The development of art and culture through greater participation, and moral support for judicial activism can go a long way in establishing their credibility. They need to build up transparent bridges with civil societies across the region and should speak on human issues without spreading themselves thin.[42] In other words, through schools, media, local activism and greater regional coordination, civil society can be more secure, effective and successful. It must realize the fact that rather than fighting against religion by simply ridiculing it or waiting for it to disappear, they must be either totally tolerant—especially when they claim to be secular—or should attempt a reconstructive discourse that incorporates the most positive aspects of both secular and sacred cultures. In other words, civic forces can build up moral and institutional pressures from various directions, offering a new daybreak for this otherwise land of much potential, and hard working people.

The governability crisis engendered by an opportunistic elitism, and a diehard militarism exposes the limitations of a middle class-centred, eurocentric definition of civil society. It equally reflects sadly on an obscurantist vision of Islam where pluralism is scoffed at. With both statist and societal regimentation on the offensive, civil societies in South Asia have entered the most difficult phase in their history. This watershed could be its death knell, or given some courage and timely institutionalization, it could be a new dawn for the entire country. The press, judiciary, women's and human rights groups, media, political parties and other independent and critical think-tanks need to come forward to mould plural South Asian states in consonance with the plural and democratic imperatives of their societies at large. To a great extent, any lasting India-Pakistani amity will prove to be the most consequential step towards a positive regional cooperation and significant eradication of poverty. Not only will the scarce resources, now being wasted on non-development sectors, be redirected towards greater uplift, but democratic and tolerant forces within the most populous region in the world will benefit as well. Inter-state harmony will surely enhance inter-communal coexistence and massive empowerment will certainly underpin democratization in countries like Pakistan while minimizing the threat to India's vulnerable minorities. Unfettered democratization and multiple regional cooperation are the greatest challenges for South Asian civic leaders. So far, the states—especially India and Pakistan—have not allowed such processes and priorities from becoming more pervasive, given their own inertia and vested interests. They have not only controlled people-to-people relationships across the borders, but have vociferously vetoed them through promoting active violence on both sides. As a result, civil societies in both the neighbouring countries, and for that matter, the entire region remain locked in a time warp. Both Pakistan and India have similar politico-economic problems, and a simmering communal predicament which can only be rectified through a fresher perspective, as was forcefully articulated by a leader:

In Pakistan, some have bent Islam to propagate hate, despite its message of peace. Similarly, in India, Hindusim is being polluted by extremists. Last year's riots in Gujarat confirmed that anti-Muslim prejudice could murderously explode if tended to by religious bigots. The nation's history is also being rewritten in Saffron ink—and being used to justify the razing of mosques on the grounds that they were built on Hindu temples. India's democracy is being battered by such forces. Damaging too is that the country's 140m Muslims have not been lifted by India's rising economic tide....Both Pakistan and India will have to move from trading insults and shells across disputed borders and become serious about treading the road to peace. There will be elements in both countries who will seek to derail any compromise or deal. Bombay's blasts [on 25 August 2003] must be seen in this light. Leaders in both nations must stop envenoming tongues and minds and offer a way, instead, to replace antipathy with amity.[43]

Civil society in Bangladesh and Sri Lanka, despite ethnic problems and other security-oriented considerations, appears to be comparatively stronger than its Pakistani counterpart, but emphasis on uniformist particularism is putting serious strains on minorities and human rights groups. While Bangladesh fought against a military regime to wrest her independence, the nation soon succumbed to a military coup, which persisted until 1991. The post-Ershad salience of Hasina Wajid's Awami League (AL), and Khalida Zia's Bangladesh National Party (BNP), in a limited sense, augurs well for a democratic gradualism, despite their unending and rather taxing rivalry. The low-key role for generals, and less assertive preoccupation with external security—unlike Pakistan—has given Bangladesh longer years of peace and stability, though complaints of corruption, fundamentalism and inefficiency also abound. Bangladesh is not inflicted with a sectarian divide, though anti-Hindu sentiments have often led to occasional riotous outbursts, especially after the Hindu-Muslim strife in India. The religio-political elements received an immense fillip during the recent Afghan war and the Anglo-American invasion of Iraq in 2003, in addition to the JI-BNP alliance in the centre. Reports of exclusion and expulsion of Hindu Bangladeshis were frequently discussed in the country and abroad, though Dhaka continued to deny a massive exodus. Other than Hindus and, Christians, Chakma hill tribes and Biharis were being singled out by fundamentalists applying coercion, exclusion and sheer violence, sometimes on their own and occasionally with a nod from corrupt administrative machinery. A free press, increasingly independent judiciary, the steady growth of accountable NGOs, especially dealing with the women's sector—within the context of a gradual democratism—still offer an optimistic future for Bangladeshi civil society.[44] On the contrary, whereas Sri Lanka enjoys the highest rate of literacy and more mobility amongst its women than anywhere else in South Asia, her enduring civil war has inhibited the island from striding towards a well-deserved economic breakthrough. However, despite the polarization among her leading political elite, democratic norms and institutions have stayed strong in Sri Lanka. The nation is not averse to learning lessons from the tragedies of the 1980s. The post-September US-led blanket campaign against terrorism, nudged the Tamil Tigers towards a more conciliatory role, though polarization remains undiminished. Nepal does not have a vocal civil society unlike its eastern and southern neighbours, which is proving further problematic due to the Maoist insurgency and official counter-measures. The continuity in party politics and non-interference from both India and China in the spirit of regional cooperation, may still offer a glimmer of hope for the Nepalese reformist groups.

The challenges to South Asian civil societies are robust, as the military and fundamentalists may disallow autonomous space, and the legacy of corrupt and inefficient political leaders may continue exacerbating the credibility crisis. Pakistan's persistent economic debilitation, thanks to ever escalating, massive non-development expenditure, a narrow tax base and unbound corruption—quite in the interest of the oligarchs—will simply not allow any politico-economic empowerment of the masses. Frankly, the army holds the key to her future politico-economic destiny, and its leaders will have to opt for bolder policies, over and above sectional and vetoing interests. In the same vein, India will have to charter a more tolerant and all-encompassing path offering security and unencumbered participation to its minorities along with pioneering a conflict-resolution strategy towards its smaller neighbours. Neither hegemony nor mere status quo oriented conflict management based on bullying or scapegoating, suits its stature and interests. Bangladesh, Sri Lanka, Bhutan and Nepal will have to further strengthen their participatory institutions and head towards economic stability by developing complementary economies and transparent policies on natural resources. Regional and ethnic feuds have to be resolved through negotiations, and not through military means or proxy wars. South Asian civil societies, unlike their ambivalent regimes, urgently need to establish stronger linkages to play a vanguard role in offering overdue alternatives to the one-fifth of humanity. In other words, their battlefronts stretch from domestic issues to pressure group politics, and from regional discords to the diverse domains of political economy.

NOTES

1. Turkey is offered as a secular state where any juxtaposition with religion is officially abhorred, but such a model, however justified in the name of Kemalism, refuses to tolerate ethnic and ideological pluralism. The state, in a rather dogmatic way, tries to impose unilateralism the way Saudi Arabia may disallow any debate or democracy in the name of Islam. Iran is still a different model while Sudan under General Omar al-Bashir, and earlier, Pakistan under General Ziaul Haq pursued Islamisation from above disallowing any dissent or debate. All these and other models seem to be wanting in characteristics allocated to unfettered democracy and universal empowerment. For a comment on Turkish ideological issues, see, Iftikhar H. Malik, 'Turkey at the Crossroads: Encountering Modernity and Tradition', *Journal of South Asian and Middle Eastern Studies,* XXIV, 2, Winter 2001. India, by constitution and its early Nehruvian stipulation is secular and democratic, but since the early 1990s, is confroted with the Hindtuva backlash. The BJP-led transformation of India is a negation of the Nehruvian-Gandhian model of pluralist coexistence.

2. For a conceptual framework, see, Iftikhar H. Malik, *State and Civil Society in Pakistan: Politics of Authority, Ideology and Ethnicity,* Oxford, 1997.

3. Within the South Asian context, there are various forms of ethno-regionalism. Some movements are simply secessionist, some are separatist, a few seek equal empowerment while others may be nativist. The separation of East Pakistan continues to unnerve Pakistani establishment, whereas the Muhajir/Muttahida Qaumi Movement (MQM) may be seen vacillating between separatism and sheer anarchy. Concurrently, some Sindhi *nationalists* may be perceived as nativist forces reasserting their cultural nationalism. The erstwhile Pushtun nationalism— sometimes referred to as *Pushtoonistan*—has already subsided largely, due to the integration of Pushtuns within the Pakistani set-up and also because of the decimation of the Afghan regimes, which more often propped up such elements. The Baloch and Pushtun elements in Balochistan may be striving towards a more equal and parallel participation in the regional affairs rather than seeking secession. For a useful overview, see, Subrata Mitra, (ed.) *Sub-national Movements in South Asia,* Boulder/Oxford, 1996.

4. Apart from many Muslim writers, Maxime Rodinson has further elaborated this view in his various books including *Mohammed,* London, 1993.

5. There were pressures on Muslim rulers like the Delhi Sultans from ulama to impose Islam on Hindu subjects but kings such as Iltutmash and Balban resisted it. Babur, the founder of Mughal empire, as borne out in his own *Tuzk,* while invading India killed many Muslim Pushtuns and built minarets from their skulls. For details, see, *Baburnama,* translated by A. Beveridge, London, 1965 (reprint).

6. This would imply focusing on a few upper class elite and individuals rather than investigating the societal trajectories. The emphasis would remain confined to a few seminaries or groups whose views would be seen typical of the entire Muslim population. For instance, the emphasis on the Deobandis, Brelvis, Tablighis or Jama'at-i-Islami may not fully reflect the diversity, as well as local strategies at numerous other levels.

7. A Pakistani Muslim of the Indian origin was quite sad with his experience of seeking Indian visa to visit his ancestral place in the UP. On the application form he mentioned the name of a known Muslim MP as an acquaintance for reference purposes. The politician had been known to him since the school days, but when approached by the Indian police for a mere authenticity, he plainly refused to recognise the applicant. (Based on an interview in Karachi, 4 April 2001). Several Indian Muslim elite have been openly decrying Pakistan as a communal creation, so as to affirm their *Indian* credentials, but privately may have different views. This dilemma of the Indian Muslims, despite their huge numbers, is rather unique as their counterparts from amongst the Hindus, Sikhs, Christians and other plural communities do not have to disown their *cultural* identity. (Based on interviews conducted in India in August 1997). An Oxford-based academic with avowed commitment to communism does not find any hesitation in acknowledging his *Sikh* credentials and finds Guru Nanak to be far superior an intellectual and leader to Karl Marx. To this intellectual-activist, some Muslim elite intentionally try to create this dilemma for exploitative purposes. They like to portray Indian Muslims as an impoverished and dilemmic community whose rights have to be preserved through *them*. The religious, as well as secular leaders would avoid fresher perspectives on Islam, Indian nationalism, Pakistan, and so on, otherwise, as posited, it may cause new challenges. (Interview held in Oxford on 30 May 2001). In a query to this affect, Salman Khurshid, a former Indian [Muslim] foreign minister accepted the fact that his party—the Indian National Congress—was not thinking of developing any new perspective on India-Pakistan relationship, so as to improve inter-community relationship. His lecture, 'Indian Democracy and Muslims', was held at the Centre for Islamic Studies, Oxford, on 22 May 2001.

8. This is the ideology of ultra Right from amongst certain middle class Hindus, to whom secularism is basically an appeasement of minorities like Muslims. To them, it is equally divorced from the Indian socio-cultural realities. Just by refuting pluralism, these exponents see, Hinduism as an overarching ethnic, cultural and historical essentialism to which everyone else has to conform. It is also defined as a 'New Hindu' movement.

9. Her *The Sole Spokesman* (Cambridge, 1985), despite its significance, simply reiterated the well-known Cambridge school of South Asian history, though in her later books, she has positively moved on to other factors as well. However, she is hesitant to accept the simplistic nature of imperial/high history interpretation of the Indian politics of the 1940s. Her own personal nostalgia does not allow her to seek wider and complex undercurrents, spawning the demand for Muslim separatism. To her, it was the same-old, discredited two-nation concept or a communal version of Islam rather than its diverse, atomised versions. Based on her lecture to Oxford's South Asian Students [the Majlis], 30 May 2001. She may not realise the fact that demonolithising Islam or romanticising folk Islam is as dangerous as positing it only as a monolithic, static or purist culture.

10. Aziz Ahmad, *Islamic Modernism in India and Pakistan, 1857–1947*, Oxford, 1967; Rafiuddin Ahmed, *The Bengal Muslims, 1871–1906: A Quest for Identity,* Delhi, 1981; Farzana Shaikh, *Community and Consensus in Islam: Muslim Representation in Colonial India, 1860–1947,* Cambridge, 1989; and, Taj-ul-Islam Hashmi, *Pakistan as a Peasant Utopia: the Communalization of Class Politics in East Bengal,* Boulder, 1992. Without any irreverence to his established research, Hasan

ends up justifying India by denigrating Pakistan as an historical incident and rather harbinger of problems for the Indian Muslims. See, his *Legacy of a Divided Nation: India's Muslims Since Independence,* London, 1997. For a review of various interpretive strands in recent South Asian historiography, see, Iftikhar H. Malik, *Islam, Nationalism and the West: Issues of Identity in Pakistan,* Oxford, 1999.

11. One wonders how, even after fifty-seven years of separate existence, the Indian Muslim problem can still be burdened on to the creation of *an un-Indian Pakistan.* If Pakistan has proven such a bad omen for Indian Muslims then even without a territorial state what could have been the fate of Muslims (especially in minority regions) in a united India? The view that they could have fared well by being in one India is again based on appeasement to a majority and also by essentialising secularism as the core of Indian nationalism. With the ascendancy of the BJP and the other communal forces in India, such a view based on secularist essentialism and the static nature of Indian nationalism has turned out to be wishful thinking. The fact is that even before the demand for a territorial state, the Mahasabha and such forces were powerful in India and to them India was to eventually revert to its *true fold.* It was on 8 March 1947 that the partition was forcefully demanded by the Congress—not by the Muslim League—to appease the Mahasabha, something that many historians tend to gloss over.

12. Along with Mushirul Hasan, Professor S.A.K. Rizvi and some other Indian Muslim scholars would seek syncretism in Indian Islamic experience, whereas I.H. Qureshi and Pakistani historians have only essentialised separatism. However, historians like Muzaffar Alam would definitely seek a wider role for classical Indo-Muslim culture even outside the present-day South Asian boundaries.

13. Both the Muslim rulers of Mysore, a predominantly Hindu state, resisted the European incursions into India. Tipu Sultan, the son of Hyder Ali, and a hero of the India-Pakistani nationalist and folk traditions, died fighting the British East India Company in 1799, at Seringapatam.

14. These movements, mostly occurring in northern India, were based on a sustained concept of resistance to the British *(feringi)* rule. Except for Kharral in Punjab the rest were largely inspired by a religious ideology.

15. For a useful commentary on these early Muslim observers and commentators of the West, see, Gulfishan Khan, *Indian Muslim Perceptions of the West During the Eighteenth Century,* Karachi, 1998.

16. In that case the Indian Muslims were not unique, as their cultural nationalism eventually matured into political nationalism, though remained polarised between traditional elite and their westernized counterparts. One sees similar processes at work among the contemporary Hindus and Sikhs in India where revivalism and reformism seem to be contesting for the same space.

17. For an early analysis, see, Leonard Binder, *Religion and Politics in Pakistan,* Berkeley, 1961. Several important studies by Louis Hayes, Khalid B. Sayeed, Anwar Syed, Charles Kennedy, Ishtiaq Ahmed, Lawrence Ziring, S. Vali Reza Nasr, Ian Talbot and others have appeared over the last three decades.

18. For a polarisation between a reluctant state and the nascent civil society during the 1980s and early 1990s, see, *State and Civil Society in Pakistan.*

19. The general impression in Pakistan is that the judiciary has usually been less assertive and vocal on democracy, constitutionalism and the illegality of the military coups, whereas some analysts may see, Pakistani higher courts still being able to

safeguard their autonomy. The latter view is carried in Paula Newberg's *Judging the State: Courts and Constitutional Politics in Pakistan,* Cambridge, 1995.

20. There has been a profusion of literature on these outfits in recent months. For instance, see, Jessica Stern, 'Pakistan's Jihad Culture', *Foreign Affairs,* November-December 2000. During the local bodies elections in the summer of 2001, the religious parties such as Maulana Sufi's Nifaz-i-Shariat Movement banned women in the Malakand and Dir districts from participation in the electoral politics. Later on, he incited thousands of his followers to fight a holy war against the Americans in Afghanistan. Many of these innocent tribals were either killed or were taken prisoners while Sufi himself escaped back to Pakistan and sought official protection from the families of his detractors.

21. Based on interviews with Maulana Sami ul Haq of Akora Khattak in northern Pakistan on 10 August 2000, and with Maulana Akram Awan in Munara on 15 April 2001. However, by the summer of 2001, it was being suggested in official quarters that the military regime was planning to put curbs on military training and such militarist agendas at the religious schools. In August, two sectarian outfits—Lashkar-i-Jhangvi and Sipah-i-Muhammad—were finally banned, though the regime stopped short of taking any similar action against the Jihadi groups until American pressure led to further marginalisation of the Jihadi groups towards the end of 2001.

22. For further details on the circumstances leading to the coup and the situation soon after it, see, Iftikhar H. Malik, 'Military Coup in Pakistan: Business as Usual or Democracy on Hold!' *The Round Table,* 360, 2001, 357–77.

23. 'Precarious in Pakistan: Musharraf lacks a firm footing' (Leader), *The Guardian,* 26 March 2002. In fact, under a mounting Indian and global pressure, Musharraf had to change the military-led policy in May-June 2002 on Kashmir. Like Afghanistan, here again the GHQ and ISI had to retreat from a forward policy by reining in Jihadi elements. Pakistan, despite her active role in the US-led coalition was again isolated and directionless, prompting Bhutto to demand Musharraf's resignation, whereas, some other political groups demanded the formation of a national government. The military regime simply ignored these demands for civilianisation. However, Musharraf, after a rigged referendum on 30 April, a retreat on both the borders, and by pursuing a militarist policy in South Wazirisitan agency—the semi-autonomous tribal territory—and by banning Jihadi groups appeared quite isolated. His proposed amendments in the country's constitution were seen as a desperate effort to amass political powers in a rather precarious situation. See, *The Guardian,* 29 June 2002. It was also feared that several groups now simply wanted to eliminate the general. *Dawn* 29 June 2002. The imposition of Sharia in the NWFP, amidst a growing anger towards Musharraf's LFO and pro-US policies posed serious challenges for Islamabad. See, Isabel Hilton, 'Pakistan is losing the fight against fundamentalism', *The Guardian,* 29 May 2003. On 2 June 2003, several police trainees were ambushed in Quetta and killed through a hit-and-run attack. They belonged to the Shia Hazara community, who were targetted by Sunni militants revealing an undiminished sectarian divide in the country.

24. This is a South Asia-wide phenomenon when one looks at the BJP, Shiv Sena, and such other parties in Bangladesh, Pakistan and Sri Lanka which are pushing the agenda towards an extreme right by proposing intolerant forms of nationalism and cultural redefinition.

25. In a TV interview, Dr Nasim Hasan Shah, the former chief justice of the Supreme Court, defended the highest judiciary all the way from 1954 to 2000, when so many verdicts were given in support of executive's dismissals of the elected regimes under the all-too-familiar law of necessity. He, however, took the credit for restoring Sharif's first government in 1993, when it had been dismissed by the then President, Ghulam Ishaq Khan. Interview on Pakistan-ARY Channel, monitored in Oxford, 29 May 2001. However, the general feeling is that the judges have generally legitimated the dismissals and the take-overs.

26. It all began in 1953–4 with the dissolution of the first Constituent assembly when the Governor-General, Ghulam Muhammad simply dismissed the elected house as it was becoming more vocal on the legislative front. The petition against the dismissal was heard first by the provincial court in Sindh which declared the executive decision to be unconstitutional but the highest court—the Supreme Court—upheld the governor's order on the basis of a dictum of 'law of necessity'. It rationalised such a decision on the basis of special and critical circumstances affecting national security. This damaging decision by Justice Munir-led apex court became a precedent for all future such dissolutions by Ayub, Yahya, Zia and Ghulam Ishaq Khan. For details on all such crucial cases and the rulings by the highest court, see, Paula Newberg, op. cit.

27. In April 2001, a senior judge of the Punjab High Court, Malik Abdul Qayyum, made headlines in the national and international media when it was revealed that while hearing petitions against Benazir Bhutto, he had allowed himself to be influenced by the ministers from Nawaz Sharif's cabinet in 1998–9. His secretly recorded tapes, available now on the internet, show Malik seeking guidelines on the case from one of Sharif's colleagues. However, the judge resigned under public pressure in June 2001.

28. It is true that a former admiral, hiding in the United States, has been brought back to face the charges on receiving kick-backs in an arms deal, but many observers predict his emancipation in the near future. The military regime is using him it as an example of a holistic accountability but the fact remains that the entire focus is on the politicians who interestingly were first corrupted by the generals in the near past.

29. See, Stephen Cohen, *The Pakistan Army,* Karachi, 1994; Hasan Askari-Rizvi, *Military and Politics in Pakistan,* Karachi, 1998; and, Brian Cloughley, *The Pakistan Army,* Karachi, 1999.

30. The opinion remained divided over the role of generals and politicians all through this time.

31. These opinions were gathered in 1999–2001, following extensive interviews with the various opinion groups in Pakistan and elsewhere.

32. In a speech at the Rhodes House, Oxford, in late May 2001, the former US President, Clinton, expressed his worries about the future integrity of a nuclear state like Pakistan. At Hay-on-Wye book festival in the same week, he again mentioned Pakistan in his observations.

33. Such apologists trying to rehabilitate their own images include retired generals like Gul Hasan, Farman Ali, A.A.K. Niazi, K.M. Arif, Jahandad Khan, Sher Ali, Faiz Chishti, and few others.

34. For an internet or print version see, *The Nation,* 14 August 2000.

35. Other than their separate hospitals, schools and servants, the officials, on their retirement, are allotted agricultural lands in Sindh and border regions, which has been causing serious consternation among the local people. Further, officials are appointed to all the senior government positions including the governorship, cabinet, ministries, embassies and semi-autonomous corporations. The present regime has appointed a number of retired generals as vice-chancellors as well. For an early report of a huge number of military officials—the former and serving—in civil departments and corruption in military-related deals, see, Kamran Khan, 'Evidence of Corruption in Defence Deals', *The News International,* 15 and 19 August 2000.

36. General Rashid Qureshi, the head of ISPR—the Inter-Services Public Relations Department—in one of his interviews with journalists in 2000, observed that Pakistan was the winner in the Kargil clashes so there was no need to hold an inquiry of the winning party. Such a travesty took place when the Indian generals and government were being lambasted for their neglect of the security of these strategic heights. In an interview, circulated on the Internet and sent as a message on Independence day, Nawaz Sharif, the deposed Prime Minister, for the first time, made some revelations about the Kargil campaign. According to him, 4000 Pakistanis were killed while the country was on the brink of a complete defeat. Sharif rushed to Washington to seek a face-saving device and did not go public on Pakistani losses since this, according to him, would have emboldened the Indians for an all-out attack on the country. Nawaz Sharif also held General Musharraf responsible for scuppering growing India-Pakistan amity following the Lahore Summit in February 1999, when the Army Chief refused to welcome the visiting Indian Prime Minister. To Nawaz Sharif, the military top brass did not want any solution to the Kashmir dispute and thus began the Kargil attack without his prior knowledge and permission. http://www.rediff.com/news/2003/aug/16pak.htm, 16 August 2003.

37. It was deeply encouraged by the CIA during the Afghan war against the Soviet Union. It even carried out certain projects including the alleged blow-up of the Ojhri Arms Dump in Rawalpindi in 1988, which cost scores of innocent Pakistani civilian lives. The report ordered by the then Prime Minister, M.K. Junejo, remains shelved as it points fingers at the ISI. In fact, Zia dismissed him unceremoniously soon after Junejo's demand for its implementation.

38. Even the very choice of the name, Pakistan, as a neutral term, was quite pertinent as it would not allow any regional or ethnic hegemony, nor would it symbolise any one province or specific community.

39. A number of interviews with these leaders failed to put across any clear-cut form of politics and economy in their espoused Islamic order. They all differ, and in many cases, simply hate one another. The clerics exploit the popular loyalty to Islam across the country to suit their expediency.

40. Some of the findings of that survey are as follows:
A whole majority of them (67 per cent) opposed the Taliban-style restrictions on women, whereas 63 per cent opined in support of inter-gender equality before the law. This is an open rejection of the law of evidence imposed by Zia, equating two women to a man in a court case. The 59 per cent of the men polled in this first-ever major survey favoured the view that just like men, women should also have an equal right of divorce, and 43 per cent did not mind their daughters attending co-educational schools. Still coming from a predominantly rural society, an amazing

ratio of 74 per cent supported family planning. Another 74 per cent supported joint electorates for everybody including the minorities. On the question of corruption, Pakistanis showed an amazing amount of consensus across the board. A huge majority of 76 per cent considered the generals to be corrupt whereas another 95 per cent found politicians to be absolutely corrupt. Another 55 per cent felt that Pakistan would never have true accountability as against 34 per cent of the total respondents who felt hopeful. Fifty-two per cent felt that Pakistan had been harmed by martial law as opposed to 43 per cent who supported military take-overs. Fifty-one per cent asked for cuts in the military budget. A high proportion (59 per cent) desired better relations with India. Two-thirds (65 per cent) opined in favour of Kashmir joining Pakistan as opposed to 34 per cent who favoured an independent Kashmir. However, 77 per cent opposed demarcation of the Line of Control as the international boundary. Most of them (82 per cent) had a positive view of their country and wanted to stay there forever. A clear majority of them (75 per cent) demanded a ban on the religio-sectarian parties that spawned hatred and violence and a similar ratio asked for restrictions on political sermons in the mosques. An overwhelming majority expected the state to uplift health and education facilities although nuclearisation was supported by 84 per cent as well. Fifty-eight per cent of Pakistanis, felt that the Muslims in South Asia were better off in the 1990s than the pre-partition generations. Of course, this was an overwhelmingly Pakistani viewpoint. *The Herald,* Karachi, January 1997, and *India Today,* 18 August 1997.

41. Khawar Mumtaz, 'NGOs in Pakistan: An Overview', in Tariq Banuri, et al., (eds.) *Just Development: Beyond Adjustment with a Human Face,* Karachi, 1997, pp. 171–190.
42. This was amply illustrated in the week before the Musharraf-Vajpayee meeting in Delhi, when dozens of concerned Pakistanis met their Indian counterparts to strongly recommend common agendas that both the leaders could achieve in the larger interests of the people on both sides. For details, see, *Dawn,* 9 July 2001. Even after a thaw in the summer of 2003, India-Pakistan relations seemed to have nose-dived following the bomb blasts in Bombay on 25 August, as L.K. Advani and several other BJP senior officials tried to implicate Pakistani militant groups in the arming of Indian Muslim organisations such as Students' Islamic Movement of India (SIMI). For details, see, http://news.bbc.co.uk/1/hi/world/south_asia/3184189.stm.
43. 'Prisoners of the past. Restraint needed in the Bombay debris', *The Guardian,* 27 August 2003.
44. 'Rape and torture empties the villages', ibid., 21 July 2003.

Cruelty begins at home; charity is something we export in the barrel of a gun.... It make sense for us to spend millions going to foreign parts to wreak havoc with missiles but not for foreigners to come here with nothing and look for low paid work.

— Gary Younge, *The Guardian*, 19 August 2002

Even the moderates here in Pakistan are outraged. Across the board, young and old, poor and rich, fundamentalist and secularist are united in their hatred of the US and their contempt for Britain. Such an unprecedented unanimity in a country renowned for its ethnic and sectarian divides is a huge achievement....

The same is happening throughout the Muslim world. A previously fractured *ummah* is finally uniting against a perceived common foe, leaving the fundamentalists jubilant and their pro-West leaders, despite their dependence on the US, with no choice but to join the anti-war chorus.

— Jemima Khan, 'I am angry and ashamed to be British',
The Independent, 2 April 2003

In spite of all the years of oppression, Iraqis know very well that Iraq is not Saddam. They also know that Americans and British forces are occupiers, not liberators.

— Haifa Zangana [an Iraqi novelist and painter in Britain],
'The message coming from our families in Baghdad',
The Guardian, 3 April 2003

Baghdad has turned into Afghanistan faster than Afghanistan.

— Euan Ferguson, 'A latte- and a rifle to go',
The Observer, 2 June 2003

The idealistic barrister [Lord Goldsmith] I knew 25 years ago would have been appalled at the racist treatment of these Muslims.

— Louise Christian, 'There is no defence for Guantanamo',
The Guardian, 24 July 2003

4

Kabul to Karbala:
Political Islam and the West

The angry American pursuit to arrest or eliminate Osama bin Laden and his Al Qaeda supporters after the tragic events of 11 September 2001, soon turned into an unrestrained and massive bombing campaign against Afghanistan with severe human and geo-political ramifications. Expanding it further to 'the Axis of Evil', the Anglo-American invasion of Iraq in search of never-to-be-found weapons of mass destruction and without UN legal sanction, decimated one more Muslim region. Leaving Afghanistan in the doldrums under a weak Karzai regime, Washington and London, in blatant disregard of global public opinion, undertook yet one more annihilative and unnecessary campaign. While analysts such as Samuel Huntington may have felt vindicated on their premise of 'the clash of civilisations', Western leaders became somewhat apprehensive of the growing Islamophobia as intermittent incidents of violence took place within the United Kingdom and the United States. Concurrently, Muslim immigrant communities felt they were being put under a negative societal and official spotlight, especially when hundreds of Muslim immigrants of Arab and South Asian origin were detained in the US and other Western countries, due to 'their interest to the government'. The regimes in Washington and London introduced new discretionary laws, which were mostly contested by civil liberties groups. Such strains on pluralism meant further marginalisation of the Muslim Diaspora—itself mostly belonging to a working class background. In South Asia, the states quickly awoke to new political challenges, realities and opportunities. India-Pakistan polarity further intensified in trying to woo the Bush administration, concurrently, their respective projection of the Kashmir dispute as a terrorist venture or struggle for self-determination gained a new competitive momentum. Pakistan's General Pervez Musharraf was rehabilitated from a military pariah to a frontline partner as Islamabad offloaded the Taliban, while India sought new opportunities with the Northern Alliance once again ensconced in Kabul. In Pakistan, the religio-political elements felt bewildered at the spectacle of Afghans killing fellow Afghans at the behest of the Americans and other external elements. Their early emotional outbursts had pushed hundreds of tribal enthusiasts into Afghanistan to fight a Jihad, which never came, and now the military regime sat back and watched them squirm over the great tragedy unfolding itself across the Khyber Pass. In Bangladesh, the National Party (BNP) won the elections, and in collaboration with some religious parties, Khalida Zia became the Prime Minister once again. Her predecessor and the main opponent, Hasina Wajid, known for her pro-India stance, had been marginalised with only sixty-four parliamentary seats. Khalida Zia did not seem to undertake any major change in her foreign policies, and the anti-war demonstrations did not worry Dhaka at all. Sri Lanka remained embroiled in her own difficulties and the volatile elections in December 2001 brought the opposition alliance into power, though third-party arbitration to resolve chronic ethnic problems appeared to be making headway. Nepal continued to suffer from a rising graph of militancy by Maoist guerillas, as the new monarch soon found out to his discomfort.

This chapter, after summarizing the Western ideological outlook on the Afghan imbroglio and its acrimonious realties, looks at post-11 September developments within the context of South Asian Muslims, both within the region and in Diaspora. In an aura of increased anxieties following the Anglo-American invasion of Iraq, the concluding observations delineate a unique regional consensus across the board.

AFGHAN FIASCO AND REACTION WITHIN THE WEST

The military strikes on Afghanistan exposed ideological chasms within Western societies besides an immensely violent dimension of modernity. Here was a poor country, already decimated by a former super power and the internecine civil war, now being bombed into the Stone Age by the remaining super power, duly helped by Britain. While the terrorists striking at New York and Washington were Arabs without any exception, the poor Afghans had to bear the brunt of

Anglo-American fury for hosting the former glorified and now fallen *Mujahideen*. Ironically, Osama bin Laden, his Arab and other international cohorts had been brought into Afghanistan by the same powers in the first place, which were now raining bombs on that country. The former allies had turned against each other with an impoverished country turning into an inferno. Soon, history was to repeat itself as a few months later, Iraq became the target of a similar, contentious and equally destructive military attack. Notwithstanding the support for anti-terrorism activities, still a sizeable portion of Western public opinion criticised the bombing of Afghanistan and Iraq as massive demonstrations were held across Western Europe, the developing world and North America. The proportion of peace marchers remained higher on the Continent than in the United States, where patriotic and nationalist fervour was used by the Bush Administration to justify bombing of a war-ravaged Muslim country, besides the detention of several Americans of Muslim background.

The growing criticism of the bombing and the resultant humanitarian catastrophe in Afghanistan by preeminent leaders such as Mary Robinson and other human rights activists initially unnerved the Bush administration and Tony Blair. Footage from the Qatar-based Arabic television channel, Al-Jazeera, with its on-site reporting, only added to such official frustration. However, propaganda efforts were fiercely undertaken by both the British and US governments to 'humanise the war' and CNN and British channels were told to block out or 'play down' Osama bin Laden's inflammatory harangues as they might carry 'coded messages'. Analysts like Arundhati Roy, Robert Fisk, Noam Chomsky, Tariq Ali, Gore Vidal, George Monbiot, George Galloway and John Pilger censured the US strikes inclusive of carpet bombs—'dumb bombs'—and the resultant human miseries while Salman Rushdie, V.S. Naipaul, Polly Toynbee and a few others felt that Islamic fundamentalism was a harrowing and punishable challenge. Many critics, other than the CND (Campaign for Nuclear Disarmament), socialists or such other groups and dissenters from within the Labour Party, censured Tony Blair and President Bush for continuing hegemonic policies which, rather than eradicating terrorism, could only further the support for terrorists. Western double standards in Palestine, Chechnya and a continued policy of sanctions against Iraq amidst a growing impatience for a military invasion and resultant numerous deaths and other human miseries, were flagged to draw in official attention. In addition, the worries of the Muslim communities such as in Britain and the US were highlighted to reveal dangerous strains on pluralism. George Galloway, the Labour MP from Glasgow, and a vocal critic of the anti-Iraq policy, considered the military strikes a part of 'the new imperialism' which was being unleashed against Muslims. He observed: 'Bush and Blair may not be "at war with Islam", but "Islam" is now at war with them and we will be lucky if that is not soon visible on the streets of northern English cities.' He found the Anglo-American policies towards the Muslim regions solely geared by exploitation and opportunism generating 'the rising tide of radical Islam, buoyed by our double standards towards Palestine and Iraq, and our buttressing of stooge kings, generals and 99 per cent-of-the-vote presidents of the Muslim world....'[1] The critics felt that the American media, in its jingoistic mood, was trivialising criticism from intellectuals like Chomsky and Roy.[2] Chomsky, during his lecture tours of India and Pakistan, described the US attack on Afghanistan 'illegal' and beyond international human norms.[3] Roy, in her widely published and quoted articles, saw the US bombing as a brutal act of terror against impoverished people: 'The bombing of Afghanistan is not revenge for New York and Washington. It is yet another act of terror against the people of the world. Each innocent person that is killed must be added to, not set off against, the grisly toll of civilians who died in New York and Washington.' According to her, the Americans had been traditionally using sheer force against smaller countries under different pretexts and listed such countries all the way from China in 1945–46, to Afghanistan in 2001. She felt that the brutalities being perpetrated against the helpless state were, in fact, linked with oil politics and a complex relationship that Washington had had with the Taliban. Both George Bush Jr. and Vice-president Dick Cheney had made a fortune working with the oil industry which had itself been linked with the Taliban. Roy raised a pertinent question:

> And what of the rest of us, the numb recipients of this onslaught of what we know to be preposterous propaganda? The daily consumers of the lies and brutality smeared in peanut butter and strawberry jam being airdropped into our minds just like those yellow food packets. Shall we look away and eat because we're hungry, or shall we stare unblinking at the grim theater unfolding in Afghanistan until we retch collectively and say, in one voice, that we have had enough?[4]

A whole range of specialists on Afghanistan, Political Islam and Osama bin Laden emerged on television screens, often seen voicing their

views on the war against terror.[5] Many serious analysts felt that the
Muslims had been put into a negative spotlight and especially the
early use of irresponsible terms like 'crusade', war of 'civilizations'
and 'value systems' unleashed racist attacks on Muslims, their
properties and mosques. For instance, William Dalrymple felt that in a
vengeful spree, the world had begun to misperceive Muslims as
perpetrators, whereas the heinous murder of 8000 Bosnian Muslims in
Srebrenica was never taken into account. He censured the analysts
trying to feed into misimages of Islam over the last decade: 'Anti-
Muslim racism now seems in many ways to be replacing anti-Semitism
as the principal Western expression of bigotry against "the other".'[6]
Such reviewers, while denouncing terrorist attacks and resultant deaths,
were pinpointing the significance of resolving the conflicts which
happened to cause volatility in the Muslim regions. The selection of
Afghanistan as a scapegoat, disproportionate use of military force,
enlargement of the campaign from Osama to the Taliban and to others,
angered those writers who felt that the United States and the United
Kingdom were indifferent to the Muslim predicament. Robert Fisk
saw no justification for this military action, which was causing a new
human catastrophe, and while checking past records, documented a
great sense of betrayal amongst Muslims across the board. Enumerating
various betrayals—from Lawrence of Arabia's promises to Reagan's
heightened interest in Afghanistan, hollow promises on Kashmir and
Bush's avowal for a new world order by resolving the enduring conflict
in Palestine—Fisk noted that the Muslims felt deeply cheated by the
West. To him, it was a serious crisis of credibility which would be
further compounded due to the multiplied human miseries in
Afghanistan.[7] Columnist Jonathan Freedland opined that the war on
Afghanistan did not follow any public debate and most Americans
were being offered naïve and simplistic explanations such as the
Taliban's policies towards their fellow Afghans and their harbouring
of Osama bin Laden. He lamented the absence of 'debate about rights
and wrongs of the war in Afghanistan—none at all. A single
congresswoman spoke out against it, she has been all but ostracised by
her Democratic colleagues.'[8] In fact, all across the Continent, many
analysts felt that not sufficient information on recent secret negotiations
between Washington and the Taliban centring on oil and gas resources
of the region was being made available to the American public. Instead,
a combined dose of patriotism, revenge, falsehood and jingoism was
being fed from top to bottom.[9]

MAZAR-I-SHARIF, AFGHANISTAN'S SREBRENICA

While London, Glasgow, Oxford, Birmingham, Manchester and other British and the European continent's cities and towns reverberated with weekly demonstrations, organised by coalitions against war and also participated by some members of Muslim communities, the visual media began to focus on the brutal aspects of war. The cluster bombs and daisy cutters, despite their apparent precision, were shown causing more and more civilian deaths, in addition to an outflow of the new refugees. The drought, civil war and now aerial bombing all added up to a major human catastrophe. The bombs hit civilian populations, Red Cross facilities and refugee convoys in a country which already lacked basic facilities, and had, for a long period, suffered from famine and extreme poverty. The public relations campaign was put into motion 'to humanise the war', though Tony Blair was rebuffed by the Syrian President in his whirlwind visit to elicit support for the Anglo-American alliance. The First Ladies highlighted the demonisation of the Taliban and their denigration of women's rights only to evoke further protests against the simultaneous Western protection of similar, other oil-rich states. Following the dissolution of Taliban authority in Mazar-i-Sharif, the fall of Kabul, as enthusiastically reported by BBC's John Simpson—later to apologise for his getting carried away—was officially interpreted as the vindication of this single-pronged strategy.[10] The arrival of the Northern Alliance in Kabul, largely due to support by aerial bombardment and weapons from Russia, India and Iran, led to two very important developments. Firstly, Professor Burhanuddin Rabbani aided by General Fahim—the two main Tajik contenders for Kabul—now ruled the post-Taliban northern Afghanistan with Rashid Dostum consolidated in Mazar-i-Sharif. Secondly, and more significantly, the new regime frowned upon the presence of one hundred SAS soldiers at the Bagram air base outside Kabul and disallowed the arrival of more British troops. Ironically, within a day of the rebuke, twelve Russian military planes flew in to offload Russian troops and security agents, taking everybody by surprise.[11] However, the Americans, without showing any pronounced interest in the reconstruction of Afghanistan, largely pursued a military campaign to eliminate Al Qaeda, Osama's organizaton, though Blair promised a sustained interest in post-war Afghanistan.

After the fall of Mazar-i-Sharif and Kabul, facilitated by the Northern Alliance, the attention focused on Kunduz, a largely Pushtun town on the strategic road between Kabul and Mazar-i-Sharif. American troops, CIA personnel and the SAS advised the forces of the Northern Alliance on how to deal with the remnants of the Taliban and their Arab, Pakistani and Chechen supporters, who had been drawn in to fight a holy war against the Americans but had, instead, found themselves confronted by fellow Afghans. The negotiations between the Taliban and Dostum, the warlord from Mazar-i-Sharif notorious for his past brutalities, went on for a few days, until the Taliban decided to surrender on 25 November. The non-Afghan prisoners of war were largely disarmed and taken to Qala-i-Jangi—the personal fortress of Dostum where they were interrogated by the two CIA *apartchiks*. These POWs, in many cases, had their hands tied behind their backs and were put in a small, isolated area of the fortress. Inflamed by the CIA probe and worried about their own safety, given the lack of communication, some of them reportedly revolted, to which the captors panicked. Allegedly, when the POWs subdued a CIA agent, his colleague sought aerial help from US forces who sent in gunships and B52s to carpet-bomb the besieged POWs. Within a few hours, at least six hundred POWs lay dead with the hands of many of them still tied up. Despite the early calls by the Red Cross, Pakistan, Mary Robinson and others, US troops and the SAS elements not only facilitated the siege but also ensured large-scale slaughter.[12] The stories of the mass murder relayed through the German television crew and by other journalists made headlines in the last week of November causing grave embarrassment. Amnesty International, Human Rights Watch and other notable groups across the world criticised Western official complicity in this mass slaughter. They sought explanations for the events leading to the mass killings, number of prisoners killed, and the circumstances leading to the looting of the dead bodies.[13] In addition, they demanded details on this four-day long incident where the trapped POWs were so mercilessly massacred.[14] Tanks were rolled over the dead bodies of the POWs, whose hands were quickly unbound before Western journalists or Red Cross representatives could take pictures.[15] By the weekend, it was clear that the massacre at Qala-i-Jangi, outside Mazar-i-Sharif, had claimed hundreds of POWs in immensely brutal conditions through a close-range military operation carried out from the ground and the air. On American advice, boiling oil was rushed in to kill the few remaining POWs hiding in the gutters four days after the main slaughter.[16] Isabel Hilton, while challenging efforts to gloss over the tragedy, raised several important questions in her column. According to official sources, the CIA's probe of some non-Afghan POWs on their reasons for being in the country had provoked the revolt, which she found unconvincing: 'No doubt, the CIA is full of gallant figures,' she wrote skeptically, 'careless of their own safety, but this story seems preposterous. If they wanted to interrogate prisoners why did they not remove them to a place of interrogation singly or in twos?' She further asks herself if the volunteers 'were led into a trap in the fort, then provoked into rebellion once they realised that the promises they had been given were hollow.'[17] An editorial in *The Guardian* noted three major problems with respect to the Qala-i-Jangi tragedy: firstly, the POWs were not held in a way that was conducive to their security or to that of their captors. Secondly, the force used against them for four days raised 'big questions about the true aims of the Northern Alliance and of the US and British Special Forces who were involved.' Thirdly, while the US policies may have been driven by revenge, the same cannot be assumed about the British, and thus their involvement raises serious questions. The British Parliament was requested for a probe of the political and humanitarian aspects of the conflict, so as to seek 'hard answers to the hard questions from Qala.'[18] In the House of Commons, during the Prime Minster's Question Hour, there was no debate about the massacre at Qala-i-Jangi, and the only single point raised by a concerned MP was about the one-eyed lion in the Kabul Zoo. The few charred, starved and skeletal survivors—including an American—were discovered almost five days after the catastrophe, though ironically the attention by then had shifted to Kandahar, Tora Bora and a new spate of violence in the Middle East.

BUZKASHI IN AFGHANISTAN

Following the dissolution of Taliban power in the northern, western and eastern region, the Anglo-American alliance forces concentrated on Kandahar, the last Taliban stronghold and the home of their leader, Mullah Muhammad Omar. By early December, American troops had encircled Kandahar and it was feared that here the Western troops may be used to eliminate the Taliban and their non-Pushtun supporters. When Hamid Karzai, the Pushtun leader, offered general amnesty to all, including the Taliban, on 6 December 2001, London and Washington reacted with anger. It appears as if the Western powers, especially the United States, were expecting a major engagement resulting in large-scale elimination of Taliban personnel. Otherwise, to them, the entire campaign costing billions and hyped up emotions did not offer anything tangible to be shown to their own public. It was immaterial to them how millions of refugees had been added to the already three million in Pakistan and Iran, whereas the entire landscape had been irreparably downgraded by cluster bombing and other laser-guided devices. While Kandahar was being decimated through a sustained bombing, the cave complex at Tora Bora in eastern Afghanistan near Jalalabad, received continuous US aerial bombing and pounding by the local allies. Initially, Dick Cheney and other senior officials had proclaimed that Osama and his followers were 'holed up' in these caves, originally built by the CIA to engage the Soviets. The local tribal chieftains were induced through money and other temptations to mount attacks on the mountainous caves. The strategy pursued by the Anglo-American alliance in Afghanistan seemed to be twin-pronged: total decimation of the infrastructure including some civilian areas followed by a ground offensive mainly launched through the surrogate rival Afghan forces. Logistical and technical support was made available through the CIA, SAS and other Special Forces to direct the anti-Taliban constellations. Once having cleansed the region of the Taliban, the Western elements would move on leaving the towns and the POWs at the express mercy of the victorious warlords. This policy of 'divide and destroy' aimed at avoiding Western causalities and military blunders such as those committed by the Soviet Union when operating as the occupying force that had allowed the disparate groups to unite against a common foe.

In Kandahar, while carrying out a holistic bombardment of the city, Anglo-American troops helped Pushtun warlords like Gul Agha Sherazi to close in on the last Taliban stronghold. The American aerial bombardment killed at least 10,000 people along with an almost total destruction of the city.[19] Any Afghan fleeing on a vehicle was targeted by American marines and SAS scouting around Kandahar. The stories of rape, summary executions, looting and kidnap for ransom by the reemergence of the warlords such as Gul Agha or Dostum were simply glossed over. The parleys at Bonn on the future political set-up of Afghanistan offered a beam of hope but given the past record, many objective analysts worried that being a failed state, Afghanistan may soon revert to regionalism and heinous warlordism. General Rashid

Dostum distanced himself from the Bonn formula of an interim government of twenty-nine people by saying that he had not been given enough shares in the interim power structure. Gulbaddin Hekmatyar and Pir Ahmed Shah Gilani—the two opposition Pushtun leaders in exile—also criticised the Tajik leadership for taking eighteen out of twenty-nine ministerial posts. The promises of a possible $5 billion reconstruction package increased mutual rivalries, further fanning tribal and factionalist dissension. By the summer of 2004, neither Osama nor Mullah Omar had been arrested, whereas the military campaign initiated in late September went on claiming its toll. In June 2002, the operation had dangerously involved the tribal areas of Pakistan, especially the Waziristan Agency. Amidst the India-Pakistani escalations, Western pressure on Pakistan remained unmitigated and the generals were urged to use Pakistani troops again Pushtun elements supportive of the Taliban. This was for the first time that Pakistan had sent its troops into the autonomous tribal belt since their withdrawal in August 1947. Failing to accomplish any mentionable mission and inflicted by the controversy of inaction and the contradictory roles of peacemakers and of warring party, the British government also decided to withdraw most of its troops in July 2002. Several of them had never shot a single bullet nor had encountered any Taliban resistance. It appeared as if Afghanistan was once again being left on its own after extensive and rather misplaced military operations. The convening of the Loya Jirga of 1500 tribal elders on 11–13 June offered legitimacy to Karzai's regime and a pronounced voice to Afghan women. They valiantly rebuked Rabbani and the other warlords for spawning unnecessary deaths and destruction in the country and making so many widows and orphans. Earlier, the former king, Zahir Shah, had voluntarily decided against seeking any leadership role much to the chagrin of his Pushtun supporters. Karzai's immediate challenge, other than reconstruction of the war ravaged country, was to pacify the ambitious Tajik commanders and their Uzbek rivals who wanted to control their respective regions besides acquiring important cabinet positions. Kabul's new rulers were faced with a formidable challenge of seeking a balancing point between external pressures and domestic dissensions. Amidst a pervasive though lessening goodwill, the challenge appeared mightier by each passing day. The Karzai experience could have proved to be a formative transition for the country if he had been able to establish peace by engaging various ethnic groups along with reconstructing an institutional infrastructure within the country. His immediate priorities could have included an effective end to the US militarism, and an all-encompassing reconciliation simultaneous with a massive reconstruction programme. From his own safety to these two goals, he was largely dependent upon external forces whose own sustained but sagacious involvement could have saved this tormented country from further turbulence. However, in 2004, Afghanistan was still waiting for the delivery of funds and visible indications of the Western will to implement the reconstruction projects, especially in the wake of the Anglo-American focus on Iraq. Though Karzai was able to receive revenues from some warlords, the country needed more resources, a cross-ethnic consensus and an efficient security apparatus to put it back on the road to reconstruction. His visit to London on 3 June 2003 coincided with the Kabul troops confronting the Taliban in one of the fiercest battles near Kandahar. In the meantime, people in Afghanistan were, once again, internalising a grave sense of betrayal over the rest of the world walking away from them. By the late summer, owing to partisan policies, lack of any major external support for proper reconstruction, and also due to obduracy by the Northern Alliance leaders such as General Fahim Khan, Karzai's efficacy in Kabul had come under the spotlight. In the meantime, the disgruntled Pushtun elements had begun to intensify their guerrilla attacks on the Kabul regime's troops. The deployment of NATO troops—for the first time, outside Europe—was a significant new development, focusing on security while eliminating Al Qaeda remnants. It appeared as if the vengeful American military campaign, duly helped by Tony Blair, despite its high sounding moralism and generous promises, was never going to progress beyond a military venture and a few token measures. The fact remains that a peaceful and stable Afghanistan could be a major socio-economic bridge between Southern and Central Asia minimising threats to regional security.

ISLAMOPHOBIA AND THE ENEMY WITHIN

The selection of Afghanistan for a massive and sustained aerial bombardment, support for its factionalism, large-scale slaughter of the Pushtuns and their non-Afghan supporters, the muzzling of civil liberties within the United States and other Western democracies, the arraignment of hundreds of Muslim immigrants and a constant spotlight on Muslim religious places and rituals made it look like a massive operation. Western leaders tried to underplay the premise of a clash of civilisations, but Muslim fears and anger remained evident, especially of an uncalled for eagerness to invade Iraq.[20] Several Muslim individuals or their look-alikes were targeted for physical violence and verbal abuse, and a few mosques were vandalised. A mosque in South Shields, England, had graffiti on it, saying: 'Revenge America: Kill a Muslim Today', whereas a young scarved Muslim woman was attacked by a groups of youths in Swindon.[21] In the United States, a sweeping wave of patriotism, underlined by racist and Christian undertones, made it difficult for Muslims to offer their viewpoint. A number of immigrants were arrested or harassed by the FBI and CIA on suspicion, which reminded people of *relocation camps* for Japanese-Americans during the Second World War. According to John Ashcroft, the US Attorney General, more than six hundred Muslims of Arab and South Asian origin had been arrested for interrogation purposes. The number of Pakistanis itself was 208.[22] Within the West, the Muslim minorities felt further depressed and marginalised, whereas many analysts opined that this upsurge in anti-Muslim feelings symbolised a 'new anti-Semitisim'.[23] This is not the place to delineate the predicament as well as the prospects of the Muslim Diaspora but a mention needs to be made of the various investigative reports on the subject. The Runneymede Trust, in its landmark report (1997), had highlighted a widespread anti-Muslim idiom and the continued marginalisation of British Muslims. *Islamophobia* documents conflicting views of Islam and the political and social ghettoisation of the Muslim communities amidst an institutional peripheralisation that does not help the policies towards a more harmonious and egalitarian pluralism.[24] The developments since September have dangerously added to xenophobia in the Western democracies, helping the ultra-right and avowedly racist parties in gaining centre stage position. The strains on pluralism have multiplied with strong anti-asylum sentiments. Despite the fact that only a trickle of the asylum seekers were reaching Western Europe, the media, public and popular reaction remained highly pronounced with the EU turning into a formidable Fortress Europe.

While there is an acknowledged socio-economic unevenness in the inter-community relationship in the Western Europe, as was borne out by elections in France, Austria, Denmark, or in the North of England, still it may be wrong to assume that Muslims are totally incapacitated and that the Western societies and states are racist both by intent and content. The democratic processes, inter-faith dialogue and a continuous self-questioning by several opinion groups are positive indicators for better alternatives. In the same vein, the Muslim attitudes—either out of apologia or mere frustration—do not reflect the sentiments of 'the silent majority'. It is, however, ironic that only the extreme views, as expressed by marginal groups such as Al-Muhajiroon or of a few extreme clerics, always receive more media coverage on the presumption that they represent the entire community. There is a curious and equally dangerous game played all the time between media props and the extreme Muslim elements that excel in using each other to create more sensational and exaggerated profiles. Thus, the daily reports on certain clerics or the presumptions on a large number of British Muslims in Afghanistan volunteering against the British forces, simply increased the societal chasms. Like Le Pen in France and Fonteyn in Holland, the BNP even tried to create a wedge between British Muslims and other ethnic communities. Their propaganda literature and other communications addressed certain Hindu and Sikh elements including the Vishwa Hindu Parishad (VHP); that the former's campaign was against Muslims and not against them. It was nefariously suggested that the war was against Islamic terrorism and not against immigrants. This campaign had its impact at various levels; for instance, under the VHP's pressure, Sunrise Radio in Southall stopped calling itself the Asian network

Whereas an absolute majority in the Muslim Diaspora condemned the terrorist events, they, by similar proportions, refused to support military strikes on Afghanistan or Iraq. These opinion groups were not the supporters of the Taliban nor did they support Al Qaeda or Saddam Hussein, rather it was felt that the Western governments, in most cases, had themselves created such monsters and were now out to punish entire societies *per se* for the crime of a few. In the same manner, the Western inaction over Israeli militarism and disregard for the UN resolutions on Palestine and Kashmir or the Russian campaign against Chechnya were seen as opportunistic. Thus, Muslim anger was directed both against the terrorists and the states now inflicting misery upon ordinary and innocent masses. Serious Muslims felt that Osama bin Laden and such elements could have been extricated selectively rather than mounting mass-scale annihilative campaigns. Muslims in the West have largely felt helpless while caught between the authoritarian Muslim regimes and their own longing for peaceful and prosperous societies in the Muslim world. Muslim helplessness and frustration, as felt intermittently in the cases of Bosnia, Palestine, Chechnya, Kashmir, Iraq and Afghanistan made them mindful of their own absence from the larger political picture. Despite huge numbers— seven million in the United States and about one and a half million in the United Kingdom—Muslims, unlike some other ethno-religious lobbies, have been unable to register any impact on the foreign policies of these countries. The Muslim Diaspora in the West overwhelmingly shares a sheer sense of marginalisation and despair and the intermittent human and ecological tragedies in all these places only affirmed this helplessness. A massive invasion of Iraq by British and American troops irreverant of global opinion and international law, Ariel Sharon's unrestricted campaign against the Palestinians, increased military operations in Kashmir and Chechnya conjoined by a greater confusion amongst the younger generation have collectively anguished Muslim communities. While during the months of *Ramadhan* and *Muharram*, there were more Muslims praying and fasting, they, like their counterparts in the Muslim world, felt perplexed over the rising tide of violence against Muslims as well as the fragmentation from within. The 57-nation Organisation of the Islamic Conference and the United Nations were seen totally helpless before the prerogatives of powers such as the United States and Britain. With the darkening war over Western and South-western Asia, and the possibility of a nuclear threat and increased terrorism, the UN simply remained inactive and the Gujarat massacres in India or the invasion of Iraq failed to register any assertive condemnation. Under these testing circumstances, several Muslim youths moved towards fundamentalist extremes while many more espoused self-denial. The elements left in between vacillated between a growing Islamic consciousness and a bleak helplessness.

The overwhelming Muslim view—both in the Diaspora and elsewhere—stipulates that the conflicts in the Middle East and Asia might have caused grievous events of terror but it still did not warrant massive military campaigns against Afghanistan and Iraq. Muslim groups like the Muslim Council of Britain (MCB), Muslim Association of Britain (MAB) and Islamic Human Rights Commission (IHRC) and magazines such as *Muslim News, Impact* and *Q News*, or Pakistani, Arab and Bangladeshi television channels based in London or similar other stations in France and Germany condemned the terrorist attacks but felt that the reaction itself was unleashing further terror. The Anglo-American equation of terror with Iraq even without tangible proof was further discomforting. While Muslim moderates felt that Islam was a religion of peace and that various fundamentalist outfits used it for their own narrowly defined or misdirected purposes, Western perceptions of Islam, in general, were not positive. The sudden outburst of Western anger at the Taliban was not out of any moral reason or some fondness for Afghan men and women, rather it had complex geo-political reasons including the Central Asian oil and gas reserves worth five trillion dollars. Programmes on the Taliban's repressive anti-gender policies were seen not as altruist adjudicators but mere propaganda ploys to justify war and vengeance being wreaked on an incapacitated society. The British-American disregard for humanitarian concerns and Clare Short's total turn-around from her early criticism of the aerial bombardment to its vehment support, were all viewed as being part and parcel of a sustained, arrogant and equally vengeful military campaign.

However, it will be futile to posit that the military and public opinion campaign mounted by the Western governments, and certain specific lobbies aimed at neutralising the Muslim factor, did not have any redeeming facets. By default, it posited more attention to the issues of racism, hierarchical system of allocating jobs and other facilities to some over the rest within the entire gambit of multi-culturalism. Though the campaign's negative imprints outweigh any positive outcome, the greater curiosity for Islam as a religion of resistance and the underprivileged nature of the Muslim communities elicited some increased interest. While many xenophobic elements immersed themselves in a 'told-you-so' attitude, and the Muslims came under greater pressure, pushing the community towards increased segregation, a modicum of introspection also emerged in the process. While serious commentators sought politico-economic factors behind the apparent fundamentalist tapestry, Muslims themselves in growing numbers analysed the political models of Islam. The Saudi, Iranian or Taliban models of Islamicity were found wanting in clarity, greater regard for human rights and democratic nomenclatures. In the same manner, the regimes including those of generals and dynasts attracted more ire. Some Muslim intellectuals, in their community seminars and private meetings, resented the hold of obscurantists on Islamic discourses, both in the Diaspora and elsewhere. Many enlightened Muslims felt that the Muslim communities needed to be greatly politicised and liberated from societal and statist authoritarianism. How far such a discourse may be crucial, remains to be seen.

SOUTH ASIA AND THE WAR ON AFGHANISTAN

The anti-war demonstrations in India, Bangladesh and Pakistan stemmed from a number of sources. South Asia, home to large Muslim population sections, felt a stronger sense of solidarity with their poor and hapless co-religionists from across the Khyber Pass. But the anger was not just confined to Muslims, as many humanists—even in the West—felt that the United States was stubbornly intent upon wreaking vengeance upon an already devastated country, using it as a scapegoat. Huge demonstrations in Calcutta, Delhi, Dhaka, Srinagar, Karachi and Rawalpindi, though under-reported in the Western media, displayed anger as well as helplessness over the trans-regional action of the United States, joined by an overwhelming number of leaders from the developing world. In India, the *Imam* of the Badshahi Mosque tried to personify the Indian Muslim anger, much to the annoyance of many secular elements while in Bangladesh, some religio-political elements tried to idealise Osama bin Laden as a great hero. With the rout of the Awami League in the recent elections in Bangladesh, such sections used the opportunity to reach the masses by making Afghanistan, a major *Muslim* issue. Anti-Americanism, Political Islam, and global pacifism all seemed to join in together to seek an end to the military campaign against Afghanistan. The Anglo-American campaign against Iraq, despite massive public disapproval and global skepticism, also revealed the vulnerability of the post-Westphalia system, including the UN.

In Pakistan itself, the overwhelming majority feared more miseries and refugees, and detected brutal vengeance within the American campaign. The anger came from the realisation that, once again, a Muslim nation was being tormented because of the presumed crimes of a few, whereas the Israeli brutalisation of the Palestinians and the Indian aggression against Muslim Kashmiris remained unchecked. Some critics felt that the United States, run by hawkish elements, was contemplating 'turkey shoots' through encouraging intra-Afghan warfare, besides a massive bombardment from the air, while being heedless of its human cost. Pakistanis worried about further regional instability, and given the porous borders, feared that the retreating Taliban might end up in their tribal belt. The two factions of the Jamiat-i-Ulema-i-Islam (JUI)—a Deobandi religio-political party—and the Jama'at-i-Islami (JI) tried to make it a populist issue but the military regime was able to contain their campaign. The involvement of Western troops in Afghanistan and reports of a joint Israeli, Indian and American covert action to snatch Pakistani nuclear warheads had stirred Jihadi sentiment amongst the Pushtun tribals, whose fiery leader, Maulana Sufi Mohammad from Malakand led a huge group into Afghanistan to help the predominantly Pushtun Taliban. Islamabad avoided stopping the tribal *lashkar*, though the subsequent rout of these tribal enthusiasts vindicated the regime, despite its limited maneuverability, on the safety of these 'misguided' Pakistanis besieged in Mazar-i-Sharif, Herat, Kunduz, and elsewhere. However, the JUI, JI and Sufi Mohammad's Shariat Movement were deeply embarrassed at irresponsibly leading so many enthusiasts on a killing spree into Afghanistan's imbroglio, while the Taliban themselves had opted to surrender. The fall of Kabul to the Northern Alliance (United Front) was viewed across Pakistan as an American strategy, despite prior assurances to Musharraf to the contrary. Pakistanis wanted post-Taliban Kabul to be demilitarised under a UN-led peace keeping force until a broad-based government had been formed. US persistence in bombing the Taliban even after their dissolution was seen as a possible elimination of a trans-tribal Pushtun factor from within the Afghan body politic. The reemergence of the regional warlords and resumption of internecine warfare immensely worried concerned Pakistanis. The Russian, Iranian and Indian assistance being rushed to the Northern Alliance amidst the marginalisation of Pushtun elements, only intensified consternation in Islamabad.[25] However, the Bonn resolution of an interim arrangement led by Hamid Karzai, a Pushtun leader, was seen to be a positive alternative to a totally Tajik-Uzbek dominated Kabul.

While Pakistani support for the Taliban had not been merely confined to Pushtun elements of the JUI, JI, or the totally Pushtun party of Mullah Sufi, their sympathizers from elsewhere in Pakistan were mostly the *madrassa*-related youths who had earlier begun to idealise Taliban ascendancy and their comparatively dramatic rise over and above the ethno-tribal schisms. Now, the quick dissolution of the Taliban deeply shocked them and earned a conviction for Mullah Sufi and some others for instigating violence. However, within the military regime itself, the pro-Taliban supporters were equally shocked and hurt. Though Musharraf had sidelined such elements through an early purge, yet public criticism of the ISI and its monopolist and rather dangerous hold on Pakistan's foreign policy worried articulate public opinion.[26] Despite pervasive perceptions, Pakistani official support for the Taliban, in fact, had been wavering since 1998, though Islamabad continued to deal with them. Despite the various hypotheses on their origin, such as oil politics, and support from the CIA and ISI, the Taliban represented a streak in the dominant Pushtun ethnic groups, who had initially promised stability and peace in the war-stricken country.[27] During 1992–96, the Northern Alliance, led by Professor Burhanuddin Rabbani and Ahmad Shah Masood, had disappointed everybody whereas the Taliban promised to end regional warlordism and factionalist fighting.[28] However, having once recognised them, Pakistanis and other allies could not contain the Taliban zealotry, and their hospitality to Osama bin Laden added to existing strains. Pakistani diplomats in Kabul during the Taliban phase, as revealed in the seized papers from Kabul by the *New York Times,* had frequently expressed frustration and helplessness over the Taliban's policies.[29]

Amidst a persistent and rather unmitigated bombing campaign in eastern Afghanistan, the anti-American and anti-Western feelings increased in South Asia. Not only did Waziristan and other tribal agencies such as Mohmand in the semi-autonomous regions on the Frontier become restive, their sympathisers elsewhere plotted to focus on Western establishments across Pakistan. Pakistan was compelled by the Americans to use its troops against its tribals, who were being accused of harbouring Al Qaeda or Taliban. This pressure came at a time when India amassed her troops on the borders, demanding a total reversal of the Pakistani stance on Kashmir. A number of Pakistani troops and tribal citizens died in these battles, as Pakistan engaged her forces against the tribals for the first time since 1947. Ironically, for many Pakistanis, the Western policies were either totally partisan or simply lacked a holisitic dimension to resolve this conflict. Thus, Musharraf's Pakistan found itself fighting on several fronts and the terrorists geared themselves to implement their anti-Western agenda of killing Western personnel and damaging their establishments. The murder of Daniel Pearl, an American journalist, in 2002, the terrorist attack on a church in Islamabad in April, the bomb blast at a hotel in Karachi in May, and a suicide attack on the US consulate in Karachi on 14 June 2002, remained unclaimed acts of terror. The Karachi hotel blast killed twelve French technicians as well as several Pakistanis, whereas the suicide attack on the consulate claimed twelve lives and injured more than forty-five—all of them Pakistani nationals. This new trend of a selective, unclaimed and astutely planned bombing campaign ushers in a new phase being pursued by anti-Western groups to vent their anger on Western policies towards the Muslim world. Western criticism of Pakistan over her stance and policies on Kashmir was perceived as Indian appeasement and sheer opportunism directed against a Muslim ally. Many serious Pakistanis during 2002–03 felt that their country had become a battleground following the ill-planned and directionless 'war against terror' at a time when their situation needed more sensitivity from Washington and London. Ironically, the anti-terror campaign was hurting a predominantly Muslim population more than anybody else.

In India, the dramatic events of 11 September offered a greater opportunity to join in the world chorus to condemn terrorist groups, mainly to deny Pakistan the 'strategic depth' that it had acquired through a friendly regime in Kabul. The loss of Kabul to predominantly Pushtun Taliban was a great blow for Delhi, which had seen its interests further dwindle sharply in Central Asia, following the dissolution of the Soviet Union. India, instead of consolidating the bilateral dialogue established at Agra in July, attempted to categorize both the Kashmiri militants and Pakistan as terrorists. The BJP-led regime volunteered three bases to the United States, though Washington found Pakistan's location more congenial. Several statements by hawkish elements, especially by George Fernandes and a few measures such as a botched hijack attempt did not cause any major rupture in the new US-Pakistani alignment. With the arrival of the Northern Alliance, India, like Iran and Russia, found an opportunity to reestablish its influence in Kabul and Indian diplomats rushed to Afghanistan, whereas Pakistan was rather sidelined. Ironically, the Afghanistan crisis only intensified Indo-Pakistan rivalry, as it appeared that the new contestation had already vetoed the gains made at Agra. The amassing of Indian troops for months on Pakistani borders was seen as a multi-pronged strategy, seeking more concessions from an unstable Pakistan and to divert attention from the anti-Muslim riots in Gujarat. In addition, the BJP hawks sought to court greater public opinion within India by humbling Pakistan and critiquing Kashmiri activists. In Pakistan, Indian policy all through 2001–02 was perceived to be anchored on revenge and opportunism, seeking a pound of flesh at a time when the Western powers were pursuing a single-item agenda in Western Asia, irreverent to Pakistan's security concerns. The thaw appeared to take place in the summer of 2003, following the restoration of some confidence-building measures and Prime Minister Vajpayee's desire to establish peace in the region.

The fall of the Taliban has equally generated an interesting debate within Pakistan on a few significant issues. First, there was a debate on the future set-up in Kabul, though Islamabad demanded a broad-based regime. The mechanics of such an arrangement and the leadership of an interim regime, as was witnessed in the Bonn Conference, remained quite crucial for Pakistan. This discussion was not merely confined to Pakistan, as at one stage, even both London and Washington differed on the future Western role vis-à-vis Kabul.[30] Many elements felt that, given the past contacts with Rabbani and others, Pakistan must offer new incentives to the United Front, and should not wait any longer for a new coalition to emerge. Pakistan's role in the future economic reconstruction of Afghanistan and her links with Zahir Shah, Hamid Karzai and Yunas Khalis—the three main Pushtun figures—also gave hope to such opinions. Eschewing bitterness over the fall and fragmentation of the Pushtun elements was advised by pragmatists. Also, civic groups began criticising the total control by intelligence agencies and a small group of individuals over Pakistan's foreign policy, sometimes even in conflict with the larger national interest. The military regime, basically a status quoist bureaucracy, did not seem willing to broaden the debate on the country's vital domestic and regional policies. Second, there was a genuine concern that Pakistan's traditional enemy, India, had stolen a march over the former by offering military and economic assistance to Kabul. Some Pakistani politicians feared that 'by donning uniforms of the Northern Alliance, the Indian soldiers will now be confronting us in the Khyber Pass.'[31] Marginalisation in Afghanistan meant losing the entire Central Asia region, besides the serious security ramifications on the eastern borders, 'without gaining anything tangible in return.'[32] The decisions to be taken in respect of such vital issues were considered to be a major threat within several Pakistani circles thus further isolating General Musharraf, who through his ill-thought policies such as a referendum on 30 April 2002, appeared vulnerable. His Legal Framework Order (LFO), stipulating vital discretionary amendments in the Constitution preempted the October 2002 elections and exacerbated public uproar against his policies. He was perceived to be dependent on American support besides his army constituency. The opposition to Musharraf and America resulted in greater electoral support for religio-political parties. The spring of 2003 saw massive demonstrations on Iraq across Pakistan with simultaneous sloganeering against Washington and Musharraf. Pakistani opposition in the parliament became quite restive, both on the constitutional amendments and Islamabad's closer alliance with Washington over vital issues. Soon, the cleric-dominated Frontier's provincial assembly surprised Islamabad with its *Sharia* enactment, raising tensions between the centre and Peshawar.

The most crucial fall-out of the Afghan crisis for India was a greater intensification of ideological debate on Indian identity. While initially, many Indian nationalists and secularists saw the dissolution of Taliban power as a positive development, the subsequent introspection offered diverse scenarios, varying from a new great game in that country to increased demands on Indian Muslims to prove their loyalty towards Indian nationalism. The BJP presented itself to the outside world as a progressive party totally against terrorism, while domestically, it pursued its campaign to change the ideological moorings of Indian society and nationhood. The policy to change textbooks was pursued vehemently to the discomfort of many liberal elite. The BJP government was accused of the 'Talibanisation of textbook history,' through preening books of certain important material so as to strengthen Hindutva.[33] The debate between the Hindutva supporters and the secular group over the parameters and props of the Indian identity gained a newer momentum. Many of the secular and non-communal historians felt that through misinterpretation of its early history and misappropriation and expropriation of its recent past, the plural country was being pushed towards a fascist extreme. In a paper at a convention, Romila Thapar observed that the Vedic past was being exaggerated to suit the present day exclusionary nationalism, whereas the context was being willfully neglected. The recasting of history texts to suit Hindutva, to her, by default meant reviving the Orientalist discourse of the colonial era where India was shown as being totally incapacitated, until the Raj had revived her through a timely and scientific redefinition. She alerted the non-BJP states within India to rise to the occasion and resist this totalitarian assault on India's plural heritage and simultaneously alerted the secular elements to redefine their own ideological formulation. To her, *Sangh Parivar* presented a grave threat to Indian identity by producing 'garbled texts', and in its single-minded pursuit of romanticisation of the Vedic past, was wasting resources on promoting astrology beyond reasonable pedagogic limits. She also censured NRIs (Non-Resident Indians) for romanticising obscurantism and externalising their own diasporic identity problem to India. She differentiated between 'the open

Hinduism' and its hijacked version, which she called 'syndicated Hinduism'.[34] Another commentator compared both the Indian and Pakistani history texts to suggest that both were pursuing similar, unilateral and exclusionary policies, and denying a holistic knowledge to their younger generations. The views on Hinduism in Pakistan and on Islam in India were mostly negative and ended up supporting exclusionary nationalism besides adding to India-Pakistan polarity.[35] While the secular elements in Bangladesh felt greater strains on pluralism with an increased resentment towards the Hindu minority due to the idealisation of Osama bin Laden, in Pakistan, the English press and human rights groups demanded a more assertive policies on the *madrassa* culture. Despite a pervasive sympathy for ordinary Afghans, moderate Pakistanis felt happy over the break-down of the military-mullah axis, though they worried about its return at some possible juncture due to the army's single-minded pursuit of depoliticisation of the nation.

The events in Afghanistan may be seen through numerous prisms. On the one hand, it could be interpreted as a simple case of a super power scapegoating a poor country, while some may ascribe it to the tumultuous polarity between two civilisations. The more balanced view could locate a multiplicity of factors and forces propping trajectories like the Bush administration or the Taliban phenomenon. However, traditional scholarship in areas like political science and international relations may stay focused on state-based analyses, while anthropologists may seek a reinforcement of their theoretical paradigms, focusing on the distinctness of the trans-Indus regions. The early country-based studies by Adamec, Gregorian, Dupree, Elliot, Roy, and Rubin have to be re-read with the more recent ones on the Taliban by Rashid, Marsden, Malet, Corbin, Matinuddin, and Griffin, focusing on the extra-territorial role of the CIA, regional actors and oil politics. In addition, the Taliban factor may remain crucial in the years to come, on the back of Pushtun nationalism and a liberationist ideology of ridding Afghanistan of non-Muslim troops and their surrogates in Kabul. Political Islam will find comfortable company with hurt Pushtun nationalism, and will be seeking for an opportunity to stage a comeback, especially when the American troops move out of the country and Karzai's promises remain unfulfilled. A new alliance of warlords with newer incentives for power sharing, strengthened by anti-Western sentiment, may help the Taliban or a similar dispensation to come about. In other words, Pushtun majoritarianism, justified through post-1997 salience, helped by anti-foreign discourse could rekindle a new form of *buzkashi* in the country, unless Afghanistan does not experience another 'walk-away', and the external powers remain fully engaged in its reconstruction. Some reports during the summer of 2003 even hinted towards the resurgence of the Taliban in league with Pusthun warlords such as Gulbaddin Hekmatyar, with Karzai's control confined to Kabul. His personal dependence upon American personnel for security and a continued financial crisis did not bode well for his regime. The Pushtun majority remained resentful and restive over the *de facto* monopoly of the Northern Alliance in the new set-up. Iraq had already begun to replace Afghanistan as the main preoccupation for the Anglo-American leaders, though Straw, in his visit to Kabul and Kandahar on the heels of Karzai's high-profile visit to the West in May-June 2003, was meant to reiterate closer mutualities.

In March-April 2003, American and British tanks rolled across the ancient land of Babylon to dislodge Saddam Hussein who had held on to power ruthlessly for the past two decades after having led his population into a series of unnecessary and costly wars. The world witnessed thousands of tons of the latest devices exploding over another Muslim country, killing its people by the thousands and destroying its ecological and historical heritage. By the rivers of the Euphrates and Tigris, once again, the hordes of Anglo-American troops, posing as latter-day Crusaders, geared up for an assault led by the latter-day 'Lion Hearts'—Blair and Bush—whose cultural and moral righteousness knew no bounds. They were seeking the overthrow of a tyrant whose weapons of mass destruction presumably posed a serious threat to global security. The travesty was that neither the United Nations nor global public opinion had validated this unilateral military campaign. Neither could the Anglo-American troops discover any arsenal of mass destruction, instead they multiplied severe human hardships. A country already exhausted by unnecessary wars and a decade-long period of sanctions interspersed with the frequent Anglo-American aerial bombardment surreally was made a target of history's most debilitating military campaign from land, air and the sea. The unexplained objectives included the conquest of the oil-rich Middle East before the rag-tag Islamicists could overthrow the surrogate, dictatorial Gulf regimes, notorious for kowtowing to the West and brutalising their own people. In addition, it aimed at serving the Neo-Conservatives in the United States, drumming up anti-Muslim hysteria before the commonly-held Second Coming of Christ. Moreover, the venture was equally aimed at bolstering Israel's security besides reinvigorating the sagging American economy by helping corporate interests. In a nerve-tinging game of psychological warfare, for Saddam Hussein, his enemies were the Mongols, reincarnate, whereas to the latter he was a Hitler who understood only the language of force. Both the adversaries used religious symbols and cashed in on xenophobic forms of moralism and patriotism. The ordinary Iraqis, like their Afghan counterparts, nevertheless experienced 'turkey shoots', sanctioned by George W. Bush and his hawkish team of Donald Rumsfeld, Dick Cheney, Condoleezza Rice, Paul Wolfowitz, Richard Perle and several others. The Anglo-American alliance had already lost the battle for the hearts, though after 9/11, there was a universal sympathy for America in particular. While the invasion united the Iraqis—both Shia and Sunni—it equally turned Osama bin Laden, Mullah Omar, and Saddam Hussein into symbols of the disempowered Muslim masses. The invasion of Iraq with its powerful moralist undertones and open advocacy from the Christian and Judaic lobbies in the United States, despite a strong reprimand from the Pope and Nelson Mandela, aggravated inter-faith dissension. The former US president, Jimmy Carter, felt that the United States, under a Republican leadership, was losing global support besides sacrificing several other long-held precepts. Not only did the military action lack an 'international authority', it was going 'to undermine the UN as a viable institution for world peace'. Carter further opined: 'The heartfelt sympathy and friendship offered to America after the 9/11 attacks, even from formerly antagonistic regimes, has been largely dissipated; increasingly unilateral and domineering policies have brought international trust in our country to its lowest level in memory.'[36] The military campaign earned global denunciation because of its moral and constitutional illegality and the harrowing destruction caused to the Iraqi populace though these critics were not supporting Saddam Hussein's policies. The Anglo-American earnestness for a regime change in Baghdad signalled partisan, dangerous and hegemonic intentions, vetoing proper human exigencies, as warned by President Fidel Castro in his speech to the summit of the Non-Aligned Movement at Kuala Lumpur:

The world is being drawn into a dead end. Within hardly 150 years, the oil and gas it took the planet 300 million years to accumulate will have been depleted. In just one hundred years, the world population has grown from 1.5 billion to over 6 billion people, who will have to depend on energy sources that are still to be researched and developed. Poverty continues to grow while old and new diseases threaten whole nations with annihilation.... Authority is being wrenched away from the United Nations, its established procedures are being obstructed and the organisation itself destroyed, development assistance is being reduced; there are continuous demands on the third world countries to pay a $2.5 trillion debt that cannot be paid under the present circumstances, while $1 trillion are spent in ever more sophisticated and deadly weapons. Why and for what?[37]

The large-scale destruction of a whole country merely to change an undesirable regime in a region notorious for pro-West dictatorships, only displayed serious contradictions in Anglo-American policies. Arundhati Roy, in her characteristically forceful way, took up the issue with Bush and Blair, as she noted: 'Mesopotamia, Babylon, the Tigris and the Euphrates. How many children, in how many classrooms, over how many centuries, have hang-glided through the past, transported on the wings of these words? And now the bombs are falling, incinerating and humiliating that ancient civilisation.'[38] Tony Blair's unequivocal support for Washington added to concerns of Britain becoming a target for terrorists, besides worries that like George W. Bush, the British Prime Minister was also 'tangled in the neo-conservative web'.[39]

The decimation of Iraq and its infrastructure, leaving millions without food, water and power, on the heels of a decade-long period of sanctions which had already killed half a million children, were traumatising experiences. Even otherwise sanitised television pictures of cluster bombs and incendiary devices tipped with depleted plutonium only further angered the Muslim communities. Moral justification for the invasion—to help the Iraqis regain their 'liberation' from a brutal regime—contrasted starkly with the concurrent Western support for dozens of other dictatorships in the region, as also for Sharon's ruthless policies.[40] Efforts to stoke Shia-Sunni and Iraqi-Kurdish feuds in Iraq through surrogate forces angered Muslim public opinion which already complained of 'neo-imperialism'. Such dangerous postulations in the wake of efforts to woo the Israeli lobby further dismayed the Muslims.[41] It was feared that soon after the 'conquest' of Iraq, states such as Syria, Iran and Pakistan could become the next target for an ever-expansive US involvement at the behest of hawks and neo-conservatives in America and Israel. While the Iraqi resistance did not aim at protecting a fledgling regime, and was mainly purported to be defending the homeland from an invasion, it, for a short while, 'breathed life into the corpse of Arab nationalism', and a long-time hurt pride.[42] The fall of Saddam Hussein, as expected, came about at a huge price, though the publicised WMDs (Weapons of Mass Destruction) were never to be found, causing constant embarrassment both in London and Washington. However, it was equally apprehended that a pervasive anger across the Muslim world may further strengthen the fundamentalist outfits. The incapacitation of the Muslim states—most of them unrepresentative—and that of the Organization of the Islamic Conference (OIC) in resolving these frequent crises involving millions of innocent people, only exacerbated Muslim fury, allowing fundamentalist forces greater leeway. In the name of solidarity with Iraq and Palestine—as for Afghanistan earlier on—Muslim rage filled the streets in all continents. In the Diaspora, worries about Muslim youth becoming vulnerable to a pervasive marginalization or intolerant elements in the wake of a powerful anti-Muslim idiom was being posited as Muslims being *gendered*—victims to multiple forms of violence and discrimination. Jobs, promotion and other such professional opportunities further shrank for the Muslim Diaspora, reviving terms such as '*Muslims, the new Jews of the West*'.

The build-up to the invasion on Iraq—just as in the case of Afghanistan—led to a flurry of literature on Iraq, Political Islam, terrorism, American policies and the peace movement. Noam Chomsky took the US government to task over violating international law to serve insidious corporate interests.[43] Some writers looked at the lack of a common Arab platform in resolving regional issues, showing a severe 'fragmentation' within the Arab body politic.[44] Saddam Hussein's own career, an unstable childhood of unfulfilled desires and his latter ambitions in Iraq—'the least Arab country'—in conjunction with Western duplicity was also reflected in some scholarly works.[45] The Anglo-American single-minded pursuit of Iraq, according to several analysts, only furthered the cause of Islamic fundamentalism.[46] Whereas military history and analysis of 'smart' weapons attracted some new studies,[47] the anti-war treatises, however, censured the United States itself for proliferating such weaponry in the first place. Reverberating a pervasive anti-war sentiment, it was noted: 'The Bush Administration is taking us on a dizzying ride toward a war with Iraq which will be totally unjustifiable.'[48] Some volumes, while critiquing American eagerness to attack Afghanistan and Iraq, tried to highlight the fallaciousness of Washington's pro-war arguments. Accordingly, neither did Iraq retain any WMDs, nor did the Taliban want to keep bin Laden in Afghanistan. Instead, the latter had agreed to hand him over to the United States on seeing the substantial evidence to the effect. But, a vengeful United States was intent upon seeking revenge from these two countries.[49] Other than the politico-economic fall-out from the tragedies in Afghanistan, Palestine and Iraq, the entire Anglo-American dictum of pre-emptive strikes through a use of extensive annihilative power has spawned newer strategic worries in the neighbouring regions. The inter-state chasms and imbalances are quite vivid in South Asia, and the application of similar rationale for any offensive against a weaker opponent could become a neo-Clauswitzean reality of nuclear proportions. It was no coincidence that the Indian Defence Minister, George Fernandes and the Foreign Minister, Yashwant Sinha issued several statements focusing on 'Pakistan's weapons of mass destruction', which needed to be 'taken out'. India, a close ally of the Baathist regime of Iraq for decades, but now a close partner with Israel and herself possessing nuclear weapons, found the policy of 'no dialogue' with Pakistan to be an accurate strategy.[50] However, there was a cautious optimism in the summer of 2003 for a gradual thaw in the otherwise mostly sour bilateralism. Even without a new India-Pakistan imbroglio, the economic, social and political ramifications from wars in Afghanistan and Iraq will certainly leave their imprints for years to come. Not only were these military campaigns proving to be costly and unnecessary in the first place, they betrayed a greater sense of personal urgency on the part of the Anglo-American leadership over and above the pervasive opposition.[51] The invasion of Iraq, despite its moral and legal questions, had already turned into 'a classical guerrilla-type campaign', as admitted by General Abizaid, chief of the US Central Command, and successor to General Tommy Franks.[52]

NOTES

1. He further noted: 'And if military action was seen as unavoidable, the target should have been the Arab legions in the mountains, not the poor ragged Afghans they've colonised, who never invited them in—we did—and have no way of making them leave.' George Galloway, 'We will not be silenced', *The Guardian*, 20 October 2001.

2. It was opined that Noam Chomsky's following was confined to a few leftists and anti-globalisation activists and his long-time criticism of the US foreign policy was viewed as nothing new. See, Richard Bernstein, 'Counterpoint to Unity: Dissent', *The New York Times*, 6 October 2001. Roy's essays were derided as 'vain, shrill, unoriginal, oversimplified, hyperbolic and lacking any voices but her own'. See, Cecilia W. Dugger, 'An Indian Novelist Turns Her Wrath on the US', ibid., 3 November 2001.

3. Professor Chomsky was given wide coverage in South Asia and in Pakistan, he was given a prestigious award for peace and human rights. For further details on his lectures in Lahore and Islamabad, see, *Dawn*, 27 and 28 November 2001.

4. Arundhati Roy, 'Brutality smeared in peanut butter: Why America must stop the war now?', *The Guardian*, 23 October 2001.

5. The books on Taliban by Ahmed Rashid, Paul Marsden and Andrew Griffin elicited greater demand though Rashid's meticulous research has been the major cause of its publicity. See, Ahmed Rashid, *Taliban: Islam, Oil and the New Great Game in Central Asia*, London, 2000. Osama became the most talked about terrorist in the human history with several articles, cartoons and documentaries appearing in the print and visual media. The websites carried special cartoons, serious articles and biographical details on bin Laden, Bush, Blair and Taliban.

6. William Dalrymple, 'Scribes of the new racism', *The Independent*, 25 September 2001. Seeking a higher moral upper ground, several Western authors found no qualms in calling Anglo-American campaigns directed against Muslim countries and communities a due and justified 'crusade', rather took great pleasure in narrating the killings of forty thousands Afghan 'terrorists' within three months. For details on killings by special forces and their allies, see, Robin Moore, *Taskforce Dagger: The Hunt for Bin Laden*, London, 2003.

7. Robert Fisk, 'Promises, Promises', *The Independent*, 17 October 2001.

8. 'Nor do Americans give much time to the other discussion that has gobbled up airtime in Britain. There is little serious talk here about the root causes of terrorism—not about poverty or malaise of bad governance across the Arab and Muslim world or the Palestinian-Israeli conflict. You will find more opinion pieces on airport x-ray machines and new check-in procedures than about global injustice.' Jonathan Freedland, 'Wrapped up in itself', *The Guardian*, 14 November 2001.

9. *Bin Laden, la verite interdite* (Bin Laden: the forbidden truth), by Jean-Charles Brisard and Guillaume Dasquie, two French authors, gave details of such secret overtures. The publication was widely reviewed in the journals and on the Internet. See, *Commentary*, Vol. 1, No. 11, November 2001; also, http://www.jaring.my/just.

10. The extrnal factors, once again, only exacerbated the intra-Afghan ethnic mayhem. A number of Tajik and Uzbek soldiers belonging to the Northern Alliance (United Front), while entering Kabul, started to kill Pushtuns and other non-Afghans. Even

the dead bodies were not spared from an inhuman mistreatment. For details, see, Chris Stephen, 'Afghans armed with rocks vent their hatred on the dead', *The Observer,* 18 November 2001.

11. These Mujahideen had fought against the Soviets and since the ascendancy of the Taliban had been receiving the weapons from the former foes. It is not clear whether the Russian re-entry was to counterbalance growing Western influence in their south or, it was aimed at winning over their former foes. For details, see, Rory McCarthy, *'Déjà vu* in Kabul as Russian forces return', *The Guardian,* 28 November 2001.

12. For details on the Anglo-American support for the elimination of the POWs, see, Luke Harding, 'Allies direct the death rites of trapped Taliban fighters', *The Guardian,* 27 November 2001. The British correspondent was in the Uzbek town when the atrocities took place. He sent in the details on how the Red Cross representative was shaken up by the developments and the CIA agents requested for troops and aerial bombing which came so soon. The mayhem became a major sticking point as the human rights groups censured the UK and US for sponsoring this massacre quite in contravention of the Geneva Convention.

13. 'Britain and the US faced growing pressure to explain the role of their forces in the deaths of hundreds of Taliban prisoners of war killed by warplanes at a fortress outside Mazar-i-Sharif. An AP photographer saw alliance fighters cutting the bonds from 50 Taliban corpses which had apparently been shot with their arms bound with black scarves.' Ibid., 29 November 2001.

14. Mary Robinson, in her statement in London on 30 November, further criticised the disproportionate retaliation against the POWs. The Amnesty International asked several questions regarding the number of POWs and why so many had their hands tied up. In addition, they asked for the trials of criminals involved in the slaughter. Donald Rumsfeld and several Labour ministers avoided the questions about the responsibility, and usually expressed ignorance on details or allocated it to usual war occurrences.

15. Luke Harding, 'A tank roared in. It fired four rounds. Then there was silence in the fort', Ibid., 28 November 2001. Also, Luke Harding, 'Dead lie crushed or shot, in the dust, in ditches, amid the willows', ibid., 29 November 2001.

16. Luke Harding, 'Errors revealed in siege of Afghan fort', Ibid., 1 December 2001.

17. She wrote: 'We too are responsible for the massacre at Qala-i-Jhangi'. Isabel Hilton, 'There is no excuse for this savagery', ibid., 29 November 2001. Jonanthan Freedland also raised similar questions about the slaughter in Mazar-i-Sharif. See, his column in the same issue. Long after the massacre, the video footage and eyewitness accounts continued to highlight the scale of the tragedy and the American complicity. A British documentary, 'Massacre at Mazar', affirmed by Andrew McEntree, the former head of the Amnesty International, detailed rounding up of thousands of Taliban soldiers and their transportation 'in sealed shipping containers to Sheberghan prison, then under US control'. The two Afghans admitted being forced to drive these prisoners into desert where they were shot dead. *The Guardian,* 13 June 2002. Many of those prisoners died of suffocation in the containers and were quickly interned in mass graves. The story was confirmed by *Newsweek,* which got access to some secret UN documents on these graves. For details, *The Guardian,* 29 August 2002. The media confirmed growing pressure on Washington to hold an inquiry into the matter. *The CNN report* monitored in

Oxford, 21 August 2002. The undecided and equally troublesome state of Muslim prisoners on the Guantanamo Bay, kept on making news amidst revelations of their sad plight. The photographs of the 'shackled and hooded terror prisoners' on the web sites and in the papers unnerved the US Administration, besides putting pressure on the UK, Canada and Pakistan for the restoration of their human rights. See, Stephanie Nolen, 'Photos of Hooded Terror Prisoners Rekindle Debate', *The Toronto Globe and Mail,* 6 March 2003; and for the pictures of the prisoners and their torture by the US authorities, visit: www.globalresearch.ca/articles/CRG211.html.

18. 'Justice in the dust: MPs must probe the battle in the castle', (ed.) *The Guardian,* 29 November 2001.

19. The Sky Television newsreports from Kabul and Quetta, 7 December 2001, monitored in Oxford.

20. In numerous interviews in London, Oxford, Northampton, Birmingham, Stockholm, Chicago and elsewhere, it became quite clear that Muslims, by a clear majority, resented the bombing of Afghanistan and many Muslims complained of further marginalisation. The comprehensive Muslims denunication of war mania on Iraq soon became obvious by becoming part of a global peace movement.

21. Even in certain colleges in Oxford, scarve-wearing Muslim students were advised not to venture out in the evening. At a school a Muslim boy was beaten up simply because his name happened to be Osama. (Based on personal information conveyed by a Muslim student to the author.)

22. *Dawn,* 1 and 2 December 2001. A number of letters appeared in the Pakistani press urging the US Ambassador and the Pakistani officials to move on behalf of these Pakistanis who, in most cases, had nothing to do with the terrorist attacks. In fact, about 40 Pakistanis had been killed in the bombing of the World Trade Center.

23. It was felt that instead of just outlawing incitement for religious hatred, religious discrimination itself should be banned: 'The incitement to religious hatred offence is at best a sop and at worst an attack on the Muslim community'. Madeleine Bunting, 'The new anti-Semitism', *The Guardian,* 3 December 2001; also, Ian Black, 'End growing anti-Muslim prejudice, EU report urges', ibid., 24 May 2002; for an American case study, see, Inayat Durrani, 'Anti-Muslim incidents up three-fold', 5 May 2002, www.arabia.com.; and, Human Rights Watch, 'US Officials should have been better prepared for Hate: Anti-Muslim bias crimes rise 1700 percent after September 11', 14 November, 2002, www.hrw.org.

24. The Runneymede Trust, *Islamophobia* (a report), London, 1997. The commission was headed by the former vice-chancellor of the University of Sussex and included various notables. The quality of work, documentation and recommendations has been largely seen quite authentic and valuable. Like McPherson Report on institutional racism following the murder of Stephen Lawrence (1993), this report highlights areas where significant improvements are overdue. The visual and print media have occasionally offered tangible and concrete statistical and biographical analysis on the state of pluralism in countries such as Britain. For instance, *The Observer,* in its special edition (25 November 2001) brought out a 12-page exhaustive report on 'Race in Britain'. Such cross-cultural surveys are quite revealing and also educational in their larger context.

25. It was reported that the Rabbani regime was filling up all the important posts with its own loyalists. *The Guardian,* 20 November 2001.

26. It was interesting to see, how General (retd.) Hamid Gul, a staunch Taliban supporter and a former ISI head, took refuge in suggesting that the Taliban were not yet finished and had only pursued a strategic retreat. His interview with the BBC, monitored in Oxford, 22 November 2001.

27. The support from the oil companies like UNOCAL, the CIA or other willing Western powers is already documented in various works. See, Ahmed Rashid, op. cit.; Kamal Matinuddin, *The Taliban Phenomenon,* Karachi, 1999.

28. The extensive interviews in the summer of 2000 in Pakistan revealed that the officials in the Foreign Office as well in the Military appreciated the element of stability in the country contrasted with a mild critique of their repressive policies. However, many Sunni outfits greatly idealised the Taliban across the Indus Basin.

29. Reproduced in *The Observer,* 18 November 2001.

30. Tony Blair had made several commitments on a sustained reconstruction of the country, whereas the Bush administration seemed interested only in the eradication of the Taliban and the Al Qaeda through a sustained military campaign. Simultaneously, the presence of the British troops from Special Forces at the Bagram base registered resentment from the Northern Alliance, though London tried to show that they were there for humanitarian efforts. But Afghans and other observers knew that they were combat troops and had nothing to do with facilitating humanitarian assistance. Tony Blair tried to play down divergence between the USA and UK, whereas his colleague, Claire Short, openly admitted the differences in policies. See, *The Guardian* and *The Daily Mail,* 21 November 2001. Her differences with Tony Blair came out in the open again over Iraq in March 2003, when a sizeable section within the Labour Party and across Britain differed with the Prime Minister's pro-war policies.

31. Remarks of Shaikh Muhammad Rashid, the former minister in Sharif's cabinet, in an interview with the ARY, a satellite Channel in London, 22 November 2001. Yunus Qanooni, an important member of the Northern Alliance, in his interview in New Delhi on his return from Bonn, criticised Pakistan's foreign policy on Afghanistan and Kashmir. His remarks were seen partisan, aimed at playing the India card against Pakistan. *Dawn,* 9 December 2001.

32. The politicians felt that Musharraf gave away too much too soon which would have not been possible under an elected regime. Tehmina Daultana, a Sharif loyalist and the vice-chair of the Pakistan Muslim League, felt that Musharraf's midnight decision to offer unquestioned support lacked a proper strategy, hard thinking and tough bargaining and that is why Pakistan had been so quickly sidelined by the US. Ms Tehmina Daultana's interview with the ARY Channel, 23 November 2001, monitored in Oxford.

33. Rajive Dhavan, 'Textbooks and Communalism', *The Hindu,* 30 November 2001.

34. Romila Thapar, 'Vedic Civilisation's Learning and Anachronism', her lecture at a SAHMAT Convention on education on Tehlka.com. Some scholars in pre-Gujarat massacres period felt as if the BJP had toned down its communalist onslaught and was proving more 'responsible' on plural issues. Amrita Basu, 'The dialectics of Hindu nationalism', in Atul Kohli, (ed.) *The Success of India's Democracy,* Cambridge, 2001, pp. 163–189. Of course, anti-Muslim riots in Gujarat in the early 2002 dampened such optimistic views besides highlighting the symbolic role of an ongoing Ayodhya legacy. A pertinent review of Indo-Pakistani historiography, away from communal and nationalist parametres relocates the Perso-Islamic culture in

India as a florescent Indian civilisation, contrasted with a similar and contemporary interaction between Arabo-Islamic culture with Europe. The former exceeds in terms of its contributions and diversity though its denial or even strict monopolisation for partisan reasons are not allowing it a full recognition. The evolution of Islam in South Asia and then its greater expansion 'east of Karachi' compared to the 'west of Karachi' from the seventeenth century onwards remains an exciting but less-researched area. See, Richard M. Eaton, *Essays on Islamic and Indian History,* New Delhi, 2002; also his, *Rise of Islam and the Bengal Frontier, 1204–1760,* Berkeley, 1996.

35. Krishna Kumar, 'Prejudice and Pride', *The Hindustan Times,* 30 November 2001.
36. Jimmy Carter, 'This will not be a just war', *The Guardian,* 12 March 2003. The zealots like Frank Graham, the son of evangelist Billy Graham, and known for his anti-Islam views, were preparing to bring their missions into post-war Iraq as they saw the age-old prophecies coming to fruition. Ibid., 4 April 2003.
37. Fidel Castro, 'Voice of the dark corners', Ibid., 6 March 2003.
38. Arundhati Roy, 'A strange kind of freedom', Ibid., 2 April 2003.
39. John Kampfner, *New Statesman,* 7 April 2003, p. 18; also see, Michael Lind, 'The weird men behind George W. Bush', in ibid., pp. 10–13.
40. The terms were used both by President Bush and Prime Minister Blair in their press conference in Belfast, monitored from BBC Television, 8 April 2003. It is interesting to note that such terms replaced frequent mention of finding 'weapons of mass destruction' as the main purpose of invading Iraq.
41. Secretary Colin Powell's speech to the Jewish leaders in early April 2003 was a further proof of the specific Western interests and partisan policies. In his speech, Powell had warned Syria and Iraq of a US-led retribution for helping Baghdad. Quite a few Western observers—such as John Esposito, Gilles Kepel, Malise Ruthven, Jason Burke, Robert Fisk, Jonathan Steele and William Dalrymple—tried to remind their leaders of being insensitive to Muslim sentiments and thus losing the battle of hearts and minds: 'The greatest weapon in the war on terrorism is the courage, decency, humour and integrity of the vast proportion of the world's 1.2 billion Muslims.' Jason Burke, *Al-Qaeda: Casting a Sahdow of Terror,* London, 2003, as quoted and reviewed in William Dalrymple, 'Who is the real enemy?', *The Observer,* 20 July 2003. An additional and equally dangerous aspect of this Western moral uprighteousness took the form of Christian evangelist efforts in Afghanistan and Iraq, soon after the Anglo-American invasions. Hordes of American missionaries, expecting the second coming of Jesus, not only helped Israel in its expansionism but also intensified their efforts to convert Muslims. For a detailed report on the renewed missionary enterprise, see, David Van Biema, 'Missionaries Under Cover', *Time,* 4 August 2003.
42. James Buchan, 'The return of a forgotten ideology', *New Statesman,* 31 March 2003, p. 21.
43. Noam Chomsky, *Rogue States: The Rule of Force in World Affairs,* London, 2002.
44. Geoff Simons, *Targetting Iraq: Sanctions and Bombing in US Policy,* London, 2002.
45. Said K. Aburish, *Saddam Hussein: The Politics of Revenge,* London, 2000.
46. Dilip Hiro, *Iraq: A Report from the Inside,* London, 2002.
47. For example, see, Robert Hutchinson, *Weapons of Mass Destruction,* London, 2003.

48. Michael Ratner, et al., *Against War in Iraq: An anti-war Primer,* New York, 2003, p. 7.

49. Milan Rai, *War Plan: The Reason against War on Iraq,* London, 2002, pp. 37–8. Also, Mark Hertsgaard, *Eagle's Shadow: Why America Fascinates and Infuriates the World,* London, 2002. Based on informal surveys in 19 countries, this book investigates the roots and types of anti-Americanism and also suggests some ameliorative measures.

50. See, *Dawn, The Hindu* and *The Hindustan Times,* 1, 2, and 5 April 2003.

51. According to a study, Iraq's war was to cost at over 5 billion pounds to the United Kingdom. This cost did not include several other overhead expenses. The American cost was several times more while the worst sufferers have been the people of the region and of course, international law. See, *The Guardian,* 17 July 2003.

52. 'US confused by Iraq's quiet war', ibid., 18 July 2003. The car bomb attack on the UN headquarters in Baghdad leading to the death of the UN head of the mission and several other officials in August 2003, not only confirmed the growing problems for the occupying forces but also a pervasive resentment over the incapacitation of the world body in preventing an unjustified attack on Iraq. The UN, as seen in all the Muslim cases, was viewed to be under the strong American influence, whereas states like Israel defied its resolutions so stubbornly. Even an otherwise highly pro-Western former UN secretary, Boutros Boutros-Ghali 'lambasted a pliant UN'. *The Guardian,* 21 August 2003.

More women became victims of 'honour' killings, including 'karo-kari' than ever before, while the rate of all forms of violence against women soared. Every second Pakistani woman is now believed to be a direct or indirect victim of violence.

Thousands of Hindus were forced to flee their homes in Balochistan after separate incidents triggered violent unrest....Though the precise number of Hindu families which fled was unknown, reports suggested almost half the community of 10,000 Hindus in Lasbela had been forced to leave their homes over the year.
　　　　　　　　— From *State of Human Rights in 2000,* Lahore, 2001

Forming friendship with a Qadiani (Ahmadi) is betraying Islam.
　　　— An Urdu poster in Takht Hazara, Sargodha District in Punjab

5

Religious Pluralism, State and Nation-building in Pakistan

The efforts and saga of nation-building in post-colonial societies are understandable, given the enormity of socio-economic problems, further compounded by border conflicts and external interference. The feeble nature of civil societies, preference for colonial structures and discretionary policies pursued by the monopolist elite, in most cases, have used pseudo slogans and symbols of democratisation, yet in practice, have jealously held on to their own powers. The lack of debate or sheer monopolisation of religious symbols to establish nationhood while bypassing accountable democratic institutions has only exacerbated social conflicts. Unitary nationalism basing itself on religious majoritarianism or the other way around, offers the greatest threat to minorities. The recourse to a misunderstood Islamicity in Pakistan or Bangladesh is largely due to military regimes using Islam to bypass democratic prerogatives. The military and *mullahs* (clerics) in Pakistan, particularly during the long military regime of General Ziaul Haq (1977–1988), proved totally inimical to the country's civic and plural institutions. In the name of Islamization, the country's minorities and women suffered the worst, whereas the ethno-regional forces accelerated their militancy, chasing the capital and professionals away. It was in 2002 that, following the Western pressure, the military-mullah axis weakened for a while and a rather unstable Pakistan appeared to be steering towards a more liberal course by shunning its erstwhile policies on Afghanistan and Kashmir. These policies had been anchored on a militarist strategy where the ideology of Jihad was applied to help the Taliban and other elements fighting the Indian occupation of Kashmir. These policies were pursued with the active support of the premier military intelligence agency, the ISI. Concerned Pakistanis had been demanding a reversal of these policies for a long time, only to be decried by Islamabad. However, General Pervez Musharraf's unpopular policies, and a pervasive country-wide accent on anti-Americanism have, once again, allowed the religio-political parties, to assume centre stage in national politics since the October 2002 elections, followed by the imposition of *Sharia* by these parties in the North-West Frontier Province.

Our present chapter focuses on the precarious state of pluralism in Pakistan and how an institutionalized discrimination, largely undertaken by the state itself, has been hurting its nationhood, besides debilitating minorities. The chapter also looks at the constitutional amendments and other legal injunctions inducted by General Zia, their fall-out and a valiant resistance by the nascent civil society.

Pakistan is an immensely plural country characterised by religious, sectarian and ethno-lingual diversities, which, in many cases, have engendered tensions and conflicts. It is an overwhelmingly Muslim community with more than 90 per cent of the inhabitants adhering to Islam, yet they belong to quite a few doctrinal sects. In addition, there are several Christian denominations, Hindus, Sikhs, Parsis, Bahais, and Kalashas who are identified as non-Muslim Pakistanis. In 1974, the Pakistan National Assembly declared the *Ahmadis*—also called *Qadianis*—a non-Muslim minority. They are a small community, which allocates a highly elevated religious status to the late Mirza Ghulam Ahmad, the founder of the movement in British India. Both the Sunni and Shia Muslims believe that Ahmad is projected by Ahmadis as the promised Messiah and a prophet thus refuting the finality of Muhammad's (PBUH) prophethood. Though a vast majority of Pakistanis converse or understand Urdu—the national language— yet compared to various regional languages such as Punjabi, Pushto, Balochi, Sindhi and others, Urdu remains the mother tongue of only about ten per cent of the total population. The Urdu speakers are mainly immigrants from India or their descendants, who at the time of Partition in 1947, opted for this predominantly Muslim homeland by leaving a Hindu-majority India behind. Historic and more recent migrations have immensely contributed to Pakistan's socio-cultural and ethnic plurality. All the way from ancient pre-Vedic times, several centuries back, when present-day Pakistan was the heartland of the Indus Valley Civilization, invaders and immigrants from the neighbouring Western regions and elsewhere have been migrating into this region. Thus, despite their apparently distinct ethnographic features, all the four provinces of Pakistan—Punjab, Sindh, NWFP, and Balochistan—have become immensely plural. Interestingly, the 'traditional' ethnic movements like 'Pushtunistan' (a separate homeland for Pushtuns), and 'Greater Balochistan' (a separate state inclusive of Balochi regions in Pakistan, Iran and Afghanistan) have subsided in recent times, and new ethnic configurations such as the *Muhajir* identity of Urdu speakers in urban Sindh, as espoused by the MQM have evolved as a consequence of these demographic and economic developments.

In 1947, Pakistan's independence accompanied the greatest movement of people ever known in human history. As is generally accepted, more than fourteen million people moved across the borders with Pakistan receiving more than eight million Muslims from all over India. Most of them came to West Pakistan with 1.2 million moving into the then East Pakistan. Most of the Hindus and Sikhs earlier settled in West Pakistan, left for India, whereas several Hindu communities in East Pakistan remained intact until subsequent events compelled their migration. East Pakistan, Sindh and Balochistan largely remained unaffected by communal riots accompanying Partition, and hence there were fewer incentives for non-Muslim Pakistanis to migrate. The India-Pakistan discord over the former princely state of Kashmir not only brought Kashmiri refugees into Pakistan, but also made it difficult for many non-Muslims to stay on in Pakistan. The immigration of individual Hindu families from East Pakistan into India continued even after the Liaquat-Nehru Pact of 1950 which had resulted in similar policies for refugees, migrations and evacuee properties in both countries. The Pact virtually stopped the migrations, but not so effectively. By the late 1950s, some South Asians began to immigrate to the United Kingdom, but such outward migrations did not lead to any major decrease in the population. Partition had left Muslims divided on all three sides—India, and the Eastern and Western wings of Pakistan—though Hindus and Sikhs largely remained concentrated in India. Another community to be seriously affected was that of the Christians, whose predominant concentration in Northern India was in the Punjab—religiously the most plural of all the British provinces—where religion and language had played an important role in solidifying the communitarian divide. The Partition of 1947 left Punjabis divided on both sides of the India-Pakistani borders, along with several radical changes in their political economy.

East Punjab was largely cleansed of Muslims and likewise, West Punjab of Hindus and Sikhs. The migrations and the concurrent communal killings involving Hindus, Muslims and Sikhs, especially in Punjab have seriously impacted the regional politics of both the countries. That is why, to many observers, the Kashmir conflict or Indo-Pakistani dissensions over water resources, among other factors, are symptomatic of this malaise.

Following the civil war between East and West Pakistan, and India's intervention in 1971, East Pakistan became the new state of Bangladesh, which led to another series of trans-regional migration. While the East Bengalis left West Pakistan for Bangladesh, Pakistan accepted the repatriation of a number of Urdu-speaking East Pakistanis, also called Biharis. Most of these new immigrants, as will be seen in the next chapter, settled in Karachi thus increasing the numbers of the Urdu speaking community in urban Sindh. Following the contentious language issue between Sindhis and Urdu-speakers in 1972, Pakistan became reluctant to accept any more 'stranded Pakistanis' from Bangladesh. Both these communities in Sindh had been contending for their respective mother tongue to become the medium of instruction, besides seeking more jobs and better housing. However, many Biharis and Bangladeshis continued to enter Pakistan informally all through the 1980s, and they have mostly settled in Karachi, adding to the plurality of its society.[1] However, since the late 1980s, Karachi has been quite restive due to a conflictive pluralism, where the MQM led by Altaf Hussain (now settled in London) demanded more jobs and urban amenities for Urdu speakers. He also emerged as the champion of *muhajir* ethnicity, challenged by Sindhi nationalists, as well as by Islamabad. His intermittent calls for strikes resulted in an economic downslide and official crackdowns led to various arrests and volatile encounters between security forces and *muhajir* activists. However, the MQM generally carried the majority *muhajir* votes in all the national and provincial elections, making it the third largest party in Pakistan after Benazir Bhutto's PPP and Nawaz Sharif's PML.[2] In early 2003, General Pervez Musharraf was able to hammer out a deal with the MQM which became a partner with the pro-regime coalition led by Zafrullah Jamali. When one of the MQM leaders in exile, Ishratul Ibad, was made the governor of Sindh province, ethnic tensions subsided but sectarian dissension continued.

There are several scholarly opinions on this major shift in Pakistan from a Jinnahist model of tolerance and democracy to a Ziaist model of rifts and schisms. According to one view, the relationship between Islam and politics is blurred unlike elsewhere, such as in post-Reformation Western Europe. But such an argument is ahistorical since religion is part and parcel of several polities, and even in the post-Soviet era, it has come back as a strong ally of nationalist forces across Europe and North America. To some others, the demand for Pakistan hinged on Muslim majority provinces and used Islamic symbols and thus has retained a Muslim majoritarian bias. This is a powerful argument that, despite the League's assurances to minorities, *Muslim* credentials were still to remain quite pronounced both during the colonial and national periods. But Pakistan, again, is no exception, as many Indian nationalists both from the Congress and other parties used Hindu symbols to establish India's historicity. The third viewpoint seeks the root cause in the enduring contestation between the religious and liberal postulations of nationalism. Like the League and other Islamic parties such as JI, the Indian National Congress was arrayed against the Hindu Mahasabha and such other fundamentalist outfits. The weakening of the modernist forces out of inertia, exhaustion or disarray has allowed parallel forces to seek centre stage in most South Asian countries. Like the Hindu BJP, the Islamicist forces in Pakistan have been rewriting the history of South Asia to suit their religious particularism. The fourth view seeks the rise of unilateralism at the expense of pluralism within the economic and political forces, rather than making it a contestation between tradition and modernity, or secularism and orthodoxy. To such analysts, the continued economic and political disempowerment of the masses has allowed an entry to the opposite forces and they are posing and promising an alternative, however simplistic, to the Westernised elements. The fifth opinion seeks the roots of xenophobia in the nature and direction of the middle classes in societies such as South Asia, where regional, sectarian or so-called majoritarian characteristics remain the hallmark. Sixth, the analysts would connect the major ideological transformation to the role of individuals like Zulfikar Ali Bhutto, Ziaul Haq and Pervez Musharraf, who for their own expediency, coopted and encouraged such obscurantist forces either to seek legitimacy or simply to generate populism. Finally, the globalists may see Political Islam reemerging as the rallying cry to counter the overpowering forces of Westernism, where societal underdevelopment finds convergence with global Muslim issues in Europe, Middle East and Asia. In other words,

Pakistan may be one of several battlefields between the forces of global capitalism and its Jihadist retort.

MINORITIES IN PAKISTAN

Pakistan's population is generally known to be around 142 million, though according to official census reports, it is around 137 million. Out of that, Muslims account for an overwhelming majority. According to the census of 1981, out of a total of 84,253,644 people, Muslims accounted for 81,450,057, followed by 1,310,426 Christians, and 1,276,116 Hindus. The Sikhs, Ahmadis, Buddhists, Parsis and others accounted for 2146; 104,244; 2,639; 7,007, and 101,009, respectively. Population growth within the country due to a de-emphasis on family planning and also due to millions of Afghan refugees and some Iranians has been immense. The next census could not take place for seventeen years, due to ethnic conflicts in Sindh, and a fear of exaggerated census numbers. However in 1990, predicting on the average growth rate of the population at 3.1 per cent, it was estimated that the minorities made 3.1 per cent of the total population. According to these estimates, there were 1,769,582 Christians in Pakistan, followed by 1,723,251 Hindus. There were 2898 Sikhs, 3564 Buddhists, and 9462 Parsis, whereas the 'others' were collectively estimated to be 13,640. The total figures were around 3,663,167. Two years later, the aggregate figures stood at 4,267,463, with Christians and Hindus almost equal at 2,061,306 and 2,007,743, respectively. The Ahmadis, Sikhs, Buddhists, Parsis and the others were estimated to be 163,982; 3,374; 4,150; 11,021 and 15,888, respectively. It is interesting to note that even the Parsis, despite some outward migration, had registered a slight increase.[3] The census of 1998 did not contend these figures with the total figures of the minorities, nearing 11–13 million altogether. The Hindus, Christians and Ahmadis, all claim to be four million each.

It is quite crucial, however, to note that given the disadvantages and stigmatisation, communities do not like to be identified as minorities. It is interesting to observe that the minorities make 8 per cent of the total population (11–13 million), and except for Parsis, most of them live in rural areas, which is in consonance with the general patterns of national demography. Over 65 per cent of them are young people; the rate of literacy in just a few cases is certainly higher than the national average, though other denominators are not pleasing. The Christians and Sikhs live predominantly in the Punjab whereas Hindus live mostly in Sindh, with smaller communities elsewhere. Most of the Sikhs are again in upper Pakistan, with a few families even in the Khyber Pass. Almost 50 per cent of the Christians live in urban areas—predominantly in Punjab—while Ahmadis are scattered across small towns and big cities. The Bahais are also a total urban community that rather remains invisible due to the fear of a backlash, as nearly all of them are converts. The sect began in Iran (Persia) in the nineteenth century, and spread to South Asia in the subsequent decades. Pakistan has a very small, unaccounted for and almost totally invisible Bahai community, who prefer to keep a low-key profile. The other smaller groups like Zikris are, by a majority, in Karachi and Makran District, though their concentration is mainly in south-western Balochistan, where the spiritual centre, Koh-i-Murad is located. However, the recent migrations to Karachi have tilted the balance in favour of urban Sindh. The Shias are mostly settled in Punjab, with a sizeable presence in Karachi, Quetta, Hyderabad and Peshawar. In addition, in the tribal areas, Shias are a dominant majority amongst the Turis of the Kurram Agency, with a significant number from amongst the Bangash settled tribes. In Quetta, there are Shias of Hazara (central Afghanistan) and Iranian background. Most of the Shias in Pakistan are called 'Twelvers', whereas the Ismailis, Dawoodi, Bohras and Khojas account for smaller communities. Excluding the Ismailis of Hunza, Gilgit and Chitral, the rest of these latter Shia groups are urban communities engaged in business and other commercial enterprises. The Twelvers are almost evenly divided between rural and urban sections, though it is difficult to establish concrete figures. It is quite difficult to offer exact statistics on minorities, given the emotional and political issues involved. In addition, many Muslim sects or denominations refuse to be characterized as minorities.

Sunnis and Shias, Politics of Differentiation

Undoubtedly, Muslims in the north-western and eastern regions of British India were in the majority, though on the whole within the subcontinent, they accounted for 25 per cent of the total population. But these Muslim communities, despite an elitist idealism for trans-regionality (*ummah*), were characterised by ethno-regional and sectarian diversities. The nationalist struggle politicised the communities *en bloc*, but after 1947, the age-old diversities and differences became more apparent. Despite an obvious Sunni majority, their doctrinal differences became more visible and often conflictive. There were differences between the purists (followers of seminaries like Deoband demanding a purified version of Islam) contrasted with those of the Sufi-based *tariqa* (order), who felt that their version of Islam was more genuine. Sufis believe in intercession through saints, and unlike scripturalists, value folk cultures. Divided into various orders and systems (*tariqas*), they have been the main propounders of Islam outside Arabia. In the same manner, party politics and issues of ethnicity have further crisscrossed the Sunni Muslims as in the case of the East and West Pakistan relationship or the JI versus JUI or Jamiat-i-Ulama-i-Pakistan (JUP).[4] The JUI, especially the Maulana Fazlur Rahman group (JUI-F), was quite active in demonstrating against US military action against Afghanistan in 2001–02, and held demonstrations mostly in the Pushtu-speaking areas of the NWFP and Balochistan. A few of their demonstrations took place in Jacobabad (Sindh), as the airport had been given to US troops bombing Afghanistan. Maulana Fazlur Rahman himself was put under house arrest by the military government, though his following increased immensely during this time in these two regions. His old class fellow and political rival, Maulana Sami-ul Haq, the leader of a religious seminary at Akora Khattak, tried to woo the Pushtuns to his side, given the fact that his Darul Uloom Haqqania had imparted religious instructions to the Taliban. After the elections in 2002, the JUI (F) emerged as the largest component in the United Action Forum (MMA) and maintained its anti-US postulation, especially over Iraq. It was able to form its provincial governments in the NWFP and Balochistan, a development that took everyone by surprise. It was for the first time that a religio-political party was able to show such an unprecedented performance in an election.

The Sunnis make an overwhelmingly majority in the country, whereas the estimates of the Shia Muslim sects are between fifteen to twenty per cent. The Shias may tend to exaggerate their numbers, whereas the Sunnis would rather challenge such claims. In fact, the lack of any official statistics, out of understandable reasons, allows both groups to offer their own inflated statistics. Academically, there are two views on the Shia-Sunni differences. According to one school of thought, these are not major doctrinal differences but over the years, a political issue of succession to Prophet Muhammad (PBUH), fourteen centuries ago, has been exaggerated into a huge divide. Many Muslim scholars, undoubtedly aggrieved over the chasm, desire a greater dialogue and tolerance to bridge this fragmentation of the *ummah*. The contrary view, shared by some Sunni and Shia extremists along with a few foreign scholars, posits that the divide is real, multiple and unbridgeable. Other than its political or doctrinal roots, Shia-Sunni differences, also known as sectarian discord in Pakistan, are linked with the geo-politics of the South-western and Middle Eastern regions. Sunni-Shia dissensions have been pronounced during the month of *Muharram*, the first month of the Muslim lunar calendar, when many Shias congregate to mourn the assassination of Ali's son and companions in Iraq in 680. The processions and fiery speeches from both sides commemorating Imam Hussain's martyrdom have often caused riots. Before Partition, such riots were confined to specific cities such as Lucknow, but in more recent years, in Pakistan, they have assumed far greater proportions. In fact, there is a great amount of sophistry and selectivity in sectarian terrorist acts. After the Iranian Revolution in 1979, many Shias in Pakistan were deeply enthused, whereas General Zia, the military dictator, used Islamic penal codes to prop up his own rule. The Soviet invasion of Afghanistan in December 1979, offered him an opportunity to neutralise demands for representative politics. His close connections with religious clerics (*maulvis*), led to greater military-maulvi collaboration. The suppression of nation-wide political processes and the democratic system led to a debilitation of the polity with a heightened accent on ethnic and sectarian identities. While Karachi simmered in ethnic conflict, Punjab became the hotbed of Sunni-Shia feuds. In the 1980s, outfits such as the Anjuman-i-Sipah-i-Sahaba (ASSP) under the leadership of Maulana Haq Nawaz Jhangvi and Azeem Tariq, emerged from Jhang demanding the declaration of Pakistan as a Sunni state. The town of Jhang was a catalyst to this rising tide of Sunni militancy as local politics exacerbated its intensity. Traditional feudal Shia elements in Jhang had usually monopolised local and regional electoral offices, whereas the growing Sunni intermediate class, especially in the town itself, sought solidarity in their sectarian fraternity. Politics was definitely not the sole cause of this heightened polarity in Jhang, but operated as an immediate flash point which quickly spread to other parts of the country. Soon the NWFP emerged as the new battleground. The Kurram Agency bordering Afghanistan is overwhelmingly Shia with

most of the Turis and some Bangash—the two Pushtun tribes—
subscribing to this doctrine. Surrounded by Sunni tribesmen on all
sides, these Shias felt inspired by the Iranian Revolution and began
displaying Imam Khomeini's posters, much to the ire of their old
tribal rivals. The influx of Afghan refugees and *Mujahideen*—nearly
all Sunnis—also caused deeper concern among local Shias of a radical
shift in demographic realities in Parachinar (NWFP). The heightened
tensions among the armed tribesmen, both for sectarian reasons, and
for traditional grudges, led to frequent official crackdowns. The
sectarian clashes took their toll when one Shia leader from Kurram of
a nation-wide following, Maulana Mousavi, was gunned down. The
chain reaction was felt across Pakistan with frequent selective killings
in Jhang, Lahore, Karachi and Peshawar. To counteract the ASSP, the
Shias had established their Tehreek-i-Nifaz-i-Fiqh-i-Ja'afria (TNFJ)
which, in fact, demanded the implementation of the Shia version of
Islamic law. Zia's promulgation of the Zakat Ordinance and such
other codes had aggrieved the Shias who felt that their interpretation
of *Sharia* was being ignored. Successful demonstrations by the Shias
in 1980 compelled the military regime to make special concessions for
Shia jurisprudence. Such backtracking only further agitated Sunni
militants. It may by mentioned that these outfits are totally male-
dominated and aggressively militant.

It must be remembered that both the ASSP and TNFJ have retained
nation-wide networks through mosques and *imambaras* but have also
spawned militant outfits to undertake specific assassinations. The
murders of Haq Nawaz Jhangvi and Syed Mousavi were carried out
by secret, well-organized outfits called the Sipah-i-Muhammad (SM)
and Lashkar-i-Jhangvi (LJ) respectively. Both Sunni and Shia militant
groups have tried to transform the Pakistani state into their own
sectarian version with the help of Middle Eastern backers according to
Iranian-Arab chasms. In recent years, the LJ seems to have gained an
upper hand. Just in the year 2000, there were 150 selective killings,
whereas in 2001, until late September, 120 middle class professionals
and scholars were killed through selective targetting and bomb blasts.
Nearly all of them were Shia, which has caused serious concern and
awe among the Pakistani Shia community. In the late 1980s, the SM
killed General Fazl-i-Haq, the former governor of the NWFP and a
close associate of Zia, but since then the tide has turned in favour of
LJ, the Sunni outfit. In the early 1990s, the LJ killed the head of the
Iranian Cultural Centre in Multan along with two other employees,

which seriously impacted the Pakistan-Iran relationship. It took many years for the Nawaz Sharif regime to seek out the culprits. When the decision to hang the culprits was announced during 2001, several threats were made by the LJ. A few Iranian military officials, while on a training mission in Pakistan, were also gunned down by the LJ. It is important to note that their urban and small-town based terrorism in the Punjab and Karachi continued unabated even after the military take-over in 1999, and the international campaign against terror in 2001.[5] In his speech on 12 January 2002, Musharraf strongly admonished these extreme sectarian tendencies and promised further bans on such militant groups. Five weeks after his famous speech, Sunni militants struck in Rawalpindi, just a few miles from Pervez Musharraf's office, and attacked a Shia mosque. They killed twelve worshippers and injured several others. Many Shias have been immensely scared of Sunni unilateralism.[6] Letters appearing in newspapers revealed a growing accent on sectarian fundamentalism especially after the total decimation of Afghanistan and the resultant social conflicts in Pakistan.[7] During the invasion of Iraq in 2003, for a while Sunni-Shia discord, especially during the month of *Muharram* disappeared in the wake of a common anti-American sentiment. However, with the absence of a stable government in Afghanistan and instability in other West Asian countries, Pakistan's sectarian travails soon resurged. Since the Hazaras in Afghanistan were opposed to the Taliban and their sympathisers, they have been bearing the brunt of the latter's fury. The Hazara-Pushtun divergences in Afghanistan periodically spill over into Quetta, where the Sunni militants target Pakistani Shias. In June 2003, twelve Hazara police cadets in Quetta were killed in an ambush, whereas a few weeks later on 4 July, fifty-three Shia worshippers lost their lives in an attack on their mosque. In addition, scores were seriously injured in the suicide and grenade attack. The three perpetrators belonged to the banned LJ, according to the documented videotapes subsequently handed over to BBC correspondents in Balochistan. It is a fact that domestic rivalries are exacerbated by ethno-doctrinal tensions in the neighbouring Muslim countries, seriously affecting Pakistan's pluralism and efforts towards nation building.

THE CONSTITUTION OF 1973 AND EXCLUSION

The separation of East Pakistan led to Zulfikar Ali Bhutto's meteoric rise in the remaining Pakistan, whereas the left-leaning NAP (National Awami Party), and the rightist JUI established coalitions in the NWFP and Balochistan. Bhutto, while assuming power as the president and civilian martial law administrator, had promised a new constitution and restoration of full-fledged democracy. Despite his own authoritarian tendencies, he presented the nation with the Constitution of 1973, which, in its original form, proved a consensus document, though lateral amendments, to some observers, have radically changed its spirit and ethos. That is why at the turn of the century, there have been demands for a new constitution. However, one has to remember that the Constitution of 1973 was the first Pakistani constitution agreed by representatives elected through a universal vote and thus largely reflected opinions across the country. Since it remains the major reference point and has been the cornerstone of several other codes and policies impacting the status of minorities in Pakistan, it is important to look at this constitution rather closely. The original document offered a parliamentary form of government within a federation, which would be headed by a president who, like his Indian counterpart, would have ceremonial powers.[8] The elected prime minister would enjoy the confidence of the majority in parliament and head the government. The provinces were given more rights as the federating units, though the federation would appoint the governors. The chief ministers in all the four provinces would be elected on the basis of a majority in the assembly. A couple of institutional arrangements were made to resolve inter-provincial disputes arising over finances, and the sharing of natural resources such as water and power tariffs. The constitution did not offer decentralisation or a more vivid form of provincial autonomy, yet went a long way in respecting provincial aspirations. It proved a good starting point after a long time in Pakistan's turbulent history of constitution-making and unilateral take-overs, but soon suffered from the authoritarianism of successive rulers, including Bhutto himself. However, it must be remembered that this constitution was prepared during the post-East Pakistan trauma where worries for further balkanisation of the country were quite vivid. Despite its various consensual points, both in symbolism and substantive areas, it tried to present itself as a reflection of the Muslim majority. The Objectives Resolution of 1949, once again, became the preamble of the constitution, whereas the two highest offices in the country—the president and prime minister—were required to be Muslim. This was a reiteration of Pakistan being a Muslim-led state with minorities not having a chance ever to assume leading roles. However, for similar offices for the provinces (governor and the chief minister), religion was not specified.

The Article 2 of the constitution states: 'Islam shall be the state religion of Pakistan...' whereas Article 2-A stipulates: 'Wherein the principles of democracy, freedom, equality, tolerance and social justice, as enunciated by Islam shall be fully observed.' In addition, Article 227 significantly ordains that no law repugnant to Islamic injunctions can be enforced in Pakistan, or Article 41 (2), that the head of the state will be a Muslim, and according to the Article 91 (3), the prime minister shall also be a Muslim, believing in the finality of the Prophethood. Such articles gave major weightage to demands by the Muslim clergy, allowing them an interpretive role. Article 228 established the Council of Islamic Ideology in an institutionalised role to oversee legislation. The Federal Sharia Court, established under Zia under Article 203 (A-J) enjoys additional powers similar to those of the Council. Under Article 203-D, the Sharia Court can declare any law defunct, if it is assumed to be against Islamic injunctions (Later on, Nawaz Sharif's Sharia Act passed in 1991 made *Sharia* the Supreme Law of the land). The government is enjoined to promote the Islamic way of life as laid down in Article 31, though Article 20 ensures each citizen's right and 'freedom to profess religion and to manage religious institutions'. Further down, Article 22 (1) ensures freedom in religious institutions, by not requiring any individual 'to receive religious instruction, take part in any religious ceremony or attend religious worship, if such instruction, ceremony or worship relates to a religion other than his own'. This clause may be seen as a concern on the part of the framers that their appeasement of Muslim clerics had gone too far and needed to be qualified. Article 33 makes the state responsible for providing safeguards to the legitimate rights and interests of minorities, including their representation on the national and provincial services, though the procedures may not be that clear. Article 36 further promises protection of the minorities, whereas Article 40 highlights the need to strengthen relationships with the Muslim world and promote international peace. But, the highest offices of the land being constitutionally closed for minorities, only suggests a second-class citizenship for them. Such a sealing, as originally stipulated in the Objectives Resolution of 1949, further institutionalized inequality.

Some people attribute Bhutto's anti-Ahmadi legislation to his own personality, egotism and insecurity, while others see in it Bhutto's efforts to woo the clerical groups to his side. In fact, when the communal movement against the Ahmadis began, Bhutto was already securely ensconced in power and did not need any such ploy.[9] By assuming this arbitrary role, the national parliament not only inhibited an equal role for plural groups in the national parlance, but also converted the Assembly—a political institution—into a forum meant to define a community's creed and religious profile. This was in conflict with several human rights conventions, as well as with the original Jinnahist vision for Pakistan. The Ahmadis had, in fact, supported Bhutto during the elections, but then both went their own ways, and Bhutto being quite vengeful, involved national parliament in a new controversy.

ZIAUL HAQ'S AMENDMENTS

The sweeping legislation introduced by Zia and further incorporated into the constitution through the Eighth Amendment—without the proper procedures as laid down in the constitution—changed the entire spectrum of policies and attitudes towards minorities and women. Zia's own religiosity, his efforts to woo religious parties like the JI and JUI, and his strategy to counter revolutionary impact from neighbouring Iran, all underwrote his sweeping amendments. Operating as the chief martial law administrator by virtue of his being chief of the army staff, his assumption of the presidency, execution of Zulfikar Ali Bhutto in April 1979, and the Soviet invasion of Afghanistan in 1979, all allowed him to acquire maximum powers. For the first time, a military-mullah nexus was installed in Pakistan. Zia favoured Sunnis over Shias and scripturalists over syncretists. Thus, the introduction of Zakat, Ushr and such other Islamic taxes caused quite an uproar from Shia groups, eventually leading to official concessions for them. Zia harshly suppressed political parties like the PPP and other pro-democracy clusters and tried to induct his own loyalists including the religio-political elements and offered himself as their head. He posed as the *Amir ul Momineen* (leader of the Faithful) and a pliant media controlled by Zia's generals projected Zia's credentials beyond normal limits. Zia set about to redirect the ideological direction of Pakistan. For instance, General Zia, while laying down the foundation of Islamic courts, introduced Chapter 3A on Sharia courts. Article 203 (D), while illustrating their purview, states:

> The court may, (either of its own mention or) on the petition of a citizen of Pakistan or the Federal Government or a Provincial Government, examine and decide the question whether or not any law or provision of law is repugnant to the Injunctions of Islam, as laid down in the Holy Quran and Sunnah of the Holy Prophet, hereinafter referred to as the Injunctions of Islam.

In other words, the Sharia courts and their verdicts were superimposed on the country's elected institutions, and the constitution became a reaffirmation of Muslim sources of religion. Part IX of the Constitution of 1973 focuses on further Islamic provisions. For instance, Article 227 states: 'All existing laws shall be brought in conformity with the Injunctions of Islam as laid down in the Holy Quran and Sunnah, in this part referred to as the Injunctions of Islam, and no law shall be enacted which is repugnant to such Injunctions.' Clause 3, however, explained: 'Nothing in this Part shall affect the personal laws of non-Muslim citizens of their status as citizens.'

Article 228 (1–3) concentrates on the composition of the Council of Islamic Ideology, its total membership, and their qualifications including that of its woman member and others representing the various doctrinal sections. The Zia-led amendment in Article 260 of the constitution declares Ahmadis claiming themselves to be Muslims as a non-Muslim minority. Clause C of Article 260 observes:

> In the Constitution and all enactments and other legal instruments, unless there is anything repugnant in the subject or context,
> (a) 'Muslim' means a person who believes in the unity and oneness of Almighty Allah, in the absolute and unqualified finality of the Prophethood of Muhammad (peace be upon him), the last of the prophets, and does not believe in, or recognize as a prophet, or religious reformer, any person who claimed or claims to be prophet, in any sense of the word or of any description whatsoever, after Muhammad (peace be upon him) and;
> (b) 'non-Muslim' means a person who is not a Muslim and includes a person belonging to the Christian, Hindu, Sikh, Buddhist or Parsi community, a person of the Qadiani group or Lahori group (who will call themselves 'Ahmadis' or by any other name), or a Baha'i, and a person belonging to any of the scheduled castes.

In other words, the state had taken upon itself to define the religions of its citizens, in addition to offering an exclusionary definition of Islam. Within a few decades of its formation, the Pakistani establishment had shifted from an egalitarian espousal to a front-line role on defining citizenship in reference to 'majoritarian' Islamic parameters. The Second Amendment (1974) had declared the Ahmadis a non-Muslim minority, which they never accepted as they claim to be Muslims. However, they became the main focus of victimisation at different levels and eventually many left Pakistan for Western Europe and North America. Their leader, since 1984, had been living in London until his death in 2003, with other countries such as Germany retaining a number of Ahmadis. A few separate seats in the assemblies had been allocated to Ahmadis along with other non-Muslim minorities, but they have been boycotting the elections. Other than one seat in the National Assembly, the Ahmadis were allotted three seats in Punjab, Sindh and the NWFP, respectively. During Zia's rule, an Ordinance, No. XX of 1984, was promulgated and was further indemnified along with various other ordinances on Sharia, Qisas, Evidence and Zakat through the Eighth Amendment (1985), when Mohammad Khan Junejo became the prime minister. Only after getting a blanket validation for all his ordinances and martial law regulations did Zia agree to lifting the longest martial law in the country's history. The above ordinance—now part of the constitution—prohibits and makes it a punishable offence for any Ahmadi to identify himself/ herself as a Muslim. Quite a few Ahmadis have been tried and convicted under this law for calling themselves Muslims or using the word 'mosque', for their places of worship. They are not allowed to use Islamic terminology for their religious practices. The act only further solidified the exclusion of the Ahmadis from the rest of the nation, and for that matter, from the entire *ummah*.

THE BLASPHEMY CODE AND LEGAL EXCLUSION

The Zia regime, in its single-minded pursuit to Islamize the legal and political set-up, inducted a number of amendments and additions in the existing penal code resulting in a regime of severe socio-legal discrimination against minorities. The stringent rules meant to counter blaspheming of the Quran and the Prophet (PBUH) has established a very unilateral regime, where any one Muslim man can institute litigation against an individual on the allegations of blasphemy. This law, of course, did not allow women and minorities to initiate any blasphemy case. The law of evidence (*Qanoon-i-Shihadah*) passed by Ziaul Haq—equating the evidence of two women or two non-Muslims to that of a single Muslim male—further disempowers non-Muslims, while making it easier for Muslim men to pursue legal proceedings against the accused party. For the past two decades, human rights groups have been actively defending several blasphemy cases—involving both Muslims and non-Muslims—along with lobbying for their repeal. The original laws were designed by the British during the nineteenth century to control communal rhetoric and actions so as to contain violence among the religious communities. Given the plural and occasionally volatile nature of South Asian communities, British administrators in 1885 introduced a law outlawing inflaming religious hatred. This law became a part of the Pakistan Penal Code as Section 295, and in its original incarnation, had noted:

> Injuring or defiling place of worship, with intent to insult the religion of any class: Whoever destroys, damages or defiles any place of worship, or any object held sacred by any class of persons with the intention of thereby insulting the religion of any class of persons or with the knowledge that class of persons is likely to consider such destruction, damage or defilement as an insult to their religion, shall be punished with imprisonment of either description for a term which may extend to two years, or with fine, or with both.

In 1927, when communal riots occurred in India, another clause was promulgated under the title Section 295-A. Accordingly:

> Deliberate and malicious acts intended to outrage religious feelings of any class by insulting its religion or religious beliefs: Whoever, with deliberate and malicious intention of outraging the religious feelings of any class of the citizens...by words, either spoken or written, or by visible representations insults the religion or the religious beliefs of that class, shall be punished with imprisonment of either description for a term which may extend to two years, or with fine, or with both.

For the next several decades, both in British India, and subsequently in Pakistan, no further amendments or additions were made to the Code until Zia undertook some crucial changes with long reaching affects. He added two new clauses—B and C to Section 295 of the

Pakistan Penal Code. Clause B was added to the Code through Ordinance No. 1 of 1982 and stated:

> Defiling, etc., of Holy Qur'an: Whoever willfully defiles, damages or desecrates a copy of the Holy Qur'an or any extract thereof or uses it in any derogatory manner or for any unlawful purpose shall be punishable with imprisonment for life.

Zia was trying to appease the Islamicists—the fundamentalist Muslims—when a few years later, he added another clause to the Code. The Penal Code Section 295-C was rushed through the Criminal Law (Amendment) Act III of 1986 and stipulated:

> Use of derogatory remarks etc. in respect of the Holy Prophet: Whoever by words, either spoken or written, or by visible representation, or by any imputation, innuendo, or insinuation, directly or indirectly, defiles the sacred name of the Holy Prophet Muhammad (peace be upon him) shall be punished with death, or imprisonment for life, and shall also be liable to fine.

A lawyer in the court challenged this section on the plea that the only punishment for blaspheming the Prophet (PBUH) must be the death penalty. Accepting this petition, the Federal Sharia Court, in October 1990, gave a verdict in favour of the death penalty. Thus, any blasphemy case in reference to the Prophet (PBUH), since 1990, is liable to the death penalty. In 1994, on a private petition regarding the Penal Code 295-C, the Lahore High Court, in its verdict, did not find it in contravention of the constitution. Earlier in February, the Chief Justice-led Pakistan Law Commission had itself discovered the frequent misuse of this anti-blasphemy clause by the police and had felt that the clause could further inflame communal tensions. The Commission, led by the then Chief Justice, Nasim Hasan Shah, had recommended its review by the Islamic Ideology Council, and henceforth, Benazir Bhutto's government agreed to amend its operation. However, following countrywide demonstrations especially after certain official statements to the effect in July 1994, the PPP regime back-tracked. Sharif's second administration and Musharraf's regime have both remained totally evasive on this crucial issue.

These three anti-blasphemy clauses have been used quite often, both against Muslims and non-Muslims. In many cases, uneducated Christians and some educated Muslims have been subjected to trial, though the actual reason for litigation may be altogether other than religious.[10] The anti-blasphemy codes and the law of evidence—shrinking a woman's evidence to half that of a man's—have caused quite an uproar, but successive regimes have been reluctant to remove them, so as not to offend the fundamentalists. Like some women's groups, many Christians have established NGOs and support groups to help individuals being tried under blasphemy codes. According to some reports, there are more Muslims in jails accused of blasphemy than non-Muslims.[11] Other than Ahmadis and some Christians, most blasphemy cases have been established against Sunni Muslims, accused of disrespecting the Prophet (PBUH) or defiling the Quran. Irrespective of religious, sectarian or denominational divisions, the three clauses are vulnerable to misuse. Another related problem with such cases is that some of the accused individuals have been murdered before a verdict could be issued by the courts. The inflammation in such cases has usually come from clerics or local influentials. Following the Salman Rushdie affair, clerics find it easy to implicate people in blasphemy cases. The number of cases under the Penal Code has been registering a steady increase in recent years, and especially more so after the rise of the Taliban in the late 1990s, which inspired many fundamentalist elements to 'Talibanize' Pakistan. The imposition of *Sharia* under the JUI-led government in the NWFP during 2003, acutely increased such apprehensions, as crowds in the Punjab started destroying billboards displaying female portraits.

Other vital amendments in the Penal Code—aimed at Islamization and carried out by Zia—have also put severe strains on the rights of women and minorities. The Hudood and Zina Ordinance—Zia's legislation dealing with rape, adultery and fornication—is now part of criminal law, though it fails to make any distinction between rape and adultery. (The two Commissions of Inquiry established in the early 1980s and in 1997, respectively, have demanded the repeal of this law). The Qisas and Diyat Ordinance—*Sharia* laws regarding homicide and blood money inducted by Zia—is part of the Penal Code since 1990. Qisas and Diyat are age-old tribal traditions, which allow seeking revenge or blood money for the deceased. They were revived by Zia through his penal legislation. These ordinances have severely handicapped women and minorities in obtaining equal rights and due justice, especially in adverse situations.[12] Firstly, it is hard to establish cases on the basis of witnesses where both women and minorities are completely disadvantaged, and secondly, they offer a parallel system of private justice, where any kind of miscarriage of justice is possible. The consumption of liquor had been banned in Pakistan under Bhutto in 1976, but non-Muslims were allowed to consume, manufacture and purchase it through several permits. The Hudood Ordinance of 1979 had reaffirmed this lateral provision for non-Muslims, which turned out to be a major source of discrimination and corruption. While the Muslim religious elements further denigrated non-Muslims for immoral practices, corrupt officials encouraged non-Muslims to run underhand sales to the rest. This further lowered self-esteem amongst the minorities, especially Christians, as the prohibition law has undoubtedly criminalized certain sections from amongst them.

SEPARATE ELECTORATES AND ELECTORAL SEGREGATION

The people of Pakistan, in general, have never sought separate electorates, and a lower legal status for minorities since the latter never posed any threat to the majority community. It was General Zia who divided Pakistanis into Muslim and non-Muslim voters. As explained earlier, his Hudood Ordinance and the Law of Evidence had already critically disempowered women and minorities. Such a legal discrimination on the basis of gender and religion was further solidified through the induction of amendments in the constitution, and by inserting new immensely exclusionary clauses in the Penal Code. They established the segregationist regime of separate electorates for minorities. An amendment (Clause 4A) was added into Article 51 of the constitution which states: 'The members to fill the seats referred to in clause (2A) shall be elected, simultaneously with the members to fill the seats referred to in clause (1), on the basis of separate electorates by direct and free vote in accordance with law.' Furthermore, through the Presidential Order No. 8 of 1984, the law on separate electorates and communal representation was further elaborated: 'At an election to a Muslim seat or a non Muslim seat in the National or a Provincial Assembly, only such persons shall be entitled to vote in a constituency as are enrolled on the electoral roll prepared in accordance with law on the principles of separate electorate for any electoral area in that area.' In other words, the non-Muslims will have their own constituencies and their own separate representatives. Despite living side by side with the Muslims, they would not share the same voting rights and constituencies. Their constituency may be lumped with people they never met, or may be living hundreds of miles away. Similarly, their representative may be a total stranger to them. Muslim representatives, even from their own township, would however, have no concern for them because minorities have selective voting rights.

Before these critical amendments, elections to the local, provincial and national bodies were held on the basis of joint electorates and common representation, and the minorities did not face any discrimination. There were reserved seats for minorities, as well as for women, which further guaranteed participation in national politics, but the separate electorates simply wrote that off. It was in 1979 that the demand for separate electorates received a major momentum, though discussions had been going on since the 1950s. The new system of separate electorates was implemented in the party-less elections conducted by Zia in 1985, though earlier in 1983, the local bodies elections had been held under the new system of separate constituencies. Interestingly, in his own referendum cobbled together in 1984 to seek the presidency for five years, Zia used joint electorates to serve his own interests. In the local bodies' elections of 1983, 71,767 councillors were elected for 4100 councils across the country, out of whom 3472 were non-Muslims. Following Musharraf's devolution plan of 2001, several non-Muslims could not actively participate in the local elections due to the handicaps posed by separate electorates. The removal of separate electorates, as well as reservation of some seats in 2002 by Musharraf, augured well for minorities, though the backlash from the combined religious opposition (MMA) remained unabated.

Most of the minorities opposed separate electorates, but some leaders such as Joshua Fazal al Din, Bishop Inayat Masih and Michael Jawaid of Pakistan Minority Front (PMF), and some advocates including S.K. Kenneth, Yusuf Masih, Ajaz Farhat and Choudhary Bashir Gul wholeheartedly supported separate electorates. Rufus Julius, the chairman of the Pakistan Christian Alliance, and Adil Sharif (MPA), Tariq Qaisar (MNA) and Bashir Masih (MPA) also supported separate electorates, on the assumption that they would guarantee a sizeable representation for religious minorities. In 1970, Joshua Fazal al Din had boycotted elections on the plea that under the joint electorates, minorities would be under-represented. In fact, through his presidential order, General Zia had specified ten seats on the National Assembly for the non-Muslim MNAs altogether; four for

Christians; four for Hindus; one for Sikhs and Parsis together, and one for Ahmadis. Similarly, he reserved certain seats for non-Muslims in the four provincial assemblies. Just in Sindh, nine seats were reserved for non-Muslim MPAs; five for Hindus; two for Christians; one for Sikhs, and one for Ahmadis. In Balochistan's Provincial Assembly, one seat was reserved for Christians, and one for Hindus, Sikhs and Parsis combined. Now, under the new system, the constituencies became altogether separate on religious grounds and also got over-stretched, covering a vast and immensely unmanageable area. Until 1977, all the elections had been held through joint electorates, though the ideological polarity on the mode of electorates was predated, especially in reference to the disputatious issue of parity between East and West Pakistan. The issue of separate electorates became more complex, with a greater accent on Islam as a nation-building force and Pakistan's total identification with the Muslim majority. The Constitution of 1956 had, rather curiously, stipulated joint electorates for East Pakistan, contrasted with separate electorates in West Pakistan. Many analysts consider this dichotomy to be one of the main causes of Pakistan's partition. However, the elections of 1970 (in both the wings), and those of 1977 (in present-day Pakistan) were held on the basis of joint electorates, but the national and provincial elections from 1985 to 1997 were held through separate electorates. The elected governments of Benazir Bhutto and Nawaz Sharif (1988–1999) and the three Interim Governments in between the various dismissals (1990, 1993, and 1997), consistently shied away from annulling separate electorates. It put the minority leadership in a dilemma. In case of non-participation in the new set-up, they were to face total disenfranchisement, whereas by participating in it, they were seen supporting the enforced segregation. Before the elections of 1993, a minority candidate for the Punjab Assembly, Naeem Shakir, had contested the issue in a petition with the Supreme Court. The court allowed Muslim and non-Muslim voters to cast their votes interchangeably across the religious boundaries. The verdict was confined to his constituency, PP-126. This achievement, which could have become a major breakthrough, however, proved temporary as the Supreme Court, in its verdict on 4 October 1993, reversed its earlier verdict. It disallowed Naeem Shakir from contesting elections from a Muslim constituency and thus maintained the religious division within a democratic set-up. The second administration of Benazir Bhutto (1993–1997), despite its apparent support for joint electorates, shied away from taking a vocal stance. Fakharuddin G. Ibrahim, her Attorney General and a former senior judge, reaffirmed support for the Jinnahist vision of equal citizenship and joint electorates, but found it to be a constitutional matter, which could be rectified only by the National Assembly. Benazir Bhutto's supporters suggest that she could not annul the separate electorates and other discriminatory laws and amendments, largely because she did not have an electoral majority, whereas the Muslim League never appeared interested in undoing Zia's legacy. This was partly, because Sharif and many of his colleagues had been the personal beneficiaries of Zia and his set-up, and partly because the League for a long time, has been a party of predominantly conservative interests representing the capitalists and landlords who have never been fond of an egalitarian set-up.

The forced segregation proved quite inimical for non-Muslims, as representatives from the majority community simply ignored development schemes in the areas inhabited by minorities, since they did not fall within their constituencies. In the same way, most of the minorities, already being economically underprivileged, would not be able to reach their members whom, in most cases, they did not know or had no means to contact. The minority communities were just left out in the wilderness and the sheer sense of discrimination and loss engulfed them. Over the last two decades, many civic groups had been demanding the annulment of this harmful and immensely discriminatory policy, but no government until 2002, ever tried to undo what Zia had regimented into the system. On 4 September 1993, the National Commission for Pakistan Justice and Peace Commission (Catholic Bishops Conference of Pakistan) had offered the following vital objections:

- They (separate electorates) only incite religious prejudices.
- They create disorder within the nationhood.
- They segregate minorities from mainstream national politics.
- They downgrade the minorities to a third class citizenship.
- The separate electorates promote only a few individuals instead of communities.
- They further divide and splinter minorities causing more feuds and strife.[13]

However, it is to the credit of civil society in the country that demands for the repeal of separate electorates and other discriminatory practices remained high on the agenda of public debate. Even so, it was only after the American action against the Taliban, and their pressure on Islamabad for reforms that General Musharraf in early January 2002 did away with the separate electorates. Musharraf also initially abolished the written affirmation of the finality of prophethood on the voter's registration form, which, in the past, had seriously affected the Ahmadis. However, following pressure by the religious elements, the military regime annulled its decision and restored the practice on 29 May 2002. While Musharraf increased the number of seats overall for national and provincial assemblies, and also those reserved for women, it has been almost impossible for several minority candidates to win elections on their own due to their meagre economic resources and a lack of proper organizational set-up. Minority representation, in its entirety, is a delicate matter, and has to be tackled in a holistic and supportive manner, so as to generate a greater sense of participation and representation by avoiding forced models of segregation and integration.

MINORITIES AND INSTITUTIONAL SEGREGATION

After a holistic portrayal of Pakistan's historical evolution, its socio-cultural fabric, and most importantly, the establishment of various forms of constitutional, legal and electoral laws and traditions mostly working against religious minorities—intentionally or inadvertently— it is important to seek out their collective and individual experiences. In this section, we look at the overall situation of minorities in areas such as legal and electoral separatism. The exclusion from socio-economic life, higher positions in the civil and military sectors or overt issues of discrimination and racism—in varying degrees—have been occurring across the country. In other words, a combination of officially institutionalised discrimination and societal indifference or anger, add to a continuum of marginalization.

The Shias, inclusive of Ismailis and Zikris, are Muslim communities *per se*, who are deeply disturbed over Sunni demands to designate them as minorities given the accompanying stigma and marginalization. In the same vein, the officially declared minority of the Ahmadis, refuse to be categorised as non-Muslims, but the government and the majority community consider them to be outside mainstream Islam due to their disagreement on *khatam-i-nabuwwat* (the issue of the finality of the prophethood). However, Pakistani minorities would consist of Christians, Hindus, Ahmadis, Parsis, Buddhists, Sikhs, Bahais and the Kalasha of Chitral. Excepting the Ahmadis, they all agree on being non-Muslim, though the Bahais are largely 'invisible'. Within these communities, we have rural, urban, ethnic, class-based, caste-based and sect/denomination-based divisions, and any superficial categorisation can be disputatious. For instance, amongst the Christians—making almost four per cent of the total population— there is an almost fifty-fifty division between the Catholic and the Protestant denominations.[14] Cities like Peshawar, or cantonments in Quetta, Rawalpindi, Bahawalpur, and Hyderabad have always had a sizeable number of Christians engaged in various professions in the service sector. The church organization is very similar to other South Asian countries, with a definite Pakistani cultural and linguistic embodiment. Amongst the Christians, there are converts, descendants of converts, and Pakistanis referred to as Anglo-Indians, and Western missionaries.[15] The Hindus, equivalent in number to the Christians— the second largest minority group—mostly reside in Sindh with some smaller communities across Pakistan. They account for nearly four per cent of the country's population. In Sindh, the major portion consists of rural community along with a small section of urbanites and some nomadic communities. There are several castes among the Hindus besides ethnic diversity. The Ahmadis are divided into the Qadiani and Lahori groups. Both the leadership—London-based—and the elite of the movement, are predominantly Punjabi, with smaller communities in other provinces. Most of the Ahmadis are located in central Punjab and after their designation as a non-Muslim minority, a huge section has moved to Western Europe and elsewhere, though familial, lingual and cultural links remain very strong with the Punjab.[16] The Sikhs are again mostly Punjabis, with smaller traditional communities in the NWFP and Karachi. There are a few Sikhs in the tribal areas who are bilingual and have had close relationships with co-religionists in Afghanistan. During the Taliban's ascendancy, many of the Afghani Sikhs migrated abroad and just a few filtered into Pakistan. The Sikhs remain comparatively more secure than other religious communities, as most of the public ire is reserved for the Hindus and Christians. Similarly, the Parsis are strictly an urban, small and enterprising community based in Karachi and Lahore, with a few families in other major cities. Due to their strong economic and commercial links, the non-evangelical nature of the faith and a steady outward migration to North America, the Parsis remain 'less visible' in Pakistani pluralism, and there are no reports of harassment or anger, specifically directed against them. Some Parsis like Bapsi Sidhwa, Dorab Patel, Bahram Avari, the Markers, the Dinshaws and the well-known columnist, Ardeshir Cowasjee, are national role models. The Bahais are, in general, converts and middle class urbanites, who publish magazines and books but keep a low-key profile.[17] So far, they have escaped any collective anger from other majority communities due to their small numbers and less publicity on their activities. The Kalasha of Chitral are an old community, who have usually held a romantic fascination for the British and Pakistani popular media and also the present-day anthropologists. There are various myths about their origins, including presumably, some Greek ancestry. They have been the past rulers of Chitral, though they now live in three small, land-locked hamlets and are immensely poor. However, since the late nineteenth century, the Kalasha (locally called Kafirs as well) have been under great pressure for conversion to Islam. Their division across the Durand Line—the Pak-Afghan borders—did not help them either. In the 1890s, Amir Abdur Rahman, the religious king of Kabul, forcibly converted many of the Afghan Kalasha to Islam. Some of them sought protection on this side of the Line.[18] Their mountainous region and existence in the isolated valleys protected them for long from outside influences. Their ever-dwindling number is around three thousand altogether, and even national statistics tend to ignore them. However, the tourist attraction of their valleys in the Hindu Kush, the gender-based equality, and a growing accent on Islamic activism, all around since the 1970s, have put these small communities under the spotlight. The uniform school syllabus and emphasis on Urdu and Arabic in the official schools in the valleys are not helping the Kalasha in maintaining their own religio-cultural identity. There have been reported cases of kidnap of their women and forcible conversions as one travels across the region.[19] During the 1980s, several cases made international news, including an American taking a Kalasha woman with him to the United States. Personal visits to the area also revealed such stories of kidnapping or elopement.

More than conversion, the physical attacks, social stigmatisation, psychological insecurity and continued segregation from the national ethos add to the woes of religious minorities in Pakistan. The recent anti-Shia attacks also show a growing sectarian intolerance towards fellow Muslim 'minorities'. Even after the banning of ASSP and LJ, the sporadic killings went on. On 20 February 2002, five members of a Shia family in Chichawatni, near Multan, were brutally murdered by Sunni militants. Six days later, twelve Shia worshippers were gunned down in Rawalpindi in a mosque while several others were critically injured. On 2 June 2003, eleven police trainees were gunned down in Quetta and several more were injured in an ambush attributed to Sunni militants. All the trainees in the police van happened to be from the Shia Hazara community in Balochistan. Still, it is unfair to suggest that Pakistani society is intolerant and intent upon eliminating pluralism; it is a small section of militants who exploit the politico-economic frustrations of the rest and also grow within a non-democratic set-up. The politics of disempowerment and Western or regional geo-political factors characterise this backlash, which is augmented by prevailing prejudices stemming out of ignorance about other religious traditions, and are refurbished by stereotypes about Hindus, Christians, Kalasha and the Shias. Religious bigots inflame hatred through the mosques and on the streets against non-Muslim minorities, as well as against Ismailis, Twelvers and Zikris. Unlike the trends of globalisation and regionalization in the north Atlantic regions, poor countries like Pakistan are undergoing different processes of fragmentation and exclusion, a phenomenon which deserves deeper analysis since religious feuds may not be religious *per se* and could be rooted in several mundane factors.

In this kind of malaise, the role of the various think tanks, activist groups and human rights groups representing the civil society of Pakistan, obtains centre stage. On the one hand, these groups try to restrain statist unilateralism, whereas simultaneously, they try to create a greater awareness amongst the masses on the sanctity and inviolability of equal citizenship. At another crucial level, through documentation and active lobbying, they organize civic groups to play an effective role at the local levels, so as to safeguard the plural nature of Pakistani society. Such a tri-dimensional strategy is understandable as it offers a buffer against official unilateralism and societal nihilism. Such groups, still many in their infancy, emerged in the last decade or so and are still struggling to survive in South Asia where fundamentalist forces and exclusionary nationalisms abound. The annual reports of Amnesty International (AI), or the Minority Rights Group (MRG) have raised these issues, but all along, there was a need for indigenous networks and pressure groups for investigating and documenting the various domains of human rights, in reference to underprivileged sections. These organizations face tough challenges and numerous pressures but over the years they have built up their credibility as effective channels of information and reformation. In the same vein, the psychological, official, societal and fundamentalist pressures on these organisations and their personnel remain unabated, yet moderate elements deeply value their untiring work. Organizations such as the Human Rights Commission of Pakistan (HRCP) are nation-wide, non-sectarian and non-profit think tanks, whereas each community may have its own respective safety networks.[20] The Christians in this sense seem to be better organized where church-based as well as secular organizations are emerging to focus on human rights.[21] The Hindus in Pakistan suffer from a wide variety of morass and the rural nature of a predominant section of their society in Sindh precludes the possibility of such a civic initiative. The Sindhi land-based influentials rule the roost, whereas a very small class of Hindu professionals remain on the defensive. On the other hand, Parsis and Ismailis (the latter not characterised as a minority) are the most organised and well-knit communities. The Ahmadis are well organized, affluent yet officially a minority, and societal wrath puts many restrictions on their social and religious mobility. Their characterization as a non-Muslim minority often feeds into strong reservations about their loyalty. The Zikris in Balochistan are becoming less visible as they are routinely differentiated from the Sunnis/Namazis and despite the official reluctance to declare them as a minority, are gradually being socially isolated from their kith and kin.

The Zikris of Balochistan—a predominantly Baloch ethnic group in Makran and the adjoining areas—fear the fate of the Ahmadis as there are demands from certain groups for their designation as a non-Muslim minority. The Zikris have largely remained an under-researched community, whose folk culture retains a special fascination for anthropologists. However, many Baloch nationalist leaders and writers have expressed a greater sense of solidarity with the Zikris considering them as the archetypal Baloch.[22] The Zikris have usually subscribed to the idea of a revealed imam—*Mahdi*—and while believing in all the basic tenets of Islam, they consider Syed Mohammad Jaunpuri, a contemporary of the Mughal Emperor Akbar in the sixteenth century, to be their Mahdi. According to them, the *imam* appeared on Koh-i-Murad, an arid hilltop near Turbat in Balochistan, where he performed religious and spiritual practices before disappearing in Afghanistan. His *jalwah* (appearance) on the hilltop is deemed miraculous and towards the end of *Ramadan* (month of fasting), a huge assembly takes places at the sacred place to commemorate the occasion. This assembly is not at all a substitute for Hajj (Muslim pilgrimage to Arabia), and commercial and other activities take place as well in a traditional manner. They are called Zikris because they remember and recite the names and attributes of God verbally all the time either on an individual basis or collectively.[23] Most of the Zikris are poor peasants or nomads who enjoy coming to Koh-i-Murad like people elsewhere visiting shrines. The exact number of Zikris is not known since they identify themselves as Muslims. Their leading intellectual believes that they are in several millions living in Pakistan, India and Iran. The four-million strong Mahdawis in India are also deemed members of the Zikri community. In addition, there are huge Zikri communities in Karachi, Lasbela and Quetta though Turbat remains the main spiritual centre. There are more Zikri Baloch in Karachi than anywhere else, but many of them have migrated only recently for economic reasons and stay in touch with their native Makran. The cultural and commercial significance of the festival is equally considerable.[24] The Zikri intellectuals challenge the claims by Sunnis and others of adding something extra to the *Kalima* which they think is not true though they respect Syed Jaunpuri as the *Mahdi*, like every Muslim believes in the ultimate appearance of a *Mahdi*. However, their religious leaders—*Malais*—believe that the Zikri prayer is 'a bit different than the others'.[25] Abdul Ghani Baloch does not consider them to be heretically different from other Muslim sects and finds similarities with many other doctrinal interpretations.[26] Their opponents, however, believe that the Zikris do not pray regularly; have added an extra phrase about the *Mahdi* to the original *Kalima,* and do not go to Mecca and Medina on pilgrimage but rather substitute it with a visit to Koh-i-Murad. They also reject their elevation of Syed Jaunpuri to the status of a *Mahdi.*[27] Their *zikr khanas*—not many in number unlike the growing number of mosques across Makran—are like mosques but do not have pulpits pointing towards Mecca. Instead, there are stones and mats on which they sit and do the *zikr*. However, on a visit to the prayer places at Koh-i-Murad, a few copies of the Quran were found in the shelves. The Sunni/Namazi Muslims, belonging to the JUI and JI have been attacking the Zikris for being a heretic sect and sometimes full-fledged campaigns have been mounted to stop the Zikris from congregating at Koh-i-Murad. Over the last several years, a police and constabulary protection has been provided to Zikri visitors. To many observers, the emphasis on re-conversion or designation as a non-Muslim minority is linked with the growing accent on Islam in Pakistan under Zia, and in neighbouring Iran under Khomeini. The Zikris had been traditionally victimized in Iran and in Afghani Balochistan and the recent emphasis on Sunni and scripturalist Islam gave impetus to the JUI to make inroads into Baloch regions, as the party henceforth has largely remained confined to Pushtun areas of the NWFP and Balochistan. The publication of anti-Zikri material, use of mosques for inciting hatred, and individual attacks have been recent features of the anti-Zikri movement which has involved demands that they be declared a non-Muslim minority.[28] The Zikri status remains unchanged but they are apprehensive and thus, find solidarity with a secular version of Baloch ethnicity. The HRCP, several local activists and NGOs have become involved in creating a greater awareness of the Zikri predicament to forestall a majoritarian backlash against this scattered and rather impoverished community. Efforts are largely directed to counter demands for a minority status and also to educate both Zikris and other groups on civic rights and tolerance.[29] However, there is an urgency to undertake further serious research and publications to counter any anti-Zikri vengeance.

Pakistan is a plural country where equal citizenship based on unfettered human rights could guarantee a better and peaceful nationhood. Such an ideal is possible, only if the country's leaders and opinion makers act more responsibly, and instead of inciting hatred, preach tolerance and coexistence. It is imperative for the Pakistani ruling elite to revisit Jinnah's vision of a tolerant, plural and democratic Pakistan, anchored on the principles of equity of citizenship and other rights, irrespective of caste, creed, gender and class. Such an ideal was the original creed of the movement for Pakistan, and it is a consensus point amongst a vast majority of the population even today. The non-representative regimes and difficult inter-state relations have only worsened inter-community relationships in South Asia. Pakistan's overwhelming majority is tolerant and in favour of giving equal rights to women and minorities. They deserve an honourable existence, protection and proper incentives to steer out of a growing morass. They should not be viewed as foreign agents or second-class citizens, and the media, as well as the academia must fully highlight their plight. The regimes should not seek expediency through *ad hoc* measures and so-called majoritarianism, which eventually further disempowers minorities. The instigation of violence, establishment of false cases, land grabs, incidents of rape, harassment and encroachment on human life and rights must be quickly and judiciously dealt with, without any distinction or hesitation. Pakistan needs to follow a new citizens charter; honour its NGOs like the HRCP, and in cooperation with its neighbours, must pursue a discourse of peace and tolerance. In the same vein, security must be redefined in reference to civic, cultural, political and economic needs of her citizens, so that a country otherwise endowed with a hard working population and unexplored natural resources moves forward as a peaceful and prosperous society.

A greater awareness of the obligations and attributes of pluralism is an urgent prerequisite of the time. Pakistani nationalism—and likewise, its other counterparts in South Asia—must symbolise and reflect the plural realities of its society, rather than demanding or imposing a unitary nationhood. The concept of human rights for all, inculcated through educational institutions and civic policies, and implemented through judicial, electoral, educational and legal institutions, can usher Pakistan into a more tolerant era. It can also resolve her enduring problems of governance. In addition, while abolishing separate electorates, Islamabad must be urged to enhance seats for minorities—just as it has done for women—so as to guarantee their representation in a spirit of positive discrimination. The state must outlaw sectarian and intolerant outfits and de-weaponise the country by offering proper security to its inhabitants. The tribal agencies and their so-called autonomous status should be abolished, so as to stop gun-running and drug-trafficking. Moreover, the tribal Pakistanis demand to be treated as equal citizens, rather than be left to the whims of an anachronistic system. In the same spirit, long overdue and substantive land reforms need to be implemented to lead Pakistan into the modern age, away from localism and the ills of feudalism. In a significant way, the rule of law and democracy will certainly guarantee a greater sense of participation, whereas religion should not be exploited to seek legitimacy. Pakistan is a predominantly Muslim society, but even amongst Muslims, there are several doctrinal and sectarian diversities which need to be acknowledged, and an atmosphere of tolerance and discourse should be allowed to flourish, instead of snubbing this religio-ethnic pluralism. The police and secret agencies have to be prohibited from meddling in inter-religious or sectarian diversities. As enunciated by Jinnah, the regimes must follow a policy of non-interference in the religious affairs of its citizens. The blasphemy clauses have already caused severe chasms and should be abolished in the larger human and national interest. The media and proper textbooks should be amply used to create a greater awareness and respect for plural communities. Since most of the crimes against minorities take place at the local and regional levels, there is a greater need for regional ombudsmen. In the same spirit, the noble work done by some NGOs such as the HRCP, should be openly acknowledged instead of denigrating them as foreign agents. The media, especially in the local languages, must act responsibly, and journalists must be awarded for their investigative reports on human rights and citizenship. Popular culture must reflect and celebrate Pakistan's diversity and every effort should be made to inculcate responsible civic behaviour. It is not a tall order, and in the true spirit of social justice and equal human rights, Pakistan has all the potential to offer itself as a role model to several other, similar societies. Pakistan's own people—especially its minorities—are its assets, and have an undeniable birthright to fully enjoy security, equal rights and dignity like anybody else.

NOTES

1. For more on Biharis and their continuing travails, see, Ben Whitaker, et al., *The Biharis in Bangladesh,* MRG Report No. 11, London, 1982. The next chapter in this volume is devoted to the same subject.
2. For conflictive pluralism in Sindh and the MQM, see, Iftikhar H. Malik, *State and Civil Society in Pakistan: Politics of Authority, Ideology and Ethnicity,* Oxford, 1997, pp. 168–256.
3. Government of Pakistan, *Pakistan Year Book 1994–5,* Karachi, 1996, pp. 5–6.
4. The JUI, for a long time, has been factionalised due to some inter-personality differences. Maulana Fazlur Rahman and Maulana Sami ul Haq lead its present two factions, respectively. Both of them have similar Pushtun background and believe in the Deobandi doctrine yet have been competing to gain further ground in Western Pakistan and Afghanistan. The JUP, on the other hand is largely representative of Brelvi Islam allocating greater status to saints and *pirs.* Like the Deobandi counterparts, the JUP also traces its origin from the UP whence during the nineteenth century the reform and revivalist movements emerged in British India.
5. It is reported that Riaz Basra, Malik Ishaq and several other leaders of the LJ had been trained in Afghanistan. The Iranian connection is cited in the case of SM. In an interview to Pakistan Television, Moin Haider, the interior minister, complained about continued resistance on the part of the Taliban in handing these militants back to Pakistan (Prime TV monitored in Oxford, 26 October 2001).
6. The interviews in Pakistan through the fieldwork conducted during 2000–2001 and in 2003 amply revealed that quite a few Shia professionals feel scared and have been seeking political asylum abroad. For more on Shia-Sunni discord, see, Afak Haydar, 'The Politicisation of the Shias and the Development of the Tehrik-e-

Nifaz-e-Fiqh-e-Jafria in Pakistan', in Charles H. Kennedy, (ed.) *Pakistan 1992,* Boulder, 1993, pp. 75–84.

7. For instance, see, a letter from Dublin from a Pakistani lady doctor in *Dawn,* 21 October 2001.

8. For useful introduction and the text of the Constitution, see, Makhdoom Ali Khan, (ed.) *The Constitution of the Islamic Republic of Pakistan,* Karachi, 1986.

9. For more on Bhutto, see, Stanley Wolpert, *Zulfi Bhutto of Pakistan,* Karachi, 1993; and, M. Anwar Syed, *The Discourse and Politics of Zulfikar Ali Bhutto,* New York, 1992.

10. For details, see, Dominic Moghal and Jennifer Jivan, (eds.) *Religious Minorities in Pakistan: Struggle for Identity,* Rawalpindi, 1996. The author is deeply indebted to Jennifer Jivan for her time and help.

11. Interviews with Joseph Francis, a leading humanist and activist, in Lahore, July 2001. His organization of young Christian lawyers has been defending the victims of blasphemy allegations.

12. For more details on the affects of these laws on women and other underprivileged groups, see, Jennifer Bennett, 'Religion and Democracy in Pakistan: The Rights of Women and Minorities', mimeo, Islamabad, SDPI Paper, n.d., pp. 1–23.

13. Quoted in Ahmad Saleem, *Pakistan Aur Aqlieetain* (Pakistan and Minorities,) Urdu, Karachi, 2000, p. 267. In several interviews with the author during 2000–2, Christian leaders, scholars and other human rightists across Pakistan confirmed these views. A number of Pakistani politicians like Asghar Khan, Abdul Wali Khan and Benazir Bhutto and other secular and progressive elements strongly resent this politics of separatism and exclusion.

14. Based on interviews with Christian leaders including Bishop Alexander Malik.

15. The Christian community underwent radical changes in 1947 when they lost landholding and many of them turned to menial jobs. Even among Muslims there are sweepers (*Musallis*) who are socially stigmatized. The educational and health services rendered by Christians are overwhelming. See, The Rt Revd Dr Michael Nazir Ali, 'Pakistani Christians', (London, 1991), a mimeographed article.

16. It will not be helpful to divulge the names of my Ahmadi respondents in Pakistan and Europe.

17. For a useful backgrounder see, Salamat Akhtar, *Tehreek-i-Pakistan Kay Gumnaam Kirdaar* (The unknown heroes of movement for Pakistan), Urdu, Rawalpindi, 1997. The publications by the Christian Study Centre offer valuable information on a little known subject.

18. It was in the late nineteenth century when the British military and civilian administrators 'discovered' Kalasha communities in Chitral and pioneer academic and fictional books appeared on them. George Robertson's two volumes and Rudyard Kipling's fictional accounts of Kafiristan are noteworthy.

19. Whenever there is a conversion to Islam, the local ulama organise celebratory procession. The extreme poverty and lack of resources and other such handicaps are making it difficult to retain their collective identity. Based on personal visit and interviews in Chitral, Ayun, Rambir, Berar and Bhamboriyat.

20. The HRCP has not only published annual reports documenting the state of human rights in the country, it has defended several cases as well. In addition, its workers have trained several Pakistanis across the country on human rights issues. Their reports and workshop are the most influential and constructive arms of Pakistani

civil society. See, HRCP, *State of Human Rights in Pakistan in 2001,* Lahore, 2002. Also see, the earlier yearly reports of 2001, 2000, 1998, 1997, and other Urdu publications.

21. Other than Christian Study Centre and the various churches or prominent bishops including The Right Revved. Michael Nazir Ali (based in the UK) and Bishop Alexander Malik and several others have often tried to raise consciousness on plural issues. Various publications by Peter Jacob of Catholic Bishops Conference, or by Joseph Francis's Centre for Legal Aid, Assistance and Settlement (CLAAS) have been quite fruitful and effective. For recent reports on such work, see, National Commission for Justice and Peace, *Human Rights Monitor-2001,* Lahore, 2001. CLAAS has been publishing special case studies and periodic extensive statistics on all types of incidents rights violations and litigation.

22. Based on interviews with several Baloch intellectuals and political leaders in Balochistan and Karachi in August 2001.

23. Abdul Ghani Baloch, *Zikri Firqa Ki Tarikh* (The History of Zikri Sect), Urdu, Karachi, 1996, p. 51. Mr Baloch is the leader of the All-Pakistan Muslim Zikri Anjuman and has worked for different official departments before his retirement. A native of Turbat, Mr Baloch lives in Karachi and is a widely respected Zikri intellectual. He is an author of several well-read books and in more recent times, has forcefully tried to remove stereotypes about Zikris. His brother, Shah-i-Haider is the leader of the Zikri community in Makran and supervises the arrangements of the visitors at Koh-i-Murad. Shah-i-Haider often lives on the premises built for visitors, and offered elaborate information of Zikri annual festival. He accompanied the author to Koh-i-Murad, which is two kilometers from the main settlement and consists of three small hills. A vast area around Koh-i-Murad has been walled for security reasons as well as to preserve the sanctity of the place. The author is thankful to both these leaders and countless Baloch members of the Zikri sect, Sunnis and members of the various political and ideological backgrounds for offering hospitality and sharing information on this least-known but increasingly important subject.

24. Abdul Ghani Baloch, *A Short History of Zikri Faith,* Karachi, n.d., p. 2.

25. Syed Naseer Ahmad Malai, *Asalathul Zikirin* (The reality of Zikris), Urdu, Turbat, 1994, p. 1.

26. Based on interviews and also, Abdul Ghani Baloch, *Zikri Mazhab Islam kay Aiynnah Mein* (Zikri faith through Islamic prisms), Urdu, Karachi, Turbat, 1993, pp. 18-22. Also, Inayatullah Baloch, 'Islam, the State, and Identity: The Zikris of Balochistan', in Paul Titus, (ed.) *Marginality and Modernity: Ethnicity and Change in Post-colonial Balochistan,* Karachi, 1996, pp. 223–249.

27. Some of their opponents include the members of JUI and JI. They pinpoint a number of major doctrinal differences with them. Privately, many Sunni Baloch—called Namazi Baloch by Zikris—do not like to intermarry with Zikris. Some believe that it was not Syed Jaunpur but a Mullah Attocki who came down from north and propagated his version of Islam and exploited the poor, uneducated people to follow his own whims. But, Ghani Baloch, Shah-i-Haider and other Zikri individuals rejected the existence of Attocki as the founder of the movement.

28. For such a material see, Maulana Abdul Majid Qasrqandi, *Zikri Mazhab aur Islam* (Zikri Religion and Islam), Quetta, 1978. The pamphlet attributes quite a few controversial beliefs and practices to Zikris and their priests—*Malais*—and advises

Zikri youth to convert themselves to Islam. Ghani Baloch and several other authors have been writing books to refute such claims but are worried about communal violence due to a growing accent on fundamentalism.

29. For instance, see, Azhar Munir, *Zikris in the Light of History and Their Religious Beliefs*, Lahore, 1998. Originally published as a series of sympathetic articles to educate Pakistanis on the Zikri beliefs and practices and to create a greater sensitivity to their rights, this book is the translated version. It is widely quoted as a vital support for the Zikris. I am thankful to Asma Jahangir, Syed Husain Naqi, Darr Paddar and I.A. Rahman at the HRCP for helping me in building up useful contacts with the Zikri community in Balochistan and Sindh. My thanks are due to a number of individuals and organisations in Pakistan for their assistance, though I am hesitant in divulging their names for the fear of their security.

Perhaps no other class of people in the world today are as ruined, economically and socially, as smitten and smashed up as the community of the former Indian refugees in Bangladesh who are known here by the general term Bihari.... Today in Bangladesh, to be a Bihari is the worst crime...

— Basant Chatterji, *Inside Bangladesh Today,* 1973, 101–13

6

Statelessness and Human Rights:
Biharis in Bangladesh

This chapter addresses the intricate subject of human rights as an intra-state contestation where several identities appear collaborating as well as conflicting by focusing on the undefined and equally arduous case study of the Biharis in Bangladesh. It is an almost forgotten issue of human rights where two South Asian states (even three!) have consistently refused to empower *their* own citizens, and thus raises serious moral, humanitarian and legal issues. While Bangladesh would like these *stranded* Pakistanis to be repatriated to Pakistan, the latter insists on their indigenization and also uses the conflictive pluralism in Sindh as an alibi. Concurrently, international organizations like the UNHCR (United Nations High Commission for Refugees) and ICRC (the International Committee for the Red Cross) refuse to allocate them refugee status. India, another party to the entire imbroglio by virtue of Partition and then through a blatant intervention in the former East Pakistan in 1971, has equally posited itself as an 'outsider'. The exaggerated threat of Bangladeshi economic refugees in India is also offered as a justification to avoid discussing any trilateral solution to this ongoing human agony. Curiously, in all the three countries, the societies have also tended to ignore the plight of the Biharis, rather, in many cases, they simply end up supporting the ambivalent stance of their respective regimes. The civil societies in all the three countries, once in a while, mention the ongoing dilemma, eventually to highlight their respective *national* policies. The Bangladeshi political elements, especially the hard core Awami Leaguers, continue to misportray them as 'collaborators' and 'insiders-outsiders', though most of the new generation Biharis were, in fact, born in Bangladesh. In Pakistan, successive regimes have more often shirked from accepting more Biharis by offering two explanations; we have already accepted sufficient numbers as agreed in the Simla Agreement of 1973 and the Delhi Agreement of 1974, and secondly, any more influxes will seriously affect the inter-ethnic relationship in Sindh, by tilting the demography in the favour of the Urdu-speakers. The Muhajir Qaumi Movement (MQM), an urban political party of the Urdu speakers, in its early career, demanded their repatriation, but over the years their support has withered away, besides which it has caused bitter resentment among the Sindhis. Thus, about 250,000 denationalized, stateless and marginalized 'non-citizens' have been subjected to live in immensely inhuman conditions in squalor and dirt since the early 1970s, and have been continuously denied their basic human rights by all the concerned parties. Bangladesh, Pakistan, India, and the international organizations, have all used similar arguments against owning up this community and have equally refused to face up to their responsibilities. Their respective elite, in most cases, have used the Bihari issue to drum up an exclusionary form of nationalism, and also to score cheaper points against each other. Globally, such a great tragedy seems to have been overtaken by tragedies in Afghanistan, the Middle East and the Balkans.

The initial section of this chapter problematises trajectories as globalization and modernity, before moving on to the politics of identity among Muslims in British India. The convergence of various interests and ideals on the utopian concept of Pakistan is discussed in this section where the subsequent politics of state versus society puts Biharis in the crossfire. Whereas global and national ambiguities have aggravated the dilemma of minorities in South Asia, unilateral demarcations of international boundaries and an exclusive definition of nationalism, appear to be the core problem underwriting the less-than-smooth operation of pluralism.

GLOBALIZATION AND THE POLITICS OF IDENTITY

Undoubtedly, globalization is spawning various trans-regional influences, which mostly have their origins in the North Atlantic region. While this *core* region itself is heading towards a greater sameness and a sustained hegemonic power, the *peripheral* countries, especially in the post-colonial world find themselves in a unique and rather ironic position. On the one hand, development and self-sufficiency remain their ideals, yet alienation with Western cultural onslaught and selective policies stays pervasive. Modernization, in most cases, is perceived by them as a new post-colonial regimentation, aimed at thwarting the indigenous languages, economies, ecologies, religions, and cultures towards a rootless and abrasive McDonaldization. Such an ideological conflict—in several situations—has serious and volatile portents. The forces espousing Hindutva, Jihad, Talibanization, and ethnic cleansing, largely bank on the nativist authenticity, and cashing on such anxieties, have been attempting to create monoethnic and fundamentalist statehood, intent upon imposing ideological uniformity at the expense of ethno-religious pluralism. These concurrent trends of regionalization and fragmentation are the post-1991 realities in the world, though the processes were unleashed in the near past when the modern state system evolved itself.

Though defining globalization is a rather testing task given the ideological polarization it has engendered, its main trajectories are economic, cultural, political, and of course, ideological. It is modernity, post-modernity, as well as Westernism all put together, where institutional frameworks despite their regional specificity remain trans-regional. Salience of globalization took a new turn in the 1990s following the dissolution of the Eastern bloc when a Fukuyamian kind of sameness seemed to be on the ascendance. Globalization as a holistic process emerged in the 1960s, though in its McLuhanian sense, it largely meant a greater mobility and crucial leaps in the areas of communications. Though information technology remains a major component of contemporary globalization, the processes have become complex and more autonomous of state-led forces. A leading columnist felt that several cultures and communities had suddenly become vulnerable to this multiple onslaught coming from the West:

> Global culture and its detritus wash everywhere, nothing sacred, nothing wild, nothing authentic, original or primitive any more....Theocratic imams, military dictators, ethnic-cleansing demagogues and the few remaining Communists will all fall in time. Historical inevitability is with us and the western way is the best when it comes to the things that really matter—freedom, democracy, liberation, tolerance and pluralism. And that our culture is the only culture of universal human rights and there is no compromise... (Polly Toynbee)

However, this tidal wave of Western culture has its drawbacks, which like a milkshake 'oozes over the planet, sickly, homogenous, full of "E" numbers, stabilizers and monosodium glutamate, tasting the same from Samoa to Siberia to Somalia'.[1] But the question is: how do we define it. In a categorical sense, globalization is perceived to be *internationalization, liberalization, universalization,* and *deterritorialization.* Of all these processes, it is the last set which seems nearer to the truth as the other three are contestable. Globalization, in that sense, may be defined as a transformation of social geography which is highlighted by supra territorial spaces.[2] While to its critics it is a new phase in ever-growing Western hegemony, to Anthony Giddens it is not all bad, and in a positive sense, could be 'the third way', though he is aware of its cultural and ecological costs.[3] The social and economic modernization of Western Europe (and North America) following the Protestant revolution as posited by Weber and Parsons, is considered to be the beginning of globalization which, unlike many *traditionalist* societies are more prone to secularization. However, the subsequent sociologists including Berger, Bellah and Martin have further refined and enlarged the scope of modernity by attributing secularization to monotheistic traditions where individualism succeeds over collectivities. In that sense, globalization becomes a historical process with secularization, reformism and individualism as its core.[4] While the *classical* theories will uniquely focus on the interface between Protestantism and capitalism, the latter day studies enlarge the scope to various other monotheistic faiths. However, the views about Islam remain ambiguous. Unlike the Orientalist certainty and fixity, one particular school of contemporary Western writers considers Islam to be non-static, yet resistant to certain features of modernity. To others, Islam is simply the opposite of modernity—thus unique, fixed and antagonistic to the Western heritage.[5] Globalization, in a nutshell, has intensified the debate on Islam and modernity, though it will be dangerous to posit them simply as two poles apart.

Globalization, to a great extent, is viewed by its critics as the monopoly of Western—more specifically American—economic interests as reflected in the 'New Military Humanism'.[6] Other than sociologists, a host of definitions and commentaries have been offered by political scientists, politicians and economists. Tony Blair, Henry Kissinger and Bill Clinton may see globalization in terms of social democracy, free marketism and *laissez faire*, the environmentalists see in globalization an unhindered exploitation of human and natural resources.[7] To David Harvey, global capitalism and the resultant changes are the features of post-modernity,[8] whereas to feminists, there is not much to celebrate in globalization as it is inherently hierarchical and exploitative.[9] The feminist position is closer to that of the developing world critique, which abhors unilateral powers, enjoyed by Western powers and institutions such as the International Monetary Fund (IMF) and the World Bank. The critics, however, are all in unison in their criticism of cultural imperialism, which remains an essential accompaniment of globalization processes. Political scientists and economists foresee greater integration of North Atlantic regions, with the state becoming a facilitator and agent rather than a hurdle, though they are equally mindful of concurrent processes of fragmentation in diverse regions.[10] While looking at the Biharis within this perspective, globalization seems to have no space or even definition on offer for such communities lost between the various border-posts and destined to live on a no man's land.

PARTITION AND MIGRATION: ORIGINS OF THE BIHARI COMMUNITY IN EAST BENGAL

Irrespective of its definitional and conceptual problems, globalization has reinvigorated the role of state, regional cooperation and contestation between religion and society. On the one hand, economic forces and technological changes, especially in the information sector are shrinking the distances, yet the North-South divide and the issues of poverty and stratification seem to be increasing. In the same vein, many of the post-colonial societies appear to be losing their autonomous space in global affairs with policies being imposed on them. Such unnerving challenges are leading to multiple responses including a reinforced religion-based activism and exclusionary forms of nationalism. The debate on civil society may be positive yet the sense of insecurity owing to extra-regional 'interventionism' has, in several cases, aggravated nativism where the state and some xenophobic elite may join hands together to define national identity through a rather intolerant postulation. The current focus on civil society, not just by Western pundits, but also by human rights groups elsewhere is a positive development, which needs a better understanding and holistic nurturing. Alert and active civil societies will have restraining influences on the West-led politico-economic globalism and can also empower weaker societies by curbing the statist and societal unilateralism.

The way the post-colonial states—democratic as well as pseudo-democratic—are single-mindedly creating unitary nationhood has already betrayed their majoritarian or elitist prerogatives which has put the ethnic and religious minorities in a nut-cracker situation. For instance, the Kurds are caught not only in a severe Middle Eastern tug of war involving Turkey, Iraq, Iran, Syria, Israel and Armenia but several majoritarian forces within them, and the regimes (through intense Turkification, Persianization, Iraqization, Arabization and so on) are determined upon their forced amalgamation. There are parallels with several Muslim communities in the Balkans—on the patterns of the Spanish Inquisition—where an all-out integration has remained the objective of immensely aggressive polities. The delineation of borders by the receding colonial empires, have in most cases, caused these inter-state dissensions. On the other hand, the break-up of the post-colonial states leaving minorities across new borders or amongst hostile/indifferent majorities has led to a new set of internecine communalism. Asia and Africa abound in such case studies. The Palestinians in the Middle East, Muslims and Christians in India, Hindus in Pakistan, Baloch in Iran, Hutus in Rwanda, Muslims in Greece, Albanians in Macedonia, Kosovars in Serbia, Catholics in Northern Ireland, and so on are several such reminders of ongoing divided ethnicities causing several human miseries. The issue of human rights of the Biharis, sometimes called stranded Pakistanis, Urdu speakers, or non-Bengali Bangladeshis, is a unique case where, as stated above, the three states and their elite continue denying citizenship rights to a marooned community. Globalization may offer newer opportunities to such minorities elsewhere, but in South Asia, the majoritarian insecurities and proclivities are antagonistic to religious, ethnic or lingual minorities. The most plural region of the world needs to undertake fresher and multiple perspectives away from a vengeful unilateralism and exclusionary nationalism.

The 250,000 Biharis in Bangladesh today comprise those who originally opted for Pakistan in 1947, and migrated to the region from India during the time of Partition or their descendants. Most of them originated from the state of Bihar, whereas there were Muslim refugees from other regions as well, all collectively referred to in Bangladesh as Biharis. In fact, riots in Bihar in 1946 led to a mass exodus of Muslims from this comparatively poor region to the neighbouring east Bengal. Between 30,000 and 35,000 Muslims were killed in Bihar in late 1946, in retaliation to anti-Hindu riots in Noakhali in Bengal.[11]

Despite the fact that Muslims in Bengal were in a slight majority vis-à-vis the Hindus, the latter were economically strong and were mostly known as *bhadralok* (a term denoting a cultured and respected person). In many cases, they were absentee landlords living in Calcutta or were middle class professionals. The Bengali Muslims were predominantly rural and landless peasants, excepting a few Urdu speaking Nawab families in Dhaka and Murshidabad. The early movements[12] for an Islamic renaissance such as the Faraidhis had politicized the Muslim rural communities, whereas the Partition of Bengal under Lord Curzon in 1905, and the subsequent Hindu uproar in the form of the Swadeshi[13] agitation created a gulf between Muslims and Hindus in the province.[14] Due to a massive uproar, the partition was annulled in 1911, but simultaneously, two new provinces of Bihar and Orissa were carved out purely for administrative reasons. The Muslims in Bihar mostly consisted of landless peasants and artisans, and by 1946, were four million in a population of about 30 million inhabitants, accounting for 13 per cent of the total. Overall, the Muslim population in India on the eve of Partition was about 110 million out of a total of 530 million. By the late 1940s, the movement for a Muslim state had become a major consensus point, especially in East Bengal and the Muslim minority regions in British India. Pakistan appeared to be an ultimate utopia for landless peasants and a thin emerging Muslim middle class who sought to preserve their economic and cultural interests in a Muslim majority state instead of turning into a permanent minority. The failure of the Indian National Congress, the Communist Party of India and of the regional parties in providing a tangible solution to the predicament of these Muslim sections led to the popularization of the idea of Pakistan.[15] By 1946, communalization had already reached its zenith and with the November riots resulting in thirty thousand Muslim deaths, many Muslim families began to migrate to neighbouring Bengal.[16] However, the major migration and accompanying ethnic mayhem took place soon after the announcement of the Partition Plan in June 1947. As seen in Table 1, more than one million Muslims just from Bihar, opted to move into Pakistan—many of them reaching the Eastern wing—along with 350,000 Muslim refugees from Orissa, Madras and other adjoining Indian regions.[17]

Collectively, there were more than one million, mainly Urdu speaking refugees from Bihar, and other states/regions (West Bengal, Orissa, Assam, Manipur, Nagaland, Tripura and Sikkim) who migrated to East

Pakistan, in addition to a huge majority of Muslim Bengalis moving eastwards from West Bengal. Along with their religion, the Urdu

Table 1. Urdu Speaking Refugees in East Pakistan, 1951

Settlement District	Bihar	Uttar Pradesh	Punjab-Delhi	Total
Dhaka	27,530	6,986	1,193	32,706
Rangpur	24,885	3,119	46	28,050
Dinajpur	22,914	2,519	302	25,735
Chittagong	6,313	2,626	331	9,270
Rajshahi	4,302	620	29	4,951
Bogra	4,285	332	12	4,629
Pabna	3,078	650	2	3,730
Jessore	3,022	571	50	3,643
Mymensingh	2,624	752	42	3,418
Kushtia	1,396	644	6	2,046
Total	97,349	18,819	2,002	118,17

Source: A.F.M. Kamaluddin, 'Refugee Problems in Bangladesh', in L.A. Kosinski and K.H. Elahi, (eds.) *Population Redistribution and Development in South Asia,* Dordrecht, 1985, p. 224.

language, and Pakistan as the new common homeland were other shared mutualities amongst these non-Bengali immigrants who were soon designated as Biharis, largely because an overwhelming proportion of the refugees coming from Bihar (95 per cent)[18] outnumbered the other ethno-regional groups.[19] In the midst of the world's largest migration on the subcontinent, around three million Hindus also left East Bengal (Pakistan) for the safety of West Bengal, and their houses and urban properties were mostly allotted to the incoming Muslim refugees who were initially well-received by their Bengali compatriots.[20] About ten million Hindus, however, stayed on in East Pakistan, whereas forty million Muslims opted to remain in India. The anti-Muslim riots in 1950, 1959 and 1964 pushed many more Biharis towards neighbouring East Pakistan. However, agrarian land being scarce, most of the Bihari immigrants chose urban professions such as railways, mills, hospitals, post offices, schools and bureaucracy.[21] However, it must be noted that there were several prosperous migrants from India such as the Bawanis, Ispahanis, Adamjees, Aga Khanis (Ismailis), who established businesses in Pakistan. For their own survival, the refugees, irrespective of their

class background, worked hard and built up a closer collaboration
with the West Pakistani Urdu speaking and Punjabi elite. On the
sensitive language issue they usually sided with the dominant West
Pakistani establishment and advocated the case for Urdu as the national
language. Such an interdependence and reservations against Bengali
deeply disturbed the Bengalis who began mistrusting their loyalties.
After the volatile language riots on 21 February 1952, and amidst the
growing popularity of a nationalist Awami League, the Biharis
continued to support the ruling Punjabi-Muhajir axis usually
represented by bureaucracy and the Muslim League.[22] Following the
military coup of 1958 led by General Ayub Khan, they visibly aligned
themselves with the Pakistani armed forces, which were
disproportionately Punjab-dominated.[23] The Punjabi and Muhajir ruling
elite not only ignored the cultural and economic aspirations of East
Pakistanis, they also exhibited negative attitudes towards Bengalis.
Jute and tea were the two main cash crops, accounting for a major
share of foreign exchange earnings, but East Pakistan received only
half of its due share from the exports. Most of the resources were any
way spent on defence, which was largely dominated by Punjabis. In
the civilian sector, East Pakistan did not see any major improvements
as very few East Pakistanis held higher offices in bureaucracy and the
cabinet. The West Pakistani ruling elite kept the political forces and
electoral politics at bay because they feared a Bengali majority would
deny them their hold over the country's affairs. From 1950 onwards
various strategies were used to thwart political and constitutional
processes in the country, exacerbating the sense of deprivation in the
eastern wing.[24]

On 30–31 October 1969, the Biharis held a convention at Rangpur
and decided to contest the elections without realizing that amidst a
growing support for the Awami League-led demand for autonomy
based on Six Points, they had few chances to be heard. The elections
in 1970 held under General Yahya Khan's military regime resulted in
the absolute victory of Sheikh Mujibur Rahman's Awami League in
East Pakistan, which obtained 167 seats of a 300-seat National
Assembly whereas in West Pakistan, a motley of several regional
parities emerged as power brokers. However, Zulfikar Ali Bhutto's
Pakistan People's Party (PPP) won 85 seats—mostly in Punjab and
Sindh, whereas the Awami League had won all except for two in East
Pakistan. Constitutionally and legally, Sheikh Mujib should have been
allowed to form the new government but the generals refused to hand

over power with West Pakistani leaders including Bhutto supporting them. The Urdu speaking East Pakistanis had voted for various parties including the Muslim League that had failed miserably to win any seats. The Mujib-Yahya-Bhutto parleys in the backdrop of the suspicion about convening the Assembly's session, resulted only in exacerbating mutual acrimonies, and eventually led to riots across the eastern wing. The Awami League felt as if it was being denied its right to form the government and began a series of strikes concurrently taking the Biharis as scapegoats. They were called collaborators and in early March 1971—three weeks before the Pakistani military crackdown began on the 25th—Awami League mobs killed 300 Biharis in Chittagong and several hundred Urdu speaking East Pakistanis at Shantahar in Bogra. Similar other incidents where Biharis were killed took place at Jessore, Khulna, Rangpur and Saidpur resulting in serious inter-community chasms.[25] The Biharis and other such elements sought protection with the armed forces, which began a massive operation on 25 March 1971 to suppress the Awami League.[26] The organized massacre of the Biharis reached its crescendo when on 28 March 1971, Zia-ur-Rahman, the Bangladeshi commander, ordered his troops to shoot male Bihari prisoners in Chittagong, and permitted his troops to violate the modesty of the female prisoners.[27] In May 1971,[28] several Bengali workers, resentful of prosperous Biharis in Chittagong, killed them in large numbers, whereas in Khulna, thousands of Biharis were 'tied to the frames especially set up to hold prisoners for decapitation'.[29] Some Biharis[30] established *razakar* associations such as EPCAF (East Pakistan Civil Armed Forces) for self-protection, as well as to help Pakistani troops, though attacks against them went on unabated.[31] The refusal to transfer power to the elected representatives, followed by a brutal military operation resulting in large-scale killing of fellow citizens by the Pakistani armed forces in connivance with several West Pakistani politicians, only pushed East Pakistan towards full-fledged independence. The brutalities committed by Pakistani troops caused an influx of refugees into neighbouring India, which used this opportunity to malign and humble its old arch enemy. Concurrently, the dismissed members of East Pakistan Rifles, many Bengali volunteers and students organized the Mukti Bahini, a guerrilla force, to attack military installations and to harass West Pakistanis and Biharis in East Pakistan. Trained and equipped by Indians, the force undertook several operations including attacks on Biharis by denigrating them as collaborators.[32] In the meantime, the Provisional

Government of Bangladesh was established in India, which fully spearheaded the secession from Pakistan. The continued military operation without any effort to resolve the political impasse through proper constitutional measures only worsened the situation.[33] India's formal entry into the war under the pretext of liberation in December 1971 delivered the state of Bangladesh,[34] following which revengeful mayhem took place directed against West Pakistanis and Biharis. Whereas there are estimates of one to three million Bengalis being killed by Pakistani troops, the numbers of murdered Biharis and West Pakistanis remain unknown, but 'not insignificant'.[35] Some Biharis even became 'freedom fighters' and joined the band of unruly miscreants looting households and valuables of fellow Biharis and other West Pakistani residents, in addition to committing serious crimes such as rape.

THE ENIGMA

Following Pakistan's defeat and the creation of Bangladesh, Zulfikar Ali Bhutto became the martial law administrator and president of Pakistan. While there were four hundred thousand Bengalis (East Pakistanis) in West Pakistan, there were almost an equal number of West Pakistanis in Bangladesh. Of these, Pakistani military personnel and several senior officials were now prisoners of war in India, while the Biharis were generally left to the mercy of the mobs in the new country where emotions were running so high. Their role as collaborators has been highly exaggerated but it is a fact that many of them had organized volunteer groups such as Al-Shams which helped Pakistani troops in their operations against a totally non-cooperative civil populace. In addition to the Biharis, many Bengali *razakar* such as Al-Badar had collaborated with the army and in several cases were responsible for the massacres of several fellow Bengali intellectuals. Some of the Biharis, for the sake of their own safety, had in fact collaborated with the Mukti Bahini but such things were forgotten in the state of frenzy though Sheikh Mujib, in his various speeches before and after his imprisonment by West Pakistani generals, had urged for tolerance. [36] In a speech on 10 January 1972, soon after his return to Bangladesh, he observed: 'I tell you, there are still four lakhs of Bengalis living in Pakistan. We have to take care of them. These non-locals living here are to be Bengali henceforth.'[37] He had given his personal assurance of the safety of Non-Bengalis in Bangladesh.[38] Following the Indian victory and Pakistani surrender led by General A.A.K. Niazi, several West Pakistani officials and military personnel came under Indian custody, while many others took off for Burma, Nepal and Sri Lanka. The local press, Awami League students and the Mukti Bahini activists pursued a very exclusionary nationalism where West Pakistan and Urdu speaking East Pakistanis were perceived as the enemies and colonizers who had to be taken to task. Individual and collective cases of retaliation, rape and looting continued to take place as desperate Urdu speakers sought shelter in the suburbs of Dhaka. This is how the *bastis* of Muhammadpur, Saidpur and Mirpur came into being, with thousands of Biharis congregating to escape attacks by Bengalis. Some of them, like Mirpur, had been traditionally predominantly Bihari localities since the early 1960s. In many cases, Awami League workers and Bangladeshi officials would prevent the ICRC access to the camps so as to exact their revenge on the Biharis.[39] With Pakistan's break-up, the administrative machinery had completely failed, and as happened in 1947, the police and other such agencies turned communal. Thus, the Biharis were left to the mercy of the ICRC, who were reluctant to classify them as refugees. When on 27 January 1972, Indian troops left Dhaka, a major struggle took place at Mirpur Bihari camp. The Bangladeshi soldiers from the Bengal regiment started a search operation to arrest hidden Pakistan army personnel. A few days earlier, Zahir Raihan, well-known Bengali author and film-maker, had ventured into the camp looking for his kidnapped brother, Shahidula Kaisar, reportedly being kept there. He was mysteriously killed with the Biharis being singled out as the accused party. Now, the Bangladeshi soldiers and a few Mukti Bahini activists invaded the camp during the night of 28–29 January, ostensibly to carry out a search for arms under the orders of Sheikh Mujibur Rehman, but it turned into a killing spree. Hundreds of people were killed on both sides—though more on the Bihari side—strengthening the Bangladeshi view of the Biharis as the 'other' and 'remnants' of Pakistani *colonialism*. Actually, Sheikh Mujib's own wife had been protected by Biharis in March 1971 during the Pakistani military operation, but now his sympathies lay with the Bangladeshi majority and 'he made little effort...to translate this ideal into practical steps'.[40] In Dhaka, while many Biharis had sought refuge in the cramped and undersupplied make-shift shelters, others in outlying areas proved easy victims for mobs. After the withdrawal of the Indian regulars from Khulna on 10 March 1972, hundreds of Biharis were killed and the rest were driven out of their homes. All over the country, thousands of Biharis were arrested on allegations of collaborating with Pakistani troops, and a huge number simply disappeared. The contemporary Bangladeshi press, including some left-wing Sunday papers like *Holiday* chose to gloss over these violations. The facts about the Biharis, their pitiable conditions in the camps, disappearance of so many male members of the community, large-scale incidents of rape, pillage and loot were all ignored; instead the frenzied press rather inflamed the campaign for ethnic cleansing. Bengali leaders and media were irresponsibly fanning anti-Bihari sentiments, and in a kind of anarchic situation, generosity and tolerance were scant. In a public meeting in Dhaka on 1 May 1972, a Lal Bahni (Red Shirt) leader announced to a cheering crowd that his organization would try the inmates of the Mirpur Camp if the government did not. The exaggerated stories of Bihari atrocities in the wake of temptation to grab their properties and jobs put the Awami League regime on the defensive, and it chose to go along with the inflamed mobs.[41] It was forgotten that most of the people in these camps were women and children whose men had simply 'disappeared'. Given the frenzy and all-out anger, many Biharis sought the security of international agencies and demanded repatriation to Pakistan, which, inadvertently, cast them in the dubious role of *Pakistani agents*.

Despite the fact that they have been usually categorized as Biharis, the non-Bengali population included all kinds of ethno-lingual groups. Of course, most of them spoke Urdu and before 1971–2, their number was thought to be several million. In the 1961 census, a million citizens of East Pakistan had stated their mother tongue to be other than Bengali; half of them spoke Urdu, followed by 140,000 Hindi-speakers, and another 300,000 Chakmas of the Chittagong Hills. According to the 1961 census, 434,081 citizens had been born in various parts of Eastern India but now resided in East Pakistan. The figures of five million non-Bengali speaking East Pakistanis in 1972 may appear to be on the inflated side, yet the camps were usually an easier place to carry out calculations. However, one must not overlook the fact that many Urdu speakers refused to be identified as Biharis for fear of revenge and their own bilingualism may have helped them in assuming a newer identity as Bengali-speaking Muslim Bangladeshis. Moreover, many prosperous families like the Adamjees, Ispahanis and some affluent Ismailis were able to fly to Pakistan benefiting from their own resourcefulness and communitarian networks. Some Bihari activists were also able to slip across the borders, eventually to reach Karachi, though the numbers remain unquantified. During this difficult time, a few Bihari intellectuals like S.G.M. Badrudin and Salahuddin Ahmed met in the Geneva Camp due to the Geneva-based Red Cross—to review their situation in Bangladesh.

Table 2. Biharis in Camps across Bangladesh in 1972

City	Number
Dhaka	278,500
(-Mirpur	150,000
-Muhammadpur)	95,000
Murapara	9,500
Adamjee	16,000
Ispahani	3,000
Saidpur	275,000
Rangpur	7,000
Chittagong	60,000
Khulna	60,000
Ishurdi	30,000
Bogra	14,000
Rajshahi	4,500
Mymensingh	3,100
Comilla	1,200
Sylhet	1,000
Jessore	700
Dinajpur	180

Of them, a clear majority opted for repatriation. The Biharis in outlying areas were more vulnerable to physical violence, and thus started trickling into Dhaka. In 1972, according to Ben Whittaker and his colleagues, the camps mentioned in Table 2 accounted for most of the Biharis who consisted of the poor, jobless, elderly, women and children.

Altogether, in mid-1972 there were 735,180 Bihari accounted for, whereas the total number was estimated to be one-and-a-half million.[42] The Biharis in Ispahani Camp were usually from the affluent urban community whereas those in other camps were not so privileged, and according to a survey conducted by the ICRC, 95 per cent of them wanted to be repatriated to Pakistan, with 5 per cent even willing to go back to India. The Saidpur Camp in north-western Bangladesh was comparatively safe from individual and/or collective reprisals because the almost 300,000 Biharis outnumbered the local Bangladeshis in that area. Elsewhere, the situation was not so secure. For instance, on 10 March 1972, one thousand Biharis were killed on the instigation of militant students. Most of them lived in very small tents provided by the ICRC, which distributed food and supplied water. The Committee, without properly understanding their precarious situation and without seeking prior approval from the governments of Bangladesh and Pakistan, took upon itself to register the Biharis. This anomaly made it easier for both the governments to evade their responsibility of offering citizenship to these stranded families, whose plight was depicted by a contemporary observer as follows:

Perhaps no other class of people in the world today(are)as ruined, economically and socially, as smitten and smashed up as the community of the former India refugees in Bangladesh who are known here by the general term Bihari.... Today in Bangladesh, to be a Bihari is the worst crime.... Thousands have been discharged from service on the ground of 'long absence without leave'. But their salaries and funds have not yet been paid.... Many persons rejoined duty on the strength of 'clearance chits' given by the Awami League MPs. But they did not return; even their bodies remained untracked.[43]

Following the Delhi Agreement of 28 August 1973 between Pakistan and India, and the tripartite agreement between India, Bangladesh and Pakistan of 1974, the former agreed to take a 'substantial number of non-Bengalis' from Bangladesh who had 'opted for repatriation for Pakistan'. In exchange, the Bengalis in West Pakistan were to be repatriated, besides the release of Pakistani troops and other officials from India. All the 128,000 registered Bengalis were to be sent back to Bangladesh from Pakistan, though due to official protection none of them had suffered any physical reprisals. However, their properties and jobs had been taken over by the government on the plea of compensation for the 'returnees'. Pakistan had agreed to accept all government officials of the former East Pakistan as well as 25,000 hardship cases, and thus by late 1974, had accepted 108,750 personnel altogether. Of these, 58,000 were from the armed forces and their families; 9000 had been transferred by sea and the remainder through the UN airlift. The ICRC had listed 470,000 Biharis for repatriation, but 350,000 of them remained stranded.[44]

According to another study, Pakistan accepted 178,069 Biharis between 1973 and 1993, as illustrated in Table 4. When the Bangladesh Red Crescent Society took over from the ICRC in 1972, it estimated the number of Biharis to be around 735,180 in sixty-six camps. During 1973–74, the ICRC flew 12,915 people from Bangladesh to Pakistan while 27,000 escaped to Pakistan along with the POWs. Since 1974, the various regimes in Islamabad have shown resistance to repatriation by suggesting that the agreements offered only a conditional facility, whereas Bangladesh has equally remained ambivalent towards them. The latter could have pursued an integrationist approach while Pakistan could have been more accommodative. The ICRC and other international agencies have been unable to influence either government, whereas the remaining Bihari communities remain largely cooped up in small, unclean and highly pitiful shacks in various camps. Though initial Bengali rancour against them has lessened over the last thirty years, the stigma remains and Biharis are refused jobs, regular care and other rights that should be theirs by right because more than 50 per cent are now native born and also multi-lingual. The food and other commodities of daily need are distributed by the ICRC, Rabita-i-Alam-i-Islami—a Saudi funded charity—or other Western

Table 3. Biharis Repatriated to Pakistan, 1974–98

Year	Number Repatriated	Total	Left Behind
1974	108,754	108,754	470,000
1979	121,212	–	–
1981	7,000	163,072	300,000
1993	325	237,440	–
1998*	8,000	171,397	–

Source: Ben Whitaker, Tazeen Murshid, op. cit., and Bangladeshi official estimates in ibid.
* Was planned by Nawaz Sharif, as earlier in 1993, Pakistan had accepted 325 individuals belonging to 45 families for settlement in central Punjab.

Table 4. Biharis Repatriated to Pakistan, 1973–93

Year	Number
1973-4	163,072
1979	9,872
1982	4,800
1993	325
Total	178,069

Source: The News, 8 September 1992; and, The Guardian, 11 January 1993, as tabulated in Sumit Sen, 'Stateless Refugees and the Right to Return: The Bihari Refugees of South Asia—Part 2', International Journal of Refugee Law, XII, 2, 2000, p. 62.

charities have been meager, though over the past two decades, the Biharis have tried to develop their own small-scale economy. Many of them are cycle rickshaw drivers, while others work as menial workers in the cities. A few shops selling food, books, cassettes and utensils have emerged within the camps and are trying to keep up with local demand though the scarcity of capital, space and market pose serious hindrances. The lack of clean water, especially during the rainy season, scarcity of hygienic toilets, especially for women, and proper jobs even for otherwise qualified artisans and professionals remain persistent. The Biharis have developed their own committees, some of which may be inflicted with schisms and inter-personal rivalries, but they have tried to cater to the need for education for the new generation and have also tried to influence politics in Pakistan and Bangladesh. Some of them have moved out or have slipped into Pakistan by taking all sorts of risks but many continue living in the camps because residing elsewhere may weaken their bargaining position. The camps are located on expensive urban property, and elements in the Bangladesh government have tried to resettle them elsewhere, both for mundane and humanitarian needs, but the Bihari leadership is resistant to such proposals. In the meantime, their existence remains pitiable and precarious in the camps. Though a visitor is often greeted with sentences like: 'Humain Zehr Do' (Give us poison), dissatisfaction with the status quo remains ascendant. Any change in regimes in Islamabad and Dhaka rekindles temporary hopes soon to be dashed by the same old 'official' considerations. The opening up of a Pakistani embassy in 1976 in Dhaka was received with great optimism, which has been replaced by criticism of a successive line of diplomats and bureaucrats who have remained 'insensitive' to fellow Pakistanis. Secular Bangladeshis routinely avoid the issue and merely put the responsibility on Pakistan which, since 1971, has emerged as the *other* in the nationalist discourse. By taking such a stance they feel relieved of all responsibility or guilt towards fellow citizens who are all categorized as Biharis, *Muhajirs* and stranded Pakistanis. Nationalist elements have been stubbornly refusing to own their due share in the malady and miss the point that if the former East Pakistanis could become Bangladesh on 18 December 1971, how come the generations born on their soil and sharing their language remain alien. Individually, both Bangladeshis and Pakistanis express grief over the plight of the Biharis, but collectively, end up towing the official line. Conversely, both Pakistan and Bangladesh allow dual citizenship to their expatriate communities in Britain, but are reluctant to offer citizenship to these native-born individuals.

In the 1970s, both Pakistan and Bangladesh suffered serious economic and political problems and in their own ways felt that adding the Biharis to their citizenry may result in socio-political complications. During that decade, Pakistan's nationalization process under Zulfikar Ali Bhutto, low morale after the war and separation of East Pakistan had curtailed any interest in the Bihari issue. By 1972, Karachi had become restive over the language issue, with local Sindhis demanding replacement of Urdu with Sindhi as the medium of instruction. The clashes between Urdu speakers and Sindhis became volatile, with Islamabad shying away from accepting more Bihari hopefuls. In the 1980s and 1990s, Sindh remained volatile with serious ethnic clashes in Karachi and Hyderabad, as the MQM demanded more political and economic rights for *Muhajireen* to be confronted with a similar grudge by the Sindhis who complained of 'turning American Indians' on their own soil.[45] The MQM, the largest electoral party in Sindh all through the 1990s, demanded the repatriation of 'stranded Pakistanis' and were opposed with full force by Sindhis. The various governments have worried that the influx of more Biharis would further tilt the demographic balance in favour of the *Muhajireen* who alveady make up more than 50 per cent of the urban population of Sindh further alienating the Sindhis from Pakistan. The military regime of General Ziaul Haq (1977–88), and of Mian Nawaz Sharif (1990–93 and 1997–99), appeared sympathetic towards the plight of the Biharis in Bangladesh, but privately complained that even if they were rehabilitated elsewhere in Pakistan, they would trickle down to Karachi. Islamabad, that had already accepted millions of Afghan refugees, asked for financial assistance for the rehabilitation of at least a quarter of a million Biharis. The Rabita, led by Abdullah Omar Naseef, tried to determine the modalities, as well as the funds, but nothing substantial came out of it.

Following the Minority Rights Group's pioneering report on the Biharis (1972), a further writeup was added in 1977 by Iain Guest, seeking post-1974 developments. To him, the estimated figures of the Biharis in mid-1972 stood at 735,180, while the estimate from 'Concern', the relief agency primarily involved with the Biharis, showed that it had fallen significantly to just over 300,000 by the end of 1976. Amidst a serious economic slump in Bangladesh, Guest found little improvement in their conditions. Large families of six to seven members lived in one 6–8 foot shack with no sanitation or other such basic facilities. The Biharis all over Bangladesh were seen by the relief agencies as 'the "most visibly miserable" anywhere in Bangladesh', and were likened to Palestinians in the Jordanian refugee camps.[46] The Biharis themselves were caught between the dilemma of repatriation and integration, though the erstwhile hostility had by now turned into indifference. However, the precarious economic conditions, the memories of the post-war killing sprees, and other incidents of violence still made most Biharis yearn for repatriation to Pakistan. India did not offer any attraction either, and many Biharis and Bengalis attempted to get to Pakistan, still economically better off than Bangladesh, and also to reach the Gulf region for better prospects. This illegal immigration began to cause all kinds of underhand syndicated criminal activities, including the trafficking of women. The number of the people making it to Karachi and those lost on the way or in the slums and red light districts across India, will never be exactly known. Forces within the camps were blamed for working against integration in the hope that Pakistan or some other Commonwealth country may accept them. The lack of reciprocity, both from Bihari leaders and the Dhaka regimes, vetoed integration into mainstream society. While the UNHCR and ICRC avoided identifying them as refugees, Bihari organizations defined themselves as 'stranded Pakistanis', a term disliked by non-Urdu speaking Pakistanis and other officials. Relief organizations, such as CORR and especially Concern, an Irish charity, distributed relief and food amongst the camp dwellers, though at times it was difficult for international organizations to undertake direct distribution without the involvement of the Bangladeshi bureaucracy, as well as the Bihari committees. Concern had opened schools and handicraft centres for Bihari women, and through sustained efforts got scores of Biharis employed in the railway services in Bangladesh. However, the international organizations, and likewise, Pakistan and Bangladesh all shied away from publicizing the issue for their own respective reasons and considerations. The Biharis, being mainly urban people, offered no pressure on the rural sector but overall limited job opportunities in Bangladesh have indirectly created strong resistance against the Bihari integration.

In 'The Context of Bangladesh in 1977' by Iain Guest, a doctor, then working in Bangladesh reported there were sixty-six Bihari camps all across the country and despite efforts by relief agencies including the Bangladesh Red Cross, each rainy season wrought havoc on most of them. For instance, in Dhaka's Geneva Camp, out of 38,740 thatched huts, two-thirds needed urgent repairs and the water pump—ironically situated next to latrines—caused serious health hazards. In Bogra, the situation was equally worse, where the Biharis had been evicted from a warehouse in Rangpur and now formed a new camp, Ispahani 3, which suffered from serious housing and sanitation problems. Like other camps, Saidpur suffered from a high rate of infant mortality. Official efforts to disperse the Biharis into certain cities had resulted in new, smaller and equally underprovided camps. There were serious cases of starvation in Dhaka's Adamjee camp. A few efforts by Biharis, especially those settled in the United States, in reclaiming their property had been successful, but for a clear majority legal rights had been lost after 1971. However, it was recognized that some Bangladeshi relief organizations had started working for the welfare of the Biharis. The Bangladesh Volunteers Service was running two schools in the Geneva camp and there was a similar school in Bogra, but the Bihari enrolment was almost nil. In Saidpur, there were 1300–1400 Biharis and in Mirpur, another 1200 waiting to be repatriated to Pakistan, which by 1974, had accepted 110,000 of them and was reluctant to accept more. In fact, Zulfikar Ali Bhutto was asking the Commonwealth to absorb the remaining 200,000–300,000 Biharis, whereas 'the Doctor' felt that given the 'destitute' nature of life in these camps, the Biharis needed to be dispersed through officially provided housing facilities.[47] The most vocal organization urging for their repatriation to Pakistan is headed by Nasim Khan and is called SPGRC (The Stranded Pakistanis General Repatriation Committee), which came into existence on 2 December 1977. M. Moohiddin worked as the General Secretary of the SPGRC. In 1979, according to the

Ministry of Foreign Affairs of Bangladesh, there were 475,502 non-Bengalis in the country, out of them 15,000 had opted for settlement in Bangladesh.[48] But the government did not offer any major incentive for integration and instead, on 28 February 1979, implemented President's Order No. 16, dealing with properties owned by non-locals. Under this crucial ordinance immovable properties like houses, shops and industrial concerns owned by Biharis were formally taken over by the government that had also denied basic citizenship to the former. On the other hand, the properties owned by Bengalis now settled abroad or even in Pakistan, did not come under the purview of this ordinance. In some cases, even some pro-Pakistan Bengali elements were able to retrieve their properties, which in the case of Biharis was impossible. A few years later, in 1985, General Ershad's regime imposed yet another regulation known as Ordinance No. 54, which unlike Order No. 16, made it the claimant's responsibility to prove that the property was abandoned. The previous ordinance had vested the onus of proof on the government. This legislation is considered discriminatory because it contravenes the spirit of equality as ordained in Article 27 of the Constitution of Bangladesh. However the Supreme Court's ruling of 1984 was seen as a redeeming precedent, which for example in Mukhtar Ahmed's case, as reported in 34DLR (1984), has upheld the rights of citizenship even if under special circumstances one may deny it. The Division Bench, presided over by Justice Shahabuddin Ahmed (later on the President of the country), observed as follows:

> The mere fact that he filed an application for going over to Pakistan cannot take away his citizenship. The Bangladesh Citizenship order, P.O. 149/72 has enumerated different situations in which a person shall be deemed to be a citizen of Bangladesh, but has not discriminated among its citizens no matter in which way they have become citizens of this country. So, this petitioner is on the same footing as any other citizen. His citizenship, therefore, clings to him. He could voluntarily renounce it or he could be deprived of it if he had incurred any disqualification.[49]

THE BIHARIS DURING THE 1980s AND 1990s

In 1981, Lord Ennals likened camps like Muhammadpur to 'a sea of mud and excrement, an open sewer surrounding broken down shacks with corrugated iron roofs, housing of thousands of desperate people waiting, still waiting, to go to their country of choice'. Contrasted with 400,000 Bengalis from West Pakistan, only 163,072 Biharis had been able to settle in the latter, though both Sheikh Mujibur Rahman and Zulfikar Ali Bhutto had promised Lord Ennals of a 'one for one exchange'. Some had ventured out of Bangladesh on their own and by 1981, there were 300,000 left in the country. Led by vociferous organizations such as the SPGRC, they designated themselves as 'stranded Pakistanis' living in transit camps waiting to be repatriated to their *own* country. Lord Ennals met General Ziaul Haq who promised to be helpful but expected financial help towards their resettlement. Zia, in pursuance of his promise, sent the Foreign Secretary to assess the Bihari situation and another 7,000 were repatriated to Pakistan. Persuaded by the UNHCR, the governments of Pakistan and Bangladesh agreed to establish a tri-partite commission to work on resettlement schemes for the remaining Biharis. At this stage, Oxfam and the Mennonite Central Council were requested to prepare a feasibility scheme, and Saudi Arabia agreed to provide some financial assistance for the project through the Rabita Trust.[50] The situation finally appeared optimistic, but by the late 1980s, ethnic turbulence in Karachi, slow pace in collecting funds and a weakening of resolve by both regimes, did not result into any major ameliorative initiative.[51] Once again, the repatriation issue was put on the back burner because of the turbulent situation in Karachi.[52] Concurrently, the Dhaka administration was not being helpful by virtue of redefinition of citizenship laws. On 16 March 1987, Ordinance 16 (A) was promulgated, defining pre–1971 residents on Pakistani soil as non-Bangladeshis, which once again made the Bihari status in Bangladesh precarious. However, by 1982, according to Bangladeshi sources (see Table 5), there were 212,000 Biharis left in the country as many had gone to Pakistan, and others were locally reintegrated.

In 1992, the Rabita Trust carried out a special survey (see Tables 6 and 7) for the Pakistani High Commission in Dhaka, which offered figures on the number of Biharis in seventy camps across the country.

Table 5. Biharis in Bangladesh in 1982

District	Number of Camps	Number of Biharis
Dhaka & Narayanganj	29	95,095
Khulna	6	36,462
Chittagong	7	29,958
Rangpur	18	19,128
Pabna	1	16,208
Rajshahi	10	4,520
Mymensingh	1	3,757
Bogra	4	3,412
Jessore	4	2,985
Jamalpur	1	455
Total	81	211,980

Source: Ministry of Relief and Rehabilitation, Government of Bangladesh, *Stranded Pakistanis in Bangladesh*, 1982, in Sumit Sen, p. 66.

Five years later, in another survey conducted by the ICRC and quoted by the SPGRC, there were 258,028 Biharis in Bangladesh comprising of 39,779 families (see Table 8). This shows that the numbers have increased slightly from 1992, understandably due to an improving economy and lesser desire to be repatriated. Moreover, most of the Biharis seem to be concentrated in Dhaka, Saidpur, Khalispur and Chittagong. However, in 1997, it was reported by the Bangladeshi authorities that there were 426,859 Biharis in camps—many of them native born—waiting for repatriation or reintegration.[53] This seems to be a higher estimate as the actual number in 2001—after four years— is suggested by various sources to be less than 250,000 altogether. Professionally, the Biharis were working as rickshaw pullers, security guards, computer specialists, motor mechanics, electricians, welders, factory workers, doctors, drivers, businessmen, tutors, hotel staff, photographers. midwives, weavers, blacksmiths, butchers and cleaners. The large number of disabled were either terminally ill or elderly, and the number of beggars was quite small. All through the past decades, they have been keen to regain their lost middle class status.[54] The Saidpur Camp with its 60,000 inhabitants was better off than the rest because of the special attention it received from President

Table 6. Biharis in Bangladesh in 1992

Camps	Families	Camp Dwellers	Outside Camps	Male	Female
70	40,208	237,440	111,192	119,815	117,635

Source: Rabita Population Survey, 1992, quoted by Tazeen Murshid, op. cit., p. 7.

Table 7. Professional Distribution of Biharis, 1992

Profession	Number
Housewives	35,000
Business (major)	14,000
Students	30,000
Graduates	518
Factory Workers	5,300
Doctors	59
Actors	5
Beggars	163
Disabled	6,675

Source: Ibid.

Table 8. Estimates of Biharis in Bangladesh in 1996–97

Camp	No. of Families	Number of refugees
Muhammadpur	4,863	33,174
Adamjee Nagar	1,071	7,216
Narayanganj	132	895
Mirpur (Sections X-XII)	6,560	43,438
Mymensingh	318	2,227
Rangpur	936	8,526
Saidpur	912	38,045
Dinajpur	256	1,916
Bogra	503	3,757
Ishurdi	1,157	7,591
Rajshahi	453	3,470
Khalispur	2,406	14,769
Khulna	602	3,966
Jessore	442	3,336
Chittagong (4 Camps)	2,928	18,196
Gilatalla	326	1,934
Total	39,779	258,028

Source: SPGRC, Survey report of ICRC, Muhammadpur Camp, Dhaka, as quoted in Sumit Sen, op. cit., p. 67.

Ershad. The Muhammadpur Camp with its 16,000 inhabitants had comparatively better living conditions, because after having been gutted down in a fire in April 1986, it had been rebuilt with British help. Women at the Adamjee and Narayanganj Camps found no work in areas like handicrafts and embroidery unlike their counterparts at Geneva Camp. A number of articles in the early 1990s and during 2002–03 appeared in the Pakistani press, highlighting the plight of these stranded Pakistanis, though the regime has tried to evade the issue.[55]

PAKISTAN AND THE BIHARIS IN THE 1990S: PARTY POLITICS AND THE KARACHI IMBROGLIO

While Nawaz Sharif and the MQM, his coalition partner, were supportive of repatriation, Benazir Bhutto's PPP was reluctant to accept any more Pakistanis. Sindhi elements within the PPP would not allow it, since they worried that the Biharis would all end up in urban Sindh, further tilting the precarious ethnic balance in favour of the Urdu speaking *Muhajirs*. Other Sindhi nationalist groups have vociferously resisted the influx of immigrants, whether from Bangladesh or even from upcountry. During the 1980s and 1990s, many Bangladeshis and Biharis had entered Pakistan illegally and most of them settled down in *bastis* in Karachi. Their support for the MQM was guaranteed, which reaffirmed Sindhi fears. The MQM on its part all throughout the 1980s and 1990s struggled for the repatriation of the Biharis stranded in Bangladesh. A few delegations even visited the camps in Bangladesh and through print and visual media, tried to put pressure on Islamabad to repatriate their fellow Pakistanis. Both India and Pakistan in the 1990s were weary of economic refugees from Bangladesh, and the local exaggerated accounts of their numbers dangerously increased the nativist exclusionary feelings. The BJP, like the Sindhi nativists, made a big issue of illegal Bangladeshis in Assam and West Bengal, whereas the Sindhis complained of a persistent growth of the non-Sindhi population in the second largest province of Pakistan. The ethnic question, to a great extent, came to largely depend on demographic claims and counterclaims as jobs, housing and political representation all depended upon the language-based ethnic configurations in the country. While the MQM resented the quota system—the positive discrimination implemented in the early 1970s to help the predominantly rural Sindhis—the Sindhis resisted any more population pressure on their province. Islamabad was partially right in resisting any more repatriation.

Nawaz Sharif, however, took it upon himself to build some one thousand houses in Mian Channu in central Punjab with financial assistance from Rabita, and resumed a restrictive repatriation of the Biharis. In 1992, the visit to Pakistan by Begum Khalida Zia, the Prime Minster of Bangladesh, resulted in major progress on the issue of repatriation. Nawaz Sharif's government agreed to accept another 3000 families. However, many groups in Pakistan demanded support from Muslim countries in the rehabilitation of the Biharis. Ultimately, however, only 68 families comprising of 325 individuals could be repatriated by 1993, when Ghulam Ishaq Khan dismissed Nawaz Sharif's government. Nawaz Sharif's second administration from 1997 to 1999 was again riddled with polarization and conflicts until a military coup led by General Pervaiz Musharraf overthrew the embattled prime minister. Though Musharraf and many of his colleagues are themselves *Muhajirs*, economic reconstruction and repairing Pakistan's relationship with India and the outside world remain top priority. In the meantime, the relationship between Bangladesh and Pakistan deteriorated considerably. Under the circumstances it appeared as if the entire issue of the repatriation had been put on the back burner. This is not to say that many Pakistanis, especially of the Urdu speaking communities, have forgotten the Biharis, as letters from time to time in various newspapers keep appearing in as reminders.[56] General Musharraf's visit to Bangladesh in 2002, subsequent parleys with the Prime Minister Khalida Zia, and his expression of regret on the tragedy of 1971 softened Bangladeshi nationalists to some extent, however, but the issue remained unresolved amidst a growing realization that Biharis, especially those born after 1971, could always obtain Bangladeshi citizenship. While many Biharis have established themselves in different cities, the older generation still stays on in the camps. When, in February 2003, local authorities in Dhaka began demolishing their huts to acquire property for 'development purposes', several Bangladeshi civic groups supported the Biharis against their dislocation. The media in both countries has highlighted their continued undefined status, though opinions on repatriation or settlement within Bangladesh remain as divergent as ever. The continued silence of the MQM on the Bihari issue, at a time when the party was a coalition partner, both at the centre and in Sindh province, further dampened hopes among some Bihari enthusiasts.

ARGUMENTS IN FAVOUR OF REPATRIATION TO PAKISTAN

There are historical, legal, moral and social justifications for the repatriation of Biharis to Pakistan. They, and their first generation had opted for Pakistan at the time of Partition and thus, once a legal option has been accepted citizenship cannot be withdrawn unilaterally. Moreover, any mono-ethnic or mono-cultural trajectory would simply encourage majoritarian fascism, especially by strengthening xenophobic forces. That is why Hindutva, a Sunni state, a Buddhist Sri Lanka, Bengali Bangladesh and such exclusionist nativism is dangerous in any plural society such as South Asia.

The Pakistani commitment on repatriation is legally binding because Pakistan agreed to take its officials, their families and also other hardship cases. It agreed to 'receive a substantial number of those who are stated to have opted for repatriation to Pakistan (non-Bengalis from Bangladesh)'.[57] One may engage oneself in hair splitting on the resultant scenarios or economic and demographic consequences, but the fact remains that an efficient and fair screening could have helped repair the Pak-Bangladeshi relationship. Another argument in favour of repatriation is of divided families, which is a human right issue. Other than the Bhuttos, the generals and the Muslim League have been comparatively receptive to repatriation, though the MQM involvement defaulted hopes for a quick action.[58] Even in his speeches and personal interviews, the London-based Altaf Hussain does not mention the Biharis any more, either because it is too controversial or he considers their case totally insignificant. Hasina Wajid's criticism of Pakistan and her pro-India utterances are generally seen within the context of the Biharis being used as scapegoats, and a greater empathy is shown towards them.[59] With Khalida Zia in power, however, such sentiments seem to be on the wane.

PAKISTANI ARGUMENTS AGAINST REPATRIATION

Pakistani arguments against repatriation are mainly twofold: demography in Sindh and economic cost. The Sindhis, the PPP and many officials feel that Pakistan has already fulfilled its political and humanitarian commitments and is already becoming a demographic nightmare. To them, the Bihari element will beef up the MQM and cause serious dislocation in the most plural city in the country. The more moderate elements see the plight of the Biharis as a humanitarian issue, but without meaningful support, Pakistan will only exacerbate her problems if they are allowed in. Pakistanis also feel that the second and third generation Biharis are Bangladeshis, and it is the moral and civic responsibility of that country to look after them. They also cite the example of Shia-Sunni feuds largely linked with the changing political situation in the neighbouring Muslim countries, with Pakistan having become the battleground for proxy sectarian warfare.[60]

BANGLADESHI ARGUMENTS ON BIHARI REPATRIATION

Like their Pakistani counterparts, Bangladeshi arguments vary from extreme to moderation. The secular-nationalists refuse to see the Biharis as an indigenous problem and categorize them as Pakistanis. To them, they made their choice long before liberation and by siding with West Pakistani officials and then by inclining towards repatriation in the early 1970s, they have made their choice. Such secular elements consider them to be Pakistan's moral, legal and political responsibility. To them, Pakistan is the *other* and a former colonial power, which brutalized Bangladesh and is refusing to accept its *own citizens*.[61] Several hard-liners from amongst the Awami League and its student organization use the Biharis to club Pakistan, and consider the Biharis as remnants of Pakistani imperialists, who may use them to destabilize the country. Hasina Wajid has been under great pressure by such elements—many of them pro-India—to openly rebuke Pakistan on the issue of repatriation, as well as in several other areas like the role of religio-political parties in Bangladesh. Such attitudes even see the Biharis as *fundamentalists*, and the organizations such as Rabita spreading fundamentalism in Bangladesh.[62]

BANGLADESHI ARGUMENTS ON REINTEGRATION

However, there are strong elements in Bangladesh who view it as a human issue and are trying to help the Biharis, while being appreciative of their post-1972 role as marginalized inhabitants. Some of them want their citizenship restored to them and are concerned about the squalor, lack of basic infra structure and anti-Bihari sentiments. Many moderates and even religious groups like to look at them as fellow citizens and fellow Muslims who have suffered too long for the crimes of a few. There is an economic argument as well: that the Biharis have the highest employment rate and given their skills and professionalism, can contribute more effectively to the country's economy. Some Bangladeshi intellectuals also feel that a single factor nationality or citizenship based on lingual commonality is frivolous.

THE BIHARIS AND THEIR ASPIRATIONS

As we know, there is now no single opinion in Pakistan and Bangladesh on the status of the Biharis, though there is a greater sympathy for the amelioration of their situation. In the same manner, there is no single Bihari opinion on the issue of repatriation or reintegration. In fact, no holistic opinion survey has ever been conducted in Pakistan, Bangladesh or even among the Biharis, and generally, the states or a few opinion groups have continued to uphold a unilateral position. For the last three decades, repatriation alone has been seen as the way-out by Dhaka and its nationalist-secular elite, whereas gradually, more and more Biharis are now seeking citizenship and integration into local society. The older generation with relatives in Pakistan may still desire to be repatriated, but the younger generations are desirous of settling down in Bangladesh, if given equal socio-legal rights. The Dhaka-based RMMRU carried out a rare opinion survey in 1997 to ascertain the opinion of fifty-one randomly selected Biharis in the Mirpur (Tezgaon) and Muhammadpur (Geneva) Camps to seek their views on repatriation and reintegration. The survey report censures both the governments for not undertaking legal and social initiatives to help the beleaguered community. The six interviewers asked several questions about the reasons for choosing to live in camps, their attitudes towards both countries and relationship with Bengalis. The respondents included twenty-three males and twenty-eight females belonging to various age groups. Most of them (65 per cent) had been living in the camps for more than a decade. Forty-three per cent of them had opted for camps due to security reasons, with 19.60 per cent for family reasons and about 14 per cent for economic reasons. Most significantly, 59 per cent of them saw themselves as Bangladeshis compared to 35 per cent who defined themselves as Pakistanis. Fifty-five per cent desired to live in Bangladesh permanently, compared to 45 per cent who were desirous of repatriation to Pakistan. The individuals desirous of repatriation offered family reasons (39 per cent) and economic incentives (39 per cent) for their intention to settle in Pakistan. Curiously, only 29 per cent were optimistic of ever being repatriated, whereas 47 per cent saw no possibility of repatriation. Eighty-seven per cent of the respondents acknowledged the problems faced after repatriation by their Bihari relatives in Pakistan. About 43.1 per cent had no clue of political developments in Pakistan, though 35 per cent felt that the atmosphere was not favourable for repatriation.

On the crucial question of integration, 62.74 per cent of the respondents supported integration within Bangladeshi society as opposed to 33.33 per cent. An overwhelming ratio of the respondents (96 per cent) felt that the relationship between the Biharis and Bengalis was satisfactory. About 64 per cent of them belonged to various Bihari committees, though more than 50 per cent supported Nasim Khan's SPGRC, with 35 per cent not supporting any of them. The survey team found half of the interviewees totally illiterate, with very few having education above the primary level. They found no NGO working in these camps and the Biharis overwhelmingly desirous of greater official help in education, sanitation and medical facilities. The paper concluded on demanding citizenship rights for the Biharis, and urged a greater need for nation-wide awareness on Biharis. It underlined the overwhelming Bihari desire (63 per cent) for integration as a positive sign.[63] However, there are still powerful voices within Bangladesh which insist on their repatriation and reject the plea for their citizenship.[64] However, many academics and human rights activists have been urging civil society and the state to help Urdu-speaking communities in Bangladesh. The RMMRU in Dhaka, in collaboration with some human rights activists and lawyers, have held several seminars, where papers demanding citizenship for Biharis have been offered.[65]

As mentioned earlier, several Bangladeshi groups showed some concern for Biharis—officially called 'Stranded non-Bengalis'—though the secular-nationalists would simply apportion the entire blame on Pakistan for creating the malady and then evading it. In the meanwhile, it is to be remembered that the Dhaka regimes, despite several reservations, have been providing free water, gas and electricity to them over the past several years. The camps, especially in Dhaka, are located on prime property, and many official and private groups would like to disperse the Biharis from there, but their own resilience has stood the test, though the tables were turned on them in early 2003. On the other hand, cases of discrimination, violence and vandalism attributed to non-Bihari elements have been occasionally reported in private interviews.[66]

Both Pakistan and Bangladesh need to face the issue with a fresh approach and rather than staying locked in the sad memories of 1971, they must offer helping hands to these 250,000 individuals. They must face up to their responsibilities by restoring citizenship in addition to restoration of their erstwhile forcibly snatched properties. International agencies can help both the countries in terms of compensation, as well as rehabilitation. Rather than decrying and transferring the responsibility to the other, they need to work together in a plural spirit. Pakistan is under obligation to respect their Pakistani citizenship as no state can withdraw this right. Moreover, it is the 'predecessor state' which can only withdraw if the Biharis elect the citizenship of Bangladesh. The citizenship is as integral to human rights as the right of self-determination and the rights of minorities.[67] The right to return to one's own country is enshrined in Article 9 of the UDHR 48 which prohibits 'Arbitrary arrest, detention or exile'. General Ziaul Haq and Nawaz Sharif made some progress towards this but soon got cold feet. Mohammad Khan Junejo, the prime minister, Zain Noorani, Mahbubul Haq, and other cabinet ministers, made frequent statements about bringing back all the Biharis to Pakistan.[68] Funds to the volume of $278 million were made available to the GOP in 1985 by the International Resettlement Trust, but no progress could be made on building the 36,000 agreed dwellings for Biharis. A similar activity was shown by Nawaz Sharif when land and funds in the Punjab were allocated for the resettlement of 200,000 Biharis. Some papers had been issued by the Pakistani High Commission in Dhaka, but only 325 refugees were actually repatriated. In 1998, when Nawaz Sharif came back to power, he resumed discussions with Hasina Wajid but no progress was ever made due to Nawaz Sharif's own problems back home.[69] Bangladesh's Citizenship Order 1972 (PO 149) does not discriminate among its citizens. Its Article 2 is quite elaborate and establishes citizenship on the basis of one's father or grandfather having been born on Bangladeshi soil. It also establishes the continuity of citizenship of those who were citizens on 25 March 1971. Only through a voluntary option, can a citizen surrender his/her citizenship and Biharis have not done so either voluntarily or by incurring any disqualification. Thus, 'like any other residents of the territory, (Biharis) are definitely citizens of Bangladesh'.[70]

There is an apprehension that a persistent emphasis on exclusionary nationalism, largely engendered by global changes may not be helpful to minorities. Equally, globalization without tangible and egalitarian ethos is further exacerbating inter-state and intra-state tensions, especially in the developing world, where issues of identity, ideology and economy have all become acute. Like the fallacy of the so-called majoritarian nationalism, a hegemonic, profit-oriented, and power-based globalization is immensely controversial and one-sided. Whereas nationalism has to be redefined as a confederal and plural ideology, regionalization may equally facilitate further inter-state cooperation in the interest of diverse communities, and not at their expense. In the same vein, globalization has to seek the confidence of post-colonial societies such as in South Asia and must help them resolve their socio-political problems rather than defining them merely as potential markets. By simply criticizing them and their cultures in a state of higher moral righteousness has, time and again, proven counterproductive. Post-colonialism is to give way to a more equitable world order where regional and specific hegemonies do not dictate narrowly defined interests, nor do they trample on smaller countries and ethno-religious minorities. It has to be accepted, however, that most of the problems of a demographic nature seriously disallow any equitable share in the globalization processes and have to be encountered through judicious mechanics. The negative immigration policies amidst the legacies of institutional racism, as evident within the developed countries, are not helpful pointers towards an interdependent world, nor are they useful models for post-colonial societies. Globalization without an equal citizenship or open borders for the have-nots will only exacerbate fundamentalism in the backyards of already crowded and impoverished societies. In a true spirit of regionality and by rejecting discretionary precedents and through taking its pluralism aboard, South Asia can still pursue a refreshing synthesis of tradition and modernity.

NOTES

1. Polly Toynbee, 'Globalization of Culture', *The Guardian* as reproduced in *Dawn*, 7 March 2000.

2. For a comprehensive conceptualisation in reference to these four definitions, see, Jan Aart Scholte, *Globalization: A critical introduction*, Houndmills, 2000.

3. He considers it to be rooted in modernity. See, his, *Runaway World: How Globalization is Reshaping Our Lives!* London, 2000; *The Third Way and Its Culture*, Cambridge, 2000; and, *The Consequences of Modernity*, Cambridge, 1991.

4. Max Weber, *The Protestant Ethic and the Spirit of Capitalism*, London, 1992 (reprint); Talcott Parsons, *Theories of Modernity*, London, 1991. Also, Peter Berger, *A Far Glory: The Quest for Faith in an Age of Credulity*, New York, 1992; Robert Bellah, *Beyond Belief: Essays on Religion in a Post-Traditionalist World*, Los Angeles, 1991; David Martin, *A General Theory of Secularization*, Oxford, 1978.

5. Gellner and Huntington may represent two different views on Islam whereas Muslim scholars such as Muhammad Iqbal (d. 1938) and Fazlur Rahman (d. 1988) would see, a synthesis between Islam and modernity despite their weariness of clericalism in the former and self-centered materialism in the latter.

6. Noam Chomsky—the coiner of this term—and several socialist and other such critics are occasionally erroneously bundled together as anarchists. Following the demonstrations at Seattle and Gothenburg, the use of such terms by Western leaders and media has become more common. It is interesting to note that the Muslim critics of globalisation and modernity (*fundamentalists*) find themselves in the company of these *anarchists*.

7. The US withdrawal from Kyoto Treaty and the support of 'military industrial complex' for ultra-right forces may be seen the engines of the West-led globalism. A poweful and equally persuasive critique has been provided by George Monbiot where he talks of reformist and egalitarian world order based on equal , democratic participation. He suggests a radical reconstruction of the institutions such as the UN, the World Bank and the IMF, away from discretionary interests. See, his, *The Age of Consent*, London, 2003.

8. David Harvey, *The Condition of Postmodernity: an Enquiry into the Conditions of Cultural Change*, Oxford, 1989. For an interesting comparison, see, Benjamin R. Berber, *Jihad Vs. McWorld*, London, 2003; also, John Pilger, *The New Masters of the World*, London, 2003.

9. See, A.S. Runyan, 'The Places of Women in Trading Places: Gendered Global/ Regional Regimes and the Inter-nationalized Feminist Resistance', in E. Kofman and G. Youngs, (eds.) *Globalizaion: Theory and Practice*, London, 1996.

10. For a useful overview, see, Ian Clarke, *Globalization and Fragmentation: International Relations in the Twentieth Century*, Oxford, 1999.

11. Taj-ul-Islam Hashmi, 'The 'Bihari' Minorities in Bangladesh: Victims of Nationalisms', mimeo (1996).

12. For a valuable study on the growing cultural and ideological activities amongst the Bengal Muslims, see, Rafiuddin Ahmed, *The Bengal Muslims*, Delhi, 1990.

13. This movement literally stood for the boycott of non-Indian goods.

14. It is important to note that the All-India Muslim League—the first major all-India Muslim political party—was founded in December 1906, in Dhaka at the residence of Nawab Salimullah.

15. Taj-ul-Islam Hashmi, *Pakistan as the Peasants' Utopia,* Oxford, 1992.
16. The organized massacres of Muslims in Bihar subsequent to the Hindu-Muslim riots in Noakhali made Hindu-Muslim coexistence almost impossible in this poor region of British India. For further details on the Bihar riots and their chain reaction across South Asia, see, Vinita Damodaran, *Broken Promises: Popular Protest, Indian Nationalism and the Congress Party in Bihar, India, 1936–46,* Delhi, 1992.
17. Ruth West's Report on Biharis in Bangladesh quoted in Tazeen Murhsid, *A Forgotten Minority: The Biharis in Bangladesh,* Brussels, 2000, p. 16.
18. Chowdhury E. Haque, 'Non-Bengali Refugees in Bangladesh: Patterns, Policies and Consequences', in John Rogge, (ed.) *Refugees: A Third World Dilemma,* Trenton, 1987, p. 220.
19. It is generally believed that the Urdu-speaking elite preferred moving westwards whereas the poorer sections, in many cases originating from around the Bengal region, opted for East Pakistan. However, several Urdu speaking bourgeoisie and skilled professionals migrated to the eastern wing as well and established factories and other business concerns. See, Khurshid Begum, 'The Stranded Pakistanis in Bangladesh and International Implications', a paper presented at International Workshop on Internationalization of Ethnic Conflict, Kandy (Sri Lanka), 2–4 August 1989.
20. The total figures of the Great Migration vary between 14 to 18 million. While the Hindus and Sikhs moved to India, Muslims headed for West or East Pakistan. In fact, the number of refugees received by Pakistan from all parts of India was about 2 million higher than that of India. It is not fair to allocate the entire blame to any particular community, yet one has to remember the scattered nature of Muslim communities all over India necessitating a wider terrain to cover to reach Pakistan. The Mountbatten administration, in its self-glory and haste, did not impose marital law in the border regions despite all the advice to the effect, and more than one million innocent lives were lost along with abductions and rape of thousands of women. The agonies keep on dictating the mindset on both sides. For more details, see, Patrick French, *Liberty or Death,* London, 1998. In Urdu literature, the agony of the numerous victims has been immortalised by writers such as Intizar Husain, Saadat Hasan Manto, Faiz A. Faiz, Rajinder Singh Bedi, Mashkoor Hussain Yaad, Ashfaque Ahmed and several others. For an interesting overview, see, Ian Talbot, *Freedom's Cry,* Karachi, 1997. Initially, the Biharis were not designated as a minority by the fellow Bengalis. Hashmi, op. cit.
21. In fact, Sheikh Mujibur Rahman, the leader of Bangladesh, had urged the Biharis to immigrate to East Pakistan. For details, see, Basant Chatterjee, *Inside Bangladesh Today: An Eyewitness Account,* New Delhi, 1973, p. 85.
22. Mr Aziz Ahmad, an Urdu speaking Punjabi civil servant, was the chief secretary of East Pakistan, whereas another Urdu speaking official, Rahmatullah, was the district magistrate of Dhaka. Both of them treated the eastern wing as a colony and their harsh measures on the language issue resulted in the deaths of many East Pakistanis making it a threshold in Bengali separatism.
23. However, many Urdu speakers in West Pakistan turned against Ayub Khan and also voted for Miss Fatima Jinnah in the presidential elections of 1965. Later on, Karachi became the hotbed of anti-Ayub demonstartions in 1969–9. See, Hashmi, op. cit.

24. For more details, see, Rounaq Jahan, *Pakistan: Failure in National Integration,* New York, 1972.

25. Ben Whitaker, *The Biharis in Bangladesh,* London, 1982, p. 8.

26. For details, see, Lawrence Ziring, *Bangladesh from Mujib to Ershad: An Interpretive Study,* Dhaka, 1992, pp. 64–5.

27. For further details, see, Anthony Mascarhenas, *Bangladesh: A Legacy of Blood,* London, 1986, pp. 118–9 and 122.

28. 'I am an eyewitness of how Bihari businessmen and their family members were gunned down and how 700 Biharis were kept in jail and later killed by Bengalis at Sirajganj town in April 1971, before the arrival of the Pakistani troops'. Qutbuddin Aziz, *Blood and Tears,* Karachi, 1972, p. 183.

29. *The New York Times,* 10 May 1971.

30. According to a British paper, within the month of April at least 100,000 Biharis had been murdered. *The Sunday Times,* 2 May 1971.

31. Hashmi, op. cit.

32. It is important to remember that many non-military personnel of West Pakistani origin as well as the Biharis were also brutalised by the Mukti Bahini and several other militant outfits. For details, see, Qutbuddin Aziz.

33. For details on the failure of Pakistani elite to reach a settlement see, Zaheer Hasan, *The Separation of East Pakistan,* Karachi, 1994; see, Anthony Macarenhas, *The Rape of Bangladesh,* Delhi, 1971.

34. For a comprehensive account, see, Richard Sisson and Leo Rose, *War and Secession. Pakistan, India and the Creation of Bangladesh,* Berkeley, 1990.

35. Sultana Nahar, 'Biharis in Bangladesh: Their Present Status, Legal Impediments and Solutions', a paper offered at a conference on refugees and stateless people, 29–30 December 1997, p. 5.

36. For instance, 'Tiger' Kadir Siddiqui, the leader of the Kader Bahini killed several Biharis and West Pakistanis on 18 December 1971, before a crowd in Dhaka stadium, in the full glare of cameras and global media. Several more such killings took place at Tangail and elsewhere at the hands of various Bengali Bahinis. Whitaker, op. cit., p. 8. Tiger Siddiqui was granted general amnesty for his crimes by Sheikh Mujibur Rahman.

37. Quoted in Nahar, op. cit.

38. *The Times,* 11 May 1972.

39. *The Daily Telegraph,* 14 March 1972 and *The Observer,* 14 May 1972.

40. He had made a commitment towards their safety with an international delegation led by Lord David Ennals. Whitaker, op. cit., p. 9.

41. *The Daily Telegraph,* 14 March 1972 and *The Sunday Observer,* 16 April 1972.

42. Whitaker, op. cit., pp. 13–14.

43. Chatterjee, op. cit., pp. 102–13.

44. One argument the Government of Pakistan used was that the registration took place by the ICRC on its own without the proper involvement of Pakistani authorities. Moreover, indirectly, the Bhutto regime was weary of bringing more Urdu speakers into an already turbulent Sindh, where the local Sindhi speakers resented demographic changes radically working against their interests.

45. For further details on the politics of conflictive ethnic pluralism in Sindh and the MQM, see, Iftikhar H. Malik, *State and Civil Society in Pakistan: Politics of Authority, Ideology and Ethnicity,* Oxford, 1997.

46. Iain Guest, 'The Context of Bangladesh in 1977', in Ben Whitaker, op. cit., p. 25.
47. 'The Situation in the Bihari Camps in June 1977 by a Doctor' in ibid., pp. 28–9.
48. Quoted by Nahar, op. cit., p. 8.
49. Reproduced in ibid., p. 10.
50. David Ennals, 'The Biharis in 1981', in Whitaker, pp. 30–1.
51. For details, see, Qazi Anwarul Haque, *Under Three Flags*, Dhaka, 1986.
52. The present author personally knows some cases where a few concerned Pakistanis wrote letters and articles about the inhuman conditions prevailing in the Bihari camps and critiqued the Zia regime for assuming double standards on Biharis *vis-à-vis* the Afghan refugees. These individuals were harassed by the Pakistani intelligence agencies like the ISI.
53. Bushra Hasina Chowdhury et al., 'Perception of the Biharis on Repatriation and Reintegration: A Preliminary Finding from the Dhaka Camps', a study for Refugee and Migratory Movements Research Unit (RMMRU) of the Dhaka University, 1997, p. 1.
54. The present author was equally impressed by their energetic and enterprising disposition. Despite the squalor and dirt, the eagerness to gain self-sufficiency through personal diligence was quite apparent to an observer in April 2001.
55. See, *Dawn,* 19 and 22 August 1991; and, *The Nation,* 11 August 1992. During General Musharraf's visit to Bangladesh and subsequently the Dhaka Municipal Corporation's bulldozing of some Bihari 'encroachments' reminded Pakistanis and Bangladeshis of the continued ambiguous position of the Bihari community.
56. For instance, see, *Dawn,* 20 June 2001.
57. The Tripartite Agreement as quoted in Tazeen Murshid, op. cit., p. 6.
58. Many Bihari leaders both at the Mirpur and Muhammadpur Camps lamented the role of the MQM which, in its own pursuit to score easy points amongst the Urdu speakers in Sindh, ended up making the former's case disputatious. To them the MQM-led advocacy has been counterproductive. Some of them felt that the MQM, other than using the victim and persecution factor, collected funds, which it never invested towards the welfare of the camp dwellers. Based on extensive interviews in Dhaka, April 2001.
59. Based on interviews in Karachi, Lahore, Islamabad in July-August, 2000 and April and July-August 2001.
60. Based on extensive interviews across the country in 2001.
61. For instance, Murshid, op. cit.
62. Ibid.
63. Bushra Hasina Chowdhury, op. cit.
64. Fakruddin Ahmed, the former Foreign Secretary's statement in the conference on Refugees, Migrants and Stateless Persons, Dhaka, 29–30 December 1997, as quoted in RMMRU's *Udbastu* (Newsletter), April-June, 1998, p. 1.
65. The comments by Dr C.R. Abrar, Dr Tasneem Siddiqui, Advocate Nizamul Haq are quite positive. See, ibid., July-September 2000. Also, Chowdhury R. Abrar, (ed.) *On the Margin: Refugees, Migrants and Minorities,* Dhaka, 2000.
66. Several case studies were offered where individuals after being identified as Bihari were refused a job or service. The official quarters offer excuses like the lack of citizenship status whereas private businesses may simply be rude. On the other hand, many staunch elements still discriminate against the Biharis by calling them

Pakistanis and collaborators. Based on several personal interviews in Muhammadpur and Mirpur in April 2001.

67. For more on this see, Sumit Sen, op. cit., pp. 46–49.
68. *The Pakistan Times,* 25 April 1988.
69. *The Asian Age,* 17 January 1998.
70. Bushra Hasina Chowdhury, et al., op. cit., p. 5.

Our armies do not come into your cities and lands as conquerors or enemies, but as liberators.
— British General Stanley Maude to Iraqis, on 8 March 1917

The world needs order...
— Richard Perle, 'Thank God for the death of the UN,'
The Guardian, 21 March 2003

The sheer violence of it, the howl of air raid sirens and the air-cutting fall of the missiles carried its own political message; not just to President Saddam but to the rest of the world. 'We are the superpower', those explosions said last night. 'This is how we do business. This is how we take our revenge for 11 September'. Robert Fisk, 'Bubbles of fire tore into the sky above Baghdad...
— *The Independent,* 21 March 2003

...liberal and progressive force in the Muslim world would be marginalised... Pakistani contribution to the US war on terror has already led to the erosion of the human rights and a war against Iraq would exacerbate the situation.
— Asma Jahangir, human rights activist,
as quoted in the BBC report, 18 March 2003

'The current Gujarat experiment is a success', declared Ashok Singhal, after the massacre of over 2000 Muslims in Gujarat and the election of the Hindu nationalist BJP. He and the BJP leaders went to assert that this 'success would be replicated all over India'.
— Arvind Rajagopal, 'Gujarat's "Successful Experiment" ',
19 March 2003 on: www.opendemocracy.net or
www.aiindex.mnet.fr.

Do not idealise soldiers in an 'unjust war',
— Natasha Walter in *The Independent,* 20 March 2003

EPILOGUE

South Asia: The Way Ahead

South Asia has meandered its way through a half century of strifes and strides though usually preferring a middle-of-the-road course, which sometimes looks stalemated, especially when one looks at the inter-state relationship and the rising graph of exclusionary policies. Its cultural, historical, ecological and economic mutualities, and their multiple benefits for all have been more often sacrificed at the altar of antagonism and suspicion. The ruling elite and official establishments, despite the routine *mantra* of co-operation, democracy, accountability and peace, have totally failed to seek a common platform away from mutual recriminations and accusations. In the process, not only does one-fifth of humanity stay peripheralised, regionally and globally, the private outfits espousing intolerant ideologies have equally obtained centre stage. The specific articulation of Jihad merely as a militarist concept joined with Sunni statism, and full-fledged projects like Hindutva, Khas Hindu movement and Islamic Bangladesh are similar manifestations of a majoritarian fascism. Such an ethos is invariably shared all over the region, whereby exclusionary forms of nationalism and identity are increasingly being ordained in the name of history, religion, demography and such other denominators. These irredentist ideologies offer reductionist, dangerous and simplified solutions to immense human problems. Their simple formula is through a constant 'Othering', whereby, an 'enemy within' is shown conspiring in league with the enemies from outside. The Muslim and such other religious communities in India, religious minorities in Pakistan, and the ethno-religious sections in Sri Lanka, Bangladesh, Nepal and Bhutan, suffer from various forms of discrimination, displaying a growing convergence between official policies and societal clusters, all justified in the name of an *imagined* national identity. In the process, pluralism remains the main casualty, and despite a wider politicisation, comparatively freer press and vocal civil societies, the ethnic, gender and religion-based *othering* has been on the increase. These dissensions exacerbate inter-state conflicts over several unresolved issues and at populist levels, mundane problems are juxtaposed as irresolvable conflicts between Islam and Hinduism, Buddhism and Hinduism, Christianity and Hinduism, Hinduism and Sikhism, and Islam and Christianity. The Bihari issue is, of course, an exception, where an undefined citizenship has led to the statelessness of a quarter of a million people, while religion—unlike in the cases of Bangladeshi Hindus and Christians—is not a contention at all. However, in every other case, the discretionary interpretation of religion and a so-called majoritarianism appear to be feeding into each other to deny human rights to smaller communities, which in most cases, are already disadvantaged.

In a way, South Asia may not be such a unique case, as one finds the rise of Ultra Right and discretionary nationalist ethos overriding pluralist prerogatives even in the developed democracies, such as in the North Atlantic region or the former Eastern bloc. The insecurity of the majorities, though ostensibly incomprehensible, especially after 9/11 and in the wake of vengeful attacks on Afghanistan, Chechnya and Iraq, has unleashed a plethora of tensions on the existing pluralism. The saga of 'fortress Europe', the harassment of non-whites, specially the Muslim elements, and a growing accent against political exiles, despite a hyped globalisation, have increased amidst the rolling back of civil liberties. The subtle forms of institutional racism and sheer physical and verbal violence against non-whites, in several cases, have increased, and the pervasive fear is of a sudden rise in the graph in case of any new terrorist attacks in these regions. The spotlight on Islam and rather irresponsible use of disputatious terms like 'Islamic Fundamentalism', 'Islamic Terror', 'Muslim Militancy', and the 'Crusades'—not always used innocuously and value free—reverberates in the rising popularity and electoral performance of racist outfits. Like their Hindutva and such other so-called majoritarian proponents in South Asia, specific pressure groups and powerful media trajectories egg on these racist parties in the West. The dividends of a global peace movement, with its massive and immensely plural participation, may still offer hope for an alert global civil society, away from the scavenging forces of abrasive power and profit, yet its incapacitation in the United States, Britain and Australia, in the face of official regimentation, highlights the enormous problems ahead. The disregard for the massive loss of human lives in Afghanistan, Iraq, Chechnya, or of innocent civilians in Palestine or Gujarat, abysmally reveals the limitations of the local and global civil societies while confronted with statist and societal unilateralisms. The states, in all these cases, have utilised national, cultural and even religious symbols to justify their brutalisation, or have simply sat back to let the perpetrators take their toll from disempowered minority groups. The heroic role of responsible media, democratic groups, the resistance through civil disobedience and a constant exposure of immoral, as well as partisan nature of these brutalities at a time when the UN, OIC, SAARC, EU and such other international alliances remain sidelined or totally disinterested, is no mean achievement.

Looking at South Asia within this global and rather painful perspective is both an academic and human imperative. Though South Asian states and societies have their own distinct features, yet it will be equally ahistorical to posit this region, the Middle East or even the Balkans, as eternally conflict-prone regions. Their encounter with Western forms of modernity and globalisation may be comparatively recent, but their civic societies have cherished pluralism in the past, even during their imperial phases. The evolution of nation states, on the back of decolonisation, is neither unique nor totally instrumental in unleashing discretionary policies. While *partition* has been, and is, a major component of universal dissolution of empires, this process converged with the sundering of communal harmony within these former colonies. Thus, positioning the partitions of 1947 or 1971 as the total and sole cause of communal discord or inter-state dissension, may not hold the total truth. The annulment of these partitions—even in the name of undoing one *wrong*—may unleash many more *wrongs*. The states, such as in South Asia, have to grow out of this time warp and a static victimhood, to begin a new era in regional and inter-community co-operation. The reversals of territorial decisions, irrespective of their being just or bad, will only keep on exacting more human tragedies, and a taxing waste of precious resources. The EU and ASEAN offer useful parallels for South Asia though the ruling elite, as witnessed in the last half century, may persist with the politics of hostilities, either out of sheer indifference, or for the sake of sectional interests, but the respective civil societies must not leave this solely to the former. The challenges of redefining the politics of an inclusive identity, fortified by plural, democratic and participatory systems, are definitely formidable, but the alternative is a simply million volatile mutinies.

South Asian states and civil societies are vulnerable to extra regional forces in an international system, where unilateral actions by powerful nations, as seen in Afghanistan and Iraq, certainly transmit powerful challenges. In most cases, the region espouses similar concerns over events in Southwestern and Western Asia, as has been witnessed during the Afghan crisis or the three Gulf wars. Such spontaneous but real economic, social and geo-political apprehensions over similar ramifications for the entire region, underline a shared view on regional security. While religions are social and historical realities in South Asia as elsewhere, their expropriation for narrow nationalist or such other temporary benefits needs to be seen as a region-wide malady. The tolerant and plural traditions of all these religions have been forsaken to suit specific interests, with the result that the Jihadi outfits, Sunni activists, Kar Sevaks, Sinhala nationalists, Tamil separatists, or Khas Hindus now find it expedient to deny civil rights to other fellow citizens besides aggravating inter-state conflicts. The politics of competition as well as cooption to seek a greater legitimacy through religious symbols, both by the political and societal elements, have only allowed the extremist and exclusionary policies to prevail. The dependence of an entire national identity on such exclusive religious infra structure, or the other way around may yield some temporary gains for a particular ruling or aspiring elite, but its cost for the societies at large is too horrendous, as has been seen time and again across the region. Of course, Jinnahist and Nehruvian postulations on secularism have been misunderstood—sometimes not without logical reasons—yet a greater debate on their merits within the context of South Asian pluralism, equal citizenship and a due respect for all beliefs and a 'hands-off' policy on such matters are worth investigating. The de-Indianisation of Pakistan and Bangladesh is as dangerous, as is the de-Islamisation of India. Their security and identity-related concerns will be better met through a greater awareness of their historical pluralism and shared contributions towards a larger human harmony. This has to come about by withholding the transformation of textbooks to suit discretionary needs, a responsible use of media and a greater debate on collective advantages to be had from a vigorous and fresher regionalisation, without of course, surrendering sovereignty. Regional co-operation will not only preclude any more possibility of 'balkanisation' of this immensely plural and populous region, it will also usher South Asia into a long-cherished era of peace and stability.

The stigmatisation of Islam—either by intent or by content—allows Hindutva and other hostile elements to settle their scores, whereas among Muslims it creates a greater sense of despondency. As a consequence, while the BJP may use Gujarat as a triumphal case study, Muslim fundamentalists use Western and Indian unilateralism, only to become more intolerant. Certainly, Western expediency adds to regional proclivities. For instance, the early promotion of Jihadi elements vis-à-vis the Soviet Union in Afghanistan, and subsequent about-turn by the United States, created a wider sense of betrayal among several former Mujahideen and their international supporters including Osama bin Laden. In the same vein, the peripheralisation of Pakistan after the 1999 coup and its democratic imperatives became a forgotten chapter when after 9/11, Washington once again needed Islamabad as a front line ally. However, the massive number of civilian deaths in Afghanistan the American nonchalance over the resolution of the Kashmir dispute contrasted with a steadfast support for Ariel Sharon, and an unjustified invasion of Iraq have exacerbated anti-American sentiments. The unprecedented electoral victory of the religio-political parties in the army-led elections in 2002 owed itself largely to this countrywide anti-Americanism. The sentiment, in a way, is a part of a global anti-American discourse, which multiplied in the wake of Iraq becoming one more victim despite dissuasion from global public opinion. The Anglo-American impatience to attack Iraq has further strengthened fundamentalists of all hues and colours at the expense of democratic forces in the Muslim world and civil societies elsewhere. Political Islam of a fundamentalist nature grows only on the heap of unfulfilled human needs and a massive politico-economic disepowerment across Muslim regions. It is a populist rallying point for the have-nots, whose clerical leaders and militants—like the Kar Sevaks, Tamil Tigers and Shiv Sena activists—offer intolerant and simplistic solutions to complex mundane problems. It receives its sustenance from Western partisan policies in the developing world, especially in the Muslim regions and thus becomes an anti-Western campaign.

In the same vein, the extreme elements espousing a Hinduised India, despite a thin yet powerful and prosperous veneer of its leaders, is a mass of troubled humanity, among whom rather a quickly rehashed mish-mash of secularism, socialism, privatisation, and abrasive globalisation amidst a pervasive global indifference engendered a plethora of anxieties and unfulfilled desires. The *trishol* (trident) bearing rhetoricians, spouting hatred, and parading like traditional Hindu mythical heroes, are exploiting them to their best, to suit their own desires. Their expediency is to obtain power by offering a convenient yet dangerous mix of extreme religion, partisan nationalism and selective historical discourse, all in the name of a so-called majoritarianism. Only the negative portents of religion and nationalism, underwrite this discourse based on hatred, reductionism and false pride. Street power helps irresponsible politicians in their acquisition of power, but in the process it has been causing serious cracks in the Indian civilisational heritage and makes its minorities such as Muslims and Christians hostages to an unbridled fascist assault. The challenges for a responsible, courageous and accountable leadership in India are gigantic, but the country's own vitality, its valorous civil society, and other responsible elements from within the cross-ideological groups still offer a major hope. The Muslims—not just those in Pakistan or Bangladesh—may feel that while the West and the rest only focus on Islamic fundamentalism and its exaggerated threat, they shie away from accepting their own such powerful outfits and also look aside when it comes to Jewish, Christian and Hindu fundamentalists. Such arguments may go well with populist Muslim opinion groups as they fume with anger, but mere criticism of Western interventionism or a sheer indifference cannot overshadow the domestic and regional ingredients of the malady. It is in the interest of their civil societies and polities to undertake bold measures without waiting for 'sermons', and deliverance from across the Mediterranean and Atlantic. The 'turbaned groups' have to be reined in simultaneously with the prioritisation of democratic and participatory processes to ensure distributive justice for all.

While global factors may not be that conducive to regional peace and supportive of democratic forces, South Asia needs to steer itself out of a stalemated morass. The region can benefit from grassroots empowerment, and greater celebration of pluralism. It needs to offer and protect equal citizenry by building multiple avenues of multidisciplinary cooperation across borders and communities. In addition, it can operate as a vital bridge between Central, Western and South-east Asia, helping these regions achieve stability and peace. Its human and civilisational assets are definitely waiting to be explored.

BIBLIOGRAPHY

Reports and Monographs

Amnesty International, *India, Torture, Rape & Deaths in Custody*, London, 1992.

Government of Pakistan, *Pakistan Year Book, 1994–5*, Karachi, 1996.

Halliday, Fred, *Does Islamic Fundamentalism Pose a Threat to the West*, London, 1996.

Human Development Centre, *Human Development in South Asia 2002*, Islamabad, 2003.

Human Development Centre, *Human Development in South Asia 2001*, Islamabad, 2002.

Human Rights Watch, *Human Rights in India: Kashmir Under Siege*, New York, 1991.

Human Rights Commission of Pakistan (HRCP), *State of Human Rights in 2001*, Lahore, 2002.

Human Rights Commission of Pakistan (HRCP), *State of Human Rights in Pakistan in 2000*, Lahore, 2001.

Kazi, Seema, *Muslim Women in India*, London, 1999.

Kramer, Martin, *The Salience of Islamic Fundamentalism*, London, 1995.

Malik, Iftikhar H., *Religious Minorities in Pakistan*, London, 2002.

Malik, Iftikhar H., *Islam and the West*, Oxford, 1994.

Murshid, Tazeen, *A Forgotten Minority: The Biharis in Bangladesh*, Brussels, 2000.

National Commission for Justice & Peace, *Human Rights Monitor–2001*, Lahore, 2001.

Runnymede Trust, *Islamophobia*, London, 1997.

UNDP, *Human Development Report 2001 & 2002*, Oxford, 2001 & 2002.

UNDP/Regional Bureau for Arab States, *The Arab Human Development Report 2002: Creating Opportunities for Future Generations*, New York, 2002.

Whitaker, Ben, et al., *The Biharis in Bangladesh*, London, 1982.

Selected Articles and Books

Abrahamian, E., *Iran Between Two Revolutions*, Princeton, 1982.

Abu Rabi, M. Ibrahim, *Intellectual Origins of Islamic Resurgence in the Modern Arab World*, Albany, 1996.

Aburish, Said K., *Saddam Hussein: The Politics of Revenge*, London, 2000.

Advani, L.K., et al., *Hindus Betrayed*, New Delhi, 1995.

Ahmad, Eqbal, *Confronting Empire*, London, 2000.

Ahmad, Mirza Tahir, *Mazhab Kay Naam Per Khoon*, trans. by Syed Barkat Ahmad, Cambridge, 1990.

Ahmed, Rafiuddin, *The Bengal Muslims, 1871–1906: A Quest for Identity*, Delhi, 1981.

Ahuja, Gurdas M., *BJP and the Indian Politics*, New Delhi, 1995.

Akbar, M.J., *The Shadow of Swords*, Delhi, 2002.

Akhtar, Salamat, *Tehreek-i-Pakistan Kay Gumnaam Kirdar*, Rawalpindi, 1997.

Alagiah, George, *A Passage to Africa*, London, 2002.

Ali, Chowdhury Muhammad, *The Emergence of Pakistan*, New York, 1976.

Ali, Cheragh, *A Critical Exposition of the Popular 'Jihad'*, Calcutta, 1885.

Ali, Tariq, *The Clash of Fundamentalisms: Crusades, Jihads and Modernity*, London, 2002.

Ambedkar, B.R., *Pakistan or the Partition of India*, Bombay, 1946.

Anderson, Walter K., and Shridhar D., Damle, *The Brotherhood in Saffron: The Rashtriya Swayamsevak Sangh and Hindu Revivalism*, Boulder, 1987.

Armstrong, Karen, *Islam: A Short History*, London, 2000.

Armstrong, Karen, *Muhammad: a Biography of the Prophet*, London, 1995.

Askari-Rizvi, Hasan, *Military and Politics in Pakistan*, Karachi, 1998.

Azad, A.K., *India Wins Freedom*, Calcutta, 1960.

Aziz, Qutbuddin, *Blood and Tears*, Karachi, 1972.

Baloch, Abdul Ghani, *Zikri Firqa Ki Tarikh*, Karachi, 1996.

Baloch, Abdul Ghani, *A Short History of Zikri Faith*, Karachi, n.d.

Baloch, Abdul Ghani, *Zikri Mazhab Islam Kay Aiynnah Mein*, Turbat, 1993.

Banuri, Tariq, et al., (eds.) *Just Development: Beyond Adjustment with a Human Face*, Karachi, 1997.

Barber, Benjamin R., *Jihad Vs. McWorld*, London, 2003.

Baxter, Craig, *Jana Sangh: A Biography of an Indian Political Party*, Delhi, 1971.

Bergen, Peter, *Holy War Inc.: Inside the Secret World of Osama bin Laden*, New York, 2002.

Berman, Paul, *Terror and Liberalism*, London, 2002.

Blumenthal, Sidney, *The Clinton's Wars*, London, 2003.

Bodansky, Yossef, *Bin Laden: The Man Who Declared War on America*, New York, 1999.

Buchannan, Patrick, *The Death of the West: How Dying Populations and Immigrant Invasions Imperil our Country*, New York, 2001.

Burke, Jason, *Al-Qaeda: Casting a Shadow of Terror*, London, 2003.

Butalia, Urvashi, *Other Side of Silence: Voices from the Partition of India*, New Delhi, 1998.

Carew, Tom, *Jihad*, Edinburgh, 2001.

Chatterji, Basant, *Inside Bangladesh Today: An Eyewitness Account,* New Delhi, 1973.

Chomsky, Noam, *Rogue States: The Rule of Force in World Affairs,* London, 2002.

Chomsky, Noam, *9/11,* New York, 2002.

Chowdhury, R. Abrar, (ed.) *On the Margin: Refugees, Migrants and Minorities,* Dhaka, 2000.

Clarke, Ian, *Globalization and Fragmentation: International Relations in the Twentieth Century,* Oxford, 1999.

Clinton, Hillary Rodham, *Living History,* New York, 2003.

Cloughley, Brian, *The Pakistan Army,* Karachi, 1999.

Cockburn, Andrew, and Partrick Cockburn, *Saddam Hussein: An American Obsession,* London, 2002.

Coughlin, Con, *Saddam: The Secret Life,* London, 2002.

Cooley, John, *Unholy Wars: Afghanistan, America and International Terrorism,* London, 1999.

Coulter, Ann, *Slander: Liberal Lies About the American Right,* New York, 2002.

Cohen, Stephen P., *India: Emerging Power,* Washington D.C., 2001.

Cohen, Stephen P., *The Pakistan Army,* Karachi, 1999.

Corbin, Jane, *The Base,* London, 2003.

Crile, George, *My Enemy's Enemy: The Story of the Largest Covert Operation in History. The Arming of the Mujahideen by the CIA,* London, 2003.

Curtis, Mark, *Web of Deceit: Britain's Real Role in the World,* London, 2003.

Dajani-Shakeel, Hadia and Ronald A. Meissier, (eds.) *The Jihad and Its Times,* Ann Arbor, 1991.

Daniel, Norman, *Islam and the West,* Oxford, 2000.

Dubashi, Jay, *The Road to Ayodhya,* New Delhi, 1992.

Eaton, Richard M., *Essays on Islamic and Indian History,* New Delhi, 2001.

Eaton, Richard M., *Rise of Islam and the Bengal Frontier, 1204–1760,* Berkeley, 1996.

Esposito, John L., *The Islamic Threat: Myth or Reality?* New York, 1993.

Espostio, John L., and John D. Voll, *Makers of Contemporary Islam,* New York, 2001.

Fallaci, Oriana, *The Rage and the Pride,* New York, 2003.

Fox, Jeremy, *Chomsky and Globalisation,* London, 2002.

Frank, Katherine, *Indira,* London, 2001.

Friedman, Thomas L., *Longitudes and Attitudes: Exploring the World Before and After September,* London, 2003.

Frum, David, *The Right Man,* London, 2003.

Fukuyama, Francis, *The End of History and the Last Man,* London, 1992.

Giddens, Anthony, *Runaway World: How Globalization is Reshaping Our Lives!* London, 2000.

Giddens, Anthony, *The Third Way and Its Culture,* Cambridge, 2000.

Giddens, Anthony, *The Consequences of Modernity*, Cambridge, 1991.

Golwalker, Madhav S., *We or Our Nationhood Defined*, Nagpur, 1938.

Grare, Frederic, *Political Islam in the Indian Subcontinent: The Jamaat-i-Islami*, Delhi, 2002.

Gray, John, *Al-Qaeda and What it Means to be Modern*, London, 2003.

Griffin, Michael, *Reaping the Whirlwind*, London, 2001.

Gunaratna, Rohan, *Inside Al-Qaeda: Global Network of Terror*, London, 2002.

Gupta, Charu, *Sexuality, Obscenity, Community: Women, Muslims and the Hindu Public in Colonial India*, New Delhi, 2002.

Haddad, Yvonne Y., and Jane I. Smith, *Mission to America: Five Islamic Sectarian Communities in North America*, Gainesville, 1993.

Halliday, Fred, *Two Hours that Shook the World*, London, 2001.

Halliday, Fred, *Islam & the Myth of Confrontation*, London, 1996.

Hamidullah, Muhammad, *Muslim Conduct of State*, Lahore 1961.

Hansen, G. H., *Militant Islam*, New York, 1979.

Haque, Qazi Anwarul, *Under Three Flags*, Dhaka, 1986.

Harman, Chris, *Prophet and the Proletariat: Islamic Fundamentalism, Class and Revolution*, London, 2002.

Hasan, Mushirul, *Legacy of a Divided Nation: India's Muslims since Independence*, London, 1997.

Hasan, Zaheer, *The Separation of East Pakistan*, Karachi, 1994.

Hashmi, Taj-ul-Islam, *Pakistan as the Peasants' Utopia: the Communalization of Class Politics in East Bengal*, Boulder, 1992.

Haykel, Bernard, *Revival and Reform in Islam: The Legacy of Muhammad al-Shawkani*, Cambridge, 2003.

Hertsgaard, Mark, *Eagle's Shadow: Why America Fascinates and Infuriates the World*, London, 2002.

Hiro, Dilip, *Iraq: A Report from the Inside*, London, 2002.

Hoge Jr., James, and Gideon Rose, *How Did This Happen?* Oxford, 2002.

Huntington, Samuel, *The Clash of Civilizations*, London, 1997.

Hutchinson, Robert, *Weapons of Mass Destruction*, London, 2003.

Iqbal, Muhammad, *Poems from Iqbal*, trans. by Victor Kiernan, Karachi, 1999.

Ignatieff, Michael, *Empire Lite: Nation-building in Bosnia, Kosovo and Afghanistan*, London, 2003.

Jaffrelot, Christophe, (ed.) *A History of Pakistan and Its Origins*, London, 2002.

Jaffrelot, Christophe, *The Hindu Nationalist Movement and Indian Politics, 1925 to 1990s: Strategies of Identity-building, Implementation and Mobilisation*, London, 1996.

Jain, Girilal, *The Hindu Phenomenon*, New Delhi, 1994.

Jalal, Ayesha, *The Sole Spokesman: Jinnah, the Muslim League and the Demand for Pakistan*, Cambridge, 1985.

Jerichow, A., and J. Simonsen, *Islam in a Changing World*, London, 1997.

Jog, B. W., *Threat of Islam: Indian Dimension*, Mumbai, 1994.

Jones, Kenneth, *Socio-Religious Reform Movements in British India,* Cambridge, 1989.

Jones, Owen B., *Pakistan: Eye of the Storm,* London, 2002.

Jurgensmeyer, Mark, *Terror in the Mind of God,* Berkeley, 2001.

Kagan, Robert, *Paradise and Power,* New York, 2003.

Kelsey, John and James T. James, T. Johnson, (eds.) *Just War and Jihad: Historical and Theoretical Perspectives on War and Peace in Western and Islamic Traditions,* New York, 1991.

Kennedy, Charles H., (ed.) *Pakistan 1992,* Boulder, 1993.

Kepel, Gilles, *Jihad: The Trail of Political Islam,* London, 2003.

Kepel, Gilles, *Allah in the West,* Oxford, 1997.

Khadduri, Majid, *The Islamic Conception of Justice,* Baltimore, 1984.

Khadduri, Majid, *War and Peace in the Law of Islam,* Baltimore, 1955.

Khan, Gulfishan, *Indian Muslim Perceptions of the West During the Eighteenth Century,* Karachi, 1998.

Khan, Makhdum Ali, (ed.) *The Constitution of the Islamic Republic of Pakistan,* Karachi, 1986.

Khan, M. Asghar, (ed.) *Islam, Politics and the State. The Pakistan Experience,* London, 1985.

Kimmerling, Baruch, *Politicide: Ariel Sharon's War Against Palestinians,* London, 2003.

Klein, Naomi, *Fences and Windows,* London, 2002.

Kohli, Atul, (ed.) *The Success of India's Democracy,* Cambridge, 2001.

Lal, Vinay, *The History of History: Politics and Scholarship in Modern India,* Delhi, 2003.

Lamb, Alastair, *Kashmir: A Disputed Legacy, 1846-1990,* Hertingfordbury, 1991.

Lamb, Christina, *The Sewing Circles of Herat: My Afghan Years,* London, 2002.

Landau, Jacob, *The Politics of Pan-Islam,* London, 1994.

Lewis, Bernard, *Crisis of Islam: Holy War and Unholy Terror,* London, 2003.

Lewis, Bernard, *What Went Wrong? The Clash between Islam and Modernity in the Middle East,* London, 2002.

Lewis, Bernard, and P.M., Holt, (eds.) *Historians of the Middle East,* Oxford, 1962.

Limaye, Madhu, *Religious Bigotry: A Threat to Ordered State,* Delhi, 1994.

MacMahon, Robert J., *The Cold War on the Periphery: The United States, India and Pakistan,* New York, 1994.

Mahmud, Mirza Bashir-ud-Din, *Invitation to Ahmadiyyat,* London, 1982.

Mailer, Norman, *Why Are We At War?* New York, 2003.

Malai, Syed Naseer Ahmad, *Aslathul Zikarin,* Turbat, 1994.

Maley, William, (ed.) *Fundamentalism Reborn: Afghanistan and the Taliban,* London, 1998.

Malik, Iftikhar H., *Islam and Modernity: Muslims in Europe and the United States,* London, 2004.

Malik, Iftikhar H., *Islam, Globalisation and Modernity: The Tragedy of Bosnia,* Lahore, 2004.

Malik, Iftikhar H., *Islam, Nationalism and the West: Issues of Identity in Pakistan,* Oxford, 1999.

Malik, Iftikhar H., *State and Civil Society in Pakistan: Politics of Authority, Ideology and Ethnicity,* Oxford, 1997.

Malik, Iftikhar H., *U.S.-South Asia Relations, 1784–1940: A Historical Perspective,* Islamabad, 1988.

Malik, Iftikhar H., 'The Afghan Conflict: Islam, the West and Identity Politics in South Asia', *Indo-British Review,* XXIII, 2, 2002.

Malik, Iftikhar H., 'Pakistan in 2001: The Afghanistan Crisis and the Rediscovery of the Frontline State', *Asian Survey,* 42:1, 2002.

Malik, Iftikhar H., 'Turkey at the Crossroads: Encountering Modernity and Tradition', *Journal of South Asian and Middle Eastern Studies,* XXIV, 2, 2001.

Malik, Iftikhar H., 'Military Coup in Pakistan: Business as Usual or Democracy on Hold!' *The Round Table,* 360, 2001.

Marsden, Peter, *The Taliban: War, Religion and the New Order in Afghanistan,* London, 1998.

Mascarhenas, Anthony, *Bangladesh: A Legacy of Blood,* London, 1986.

Mascarhenas, Anthony, *The Rape of Bangladesh,* Delhi, 1971.

Matinuddin, Kamal, *The Taliban Phenomenon,* Karachi, 1999.

Maududi, Abul Ala, *Tafheem Al-Quran: Towards Understanding Islam,* trans. by Zafar I. Ansari, Leicester, 1988–90.

Maududi, Abul Ala, *Al-Jihad fil Islam,* Lahore, 1947.

Maududi, Abul Ala, H. Banna, and Sayyid Qutb, *Al-Jihad fi Sabil Allah,* Cairo, 1977.

McDonald, Ian, 'A nation on the brink?' *Times Higher Education Supplement,* 22 March 2002.

Menon, Ritu, and Kamla, Bhasin, *Borders and Boundaries: Women in India's Partition,* New Delhi, 1998.

Michas, Takis, *Unholy Alliance: Greece and Milosevic's Serbia,* Houston, 2002.

Mitra, Subrata, (ed.) *Sub-national Movements in South Asia,* Oxford, 1996.

Moghal, Dominic, and Jennifer Jivan, (eds.) *Religious Minorities in Pakistan: Struggle for Identity,* Rawalpindi, 1996.

Monbiot, George, *The Age of Consent: A Manifesto for a New World Order,* London, 2003.

Moore, James, and Wayne, Slater, *Bush's Brain,* Hoboken (New Jersey), 2003.

Moore, Michael, *Stupid White Men,* London, 2002.

Moore, Robin, *Task Force Dagger: The Hunt for Bin Laden,* London, 2003.

Muir, William, *The Life of Mahomet,* London, 1877.

Mujeeb, M., *The Indian Muslims*, London, 1969.

Munir, Azhar, *Zikris in the Light of History & Their Religious Beliefs*, Lahore, 1998.

Naipaul, V.S., *Beyond Belief: Islamic Excursions Among the Converted*, London, 1998.

Narain, Harsh, *The Ayodhya Temple-Mosque Dispute: Focus on Muslim Sources*, Delhi, 1993.

Nasr, Seyyed Vali Reza, *Mawdudi & The Making of Islamic Revolution*, Oxford, 1996.

Nehru, Jawaharlal, *The Discovery of India*, Delhi, 1950.

Newberg, Paula, *Judging the State: Courts and Constitutional Politics in Pakistan*, Cambridge, 1995.

Noorani, A.G., *Savarkar and Hindutva: The Godse Connection*, Mumbai, 2002.

Nye Jr., Joseph, *The Paradox of American Power*, Oxford, 2002.

Pakistan Historical Society, *Proceedings of the Pakistan History Conference*, Karachi, 1955.

Pandey, Gyanendra, *Remembering Partition: Violence, Nationalism and History in India*, Cambridge, 2001.

Pandey, Gyanendra, (ed.) *Hindus and Others: The Question of Identity in India*, New Delhi, 1993.

Parekh, Bhiku, and Upendra Baxi, (eds.) *Crisis and Change in Contemporary India*, New Delhi, 1995.

Perkovich, George, *India's Nuclear bomb: The Impact on Global Proliferation*, Berkeley, 1999.

Peters, Rudolph, *Islam and Colonialism: The Doctrine of Jihad in Modern History*, The Hague, 1979.

Peters, Rudolph, (ed.) *Jihad in Medieval and Modern Islam*, Leiden, 1977.

Pilger, John, *The New Rulers of the World*, London, 2003.

Pipes, Daniel, *Militant Islam Reaches America*, New York, 2001.

Piscatori, James, (ed.) *Islam and the Political Process*, New York, 1983.

Power, Samantha, *A Problem from Hell: America in the Age of Genocide*, London, 2003.

Qasrqandi, Maulana Abdul Majid, *Zikri Mazhab aur Islam*, Quetta, 1978.

Qureshi, I.H., *The Muslim Community of the Indo-Pakistan Sub-Continent, 610–1947*, The Hague, 1962.

Rai, Baljit, *Is India Going Islamic?* Chandigarh, 1994.

Rai, Milan, *War Plan: The Reason against War on Iraq*, London, 2002.

Rajagopal, Arvind, *Politics After Television: Hindu Nationalism and the Reshaping of the Public in India*, Cambridge, 2001.

Rashid, Ahmed, *Jihad: The Rise of Militant Islam in Central Asia*, New Haven, 2002.

Rashid, Ahmed, *Taliban: Islam, Oil and the New Great Game in Central Asia*, London, 2000.

Ratner, Michael, et al., *Against War in Iraq*: *An anti-war Primer,* New York, 2003.

Reeve, Simon, *The New Jackals*: *Ramzi Yousef, Osama bin Laden and the Future of Terrorism,* London, 2000.

Ridley, Yvonne, *In the Hands of the Taliban,* London, 2002.

Ritter, Scott, *Frontier Justice*: *Weapons of Mass Destruction and the Bushwhacking of America,* New York, 2003.

Robinson, Adam, *Bin Laden*: *Behind the Mask of Terrorism,* Edinburgh, 2001.

Rodinson, Maxime, *Islam and Capitalism,* trans. by Brian Pearce, London, 1974.

Rodinson, Maxime, *Mohammed,* London, 1993.

Rogge, James, (ed.) *Refugees*: *A Third World Dilemma,* Trenton, 1987.

Rogerson, Barnaby, *The Prophet Muhammad*: *A Biography,* London, 2003.

Roxburgh, Angus, *Preaching of Hate*: *The Rise of the Far Right,* London, 2002.

Roy, Arundhati, *War Talk,* London, 2003.

Roy, Olivier, *The Failure of Political Islam,* London, 1994.

Roy, Olivier, *Islam and Resistance in Afghanistan,* Cambridge, 1984.

Rubin, Barnett R., *The Fragmentation of Afghanistan*: *State Formation and Collapse in the International System,* New Haven, 1995.

Ruthven, Malise, *A Fury for God*: *The Islamist Attack on America,* London, 2002.

Sacks, Jonathan, *The Dignity of Difference*: *How to Avoid the Clash of Civilizations?* London, 2003 (revised).

Sajoo, Amyn B., (ed.) *Civil Society in the Muslim World,* London, 2002.

Saleem, Ahmad, *Pakistan Aur Aqlieetain,* Karachi, 2000.

Sardar, Ziauddin & Davies, Meryl W., *Why Do People Hate America?* London, 2002.

Sayeed, Khlaid B., *Western Dominance and Political Islam*: *Challenge and Response,* Albany, 1995.

Schofield, Victoria, *Kashmir in the Crossfire,* London, 1996.

Scholte, Jan A., *Globalization*: *a critical introduction,* Houndmills, 2000.

Sen, Sumit, 'Stateless Refugees and the Right to return: The Bihari Refugees of South Asia—Part 2', *International Journal of Refugee Law,* XII, 2, 2000.

Shaikh, Farzana, *Community and Consensus in Islam*: *Muslim Representation in Colonial India, 1860-1947,* Cambridge, 1989.

Shaltut, Mahmud, *The Treatise 'Koran and Fighting',* trans. by Rudolph Peters, Leiden, 1977.

Simons, Geoff, *Targetting Iraq*: *Sanctions and Bombing in US Policy,* London, 2002.

Simpson, John, *News From No Man's Land,* London, 2002.

Singh, Khushwant, *The End of India,* Delhi, 2003.

Singh, Pritam, and Thandi, Shinder, (eds.) *Globalisation and the Region: Explorations in Punjabi Identity,* Coventry, 1996.

Stern, Jessica, 'Pakistan's Jihad Culture', *Foreign Affairs,* November-December 2000.

Stothard, Peter, *30 Days: A Month at the Heart of Blair's War,* London, 2003.

Talbot, Ian, *Freedom's Cry: The Popular Dimension in the Pakistan Movement and Partition Experience in North-West India,* Karachi, 1996.

Talbot, Ian, and Gurharpal Singh, (eds.) *Region & Partition: Bengal, Punjab and the Partition of the Subcontinent,* Karachi, 1999.

Titus, Paul, (ed.) *Marginality and Modernity: Ethnicity and Change in Post-colonial Balochistan,* Karachi, 1996.

Watt, W. Montgomery, *The Majesty That was Islam,* London, 1974.

Watt, W. Montgomery, *Islamic Political Thought,* Edinburgh, 1968.

Weiner, Myron, 'Peoples and states in new order?' *Third World Quarterly,* 13, 2, 1992.

Wheatcroft, Andrew, *Infidels: The Conflict between Christendom and Islam, 638–2002,* London, 2003.

Winchester, Simon, *Krakatoa: The Day the World Exploded,* London, 2002.

Wolpert, Stanley, *Nehru: A Tryst with History,* Karachi, 1996.

Wolpert, Stanley, *Zulfi Bhutto of Pakistan,* Karachi, 1993.

Woodward, Bob, *Bush at War,* New York, 2002.

Zakaria, Fareed, *The Future of Freedom,* New York, 2003.

Zakaria, Rafique, *The Widening Divide: An Insight into Hindu-Muslim Relations,* New Delhi, 1995.

Zaman, Muhammad Qasim, *The Ulama in Contemporary Islam: Custodians of Change,* Princeton, 2002.

Ziring, Lawrence, *Bangladesh from Mujib to Ershad: An Interpretive Study,* Dhaka, 1992.

Newspapers, Magazines, Websites and Videos

Al Ahram
ARY TV
Asian Age
BBC
Channel 4
CNN
Commentary
Dawn
Die Presse
Die Welt
Economist
El Mundo & El Periodico

Emel: the Muslim lifestyle magazine.
Financial Times.
Friday Times.
Guardian.
Herald.
Hindu.
Hindustan Times.
HistoryToday.
http://www.aiindex.mnet.fr.
http://www.arabia.com.
http://www.globalresearch.ca/articles/GRG211.html.
http://www.hrw.org.
http://www.jaring.my/just.
http://www.opendemocracy.net.
http//www.peoplepress.org.
http://www.rediff.com/news/2003/aug/16pak.htm.
Independent.
India Today.
Indian Express.
International Herald Tribune.
International Institute of Asian Studies (IIAS) Newsletter.
La Figaro.
La Razon.
Liberation.
Nation.
New Internationalist.
News International.
Newsline.
New Statesman.
Newsweek.
New York Times.
Observer.
Outlook.
Pakistan Times.
Sky.
Sunday Times.
Daily Telegraph.
Time International.
Times.
Toronto Globe & Mail.
Washington Post.
Udbastu (Newsletter).

INDEX